NOT IN THE BEST OF
HEALTH

C000161717

Charles Godden

'Not in the Best of Health will entertain and shock. This is an outstanding medical narrative from Godden who records a life in paediatrics and pulls no punches documenting his experiences of clinical medicine and the frustrations of NHS administration. His integrity and experience shine throughout with equal amounts of humour and poignancy. His clinical scenarios are elegantly described such that lay readers will completely understand. This book should be read by anyone with even a passing interest in medical literature or with aspirations to work with children in the medical sphere.'

Professor Neil Wilson MB BS DCH FRCPCH FSCAI

'Spanning three decades of reorganisation, over-management, declining consultant autonomy and sleepless nights this inimitable memoir shines a sharp light on our parlous NHS. Patient focused and moving, funny but serious, it is a must read.'

Anthony Harnden,
Professor of primary care (general practice)

'WARNING! This is an honest reflection written with great humour and enviable humility of a career in medicine. Toe curling in places, totally relatable, and an essential read for those in, around, or interested in healthcare.'

Dr Craig Marshall, intensive care medicine registrar

'Whilst maintaining his effortless wit, Charles presents an honest account into the occasional highs and tragic lows of an NHS paediatrician. I really enjoyed the read and it certainly highlights the struggles I have ahead of me!'

Robbie Hill, first year medical student

In *Not in the Best of Health* Charles Godden takes us through his hectic life as a paediatrician. It is a well-written page-turner, that is by turns laugh-out-loud funny and tearfully sad. The book is delivered in bite-sized chapters that often focus on a particular patient's story – a format that works very well, with timely diversions from the medical narrative by way of entertaining travel and cricket stories – in extreme and exotic locations.

It is refreshing to read such an honest memoir from such a senior healthcare professional. Yes, Charles makes mistakes and yes, Charles admits to them. As someone who is married to an education professional, I was not surprised to discover that ongoing problems within the health service lie mostly with meddling politicians. For those in power Charles ends by offering some remedies. Let's hope they are willing to listen to them.

Simon Yates, author (*Against the Wall, The Flame of Adventure, The Wild Within*), mountaineer (*Touching the Void*) and adventurer.

'I rarely read medical books for recreation – too much of a busman's holiday. However, perhaps because we both qualified in 1983 and are both paediatricians, I found many of Charles Godden's recollections from the front line resonated with me. His views are sometimes provocative and some readers may differ with his forthright opinions but many of the personal tragedies and uplifting successes ring very true.'

Professor Sir Terence Stephenson, DM, FRCPCH, FRCP, Past chair of GMC and past president Royal College of Paediatrics and Child Health

Published by Goldcrest Books International Ltd
www.goldcrestbooks.com
publish@goldcrestbooks.com

Paperback ISBN: 978-1-913719-76-0
Hardback ISBN: 978-1-913719-80-7
Ebook ISBN: 978-1-913719-77-7

H and W

And all who work in the NHS

CONTENTS

At the Princess Margaret Hospital for Children,
Perth, Western Australia,
July 1989.

PREFACE

"Playing all the notes, but not necessarily
in the right order."

It takes time to find the tipping point. In my case an entire career that coincidentally spanned the creeping decline of the UK's much loved, and much maligned National Health Service. We love our nurses, we praise our NHS and, in the COVID-19 crisis of 2020, for weeks on end, people painted rainbows and stood in their gardens applauding, as a visible gesture of their gratitude. Or was there a hint of what some cynics called "virtue signalling"?

I will let others sift through the rubble of COVID-19. I wasn't there. It isn't my story. Mine is a memoir of the frontline, from the madness of medical college to the management-restrained frustration of a senior consultant. This is how it was, warts and all.

PART I

Should This Child Be Blue?

The truth is rarely pure and never simple.

Oscar Wilde

1

GRACE

Grace is lying, marble white, limbs splayed wide, her mouth open like that of a netted fish in its death throes. A ventilation tube snakes into her mouth, through her vocal cords and down her airway. Freed from the confines of the womb, a healthy Grace would be crying or suckling at her mother's breast, but my newborn patient, a full-term baby girl, is lying before us, feeble, pale, limp and utterly helpless, shorn of the life-spark she so desperately needs. Above her are the peering eyes of gowned and masked staff doing all they can against hopeless odds.

Bathed in stark surgical lighting, Grace lies on the resuscitaire, a trolley, not unlike those stainless steel trolleys flight attendants rattle between passengers, dispensing snacks and drinks. Only this one is equipped for life support with tubes to put into limb veins, tubes to put into blood vessels in the tummy button, tubes to put into the stomach, tubes to put into the lung and, if no access to a blood vessel can be found, our kit includes a drill to penetrate leg bones, a procedure undertaken without anaesthetic. I hate the drill. The noise and burning smell is nauseating, sickening to the pit of one's stomach. The resuscitaire is surrounded by eight members of staff, dressed in blue-green scrubs. I am the ninth.

Christmas is approaching: such a bleak time of year. I've been at work for eleven hours, yet, in my mid-fifties, with nearly twenty years' experience as a consultant paediatrician, I still dread the penetrating *beep beep beep* of the pager that undermines the comfort of life at home. It's not as if every call of the pager signals an emergency. Too often my only reward for rushing to a ward is a litany of excuses garnished with the occasional apology. For some reason the call outs are more frequent at Christmas and the excuses more wondrous — almost festive, with bells on.

An hour earlier my crash pager had gone off. I had two pagers, a personal one and a second, the crash pager, that always bodes ill. I've heard people who've experienced air raids talk about the churning in the pit of their stomachs when the alert sounds. I can relate to that.

Beep beep beep. Beep beep beep. Beep beep beep

"Emergency Labour Ward."

The screeching noise had ruptured the peaceful silence of my office. No information, just an emergency, leaving me guessing. I'd been clearing my desk, getting ready to go home. A real one, or another overreaction? No, this was real. Grace had been born in a poor state, clinging to life after a waterbirth. There'd been no forewarning of complications. Waterbirths. Having seen so many sick babies born this way I'd asked the midwives to audit them. Although the midwives had repeatedly promised me the audit, I knew it would never come. Waterbirths, designed to make labour more comfortable, were popular with many midwives. But we're not fish, we don't have gills. I didn't like waterbirths, didn't trust them.

Both my grandmother and my great-grandmother had died in childbirth, so I was aware of the perils. But that was a different era. In an era of choices, just as the life of the mother had to rank above that of her baby, I believed the health of the baby should rank beyond the comfort of the mother. Many professional organisations had urged more research into the safety of waterbirths as they grew more fashionable across the NHS. However, swathes of articles in women's magazines extolled their virtues, so few people dared submit any counter-argument. Criticising waterbirths was akin to saying bottle feeding was an acceptable option for the mother. Which, in the UK, I believed it was. If I had my way, waterbirths would be dumped into the Room 101 of failed medical ideas, like that earlier fad of chest-clamping newborn babies, born through meconium.

Meconium is a dark green, almost black, tarry substance, that collects in the guts of babies in the womb. It is made up of the cells lining the gut and bile from the liver. It's a waste product but, unlike poo, it doesn't smell. That is the only good thing to say about meconium. In the latter part of pregnancy, while still in the womb, babies make breathing actions, allowing fluid to go in and out of their lungs. This normal healthy process allows the developing baby's lungs to grow. Mature babies, when stressed in the womb, often open their bowels and, in so doing, pass this tar-like substance within their amniotic sac. Any unborn baby that inhales this meconium risks life-threatening lung damage and death.

As a junior doctor, twenty-five years earlier, I'd performed routine chest clamping.

What used to happen is that a baby born through the meconium had its chest squeezed on delivery to stop the baby from inhaling.

While one doctor grabbed, or clamped, the baby's chest, another doctor would desperately try to suck out the struggling newborn's airway, using a machine-powered suction tube. If the device failed, the doctor could use a manual system. This consisted of a plastic cylindrical safety chamber with two flexible hollow arms. One of these arms was inserted into the doctor's mouth, the other slipped into the newborn's mouth. Suck, suck, suck and pray that one's mouth didn't fill with a gooey mixture of faeces, blood, amniotic fluid and meconium.

At least the meconium procedure was doing something practiced and positive, a well-rehearsed and familiar routine. But baby Grace isn't even in the starting blocks. She's suspended in that nether world between creation and being. I'm overlooking the huddle around the resuscitaire, I'm tired and I'm angry. Grace is fifteen minutes old and her skin is waxy white. If only she'd turn blue we might have some hope. She's needed heart massage from seven minutes of age. She's been wheeled out of the birthing room and in to the corridor that affords more space for what we must do.

She lies exposed under the pearly glare of the ceiling lights and the penetrating stare of her attendants. There's a distinctive smell, that clean scent that only a new birth can produce.

One doctor cradles her two hands under Grace, eight delicate fingers supporting the spine while her two thumbs are forcefully, rhythmically compressing Grace's breast bone. Another doctor is squeezing air, via a bag, attached to a tube, into Grace's lungs. A specialist nurse is preparing drugs, fluid and a tube to insert into the vein within the umbilical cord.

The team works silently on Grace, coordinating their efforts, working in harmony. At intervals they look to me for hope. I cannot meet their gaze. It is hopeless. I in turn look at the ward clock, then the resuscitaire clock, then my watch, anywhere but my colleagues' faces, as I nervously twist my watch bezel. I try to remember how long we're supposed to continue a resuscitation. I know the sensible maximum duration of heart massage depends on a mixture of the baby's gestation, the presumed cause of the absence of a heartbeat and the facilities available. It's all in the textbook. But how long for Grace?

In the UK, at that time, ten minutes of cardiac massage were considered to be a reasonable period before stopping resuscitation. But opinions were already dividing on timing and the guidance would change through experience in the years ahead.

So how long? Nobody really knew. Eight minutes have passed since the start of cardiac massage, a long time for a newborn baby to survive with no heartbeat. I wonder whether we should stop, I again look at the watch. One hundred and twenty seconds and we will stop. Probably.

Unexpectedly, her heart begins to beat. Her skin tinges blue. Now we have a new problem. Grace isn't going to die quite yet. Grace is in an unquestionably poor condition. Even though I expect her to die very soon, I need to protect her brain as much as I can, just in case she makes a miraculous recovery. I'm thinking it's pointless, but I know I have to do something. Keeping babies cool helps protect their brains from further damage, so I turn off the overhead heater. The registrar turns to me, saying, "I have to go, the last train to Watford is at midnight." I wish I could leave too.

Grace's blood tests are astonishing. Apart from a low blood pressure, she also has a low sugar; even more perplexingly, she's the most acidic living being I've ever seen.

I insert further lines into Grace's arteries and veins. With fine tweezers I dilate the blood vessels in her tummy button and push a tube into her aorta.

Grace has a line into her umbilical artery, another line into her umbilical vein, two further lines in her arms, a tube into her stomach and a tube ventilating her lungs.

She looks like a fragile string puppet after the puppeteer has knocked off for the night, leaving his jointed doll flopped on stage, amid a spaghetti of animating strands.

Our own performance is short of medical puppeteers. We need a Giuseppe.[1] The night registrar can't be found and the day registrar has left to catch her last train to Watford. I curse the trains.

My hands are full, trying to save Grace, so I call the hospital manager. I ask about exploring the potential of transferring pregnant women on site and deflecting ambulances off site to other, less busy, hospitals. At such a critical juncture, I cannot leave Grace and start working on another sick baby. We are barely coping.

No response, or at least nothing definitive, but I am too busy to argue and neither Grace nor I have the time or energy to repeat explaining our predicament. Some sense of our plight must have registered since it's agreed that, where possible, ambulances might be diverted. Maybe. Perhaps.

Grace is anaemic as well as acidic, and shocked. The hospital baby blood reserves have run out, so we use the emergency pack on the labour ward. No other blood is available. How has it come to this? This is an NHS hospital, not a war zone.

In between adjusting the multiple knobs on the ventilator, I'm juggling discussions with the transfusion team, two separate hospital retrieval teams (both too busy to come

1. *Giuseppe, the famous Italian puppeteer.*

and help), Grace's parents, the nurses, the X-ray team and the pathology laboratories. We're making no headway with her acidosis. Despite our injecting fluid and blood into her body, her acid level just won't budge. I fear for Grace. She will die, or at least be seriously disabled.

In desperation I decide to give drugs to raise her blood pressure and to inject an alkali solution into a vein. This is not something we like to do. I'm aware it could be dangerous and counterproductive; it could make a dire situation worse.

I am alone, apart from her amazing parents and, of course, the nurses.

The sad-eyed nurses gently shake their heads. The sister in charge gives me a look.

I know her well and understand what it means. I've seen that look so often when it's time to stop trying to save a life, and she's invariably right. We're accustomed to exchanging such unspoken signals. Even behind our surgical face masks the eyes can say so much. But Grace holds on, so although we harbour no real hope, we persevere. Other babies in the same situation would have given up. Grace is a fighter.

I shuttle to and from her parents on the labour ward. They ask if she might die. Yes, I say, she might, but I add that we shouldn't give up hope quite yet. If they'd suggested I should stop, I might have stopped. I don't know.

After four hours of resuscitating Grace she hasn't improved, but neither has she deteriorated. She's still with us, clinging to life. Something in that tiny body has invested in her extraordinary resilience. Maybe there is hope after all? Grace's grandfather arrives, photos are taken for the family. We understand.

Then, seven and a half hours after we first started Grace's resuscitation, her blood tests begin to improve. Whatever it is, a steely core beyond our perceptions perhaps, something inside her is winning. Grace has found some inner resolve to live. I feel ill with exhaustion. I've been working flat out and exposed for nineteen hours, there is no bed for me, so I lie on a mattress, on the floor.

Two months pass and I need to examine Grace. It's with foreboding that I await her parents in the consulting room. I'll need to assess the extent of her disabilities so I brace myself for the inevitable.

I call her parents' names and, as they approach the doorway, I'm surprised to see that they're smiling. Grace is hidden, only her little pale face visible in the carry cot. They tell me Grace seems normal. Optimism of parental hope over clinical reality – I frame a pained smile. The discussion is going to be lengthy and upsetting. I feel her warmth and weight in my hands as I take her from her mother to carry out the examination. It's perplexing. Grace handles beautifully; she's neither stiff nor floppy and seems to focus and, is that a smile? If I didn't know Grace's history I'd say she appears normal. Although I can't be certain, at just eight weeks of age, there's no denying that the examination looks promising.

But what does her brain scan show? This has only been done a fortnight before and it's still with the radiologists. Can we find it? It's important as it should show the surely inescapable damage that I cannot yet clinically identify, and that I need to see to discuss Grace's future care with her parents.

Grace's parents sit silently and patiently beside me as I search on the system. There it is.

The MRI scan shows a perfectly normal brain.

Right, that's it.

I tell them the result and that I have decided to resign.

Sharp as a razor, her father says, "Is it because of Grace?"

"Sort of," I say.

2

JENNIFER

Five years of studying at medical school has come to an end. The shock of qualifying is quickly followed by the unwelcome reality of having to seek employment. Like most medical students I'm offered just one six-month post and, to complete the compulsory year of house jobs, I join the pack hunting for another. Flicking through the reference book of UK hospitals, starting at A for Aberdeen, I work my way forwards, phoning each hospital's human resources department. After two hours I have reached H and first up is Halifax. Where is that? No matter, they need a medical houseman.

I'm 23 and it's 1983. UB40 has a hit with "Red Red Wine" and the latest Bond film, *Octopussy*, is playing at the cinemas. I thank God for the wine. Then the Griffiths report drops, highlighting inefficiencies within the NHS. "If Florence Nightingale were carrying her lamp down the corridors of the NHS today, she would almost certainly be searching for the people in charge," it said. I have no inkling that thirty years later we will still be searching and those in charge will still be in hiding. Florence Nightingale might have been disheartened having her name attributed to the biggest inefficiency of all: a collection of expensive, ad hoc, under-used hospitals, built in the coronavirus pandemic.

"From Hell, Hull and Halifax, may the good Lord deliver us," said the Beggar's Litany, which is new to me. Aged just 23 I arrive at this West Yorkshire mill town, to be released on to an unsuspecting public. I know no one there and no one knows me. A clean slate then.

On arrival, human resources inform me that my sole junior doctor colleague and my consultant are both on holiday. What? Together? Are they an item? I am also rostered to be on call that first night. Alone. The "firm" a team of doctors based around one consultant, must have decided I can manage alone - either that, or they don't care too much about their patients. So, with no practical medical experience, on my first day I am left running the ward, and at night I am in sole charge of the cardiac arrest team for the entire hospital. Scary, heh? You be the judge, you're the patient.

No induction, nor introduction. If a patient suffers a cardiac arrest, I am expected to intubate, manage the cardiac compressions, decide on which drugs and what electric shocks to give, and when to stop the resuscitation. I receive one tip and one useful instruction. The tip is much appreciated. A warning about which patients to watch out for: "If they are wearing tinted glasses or male and have grey shoes watch out, and if in doubt about their sanity, ask them if it hurts in their ears when they pass urine."

The instruction concerns the two pagers handed to me. In those first days, these electronic companions were a badge of office, a token of "having made it" but I'd come to loathe them as if they carried the mark of the beast.

One is a personal pager, that I am told to keep on me at all times. This will be used for routine calls – if anyone wants to discuss a takeaway curry order, for example. It makes a gentle chirruping noise, like an Easter chick calling for its mother.

The other pager clings to my waist like a black plastic vampire and makes a terrifying insistent screech when it smells blood. This something-of-the-night pager is passed from one doctor to another like a hot coal, with a palpable sense of relief when the burden has been lifted. It is the ultimate hospital pass. Better known as the "crash pager" it will interrupt whatever one is doing at any time and demand immediate attention. The creature usually makes a series of rapid beeps, followed by a few short demanding words, such as "Emergency Ward Six". There is no opportunity to challenge, ask questions or delay the demands of this squatting beast that has to be slavishly followed, whatever it bloody wants and whatever time it chooses to awake from its slumber. You've seen that scene in Ridley Scott's *Alien* where the creature bursts from John Hurt's chest. That's how we perceive the crash pager – hideous and unstoppable, like a black plastic vampire bat.

The medical houseman and, if not on holiday, his registrar, and maybe a junior anaesthetist, each have one of these crash pagers. Together they make up the hospital "crash team". For the holders, the skill is to arrive a few seconds later than the others, while making sure one is still out of breath. That way, someone more experienced will have taken control, standing over a recently expired patient.

The crash calls are invariably unsuccessful. Later there was a nationwide focus on improving this area of care and, thirty years on, the odds of surviving an in-hospital arrest have improved from about zilch, to perhaps one in five.

Eighteen months after this first post finished, during an interview for a general practice rotation, a panel consultant asked me,

"I see you state in your CV that you are competent in cardiopulmonary resuscitation?"

"Yes."

"If you got this job, you would be teaching the new doctors."

"Fine."

"How many cardiac arrests did you go to in your first six-month medical post?"

"I probably averaged two a week, so maybe fifty."

"And how many of these fifty patients survived?"

"None."

I suspected he expected me to "creatively" bump up my success rate. I explained that I had always considered that if the patient survived my care, there probably hadn't been a need for a full resuscitation in the first place. False calls happen, heart leads fall off, traces are misinterpreted, people panic. I didn't get the post, but I hadn't wanted to whine about the dangerous environment we worked in, nor massage the figures.

I enjoyed my foray into Yorkshire. I remember the pleasing shock of my first pay slip and I learnt a lot about medicine and human relationships. Another plus was that we had minimal supervision. Learning was purely on the job, through mistakes and corridor chatter. On one occasion an elderly woman was admitted with a urea of ninety, a normal urea being in single figures. Urea is a guide as to how much fluid one has in the body and how well one's kidneys work. It's not that simple, but it's a clue. High is bad. She probably needed an increase in her diuretics. I hoped so, as the junior doctor who prescribed this supplement secretly hoped to get the patient's urea to one hundred. Solely because one hundred was a nice, round number. Shocking, but true.

Today such a story would be unbelievable. An investigation would follow, then a General Medical Council (GMC) referral, strike off and maybe prison. It's hard to explain or defend the behaviour of some junior doctors at that time. But I'll try. We were in our early twenties, inexperienced and out of our depth. Often working unsupported with minimal supervision, we had to develop a thick hide to survive the brutal hours and insane expectations, accompanied by the not always unwelcome presence of death.

When someone was dying it was common practice for juniors to hang around after work, to sign the "crem form" in order to get what we called "ash cash". The cash was a designated payment, always in cash, always in a small brown paper envelope, that doctors received for confirmation of the cause of a death. The sign off was necessary before a body could be released to undertakers for burial or cremation. Two sections of the death certificate needed to be completed, the first by a junior doctor familiar with the patient, the second by a senior doctor who did not need to see the body, but who needed to have discussed the case with the junior clinician and be satisfied with the conclusions. Payments for each of these duties were on top of one's normal salary. For junior doctors they were money in the pocket to spend down the pub the same evening.

Certifying death was another competency we hadn't been taught. It sounds ridiculous but it isn't easy. One old friend from medical school days certified a patient's death, then, three weeks later the patient went home, very much alive. We soon discovered that waiting half an hour after the request to confirm a death was a wise approach. Before this lesson, many of us had nasty shocks.

The text book said that death could be confirmed by listening to the patient's chest through a stethoscope for a minute and confirming there was no heartbeat. This is combined with the absence of feeling a pulse and confirmation that the patient's pupils don't shrink to a light shone into their eyes. But it isn't that simple. One minute leaning over a "clearly dead" body feels a long time. The pop group Police released "Every Breath You Take" and I silently hummed the tune to myself, as I checked the bodies. I could only remember the first fifteen seconds of the lyrics, so I did it twice. Thirty seconds seemed close enough to a minute. Even worse, during these examinations there were occasional surprises. I would then start again. Recently dead bodies can and do let out gas. At both ends. Unnerving, if the certifier is unaware of this phenomenon.

Thankfully, it wasn't all work. A romantic dalliance with the lady who put peas on my plate rather backfired. Realising my mistake and, no doubt, hers as well, I decided to avoid the canteen for a month. Mark, a surgical colleague, found the whole episode entertaining and brought food parcels for me to the doctors' mess.

The mess was a sitting room set aside exclusively for the junior medical staff. We could relax there, watching TV, eating curry, exaggerating our achievements and telling sick jokes. I confessed to Mark that I'd been surprised when she'd told me I'd been her first boyfriend. That hadn't been my impression. I was even more surprised when Mark phoned me a year later having just delivered her third child.

The second short job was back at my own medical school of Charing Cross. This six-month post was divided into an initial three months of chopping off penises, at an average of three penises a week, and three months of fiddling in and around arteries and abnormal distended veins. The gender-reassignment post was an eye opener, and a great ice-breaker at the bar.

"What do you do?"

"I chop off penises."

"Gosh! How amazing doctor. Are they all the same?"

"Don't you know?"

OK, it didn't go quite like that, but I am sure you can see it offered a fantastic opportunity to make that first impression. As a chat-up line, it seldom failed. What woman cannot feel safe in the company of someone who does a John Wayne Bobbitt routinely, and all within the law?[2]

Never a dull moment in gender reassignment. Sitting at the ward desk my attention, and that of my registrar, were drawn to a striking woman with shiny dark hair. She was visiting a private patient about to lose his privates. Sporting tight black leather trousers, her legs seemed endless. She was gorgeous and I can still see her. Curves in all the right places. The consultant spotted us leering. "He's down for the op next month," he said.

We did three sex changes a week. I was the most junior and the least experienced doctor, so my role in theatre was holding up the penis like a miniature Eddystone Lighthouse. Purple "cut here" lines were inked on the soft skin of the shaft. The penis was then incised and peeled, like a banana, before finally having its central "sausage stuffing" removed. For the uninitiated, there really is no bone. I've always been surprised how many people think there is. The residual penile skin is then sewn up (sausage meat removed) –

2. *In 1993, while John Wayne Bobbitt was asleep, his wife Lorena cut off his penis with an eight-inch carving knife. At trial she claimed he had raped her earlier that evening. Following a nine-hour operation the penis was reattached and Bobbitt demonstrated its ability to function by making a series of pornographic films.*

making a hollow, empty tube of skin, which is then pushed inside out, into a gap made between the patient's bladder and prostate. Think of the way you restore the shape of a popped-out finger on a Marigold glove.

This then is the new false vagina, lined with the old penile and scrotal skin getting ready for a new career. Sitting snug between the bladder and the lady's prostate gland. It's bad luck if you have a small penis, as you end up with a short vagina. In our clinics some patients had such small penises that their new vagina had to be extended, at a later operation, by tacking on a bit of their bowel, resected from their own gut.

*

During the long hours of peeled-penis holding I used to day dream. My responsibility was limited and my skill set was close to nil. However, on this particular day Jeremy/Jennifer appeared to be enjoying the procedure more than I was, and certainly more than she should have been. Metaphorically speaking, the lighthouse was winking. Not good. Blood started to ooze from the stiffening, peeled penis in my hand and to my horror it gave an undeniably priapic last stand. A stiff flick might have worked but could have been messy. No need. The anaesthetist saved the day, gave more gas and the erection was over. Forever.

On the post-operation ward round we filed in behind the consultant to see Jennifer.

The patients knew that, post operation, it was important to keep their new vagina functional. To aid this, National Health Service dildos were provided for the ward. I'm not sure if audits were done to see how many dildos went missing, or which was the commonest size or colour to disappear. It would have been interesting. We walked in and there was Jennifer, lying on her back, legs akimbo. Five of us stood around the end of her bed. I was biting my lip and hoping for a sudden bout of blindness, deafness and anosmia, terrified I would burst into massively inappropriate laughter.

Jennifer was inserting and withdrawing the largest dildo I had ever seen. As the pungent smell of warm oil filled her room, the dildo made a slurping sound like a plumber's plunger as it rhythmically exited and entered her new NHS orifice. I forced my lips tightly shut.

The consultant talked to Jennifer about the operation, the next steps, her planned follow up and what was going on in the world. They then moved on to who was looking after her cat, and even discussed the weather. All the while Jennifer was pumping this massive dildo in and out. Please, please, hurry up I thought. I can't bear this any longer.

Plop: out came the twelve-inch dildo. Jennifer shot a "hello boys" look at each of us in the room and said, "This feels fine, but what happens when I meet a real man?"

I looked at my shoes. I'd never felt so inadequate. I did however feel the urge to ask a question, as there were two areas connected to the engineering of sex changes that still confused me.

Firstly, I knew that most of the male ejaculate was made in the prostate and was stored in the seminal vesicles before being ejected. In the gender-reassignment surgery the prostate was left alone, so I reckoned that there should still be two teaspoons of ejaculate, expelled during orgasm. I presumed that when Jennifer, the owner of the new vagina, had an orgasm, there would follow a male-type ejaculation of fluid. But where did it go? I didn't ask.

My second worry was that, in the making of the new vagina, both penile and scrotal skin was used and the latter would have densely packed hair follicles. Even with a "back, sack and crack" hair re-grows. So I was intrigued as to how the new vagina managed with this. It would be a bit of a shock, at a moment of high romance, for a new partner to find a small internal forest. No doubt some would be excited by this variation, but I doubted many would. I imagined that it would also be a tricky manoeuvre to de-forest such an internal growth. I wondered whether nose hair trimmers worked? No, I couldn't ask that either. Could I? I decided to break the ice:

"Does hair grow inside the new vagina?"

The consultant's answer still perplexes me.

"Does grass grow under trees?"

Next up, three months of vascular surgery. This was a blend of varicose veins, piles, obstructed arteries, dilated arteries, with some major surgery thrown in. By its very nature, vascular surgery is bloody and I soon realised surgery wasn't for me. I felt nauseated and giddy and wondered whether, if overcome, I would first vomit over the patient or faint onto the operating table. My problem was I cared too much for those poor souls whom I had clerked in (admitted) and got to know. Well, most of them. Then I had a brainwave. If I tried to "hate" them and "to not care a jot" would my nausea disappear? The technique worked and I managed assisting at surgery without any further problems. I wondered whether this was what surgeons thought, when they operated? My self-taught coping strategy was tested to the limit, however, when we had to prepare Giles for a hemicorporectomy. But before Giles, an unexpected and tricky situation arose. The phone rang at the student bar. It was an angry professor.

"Please come to my office now," he barked.

The "Please" was unnecessary. There wasn't any alternative to going. I pottered up to the main building in a confused state. This had to be bad. I must have killed someone, maybe more than one. Perhaps he was worried about his statistics.

I liked the professor, was disappointed that I'd let him down, and hoped my mistake wouldn't spoil his department's reputation. I knocked on his door and went in. The summons had nothing to do with the patients. The professor had a reputation. He told me that if I published some photos I'd taken at a party, it would end the current relaxed and happy relationship between him and the juniors. He said that we all had vulnerabilities and this was his. I reassured him that I hadn't a clue what he was talking about, that I'd never published any photos, and that I didn't have any dodgy ones that I wanted to publish.

Next morning, I was summoned to assist the professor, on Giles. Giles had localised but advanced cancer in his sacrum, the bones that make the base of the spine. The only hope of a cure was to cut Giles in half, a hemicorporectomy. That meant cutting through Giles's lower back, through the end of his spinal bones and removing both of his legs, his pelvis, his penis, his testicles, his rectum and his anus. Removing the lot. Giles really wanted to live and he knew this was his only chance. Giles taught me the strength of the will to survive. The operation went well. The lower half of his body was packaged up for the incinerator. Frustratingly, being a junior house officer, I wouldn't know the long-term outcome for Giles. Apart from his immediate post-operative care, all follow up was done by experienced juniors or consultants. Rarely would we have time to drop in to a clinic, so for Giles and the majority of our patients we had no idea as to the success or failure of any prior procedure or treatment. I hope Giles lived for many years, content in his wheelchair. Paralympics perhaps? He had made a brave decision and Giles deserved his reward. But I will never know and really that's how it is in this work. We intervene in lives, hopefully for the better but, as juniors, we do not track them generally.

House jobs were nearing an end and a new post and title awaited me. I would soon become a senior house officer. At the time it sounded impressive. The prefix "senior" must mean something?

Only a week to go but the professor was in a foul mood. I had called human resources explaining that my senior house officer, registrar and consultant were away on study leave together and our firm was on call for admissions. They saw my point and appointed an experienced locum doctor. The professor was apoplectic. If he'd had a scalpel in his hand, I'd have scarpered. I started my defence.

"But, I thought....", I started.

"YOU are paid to DO. You are NOT paid to THINK," he barked back. I couldn't understand why he was in such a bad mood. It probably wasn't just my taking the initiative, forbidden as a junior house officer.

He was proud of his work and some of that carried out in his absence didn't pass muster. Elizabeth's anal sphincter was a case in point. Her haemorrhoidectomy to remove piles could have been better, he said. Instead of a tight flower, her sphincter looked a few petals short of the perfect specimen. I doubted many would notice. Unlike Simon Bramhall's later habit of liver-signing, no surgeon I knew personally initialled the anal area, post op.[3] Not even the prof. I disliked haemorrhoidectomies, not as much as

---

3. *Simon Bramhall, a prominent liver surgeon, was convicted of assault after using an argon beam machine to mark the livers of two of his patients with his initials. Bramhall was finally struck off the GMC register in 2022.*

the patients did, but I couldn't help clenching my buttocks while the patient lay on their back, anaesthetised, legs up in the air in stirrups. We call it the lithotomy position. Cut by cut, the scalpel pared around the anus, removing skin and blood vessels, before stitching up this most delicate of areas. Elizabeth's anus was not a good result, but nobody dared whisper the maxim "If a dahlia, it's a failure".

A year later and our professor of vascular surgery had his moment. I was now on my back being anaesthetised and I couldn't talk back. Not my piles. They would have to take their chances. The professor was sorting my varicose veins and I was now the defenceless patient. As I slipped into unconsciousness, all I could see was his round face, like a pink moon, an inch from mine, as he muttered through a smile: "I've been waiting a long time for this Charles." I was relieved I didn't hear him humming "Every breath you take".

On waking, I checked downstairs.

Phew! Still all there.

3

ANTHRAX

If thinking was banned, it made my job a lot easier. Thinking consumed too much energy. It really hurt. I was aware that I wanted it both ways. Keen to think again, I was wary of the responsibility that came with it. But if I wanted to progress, thinking was part of the package, so I'd better get used to it.

As the British rock band Queen released "I Want to Break Free" I left London and went to work in Jersey, as a senior house officer in accident and emergency (A&E). The hospital was welcoming and the accommodation a notch up from most junior house officer digs.

During my first week I saw Pete, a 40-year-old man with a black spot on his face. It rang a bell – that of a picture of anthrax I'd seen at medical school. But anthrax had been eradicated from mainland Britain. The only cases in the past thirty years had been imported. My interest deepened when I discovered that Pete worked for Benetton, delivering sheep's wool in his van. Could there be a connection? I went to the nursing sisters' office, found the medical reference book, and looked up anthrax.

This confirmed my recollection that animals were the usual source, but it still seemed extremely unlikely. Vaccination had started before the Second World War, eliminating anthrax in the UK. The last known outbreak of anthrax had been in Russia, five years earlier, when sixty-four people had died. That outbreak had been attributed to faulty air filters at a Soviet military microbiology facility. I doubted Jersey had such a bioweapon factory. Or did it?

I called Worty, the medical registrar. Worty maintained a steady voice on the phone, feigned interest, and said he would come down to see me. And maybe the patient.

Worty arrived immaculately turned out. Petite, rather camp, coiffured hair, swinging hips, a well pressed shirt, stiff collar, Italian trousers and a neat central knot to his tie. Worty obviously spent a lot of time in front of his mirror. He carefully brushed his locks aside, before peering at the patient's face. He hummed and hahhed before squinting at me and asking whether we had any departmental books. I played dumb. Was there a book? Worty opened the same page I'd examined an hour earlier. He stared at it for a full minute. The photo of the patient in the book even looked like my patient. Closing the book, Worty smiled, said "Nah," and walked off to find another mirror. I needed more than that and caught up with him. What features had made him come to such a rapid and confident conclusion?

"Too bloody rare," Worty said.

"However, let me tell you about women and abdominal pain. White knickers, it's appendicitis, red or black knickers and it's pelvic inflammatory disease," he said.

Worty was right, both about the knickers and the patient. He knew. It was acne.

It wasn't long before my first exposure to the uncomfortable and unnatural professional relationship between medicine and the law. A patient had been attacked by her partner and I was called to give medical evidence in court. It would be my first time in court on the right side of the law. Though unprepared, I thought for once I should put on a suit, press my shirt and also have a neat, central knot to my tie – a Worty knot. I was learning. I listed the injuries.

The assault had left my patient with severe facial bruising, a split upper lip and three broken teeth. Luckily, she had not suffered any fractures to her face, nor was my lack of experience exposed. The judge decided on a custodial sentence. The defendant's solicitor had been expecting this response and asked if his client could have Christmas Day at home with his family, as he was a "good family man". The judge looked the defendant up and down. "No," he said. All hell broke loose. The man jumped over the dock shouting "You fucking bastard. I'll kill you."

In accident and emergency, I enjoyed mixing with all that society could provide, but the dregs were over-represented. This made the job more interesting. I was spat at and kicked a few times, but I didn't mind. I was only punched once, having told a youth that he'd been "fucking stupid" trying to carve off the tattoo on his arm with a kitchen knife on Christmas Day. We both were.

I was troubled by the island's class structure; there appeared to be four grades of human. Ranked at the top were the generals, the locals, way above the rest, towering over all, and wallowing in their self-importance. Then came the captains, the tourists, often untidy, uncouth and unwanted, but tolerated for bringing in the money the generals needed to pay their staff. Third in the pecking order were the corporals, the staff, needed to clean the islanders' houses. These were mainly poor Spanish or Portuguese workers, essential for maintaining the "Upstairs, Downstairs" lifestyle of the generals. Then, down at the bottom of the barrel, less loved than the cattle, were the privates, the French farmers. This impoverished group enjoyed no rights and no respect. I regularly saw them shuffling in to A&E in a dishevelled and uncared-for state. I was as accustomed as anyone to the English class structure, but this felt feudal, almost Dickensian in its harshness. On reflection, it was little less than modern day serfdom.

Accident and emergency was exciting work. It was more varied than most other specialities and almost anything could crop up. All orifices were well represented and each offered different and often fascinating challenges. Facial orifices were my favourite, as they didn't offend my keen sense of smell. I liked eyes in particular.

I hadn't a clue how eyes worked, but they intrigued me. I enjoyed dripping yellow dye into the eye, to see where the cornea had been scratched, or, even better, rolling eyelids inside out, on cocktail sticks, making the upper eyelid and its cartilage form a beautiful pink quarter moon.

A hysterical teenager arrived. Amy had a problem with her right ear and she wouldn't calm down. "I can feel fluttering," she said. I looked inside, but could see nothing bar a small lump of hard, dark yellow wax. Amy insisted I had missed something, so I looked again. She was right; behind the wax I could see two moving strands. What were they? Peering down the auriscope, lay an earwig curled up, tight against her tympanic membrane. As usual I had no clue what to do. As usual, the nurses knew. As usual, I had the glory of doing the procedure and of getting all the credit. I told Amy to lie on her side and, as I poured olive oil into her ear, the insect made a bolt for it.

Earwigs derive their name from the old English for ear and beetle, wicga. Old wives' tales suggested they burrowed into human brains, through the ear, and then laid eggs in the brain. Thankfully this wasn't true. Well, it probably wasn't. I was sure my unofficial mentor, Worty, would have said "Nah." Amy was grateful, but the next patient was ecstatic both before, and after her treatment.

Olivia's boyfriend, Ed, was over from Leicestershire for some "romance", and Olivia had taken a bath, eagerly anticipating his arrival. Over excited, lying in the warm water, Olivia had started experimenting with a bottle of Head & Shoulders shampoo. You never saw that in the TV commercials. Unfortunately the top of the bottle had unscrewed and this cap was now stuck far up her vagina. Stuck right up at the end. No amount of Olivia delving into herself could remove it. It was a particularly tricky extraction. The cap fitted neatly over Olivia's cervix. After much manoeuvring, I managed to see the top, through the inserted metal speculum, and get a firm grip on the white plastic rim. Out it plopped, like a pea from its pod. We both smiled and the weekend was saved, free from dandruff too.

Six months of such trials felt long enough. I'd enjoyed myself too much and needed to get off the island, before being asked to leave. The mess was also being closed.

The police had raided it. They couldn't understand why the walls were splashed with blood. I think it may have been a drunken cannula-inserting training session.

On to a general practice rotation on the South Coast, starting with obstetrics, then my first taste of paediatrics. Obstetrics felt like the frontline. I struggled with the sights, the sounds and, worst of all, the smells. The smells did me in. I have a sensitive nose.

I was fortunate in having a supportive registrar with the sort of name that would have gone down a treat among the juveniles in medical school — myself included. What other nickname could there be for a man called Bates?

Bates worked out that I was pretty useless, so he didn't play the seniority game. He used me wisely to do tasks within my ability, but that were also useful, both to him and to the department. Bates was smart — not smart as in dapper, like Worty, but smart in his people-handling skills. When something beyond my skill set arose — which was nearly everything — Bates would potter off to deal with it, allowing me to settle down in the mess to watch one of the two new TV series, *LA Law* or *Casualty*.

Beep, beep, beep. Beep, beep, beep.

"Urgent call, labour ward".

I groaned and dragged myself up from the mess sofa, arriving at the delivery suite at the same time as (yes it had to be) Master Bates. We were both unprepared for the sight. A large pregnant woman was kneeling naked on the table, on all fours, trying to deliver twins. The effect of all her pushing had resulted in an impressive dilatation of her anus. All we could see as we first walked in was a cavernous dark hole. The diameter of her anus matched that of the inner part of a loo roll. Fearful we might laugh, Bates and I looked at each other, stepped outside to gather our thoughts, and then went back in to assist. It wasn't at all funny, and we suppressed our reaction, but laughter can be a natural nervous response to extraordinary sets of circumstance.

I started to worry that the focus of care was too much in favour of the mothers, to the detriment of the babies or fetuses. Perhaps my natural bias was starting to show. At the time it was normal for the midwives to place an extremely premature newborn, if regarded as not able to survive, in a cold metal Petri dish in the sluice. It would be left to die, alone in the sluice. The sluice was a small, smelly, box-shaped room, with inadequate ventilation, where faeces, urine, blood clots and placentas were disposed of. And dying fetuses. Although these babies had no chance of living, it felt wrong on all counts barbarous, dispassionate and uncivilised.

I got to know the midwives well, but remained wary of them. It was essential to learn who to trust and who to watch out for. My next post was paediatrics and that would involve working closely with this strange coterie. The dynamics of our relationship would change markedly once my own role had changed. Obstetrics seemed to be a lot of *doing* with not so much *thinking*. I appreciate now that that was because I knew so little and Bates, who really was the master, took on nearly all of the responsibility.

Daytime deliveries were manageable, but night-time was a different story. Hours were spent twiddling thumbs in the early hours of the morning, waiting, cursing the delay, in the knowledge that a full day's work lay ahead. Then, as the delivery approached, I would find myself clenching my teeth and thighs while using scissors to cut deep into a woman's vagina, opening it wide enough for the baby's head to push through.

I often felt referred pain in my scrotum while doing this. Was I alone in feeling such? Afterwards, stitching up the mess I'd made, using feet of catgut, I'd be wondering whether I had made the vagina too loose or too tight. I tried my best, but I had received no training for such an important procedure. We worked under the maxim of "see one, do one, teach one". These weren't the only thigh-clenching moments. My duties included scraping out a womb with a sharp instrument to remove either an unwanted pregnancy or the left overs of a much wanted one. Three patients on my list were all down for a dilatation and curettage (scraping), or D&C for short.

Women on their backs, legs in stirrups, gripper on the

cervix, and a gentle dilation of the central hole, known as the os. Followed by a satisfying gritty grating sensation, like scooping out a not quite ripe pear, as the products were identified and removed. The contentment was kept in check by the real fear of scraping too deep and perforating the woman's uterus. All of the time seeing nothing and going by feel alone. Learning on the hoof. Bates was right, go gentle, go by feel. Again, see one, do one, teach one.

These experiences blended with rare moments of reflection. Why would anyone choose this as a career? Why did the cervix feel like the tip of a nose? As babies' weights varied so much, why was fully dilated *always* ten centimetres? Why would anyone want to fry up and eat their placenta?

I left obstetrics as Simple Minds released "Don't You Forget About Me". I hoped the midwives would, but realised they wouldn't have time.

The following morning I returned in a different guise – this time as a paediatrician.

4

THE WEEK

The relief of finishing obstetrics and of working one weekend in three was immediately replaced by the concern of starting paediatrics and of working one weekend in two. I was now a different animal with a different set of responsibilities and priorities. Now representing children. Now a "Paed", though still very much a junior, and about to discover just what that meant in the inhuman hours regimes expected of young doctors in the seventies and eighties.

Much was written and said about it all at the time, often by those without experience of what it involved. The intensive on-the-job learning had to be weighed against the potential for mistakes and the human cost for practitioners. This was the frontline and this is just how it was, day in, day out.

Paediatrics involved much more thinking, with a fair amount of doing, but the post carried the burden of ludicrously long working hours. Every other night and every other weekend was spent in the hospital on call, often with no middle-grade support or cover. Even though these hours attracted only one third of normal pay, the on-call work was intense. No loafing around in this job. My first week of paediatric on call started with four full days of work, before the start of the much-feared weekend.

MONDAY

09.00

Arrive with trepidation, and wonder if I and my fellow senior house officer Jen are up to it. The start of the 144 hours work that I will do in the eight days ahead.

That's the equivalent of six full days of twenty-four hours, spread over an eight-day stretch, Monday to Monday. Jen has just finished the first seventy-two hours of her eighty-hour weekend. She's taken the routine bloods and she looks a complete mess. Her eyes are reddened. I'm not sure if she's been crying, or if she is just dog-tired. Together we grab a quick cup of coffee, and enjoy a whinge about the midwives before going round the ward with Dermot, the paediatric registrar, in preparation for the consultant ward round this afternoon. Jen says the weekend hasn't been too bad. We have eight children left on the ward, with four babies to see in special care. Blood results come back before lunch. We prepare for the boss's arrival. He seems in a good mood. We have to qualify the reasons for doing every test we have requested and explain why we haven't done all the other possible tests that we might have ordered. Jen leaves at five, handing me the crash pager. I head off to the mess, with fingers crossed. Thankfully Dermot is on call tonight. Good to have the back-up.

19.00

Bleep from the children's ward for a drip to re-site in Tim, an eighteen-month-old boy, admitted with Henoch-

Schönlein Purpura (HSP), a condition of unknown cause that inflames blood vessels and can damage the kidneys, joints and gut.

19.10
Trying to insert the line for a third time, and the crash pager interrupts: "Flat baby" on labour ward saves further futile attempts and I abandon Tim.

19.40
Back to Tim. The "flat baby" was fine. Another false alarm. Why do we call sick newborn infants "flat"? I have no idea. They are floppy, not flat.

20.15
After four more attempts, the damned drip is finally secure before I'm bleeped again and asked to review a worsening asthmatic child and prescribe oral steroids.

21.00
Order a takeaway curry and settle down in the doctors' mess, to watch *Miami Vice* with Dermot.

22.15
Crash call for emergency Caesarean section, "Breech undiagnosed". Bag the newborn baby Jaz, but she still looks poorly so I admit her to special care for observations. Insert a cannula, mix the antibiotic vial with sterile water, draw this solution up and give the antibiotics, check her blood gases, and order her an urgent chest X-ray. Inform Dermot.

23.00
Do the evening ward round before Dermot goes to bed, and prepare a list of bloods for Tuesday morning. Much prefer the nurses to the midwives. Reflect for a moment and shrug.

TUESDAY

00.00
Phone X-ray. They are still busy, but say they will do Jaz's X-ray soon.

00.30
Still no chest X-ray for Jaz. Frustrated, sitting in the mess.

01.30
X-ray completed, looks fine. Repeat blood gases. Jaz is just about coping, but she's needing forty per cent oxygen administered through a head-box. Go back to bed and ask to be bleeped at 04.00, to repeat Jaz's blood gases.

03.00
Crash call to labour ward for "Dips on tracing" and an "imminent" delivery.

Dips involve a decrease in the fetal heart rate and signal fetal distress. As does too fast a heart rate or, oddly, a fetal heart rate that remains fixed at one speed, unable to vary its rate. The healthy heart, that vital blood pump for the body, needs to be responsive to pressures and stress.

03.30
Still no delivery, so check Jaz's blood gases early, which are worsening. Start Jaz on nasal continuous positive airway pressure (CPAP).

04.00
Back to bed, asking to be awoken at 06.00, to repeat Jaz's blood gases. Before dozing off I'm bleeped again. The imminent delivery baby has been born and appears fine but the midwife wants me to check him over. All good. Back to bed.

06.00
Bleeped. Jaz's repeat blood gases are stable on CPAP. Sit in

the mess alone, awaiting the hospital canteen to open for breakfast at 06.30.

06.45
Bacon, beans and fried bread, with doubles and trebles of coffee, interrupted when bleeped to the children's ward. An asthmatic child is deteriorating, prescribe salbutamol (Ventolin).

07.30
Back to the now cold breakfast, then to special care for another blood gas on Jaz and do routine ward bloods, before the arrival of Jen and Dermot for Tuesday's ward round.

09.00
Ward round with Jen. I've forgotten it's Dermot's day off, lucky bugger. He's gone, but he's earned it, he's done his time. Jen still looks pale.

09.15
First patient, Tim, has all the issues you'd expect with HSP, abdominal pain and a nasty purple rash, otherwise he's stable. Bleeped away to admit an urgent referral from general practice.

09.30
Three-year-old Claire is covered in purple spots. She looks well enough, however, I notice they're finer than Tim's and I suspect leukaemia or one of the other causes of low platelets. I take Claire's bloods and hold off antibiotics.

10.30
Bleep from haematology about Claire. Her platelet count is five. A normal count would be over a hundred. The rest of her bloods look normal. The diagnosis is confirmed as idiopathic thrombocytopenia purpura (ITP). A common, usually post-viral immune diagnosis seen mainly in children.

In this condition the immune system is corrupted, causing the patient's blood clotting platelets to be mistakenly rejected and destroyed. Bruises and bleeds are common. Usually self-limiting and usually not serious. Usually.

11.30
Ward round finishes and Jen and I head to special care to see Jaz and check the labour ward board for any pending trouble. Jen droops visibly, reading on the board of a woman admitted twenty-eight weeks into her first pregnancy. The woman's expecting twins and she's had a show. Jen is on call tonight, without Dermot, and she knows the admission spells trouble and little sleep.

12.15
Lunch and coffee. Bleeped to see five-year-old boy, James, with possible nephrotic syndrome — leaky kidneys.

12.45
James has an excess fluid in his tissues, oedema. He has swollen hands and feet, and a thick swollen scrotum. His skin oozes clear fluid as I repeatedly attempt to take samples. The protein levels are high in his urine, confirming the diagnosis. The consultant can explain it all tomorrow. Kidneys are complicated.

14.00
Jen heads to the labour ward and I retreat to the mess to rest and clock watch. The minutes tick off to my 17.00 escape time.

14.30
Claire has a nosebleed. I discuss our options with the haematology registrar and we decide to do nothing. Any platelets we give Claire will be consumed rapidly by her confused immune system. I call the ENT (ear, nose and

throat) senior house officer to find a nose-pack in case her bleeding worsens.

17.00

With relief, but a palpable tinge of guilt for the mother of all hospital passes, I hand over the crash pager to Jen and head off home for a bath, pub, bed and bleep-free sleep. And I do sleep, surprisingly well.

WEDNESDAY

09.00

Arrive on the children's ward and it's immediately clear Jen has had a bad night. The twins delivered at four in the morning and are both now on CPAP, and Claire, with the ITP and low platelets, needed her nose packed at six in the morning.

In spite of all the night's trauma, Jen has carried out most of the bloods in readiness for the afternoon's consultant round. I send her off to change out of her scrubs and do the usual morning necessities, while I start obtaining bloods from the remaining children. It's a consultant ward round day, so everyone has to be on their toes.

We get two or three of these a week and they're both a blessing and a curse.

The diagnoses and management plans will be ratified, or criticised. Teaching will happen and problems will be ironed out, but at a cost. It means we'll face potential humiliation and the consultant's wrath, exposing our lack of knowledge. Thankfully Dermot, the registrar, is back this morning, so we have three pairs of hands on the tiller. Problems should have been addressed before the Wednesday night shift when I'll be left by myself. The morning is spent shuttling between special care and the labour ward, talking to the laboratory and ordering a repeat chest X-ray on Jaz, who needs yet more oxygen. Jen's twins are still fine.

12.30

Lunch. Undisturbed for fifteen minutes, then an urgent call to look at a new baby, Fi, admitted jittery, with a blood sugar level so low it doesn't register on the paper strip. She needs immediate attention. Low sugar can cause permanent brain damage in a matter of minutes.

13.30

Working out Fi's fluid infusion and glucose requirements takes longer than expected, necessitating help from Dermot. I'm bleeped, it's 14.05, the consultant ward round has started, I'm five minutes late and he's cross.

14.05

The ward round is ponderous, as every investigation must be approved and the reasons for every test not requested are challenged. The nod of approval is not given lightly. Grudgingly, I decide I like the bastard. Somewhat rotund and balding, he knows his stuff. He's done his time and has an encyclopaedic knowledge of children's illnesses. Beneath his intimidating aura I suspect lies a caring soul. The consultant is called to the phone. He returns, his face flushed in anger. Claire doesn't have ITP. Her blood sample was highlighted by a technician for scrutiny by a consultant haematologist. The haematologist's findings are grave. Claire has acute lymphoblastic leukaemia.

Jen and I hide behind Dermot, as the consultant attempts to explain the change in diagnosis to Claire's distraught mother. The ward round drags on, even slower than before, punishment no doubt for Claire's misdiagnosis. The pager has gone off four times. Six babies need checking before they're allowed home. But neither Jen, nor I, are given permission to leave.

16.30

The ward round is finally over, five new extra blood tests and an abdominal X-ray have to be performed and the six babies still need to be seen before they can go home — that's six babies plus parents, expectant grandparents and all their wider families and friends salivating over the ritual goo-goo that we rarely witness.

Not our show. More critical still is Fi's infusion review, a drug chart to rewrite, and Jaz needing an urgent blood gas with repeat electrolytes, to check her kidney function.

19.30

One of Jen's twins has developed a temperature and Dermot says it's logical to do a full septic screen on them both, including lumbar punctures. We take one baby each. Somehow, I win the race to finish first. Jen sorts out the newborn baby checks and offers to stay, but I'm stuck on site overnight, so I can tidy up.

21.00

Immediate tasks finished, but three new GP referrals await. I know one of them well. Charlie, a twelve-year-old boy, who has the neurological consequences of measles encephalitis, a subacute sclerosing panencephalitis (SSPE). He is severely brain damaged, prone to aspirating his food (when food is taken down the airway), and has been admitted with signs of pneumonia, that can often result from aspiration.

22.15

Charlie and two others are admitted and their treatment plans sorted. It helps that this is Dermot's night of on call and the workload can be shared.

23.00

Try to calm down the locum obstetrics senior house officer who's in something of a state. He's been bleeped to roll his sleeves up and explore a lavatory U-bend.

A woman on the labour ward has passed something on the toilet and the midwife wants to know what it is. A fetus? I tell him to refuse. If she's so curious, why can't she roll up her own sleeves? Why this bulldog behaviour among midwives? I wonder if pride is at the root of their territorial aggression. They are promoted as being "independent practitioners". Historically, I suppose they did once rule the roost in the maternity suite but times have changed. Today, they are highly dependent on doctors for procedures such as Caesarian sections. I guess it must grate the midwives to have so much experience but to still have to ask inexperienced, exhausted and often disinterested junior doctors for help.

23.30

All is quiet as Dermot and I head off to bed. My head is barely on the pillow when the pager goes again — another Caesarean section — "Paed labour ward".

THURSDAY

00.30

The Caesarean section is delayed as the spinal injection — the epidural — has yet to kick in.

02.00

A healthy baby boy is delivered. Gases, repeated on Jaz, are showing better, and Fi's sugar levels have stabilised. Now the children's ward needs me to review Charlie, the boy with SSPE, whose respiratory rate has increased to fifty.

04.15
Charlie settles with some oxygen and I consider waking Dermot, but decide instead to add another antibiotic, one that helps treat anaerobic infections, those caused by bugs that don't need oxygen to thrive. I hope Dermot will support me if it's the wrong decision. I feel a responsibility to protect Dermot from night calls. He's my back-up for real crises and the more difficult decisions. Plus, it could be my turn to carry that can in a few years.

05.00
Bed. But I can't sleep, so toss and turn in sweaty sheets.

07.30
Bleeped to re-site Fi's sugar infusion. Have some toast and marmalade, before calling Dermot and updating him on the night's events. He's fine about my treatment plans and we arrange to meet over a coffee before the ward round.

09.00
Jen arrives and Dermot leaves for the paediatric outpatient clinic. Jen and I split duties. I take the chores on the children's ward, while Jen goes off to the labour ward and special care. It suits me this way — no midwives. The morning is spent reviewing Claire, James, Tim, Charlie and four others.

11.30
Meet up with Jen, who says she isn't feeling well. I pray she won't go off sick.

I'm not sure I can do Thursday night in her place, including the approaching weekend. That would be five nights on the trot. Right now things seem to be under control. Without consultant ward rounds to interfere with management, I suggest Jen has a lie down, leaving me the outstanding baby checks and bloods. As I pass Claire's

Tim's pains, meanwhile, have lessened and he can be sent home with continuing open access to treatment.

But James has deteriorated. The oedema of his feet has extended up his legs, and blood, as well as protein, has appeared in his urine. I hate kidneys, never understood them, missed that bit at medical school, so I ask Dermot to take the lead here and field the consultant's inevitably complicated questions.

10.45

Our ward round finished, there are the bloods to check ahead of the consultant's round. Dermot does the tricky ones.

11.45

Special care. No Jen. She's been delayed by a forceps delivery. Fi's glucose management is no longer a problem and she goes back to the postnatal wards, but Jaz is now on fifty per cent oxygen. Dermot says he'll show me how to insert an umbilical artery line.

13.30

Line inserted. It looks a delicate procedure. Not looking forward to my turn.

13.45

Grab an egg sandwich, white sliced bread, dry crusts turned up at the corners.

14.00

Consultant ward round. Jen leaves in tears. Dermot is absent, answering his pager, when the consultant quizzes her on the different types of nephrotic/nephritic conditions seen in children. It's not a great way to learn, like a surfing lesson in a Hawaii rip tide or plunging head first down the Cresta run in St. Moritz. I suppose, like those, you'll have learnt a lot if you survive.

16.00

Ward round over, I bleep Jen, who comes back to help tidy up. The three of us Jen, Dermot and myself huddled, subdued, consoling each other over cups of tea in the mess. Jen leaves again and I cradle the pagers. It's as if they're alive, a malevolent presence on my belt and I fantasise about crunching them underfoot, one at a time, grinding them into tiny bits under my heel.

18.15

Back to the labour ward for a routine vaginal twin delivery, no issues but hang around an hour, gagging and holding my breath. I can't bear the smells.

19.30

Maybe that's why I order a takeaway curry something strong and spicy and join Dermot in the mess. The weekend seems to be going well, then three GP admissions turn up, one after the other.

20.00

Off to see Simon, a six-month-old who isn't thriving, Chrissie, a 13-month-old girl with her first febrile fit, and Zak, a known cystic fibrosis child of eight with worsening chest symptoms. I ignore Simon, glance at Chrissie, and focus instead on Zak. I'm getting the hang of triage.

21.00

Zak and Chrissie are clerked in, bloods are taken on both, and Zak started on antibiotics. Simon will have to wait as the postnatal ward have alerted me to Fred, a day-old baby with a raised temperature of 38.5 centigrade.[4]

---

4. To avoid the use of negative numbers when describing regular environmental temperatures, Anders Celsius designed his eighteenth-century scale using zero degrees for boiling and one hundred degrees for freezing. This original scale was reversed within a few years.

21.30 Fred needs a full septic screen, including a needle aspiration from his bladder, something I hate doing, and a lumbar puncture. His veins are good — a positive. I write up his antibiotics and talk to his mother.

22.30
Microwave a cold and rather sad-looking chicken madras. I know how it feels.

23.00
Start clerking in Simon, hoping to discuss the possible reasons for his failure to thrive, but his parents have left. Perform a brief examination and tell the nurses I'll finish it off tomorrow. Simon's scrawny for sure, but otherwise he looks OK and I can't find anything untoward at this stage. He should be fine overnight. I update Dermot, who offers to give a hand, but I say I'm fine.

23.30
Late night round on the labour ward, check the board for potential problems, and pop into the special care baby unit. Jaz remains on fifty per cent oxygen, but his arterial line has failed, I can't face attempting to insert a radial arterial line, and I don't want to wake Dermot, so we shall have to run him on heel pricks: painful stabs on the sole of the foot to obtain capillary blood. These are quicker and easier than sampling a vein or artery but I must take care to avoid the area where I can cause damage to the underlying bone. Heel pricks it will be.

I haven't finished the GP admissions. Should have taken up Dermot's offer of help, but I ought to be able to do this. After all, during half of the nights of my on call, I am alone, with no support other than the nurses.

SATURDAY
Hang around on the labour ward till 02.00, as a baby

is due to be born with "decelerations", a slowing of the fetus's heart in response to stress. On arrival the baby needs a few puffs by the bag, but her condition recovers quickly and I'm not worried. She can go back to her mum and I can go to bed.

02.30
Bed. Sleep.

04.00
Bleeped to review Chrissie who has just had her second fit. She's hot and cross and even though I'm pretty sure she just has a cold and a febrile seizure, I decide to perform a full septic screen, including lumbar puncture, before starting her on intravenous antibiotics. No need to wake Dermot.

06.00
Back to bed

06.30
Bleep to the labour ward for a meconium delivery. It's taking its time. Hurry up. Any last chance of sleep gone. Do I look how I feel? Bleary eyed, yawning? Not the time to face a mirror.

08.00
The baby finally arrives. Una is floppy and stinks. I don't like the look of her. We have a lot in common, but that smell spells trouble. Infection. Una needs admission to special care with another full septic screen.

08.30
Coffee with Dermot who says "Well done and good luck" and heads home.

09.00
Bleep: the nurses on the children's ward ask when am I

going to "finally clerk in Simon", the baby who is failing to thrive. Simon's parents have arrived and want to see me to discuss the plan I've made. I consider telling the nurse that I've only had two hours sleep, just twenty-four hours into an eighty-hour shift, but don't. Instead I suggest they tell Simon's parents that I'm dealing with a sick patient and will try to be there in an hour. That the "sick patient" is me, is not something they need to know.

09.30

Canteen breakfast of stale croissant and coffee. Still in my pyjamas. Can't be arsed to get dressed. Just let someone dare challenge me. Ablutions and quick cleaning of teeth. Simon's parents can wait.

10.00

Back to see Simon's parents and take a proper history. Why was a routine failure to thrive admitted over a weekend? Ridiculous. They look at my dishevelled state and shake their heads. I explain that a screen of routine bloods is needed and that Simon's feeding will need to be observed on the ward by the nurses over the weekend. The consultant will be able to sum it all up for them on the Monday afternoon ward round. I wish them a good weekend.

11.00

Head off to see five babies waiting for their routine baby checks before they go home. Lucky babies.

11.15

Glance at the labour ward board. Nothing too frightening.

11.30

Decide I will stay on the maternity side of the hospital until after lunch and phone the children's ward to explain my pending tasks. These include: a special care ward round, chasing Una's blood results and reviewing two babies on the postnatal ward. One has features of Down's syndrome and another has six fingers on one hand.

12.45

The "Down's baby" hasn't got Down's. She isn't floppy and just looks like her mother. The six-fingered monster would make a good off spinner, but I'm too tired for any attempt at humour and reassure her mother, explaining it's easy to resolve and not to worry.

13.30

Canteen curry. Oh well, it's a curry weekend, wonder what my vitamin levels are like, or whether anybody cares? I doubt it.

14.00

Start the Saturday morning ward round on the children's ward. Thankfully James has had a good diuresis and his oedema is now resolving, Chrissie has had no further seizures and Zak's oxygen requirement is reducing. Hooray! The round is disrupted by the emergency admission of a 14-year-old boy with severe asthma. The child arrives as I put the phone down. How did he get here so quick? Thomas is a known severe asthmatic. We are all scared. I take a brief history, as the nurses give him nebulisers and oxygen. Insert a drip, giving him aminophylline and intravenous steroids. Thomas will need close watching. Should I warn the anaesthetic team?

I wish Dermot was still here.

14.30

The labour ward phones the children's office. Nice not to be bleeped. Must be a rare, understanding midwife. I'm needed for a routine breech delivery. I say I can't leave Thomas, but will run across if the baby arrives in a bad state. Silence on the end of the phone. I'm not prepared to negotiate and I'll face any consequences later.

16.00

Thomas is now stable and I go to the labour ward, who have forgotten they called me about the breech. The baby is suckling on the postnatal wards. Reviewing the labour ward board, I see they have seven labouring mothers — seven hand grenades, with their pins half out — and I wonder which will keep me awake tonight. I feel sick, I'm just so fucking tired.

17.00

Walk round special care. Jaz's gases are improving and I'm thinking she's probably through the worst of her premature lung disease. Head off to the children's ward, via a fifteen-minute break in the mess.

19.30

Review the sick children on the ward. The only one that worries me is Thomas. He has reached the stage where any further deterioration of his asthma will involve ventilation.

Thomas seems calmer and his heart rate has slowed, despite the aminophylline. Is that a bad sign? Or is it a good sign? Normally this drug makes the heart go faster. I suggest that if he continues to improve, we halve the rate of the infusion, in the night. Maybe not till 04.00. I don't want to be called back before 06.00.

21.00

Takeaway curry. Thank God for curries.

22.00

Take another look at Thomas and Chrissie. Can't be bothered to write my findings in the notes. Too tired. They'd be illegible anyway. It's true what they say about doctors' writing; it's all that sleep deprivation.

22.15

Back to the labour ward to see what's in store. Not much has changed. Jaz looks good and all seems calm over on the children's ward, so I settle down to watch a late-night film. I am desperate for bed, but terrified of being woken up and know I won't sleep unless I'm reasonably confident of a few hours undisturbed peace.

23.00

The children's ward call to say that Thomas needs a new drip and that there are three drug charts to re-write.

23.30

Midwives call. They've forgotten a newborn baby that needed a first day baby check. It can wait until tomorrow I tell them. Bloody midwives.

SUNDAY

00.30

Back to the labour ward, special care and the children's ward. Nobody reports any current or anticipated problems, although I'm asked to re-site Thomas's drip again. Why does it keep on failing? No point in asking.

01.30

Bed, bed, glorious bed.

02.00

Awoken just as I'm dozing off "Just to inform you a woman has been admitted with decreased fetal movements, but all seems well." Why the fuck tell me that?

03.00

Crash call to the labour ward for a "Flat trace," on the same patient. Jump in the lift, punch the wall. Scream to myself as I head downwards. No one can hear me.

Mrs Stephens, in her first pregnancy, with a normal antenatal history has been admitted with early contractions. The cardiotocography (CTG) machine that measures her uterine contractions and the baby's heart rate has caused alarm among the midwives. No heart trace is picked up. Neither can auscultation through the mother's abdomen pick up any evidence of a heartbeat in the baby. An emergency Caesarean section is performed and a dead baby handed to me. He is a beautiful, perfectly formed, well grown, recently dead baby boy. I intubate him, perform heart massage and squeeze oxygen into his lungs with a bag. He doesn't respond. After fifteen minutes I stop. He is dead. I am pretty sure I saw his vocal cords and intubated him correctly, but I haven't done this before and hope I didn't place the breathing tube down his oesophagus by mistake. His parents don't want to cuddle him, so I wrap him up and go to the empty delivery room next door. To practice intubating him.

I know he is dead, but I think it's an urgent and important skill for me to learn so that I can become confident in the procedure. His white cords glisten, as I repeatedly insert the endotracheal tube. I'll think this through after the weekend. No time now.

I feel like I'm doing something wrong, dirty, but know this will save lives later.

04.15

A midwife sees me intubating the stillbirth and asks what the fuck I am doing? I try and explain, but she looks at me in disgust. As if I've been caught in the act of molestation or stealing from a handbag. She slams the door shut.

04.30

I leave the baby and find the matron, asking what to do

with his body. She takes him and, depressed, I stumble off to bed, but first poke my head in on Thomas and ask the nurses to halve his aminophylline infusion.

05.30
Bed. But little sleep. Sweaty sheets. Sweaty pillow.

07.00
Labour ward bleep me. The parents of the stillborn boy, Mr and Mrs Stephens, want to talk to me. The father has to get home soon, as he is exhausted. Wearily I walk over, unshaven, unwashed, and unable to taste my own halitosis. I try my best to explain. It's a cruel fact that perfectly normal babies can die in the womb for no discernible reason. It's not uncommon among stillbirths and this was one more tragic example. I don't mention practicing my intubation skills on their dead son. They wouldn't understand. Would anyone?

08.00
Canteen beans on toast, before a quick shave and a ten-minute rest.

09.00
Start the Sunday children's ward round, alone. Thomas has coped well overnight. The nurses eye me sympathetically and have kindly written out the necessary blood forms, fortunately only four today. A little kindness goes a long way. Maybe I'm not alone on the frontline after all. I hope the storm has passed and I can get round the wards by eleven. It helps that I know the children and their cases so don't have to ask any questions. Things are looking up.

11.30
Go to the mess to lie down on a sofa and share the pain with fellow inmates. The routine baby checks can just bloody wait.

13.30

Complete two of the five routine baby checks. Wonder what I missed? Starving. Enjoy the luxury of a bleep-free Sunday lunch with a medical colleague, chatting about the recent discovery of the wreck of the Titanic, before heading back to both wards, wondering what's been happening in the two hours I've been missing. Nothing.

14.30

Bleeped about an urgent admission of a six-week-old baby boy who is short of breath. Oliver has been perfectly well since birth, but is now struggling. On examination he has a respiratory rate double what it should be, a fast heart rate, and, on palpating his abdomen, an enlarged liver. He also has a loud murmur. Oliver must be in heart failure. I take the plunge and describe the situation to the consultant on the phone. He agrees and suggests I start diuretics and call him back if matters take a turn for the worse. I don't trouble him with all the other issues. They can wait.

15.00

The labour ward call for a meconium delivery. This one is straightforward and the baby only needs a quick "suck out". However, as I leave, the matron asks to talk to me. "Is it true that you have been practicing your intubation skills on a dead baby?" I say it is completely correct, I explain why, say I am too tired to argue about it now and suggest that, if she believes my behaviour was unacceptable or unprofessional, she takes it up with my consultant on Monday. Fuck them.

16.30

Back to both wards. All calm. But I've forgotten the three outstanding new born baby checks and am bleeped, asking where I've been?

17.00
Half way through one of these examinations I am crash called to the labour ward. Imminent delivery of a baby with a poor trace in a diabetic mother.

18.00
Clearly imminent means different things to different people.

19.00
Very different.

19.30
It's now been two and a half hours. If it was urgent at the beginning it won't be now.

19.45
The baby finally arrives. A failed ventouse suction, followed by a failed forceps, ends up with a Caesarian section. The baby, Alex, is alive but in a poor state.

20.00
Alex is fitting. Lines are inserted, antibiotics given, blood gases taken. The prognosis is worrying. Alex will probably be a court case. Not my fault.

21.00
I head off to do the remaining baby checks, but am told it is too late and they will be added to my list for tomorrow. Could I start early at 07.00?

22.30
Rounds on both sides. Alex won't feed and is having nasogastric expressed breast milk. The rest will be fine until Monday. I'm starting to lose track of whose results are outstanding and which tests I've promised to do and in what order. It doesn't help that I've lost my sheet of clinical patient notes.

23.00

Early to bed, can't wait any longer. I'll take my chances.

MONDAY

04.00

Bleep. Alex's drip has failed again, we call it "tissued". Although I can barely open my eyes, a new line somehow slips in, probably, and I go back to bed.

05.00

Bleep. Alex's drip isn't working. Not surprised. I didn't really think it had gone in, a combination of wishful thinking and extreme exhaustion. I re-site it and, to punish myself, go to both wards for a quick check on the patients.

06.30

Bed.

07.15

Bleep. "Where are you? It's baby check time." Where the fuck did the midwife think I was? The cavalry is arriving in ninety minutes, but bugger it, I'll do the baby checks that I missed yesterday. But I'll refuse to see any new ones.

08.15

Yesterday's babies examined, apologies given to bemused parents, followed by canteen beans on toast and more coffee.

08.30

Jen and Dermot arrive. Dermot has seen a band over the weekend and Jen has spent the weekend in bed. I explain my issue with the midwives and the dead baby. They understand.

09.00

I join Dermot on the children's ward while Jen goes off to

the labour ward, special care, postnatal wards and to do the baby checks that I couldn't face.

11.30
Both rounds finished. Next job, bloods for the afternoon consultant round. Dermot says I should shower. Apparently I smell.

13.00
Dermot, Jen and I meet for lunch. Toad-in-the-hole.

14.00
Consultant ward round. Three hours to go, then home. I'm criticised for reducing the aminophylline at four in the morning. This should have been done at midnight. Also, I've missed some screening bloods on Simon. I'm given sympathy and support when I explain my dead baby experience and I'm congratulated for sorting Oliver's heart failure.

16.00
Ward round finishes and the consultant leaves. I help with the post ward round form-filling, take two sets of bloods and rewrite three drug charts. My writing really is deteriorating, but I no longer care.

17.00
I stagger off to the car park to drive home, then pub, bugger the shower. On the back of a beer mat I tally up the week's work, spread over eight days on the general, labour and baby wards.

This is the end of my 144 hour "busy" week, rotating every other week with a "quiet" five-day week, of just seventy-two hours. It doesn't help that annual leave can only be taken during these so-called quiet weeks.

The beer mat makes distressing reading. Surely this can't be true.

No wonder nobody believes us.

Over the last consecutive 188 hours:
Time spent in hospital: 145 hours.
Time spent not in hospital: 43 hours.
Sleep obtained in hospital, over five nights: 18 hours.
Number of disturbances, during the 18 hours of sleep: 10.

This hadn't been an exceptional or particularly un-pleasant "busy week." Same again in a fortnight. I wonder how Jen will cope with her own "busy week". I order another pint, and settle down in my own private bubble, pager-free, to think through the challenges I faced over the past eight days.

The intubation of the dead baby ticked all the boxes as the most significant event, because of ethical considerations. Was it ethical to do what I did? Was it ethical not to? What would I have done, or felt, if the dead baby's father had walked in and seen me, repeatedly sliding the cold metal instrument into his dead son's mouth?

Practicing inserting the plastic breathing tube, deep into the collapsed lungs? If the roles were reversed, I knew I would be furious. Was what I did even legal?

The law of Moses rendered anyone making contact with a dead body unclean for seven days. That much was true. Had I sunk to the level of the Anglo-Saxon phenomena of nineteenth century grave robbing, where teams, often comprised of medical students and junior doctors, dug up fresh corpses on which to practice dissection? I hoped not. Twenty years later the Human Tissue Act was passed, clarifying that any human parts could only be used if done so ethically, safely and with proper consent.

I obtained no consent for what I did, but this was the unsanitised frontline in the 1980s. I doubt I would have been given parental consent, if I'd asked. But I had to learn this life-saving procedure somehow. Wind forward a decade and experience would be gained with plastic dummies, and with senior doctors usually at hand.

We didn't have that luxury. I was confused. The practice at intubation was the ideal opportunity for me to gain the necessary skills to save lives later. A unique opportunity to gain much-needed competency. There were no consequences of failure, there were no spectators, no secretions obstructing my view of the cords and, there was no sense of urgency or pressure.

There's another question. If I reckoned practicing intubation, without consent, on a dead baby was reasonable, then why didn't I also feel it would be reasonable for me to practice other procedures? Such as inserting lines into umbilical blood vessels, inserting a chest drain or tapping the brain's fluid? I would have to do all of these procedures later and I needed the practice for those future cases too.

But I didn't think any of those procedures would be reasonable to practice on a dead child. I thought they would be a defilement of a dead body. But that was just my opinion and I knew many others would disagree. The distinction to my mind is that those procedures involved the breaking and damaging of the corpse, whereas the intubation didn't and it was an urgent skill to learn. One that I needed there and then. One where I had no other means of learning and one that I, and the newborn babies, needed my immediate confidence to perform.

I left the pub, settled in my own mind. Certain that this practicing may have been illegal, and might shock many, but in the privacy of the room, I believe it did no harm.

I'm sure there are powerful ethical arguments on both sides. But this is what I did and, whatever the midwife thought, I was then, and remain today, comfortable with my decision. Having trialled the procedure in this way, I gained the necessary confidence in a life-saving urgent act that I would use hundreds of times later, saving dozens of lives.

The lack of any other opportunity to practice these skills at this time consoled me that my approach was pragmatic and indeed necessary to be able to provide safe labour ward care in the future.

There were no plastic dummy heads to practice on.

No corpses whose parents had given prior consent.

This was real life. Real death.

The stuff that happens behind closed doors.

The truth that many would struggle to confront.

If I got into trouble, then fuck them, I would go back to the farm.

I slept well. But the established practice of leaving dying premature babies in the sluice – that did trouble me. That wasn't right.

That shouldn't happen.

In the following thirty years, I never failed to intubate a baby.

6

NECKTIES

In 1986 two catastrophes shook the world. The Space
Shuttle Challenger exploded, killing all seven crew members,
and then, three months later, number four reactor at the
Chernobyl nuclear power plant suffered a calamitous
failure. During this unsettling time I was still employed
on the West Sussex general practice rotation, sharing my
first real home, a small house in Lancing, with a friend
called Herman. Herman was tall, dark, bespectacled and
charmingly insincere, the Clark Kent of the junior doctors.
Herman made the perfect housemate since whatever
superhuman abilities he may have mustered were focused
wholly on seducing women. His kryptonite weakness was
any hint of domesticity. It didn't start well. Our first cooker
was delivered. It was a two-oven gas cooker. The delivery
men brought it into the kitchen. We didn't know if we
would understand how to use it. No matter, I guessed it
would be like obstetrics. We'd just have to learn on the job.

The men asked where the gas was. I looked around.
Herman looked around. They looked around. There wasn't

any. They carried the cooker back out and a week later it was swapped for an electric one, free of charge. Otherwise the house was fine. No gas though.

Herman and I stood naked on the Sussex Downs with lampshades on our heads. Herman's girlfriend, meanwhile, took photos of us as I rubbed a donkey's nose. Invitation cards were sent in the post, inviting all to a "Nearly Naked Party". Dozens of partially clad friends arrived. It was going well, until an elderly neighbour rattled her walking stick on the window and shouted: "People like you should live in a flat in Brighton, not in a house in Lancing." She had a point, we were rather out of control.

To a party in London thrown by Worty and his wife Nicky. After leaving the bar I made my way unsteadily on a short cut through St Stephen's Hospital accident and emergency unit. I didn't work there, but was spotted by the casualty officer who knew me, and also knew I had a reputation for being good at relocating dislocated shoulders. I'd always found the sensation of a shoulder popping back into its socket gratifying. He asked me if I could deal with his patient's shoulder. They'd tried every trick in the book, he said, but the shoulder just wouldn't go back in. Would I mind? He wasn't my patient. I wasn't on call. I didn't work in the hospital. I didn't check the X-ray. I didn't examine the patient. I wasn't even sober. Shocking now, but at the time it didn't seem out of the ordinary. Try as I might, I couldn't get his shoulder back in. The reason was simple. The shoulder wasn't dislocated. The shoulder was broken. What can I say? We had no brakes. Appalling. Embarrassing.

Oddly, the more tired I became during this paediatric rotation, the more I became accustomed to the lack of sleep. When weary, the first part to fail was my manners. Politeness and patience were sacrificed, before competency and capability.

Despite all of this, the post had its attractions. Our paediatric consultant was a legend. He could be intimidating, but he was invariably loyal and supportive to his team, qualities I needed, critically, when I was called to a formal disciplinary hearing for allegedly calling the senior midwife "fucking stupid".

I will call the midwife Eva. It was she who said, quite abruptly, "Come to see a baby," after I'd been woken at 5 a.m., the fifth time that night. I asked Eva what the problem was, not an unreasonable request. There are sound medical reasons why it's good to know the problem from the off. It's simply sensible to know whether you'll be needing to calm down a furious parent, be giving drugs to a fitting child, be certifying a death or inserting a difficult drip. If the job requires some analysis, then an idea of what's involved enables useful thinking and preparation time on your way over.

I'll admit to some tetchiness since, quite apart from my lack of sleep, I knew Eva had form. It had been Eva who'd bleeped the locum doctor, telling him he needed to search around a toilet U-bend for whatever a woman may have passed while sitting on the loo. And I'd been the one who'd told him to refuse.

On the phone, Eva told me that an hour previously a baby girl had been born seventeen weeks prematurely, at twenty-three weeks' gestation. Following the practice at that time, having decided the baby had no hope of survival, Eva had put the baby into a steel Petri dish in the sluice to die, but the baby was still breathing, alone in that claustrophobic cupboard. The baby had been expected to die, but she didn't. I said "That's fucking stupid". Leaving a baby for an hour and then asking for help is inexcusable. To describe it as fucking stupid was an understatement. There are far more damning words I could have used.

If a baby is born extremely prematurely, the best and only realistic chance of a good outcome is if the baby receives optimal initial care. The first fifteen minutes of life are critical. Alone in a cold steel dish is a hopeless start. A generation later this wouldn't have happened. If it had, the midwife would have been suspended and following an enquiry, in all likelihood been sacked. Respect and privacy would be paramount. Mementos of the dead baby's hair and ink prints of the hands, or feet, would be offered to the grieving parents as keepsakes.

I'd slammed the phone down, got in the lift, punched the wall and marched off to see the baby. She was icy cold, had no chance, and died thirty minutes later. Eva submitted a formal complaint about my conduct. A panel was assembled to explore the circumstances. My paediatric consultant was there, with my previous obstetric consultant and my paediatric registrar, Dermot. I explained what I'd said, clarified that I hadn't called *Eva* "fucking stupid" but that the situation, in my view, was fucking stupid. I apologised for using the F word, explained that I'd had less than forty hours sleep all week, and agreed I should instead have just said "That's very stupid". At the panel, the paediatric registrar, paediatric consultant and the obstetric consultant all agreed with me. As I moved on to my next post of geriatrics (care of the elderly) I hoped Eva wouldn't decide to make the consultant obstetrician's life miserable.

It didn't take long to decide that care of the elderly and general practice weren't for me. I'd enjoyed the past twelve months of hospital cut-and-thrust too much. Blissfully unaware of the Eva-fed paediatric worm eating away inside, I considered a career in genitourinary medicine. That would be useful, I thought, not to mention a source of many an interesting tale.

I enlisted the help of Freddy, a friend from medical school, who'd embarked on a career treating sexually transmitted diseases. Freddy was one of those people who knew how to work a room. Compact in stature, he could size up career opportunities or promising women with a radar sharpness, prioritising and grading those in his immediate surroundings, marking their potential. Freddy kept a little red book of useful contacts and said he could help get me a job interview.

Interview secured, a consultant on the interviewing panel noted a spell I'd spent working in KwaZulu, South Africa, and asked me about STD.

What a weird question. Perhaps he thought I'd never been there and this was some kind of a trap. I'm good with numbers.

What was the phone code? I knew it started 035...

Oh my God! How embarrassing.

Having muddled the STD of subscriber trunk dialling with the STD of sexually transmitted diseases, my cover was blown. The door closed on that avenue. The career choices were narrowing and the urgency to choose increasing. In the end it came down to neckties. I disliked wearing a tie and was running out of tie-exempt specialties. I couldn't see myself as a sedentary anaesthetist and, having been exposed as a fraud in genitourinary medicine, there was only one specialty left: paediatrics.

The decision to train for a career as a paediatrician still took me, my family and friends, by surprise. I didn't even like children.

Much to the irritation of my GP trainer, I rapidly obtained a post in London, on a two-year paediatric training rotation.

7

MANEATER

So this was it, specialty training in paediatrics.

The first attachment was with an apparently important, orthopaedic consultant. I hadn't met an orthopod before. But I knew the old joke: 'There are three types of orthopod, those that can count and those that can't.'... (get it?!) I wondered which group he fell into.

On the first day, on my first ward round, I was ticked off for not wearing a jacket.

"I don't know what paediatric docs do, but proper docs wear jackets. Make sure you do for the next ward round," he said. Bloody cheek. I was working, as a junior paediatrician, in a famous children's hospital and from my point of view the *proper docs* were the paediatricians. Orthopods were overrated and overpaid carpenters. I decided to make a stand.

A friend who worked in entertainment lent me his jacket: stark, white, with broad lapels, and covered in wild splashes of primary colours. Claire, the porter, whistled on seeing me and, turning into the mess, I met Ciaran, the go-to senior registrar. Ciaran was famous for risking his career by deflecting a patient, in an ambulance, to another hospital. He hadn't trusted the paediatric consultant on call that night. Ciaran was a rule breaker. To his disgust, the doctors' mess had been turned into a no-smoking zone. Not for Ciaran. With cigarette in hand, he sat on his throne, puffing away in the corner, pulling on his tatty beard, watching *Inspector Morse* on TV. Ciaran had declared the far left-hand corner of the mess, a separate zone, like Burgundy in *Passport to Pimlico*. "Very brave," he said when he saw the jacket.

Some said I'd be sacked. I didn't care. This was a non-negotiable matter of principle.

I went to start the ward round, and half-a-dozen others trailed behind like vultures, waiting for the pickings. Sir Lancelot didn't blink. We completed the ward round and he looked me in the eye: "See you in theatre, at half past one. Charles, don't dare be late."

Just time for the doctors' mess, an exchange of smiles with Ciaran still puffing away on a cigarette, then a change into green scrubs and a deep breath before entering theatre three. Sir Lancelot looked up and turned to the consultant anaesthetist.

"Jimmy, this is the young doctor who has been taking the piss out of me all day," he said, peering over his half-moons, as he inserted screws into the child's lower leg.

"Well done. Point well made."

Sir Lancelot liked legs. He liked lengthening them. At this time growth hormone treatment was only available for those patients with a significant deficiency in the pituitary gland. Sir Lancelot was at the cutting edge of the technique. If children had uneven leg lengths, a couple of centimetres added on one side, to balance the body, transformed their lives. Other children were just very short and adding a little length would make a big difference.

The lower limb bones were sawn through with external fixators screwed into place. A few times a day the leg would be stretched, very slowly, little-by-little, aiming for around one millimetre of growth per twenty-four hours, maybe half a centimetre a week. Two inches could take two months.

A week later, colourful jacket returned to its rightful owner, I was called by the hospital dentist to see the palate of an infant with a rare malignant tumour, a melanotic neuro-ectodermal tumour of infancy. I had never heard of this condition and was touched that he had the time and inclination to teach me. Maybe I wasn't beyond help after all. "It's usually found in early infancy, is rapid in growth and invades locally," he said. I was told this was a classic one. I peered into the baby's mouth and said, "Incredible. To me it looks like a bit of black plastic." A week later, baby Logan was prepared for theatre and a major procedure. Four units of blood were cross-matched, a senior anaesthetist booked and two hours of theatre time allocated, for a complex and dangerous operation. A significant excision of Logan's palate was planned, with chemotherapy later. Logan's parents were grey and tense. Logan's name was alone on the theatre list. He was anaesthetised, and the initial incision made, a small cut of just two to three millimetres into the roof of his palate. Then snip, snip, snip into the beautiful soft corrugated pink mucous membrane covering the bone and, out popped - a bit of black plastic. I wanted to publish the case but was told: "You'll get us closed down." Where did the plastic come from and how did it get lodged in Logan's palate? Was there a safeguarding issue that we missed? Did the concealment of the misdiagnosis lead to Logan being unnecessarily exposed to further risk? Or was it simply an accident? Since this concern was never raised with Logan's parents, we'll never know.

On a glorious Saturday morning, a month after Logan's operation and twenty-four hours into a continuous eighty-hour on-site shift, I was pushing my ward trolley thinking about what I needed this weekend. How my ducks had to line up. On the Thursday night I'd dreamt of ducks bobbing around on a pond. The ducks were obstacles awaiting me, threatening to disrupt the long weekend ahead, starting Friday morning and ending eighty-hours later, after a Monday afternoon clinic. The ducks were a sign of something. I was tired and needed a break. I gave them names, each representing a significant worry.

My first duck was the "nutrition duck". There was no canteen, or food dispenser, on site, so I was concerned about getting enough food to keep me going. The second, was "hygiene duck". I prayed that I would be able to have at least one quick bath, as otherwise I knew I would smell bad.

Duck number three was the "assault duck". I crossed my fingers and toes that I wouldn't get a child abuse case to explore. That would wreck the weekend.

"Alert duck" was next. My aim was to avoid falling asleep again in the Monday afternoon paediatric cardiac clinic. It didn't give a good impression to the parents. My fifth and final duck was the "sick duck". If the colleague replacing me became unwell, I'd be stuck and I knew if he died, I'd be a stuffed duck. More likely, if the Monday doctor was off sick, I would just have to do a fourth consecutive night of on call. And this would be after all the day hours, with no break time. No locums. No negotiation. No whingeing. No rights.

That sunny Saturday morning I was weary. I hadn't done much work hitherto, it was a mental exhaustion from the anticipation of a further fifty hours on site and from the frustration of wasting a beautiful day. As I went around one of the wards, checking on my paediatric patients, I pointedly bypassed those belonging to the other specialties.

As usual, I sought to do no more than the absolute bare minimum. I had to maintain my energy and enthusiasm for the long haul. Close by, an eight-year-old boy screamed and doubled up in pain. He wasn't my patient, but I'd heard about Pierre. We all knew his story. Pierre had been around the London hospitals with his abdominal pain and, after an initial diagnosis, then second and third opinions, Pierre had ended up with us — for psychiatric treatment. No medical cause could explain Pierre's pains. The problem was solely between Pierre's ears. I wondered whether he'd been badly treated at home. His parents seemed cold, for sure. I tried to ignore Pierre's screams; I was tired and knew no psychiatry, the nurses could deal with him, not my problem. I really didn't care as much as I should have. Yet, somehow, my trolley stopped by his bed. Irritated, I asked Pierre what he was screaming about. Pierre just groaned, making faces, clutching his abdomen.

So I did the doctor thing, partly to save face with the nurses, and put my hand on his stomach with a quick exit in mind. I'd never felt anything like it. An alien was trying to escape through Pierre's abdomen. I felt again. No doubt about it, he had a hard tender mass, like a small orange, in the middle of his abdomen. Poor Pierre had a volvulus.

In the womb, due to the restricted space within the abdominal cavity, fetal intestines take up temporary residence, outside of the developing baby, at the base of the umbilical cord. At three months of gestation they start moving back in, making two rotations, before settling into the correct location in the abdomen. A complicated process; no wonder it sometimes goes wrong. If the guts don't go back it results in a condition called gastroschisis. Alternatively they may go back inside after an incorrect rotation. The guts return, but not in the right position; this is called a malrotation. With a malrotation the bowel functions normally most of the time, but can suddenly twist. And this is a volvulus. A loop of bowel swivels around its supporting tissues, obstructing everything, including most importantly, the gut's own blood supply. Children can die from this.

Pierre had been shifted from pillar to post, effectively having been diagnosed as a fake, causing untold misery to himself and his parents, when he had a serious, potentially fatal missed diagnosis. Poor Pierre. Even if Pierre had been faking, there would probably have been a psychological explanation for his behaviour.

Even today, medicine, and society, are more sympathetic to those with tangible medical problems, rather than the equally important, but usually looked down upon, psychiatric ones. We're more responsive to conditions we understand than to those we cannot comprehend. Luckily for Pierre, and for those who had previously misdiagnosed him, he had twisted his gut just at the right time. The ducks flew away and the remaining fifty hours of on call also flew by. I felt euphoric, didn't fall asleep in the cardiac clinic, and on Monday a doctor came to take my place.

An exciting weekend behind me, I was home at last. Bathed and well lubricated, feeling dangerously disinhibited, a friend and I spotted a dumper truck. Why did dumper trucks excite me when I was running on empty? The police saw me clambering aboard, shouted and gave chase. We ran back to the flat, opened the main door, jumped down five steps, through our front door, and lay down, panting hard. Seconds later we heard the police charging upstairs. Were we stupid? Yes, of course we were, but we weren't functioning like normal adults.

Within twenty-four-hours of this childish behaviour, we had a serious ethical problem to solve. Ciaran, not content with his earlier diversion of a seriously ill patient, had hidden a different patient, William. Much debate ensued. It was a moral problem. Was it reasonable to treat a child, with a potentially fatal condition, who had arrived under our care, but technically wasn't allowed this support from the NHS?

William had HIV/AIDS, but was not a British citizen. The doctors' mess was split. We discussed what ought to prevail: the professional duty to the patient or the duty to the tax payers and the country? There was no easy answer. I was unsure. In the end Ciaran, compassion and William won and the NHS picked up the bill.

Then another problem, we discovered we had no registrar booked for the next, and rapidly approaching, eighty-hour weekend. One of the seven senior house officers (SHOs) would have to step up and act as a registrar. That would involve a new responsibility of overseeing one's colleagues and equals. Unfortunately, I was the chosen one.

I was reminded that I was by no means the smartest, nor the most knowledgeable, nor the hardest working, nor even the most senior. I knew I wasn't the prettiest, the best dressed, the most polite, or the most caring. I was told, however, that the top brass believed I was the most likely to ask for help if, or rather when, I was out of my depth. I hoped I wouldn't have to ask too often.

The on-call weekend, my first working as a registrar, started quite well.

Admittedly, having the door held open and being sarcastically addressed as *Sir* and being asked trivial questions to rile or test me had become wearing. The peace was about to be broken as a fellow senior house officer, "Rita the Maneater", was preparing to put me in my place.

Rita was an inch or two taller than a pillar box, with broad shoulders, cropped blond hair and a steely demeanour. She was a perceptive clinician who did not differentiate between fools or junior doctors, and suffered neither. Perhaps her nickname was harsh, but probably not. She scared me. She had previous, and had a definite sexual allure, if one dared. I certainly didn't.

Off Rita and I went to do the round on the surgical ward. In fact, we were three: me, as the acting registrar, the Maneater and the ward sister. As acting registrar, it was my responsibility to draw up a list of tasks.

First, was a sick baby with gastroschisis. The glistening bowel lay outside of the abdomen, resting on the baby, and was quite beautiful. Nature at work as the peristalsis, waves of bowel constriction, moved the hidden inner contents southwards. Wake up, I thought, you aren't here to be mesmerised by the allure of nature gone wrong, you are supposed to be in charge and supposed to make things better. I made what I thought was a good plan. I think the sister agreed. She would have, as we'd become close. "Rita, please do the electrolytes, full blood count and CRP." The Maneater looked at me. Cleared her throat. Pushed out her ample bosom, leant over her balcony, and said loudly and clearly, "Why the fuck don't you do it, Charles?" I wanted to laugh. I could see she had a point. It's just not how it worked.

The challenge of acting registrar used brain energy and made me hungry. There was no food on site and duck one was calling, so I popped out for a kebab and to escape Rita's glares. I had to eat. On the way back, kebab in hand, I checked the traffic on Vauxhall Bridge Road. I looked left, right and left again. Nothing was coming so I stepped out, towards the central island. I immediately sensed something was wrong and, looking left again saw a car being driven south, by a man, heading towards me at speed and on the wrong side of the island. Smack. The bumper came off. I lay on the road, waiting for the searing pain, from the compound fractures in my legs. Not much. I was grateful and waited to slip into unconsciousness and death. Must have suffered a significant head injury and be totally numb. Ten seconds later I still felt OK, so got up and ran after the car. The driver was now running back towards me. He had gone a further 800 yards down the road before stopping. He claimed later that his girlfriend had been driving. An ambulance took me to the main hospital. I was assessed, bandaged and then hobbled the half mile back with my three pagers, to the children's hospital. Nobody offered me a lift back. I'd left for a kebab at 19.30, collected a kebab at 19.40 and been run over at 19.45. Ambulance and hospital treatment complete, I was back at work before 21.00. Less than ninety minutes after I had left for some food. Pretty good.

With three pagers on my belt, all remarkably intact, I limped back to paediatric accident and emergency. This wasn't the TV series *Casualty*. There was no round of applause. Instead, the sister, a different sister, turned and said, "Where the bloody hell have you been? The senior house officer is very busy and some patients have now been waiting for nearly an hour. There are also triplets on the way for you, with an allegation that each of them has been a victim of sexual abuse." Was she serious?

Please, not the third duck. One alleged sexual abuse case could take me hours.

Triplets were unbelievable. My first weekend as a registrar. I didn't believe her.

But it was true. It was also, of course, a Sunday night, with separated parents – a popular day of the week for one parent to make sex abuse assertions against the ex. It tends to happen as children are returned to one parent, having been temporarily in the care of the other parent over the weekend. The idea of triplets mixed up in sexual abuse allegations on my first middle grade weekend was incomprehensible. Some concerns may be genuine, but a lot of this appeared to be point scoring, to boost maintenance negotiations and/or obtain greater access. I knew my triplets would be a time-consuming, difficult and dangerous sequence of examinations. I wished I hadn't bounced off the car quite so effectively.

Being treated for two broken legs in a hospital bed, by caring nurses, with no pending eighty-hour shifts, on paid sick leave, away from the glare of Rita the Maneater, seemed like a state of bliss in comparison. Two hours later I'd examined all three triplets and could find nothing abnormal. I knew that didn't prove much, either way. Unfortunately barring sexually transmitted diseases, pregnancy, significant trauma, video or photographic evidence, sexual abuse is hard to prove.

I was wary about the pitfalls surrounding safeguarding. Paediatricians were at risk of being accused of either over diagnosing or under diagnosing abuse. The process is fraught with emotional tension and there are serious consequences to making a mistake. It's also an area where hard science is scarce. I called social services. They were supportive and helpful and told me that they knew this family well and were not at all surprised. It wasn't the first time this bloody mother had taken her children to an NHS hospital, on a Sunday evening. They doubted it would be the last. I hoped that next time she'd go elsewhere.

I was right to be wary. Child protection (safeguarding) trips up many a paediatrician. A year later, in the summer of 1987, two consultant paediatricians in Middlesbrough, Marietta Higgs and Geoffrey Wyatt, made over a hundred diagnoses of child sexual abuse. So many children were taken into care that the hospital had to house them in a place of safety. The two consultants had relied on a test called reflex anal dilatation, whereby a diagnosis of anal penetration was thought to be secure if the anus dilated when the adjacent buttocks were lightly brushed. This theory was later dismissed, as the anal dilatation reflex was also found to exist in chronically constipated children.

Baroness Elizabeth Butler-Sloss reported in her findings from the subsequent Cleveland Child Abuse Inquiry that most of these diagnoses were incorrect. The vast majority of the children were later returned to their parents.

It would be a further eighteen years before the President of the Royal College of Paediatricians, Sir Roy Meadow, fell foul of this area of care, and the GMC struck him off the register for serious professional misconduct. Meadow was an expert in child protection, the source of Meadow's law: "One sudden death in a family is a tragedy, two is suspicious and, three is murder unless proven otherwise."

He was alleged to have applied flawed statistics, in a case where a mother was accused of suffocating two of her children. Sally Clark, an English solicitor and daughter of a senior police officer, had inexplicably lost two of her infant sons. Meadow had erroneously squared the odds of a second child dying from a cot death.

Only Sally Clark knew what happened, but Meadow was wrong to extrapolate. His estimate of a seventy-three-million-to-one chance of this tragedy happening was incorrect. Meadow was a paediatrician and not a statistician; he had made a mathematical mistake. Meadow immediately appealed to the High Court, which ruled in his favour. The GMC objected to the High Court's decision and applied to the Court of Appeal, which decreed, eight months later, that Meadow was not guilty of the GMC's charge.

There were no winners. There seldom are in safeguarding.

8

TOM

Monday morning arrived. I was sore after having been run over. Tired from having done eighty hours continuously on call. Emotionally drained by having to act up as a registrar. Scared, or maybe aroused, by managing Rita the Maneater. Frustrated by that damned mother and her child abuse allegations. Back to the comfort of senior house officer; I was expecting a quiet day in the mess, watching *Star Trek: The Next Generation*.

Ciaran put his cigarette down. Nobody had dared challenge the mess guru about his filthy habit. Erudite, scholarly and supportive, he commanded the room like a dowager aunt whose pronouncements demanded attention. "Someone needs to tap the pleural effusion of an eight-year-old boy," he said. The procedure involved draining fluid from Tom's lung, unpleasant for both patient and doctor and risky as it could go wrong without care and precision. The needle could penetrate the lung, causing it to collapse and create a troublesome pneumothorax; or, if puncturing a blood vessel, an internal bleed, a haemothorax. This would then need an even larger incision and a wide bore drain. A supposedly minor procedure could, in seconds, become something major. We were still working on the principle of see one, do one, teach one, and I'd done a handful previously so felt confident enough to volunteer.

I reassured Tom's parents and explained the process, before cleaning his back in preparation. As I injected local anaesthetic and inserted the thoracocentesis needle, my eyes fixed on the fifth space between his ribs. The first space lies between the first two ribs, so this was just above the sixth rib, about three inches to the left side of his spine. Being above the rib, rather than below, I hoped to avoid the blood vessels and nerves that ran just below the ribs. Pushing the needle further into the back of Tom's chest, I gently withdrew on the syringe, anticipating a flush of straw-coloured fluid. Nothing. I re-examined Tom. His chest was stony dull on the left side, confirming an effusion on that side. I re-inserted a new needle, one space higher and pushed further into Tom's chest. Then, a further inch. Still nothing came out. The needle was now over two inches through the skin, getting closer to Tom's heart.

The thoracocentesis needle was big. A much larger bore than a needle for taking blood. If I punctured Tom's heart, I would kill him. I withdrew the needle and repeated the procedure twice more. Still no fluid. What was going on? I stopped.

I should have stopped earlier. This wasn't a collection of fluid. There was no fluid to drain. Tom had a rare, paediatric solid lung malignancy. It sounds incredible now, as radiological investigations would have shown this, but with the limited tests available at the time, even in a centre of excellence, these things happened. More damning, perhaps, is that there was no system for reporting such incidents; no complaints, no later analysis of why it went wrong, no apology, and nothing learnt. I made a short entry in Tom's notes and that was the end of the matter, though, sadly, not for Tom. Tom needed surgery and chemotherapy. We needed a better system to learn from our mistakes. I wondered what would happen to Tom, but knew I would never find out. I would rotate away to another hospital, before he was either cured or died.

I enjoyed performing practical procedures and was becoming slicker at taking blood (phlebotomy) from children. At the time phlebotomists didn't exist for children. This was our job. It was the bread and butter of life as a paediatric senior house officer.

Phlebotomy on a cooperative, trusting child was more likely to be a success. Both the parent and the child had to believe you knew what you were doing. And so did you. This only came from practice and, at last, I was pretty competent. Our usual blood taking technique would soon be deemed dangerous and outlawed. Breaking the metal needle off the plastic hub and inserting the sharp tip into a small vein, letting the blood drip into the pathology container, nearly always worked.

The common sites used for finding children's small veins were the back of the hand or foot, between the fingers, at the elbow or even on the tender, soft underside of the wrist. When no veins could be seen, we went by feel alone or serendipity as we probed beneath the skin. Occasionally large amounts of blood were needed and options then included using an artery, a large scalp vein in a baby, the femoral vein in the groin or accessing the child's neck veins. None of these four was an attractive proposition. The arterial stab was painful and potentially hazardous; the scalp vein involved shaving a section of hair and risked leaving the child with half a mullet. The femoral stab was another thigh clenching procedure, guaranteed to make my scrotum tighten in sympathy as the needle probed deep into such a tender region. The last and most effective, but also most unpleasant method, was to wrap the child up in a towel, have a nurse hold the child, with its head hanging over the edge of the table, and then to sample the bulging neck veins, Dracula-like. I reserved that technique for young children where a large blood sample was needed.

It wasn't long before I realised that most of what we did in medicine was under constant Government scrutiny. However we tried to execute our duties, the Government interfered, publishing papers, directives and instructions, few of which we appreciated. As a senior house officer this mattered little. We were left to do our jobs. For consultants these changes were more troublesome. Some of the papers had ridiculous titles such as *Project 2000*, published in 1986, with fourteen years to go. Plans were announced to raise nursing qualifications to degree-level. It sounded good, thought the nurses, but it would take more than twenty years to happen. When it finally did, in 2009, the experience did not match the vision. Nurses were trained in universities and, as a result, many of them missed the hands-on traditions of a caring vocation. Then another White Paper emerged called *Promoting Better Health*. We neither knew nor cared about the difference between White Papers, Green Papers or paper napkins. The consultants tore out any residual hair, while the junior doctors partied in blissful ignorance.

Meanwhile my career began gathering momentum. At about the same time, too much momentum on the ski slopes led to an unscheduled somersault, landing on my head. The consequences of this accident would shape the next three years. A week after the skiing accident, my neck pain was worsening, with severe burning pains down my right arm. When lifting a pint of beer became a struggle, I knew I had to see a doctor. It turned out I'd pushed the top five neck vertebrae forward on the rest of my spine. I liked the radiographer, Rhian, who had taken the films. In one of life's *Sliding Doors* moments she entered my tube carriage on the way home and we arranged to meet for a drink. She was going to Australia to work, she said. Why didn't I join her? Well, indeed, why not?

First, however, I needed some proper training in the medical management of very prematurely born babies. A friend recommended Oxford, so I headed off for a discussion with the professor. I was hoping for a job without an official interview. When I got to Oxford, I was still in jeans and had forgotten to bring a suit. I phoned Anthrax Worty. He was a man with a finger in every pie and knew people everywhere.

Worty gave me a telephone number of his friends, Rupert and Ruth. Rupert was a larger-than-life orthopod, generously proportioned, with a good brain, proving there are few absolute rules in life.

"Of course, no problem," said Ruth when the stranger appeared on her doorstep.

"You can wear my husband's suit, he's out at work wearing another suit. Rupert has plenty of suits," she said.

I had thirty minutes before the interview. She showed me into their bedroom and told me I could take any suit I liked. Rifling through Rupert's wardrobe, I'd never seen so many smart clothes. Had Worty met Rupert at some fashion show? The suit fitted well. Leaving my clothes in a heap on the bedroom floor, I charged off down the stairs to the front door, which opened just as I got there. In walked Ruth's parents, to see me standing, flushed and dishevelled, wearing their son-in-law's suit. It was classic Brian Rix farce at the moment the curtain falls.

The professor couldn't have been more helpful, agreeing to lay on some intensive training of the very premature and sick newborn before I set out for Perth, Western Australia. Worty, my new Mr Fixit, also knew one of the more senior paediatric doctors at the Oxford hospital. Slimes was as dapper as his friend. With thick, flowing dark locks and an engagingly hearty laugh, he could have been medicine's Heathcliff or possibly a blend of Lord Byron and W.G. Grace. And he was looking for a tenant.

The neonatal post offered high-quality training and, as usual, things went wrong.

Each morning one of the junior doctors pricked the heels of the sick babies and collected their precious blood into separate, thin, three-inch-long glass tubes. This is referred to as "doing the bloods". Having labelled twenty of these blood samples, I gingerly put them into a centrifuge, plugging the end of each glass tube with plasticine before placing each tube into a groove, then securing a metal plate on top to hold them firm. The idea is to turn on the machine, then wait five minutes for the blood and plasma to separate. After taking the lid off it's easy to see how much clear plasma there is and how much is thick blood. Dividing the percentage of blood by three gives the approximate haemoglobin. If the red bit is under a third of the tube's length, the baby has a haemoglobin of under eleven and might need a blood transfusion. The whole process is simple and fun, was well within my capabilities and indisputably worthwhile. Only this day I was a little jaded. Slimes had been testing his home brew on me and running through his love life. There was a lot to tell. It had been a long night.

I thought I'd screwed down the centrifuge plate. I hadn't. Inside the centrifuge was the debris from twenty broken glass tubes, carefully collected from the pricked heels of twenty sick newborn babies. I must have been particularly forgetful that day, as I also sent the cerebrospinal fluid that I'd drained from a child's spine off to the laboratory without putting the top on the glass bottle. I correctly put the silver foil over the end, but forgot to screw a glass lid on the sterile container first. How could I have been so inept?

Prior to departing Oxford I went to see one of the consultants about a minor issue. "You got away with it," he said. I hadn't a clue what he was on about. Centrifuge? Spinal fluid? "I got away with what?" I asked. He told me that, two months earlier, I'd made a common, but serious, drug error. I'd written up ten times the correct dose of morphine for a newborn baby. When babies weigh under one kilogram, it's much easier to make this error. The morphine overdose could have made the baby stop breathing and make his blood pressure crash. By good fortune for us both, the baby came to no harm. I was amazed. Not at making the error, but at only finding out two months later. My junior doctor colleagues had hidden my mistake from me, as they were rightly concerned that I would be devastated.

Australia beckoned, but before leaving for Down Under I dabbled for the first time in medical research as the most junior member of a team puzzling over ventilation rates for sick premature babies. Was it safer to ventilate a sick premature baby quickly or slowly? It was a simple, reasonable, question to which nobody knew the answer: which was better, forty breaths a minute or sixty breaths a minute?

My job was pretty menial — entering the data that would back up the subsequent paper. This basic groundwork involved filling in dozens of sheets of data. If it came to be published, doctors would get their names on the paper, after peer review. Not mine. Unjust, perhaps, but that was the junior's lot. I didn't mind; my time would come.

I'd collected six months of records: weight, gestation, blood pressure, inspiration time and ventilation rate. There was even a row for mean arterial pressure (MAP). Why did they want that? Sheets finally completed and handed in for analysis. Whoops! I'd misunderstood MAP. It wasn't Mean Arterial Pressure. It was Mean Airway Pressure.

"Bad Medicine" by Bon Jovi had reached number one in the US. Time for my transport to Australia.

First, my old Sussex friend Jules was getting married, and I was to be his best man.

The stag do was in drag at the *Goat in Boots* pub on London's Fulham Road. Standing at the bar, I noticed that women seemed to respond better to me in drag. I'd been distracted and, looking around, I became aware I'd been abandoned, no longer safety in numbers. I tottered outside to catch up as fast as my high heels and tight red dress would allow.

I saw Rhian's best friend walking towards me on the pavement so turned my head and ignored her as we crossed.

"It's no good," she said. "I know it's you."

9

PERTH

Perth was searing heat, persistently irritating flies, giant magpies, flocks of parrots, weird quokkas and even weirder locals. As soon as I could, I headed to the hospital human resources department, to sort the necessary paperwork and discuss my job options. "I'll do anything, but please no more neonates," I said. So they gave me a year in the largest neonatal unit in the southern hemisphere. It was good to find out early that we Poms were at the bottom of the social stack. Well, not quite. The very bottom was reserved for the indigenous people. It nagged me that the true Poms, the Prisoners of Her Majesty, were ancestors of the locals. So why was I supposed to be one? But a Pom I was, and being a Pom made everything a little harder. At first I found the label irritating, but came to wear it with pride. Having studied Homo Australiensis for a while, the breakthrough in relations came when I discovered the best approach to hostility was to be abrasive back. This worked a treat.

Before starting work, now as a registrar caring for the sick and/or extremely premature newborn, there were a few days to kill. Rhian and I drove north in my new purchase, a pale green, twelve-year-old, automatic Valiant station wagon. We entered Broome, part of untamed Australia, and rodeos were in town. As Rhian and I settled down in the pub to scampi and chips, an Aborigine walked in. He was promptly thrown out.

We glared at the expressionless square jaws below wide-brimmed fur felt hats. They squinted back, men with no names, feigning disinterest. A ruddy-faced local leant over my plate, removed and then slowly bit into one of my fries, before returning the dog-end to my plate. This was going to end badly. I glanced apologetically at Rhian, cut the remains of the chip in half, flicked the contaminated part onto the floor and waited. The room went silent. You could cut the atmosphere with a knife. In the Wild West someone would have shot the bartender. We ate quickly. As we left, the cowboys lined up and we received a guard of honour. But no fists flew. I'm not sure why. It was going to be a testing couple of years.

I was now a paediatric registrar, but there weren't any senior house officers. So it was really no more than a label, acknowledging my previous medical experience. It didn't change the role, although it did make me feel more important. I hoped my title would give me the right to think. Meanwhile Rhian, the radiographer, saw the light, and flew the nest. People were taking flight too easily; two parents disappeared after we'd saved their child, Annie. They refused to take their baby home. They were Jehovah's Witnesses and we had given a blood transfusion to their baby girl. Their interpretation of scripture meant that they would not accept blood in any circumstances. Not even their own blood, stored for later re-transfusion back into their own body. I wondered if that was why you never saw Jehovah's Witnesses taking up professional cycling.

Annie had been born four months prematurely and her bone marrow couldn't produce enough red blood cells to oxygenate her small body. She was going to die unless we transfused her.

Despite full knowledge of her parents' wishes for us to let Annie slowly asphyxiate through a lack of oxygen, we obtained a court order, transfused her, and she recovered. That was when her parents refused to have her back. Annie had been orphaned through religious orthodoxy.

The neonatal unit was of a size I had never conceived. Four rows of ventilated babies, eight to a row. I tried to work the English system I knew, starting my ward round at one end and moving slowly forwards. One baby at a time. Only one registrar worked in the unit at any one time so I barely saw the other doctors, apart from an Englishman, called Lurch. At six feet six inches, weighing well over 100 kg, it was always reassuring to have this giant by your side in some of the rougher bars we visited. But now he was upsetting the nurses since he doggedly refused to get out of bed when on call.

The first day proved stressful. After eight methodical hours I'd only reached the twelfth ventilated baby, just one third of the way. It seemed I was being too thorough.

Here in Australia the nurses did nearly all the work and made most of the decisions. The paediatric registrars were there to help, but not to run the show. I'd also been delayed trying to feed a catheter into a 500gram baby's radial artery, in her wrist.

At the time she was the smallest baby to have survived in Australia, and using the smallest catheter we had, I found it stretched her artery as I carefully threaded it under her transparent pink skin; fascinating and beautiful, but time-consuming.

As I settled in, the new medical system was starting to work better and I'd found a new friend in Frank, who had moved in when Rhian moved out. Frank's real name was Ian, but he had a dimpled chin like the footballer Frank Worthington and the name stuck. Frank, a worker in the gold mines in Kalgoorlie, was the perfect flatmate. He drank like a fish, partied endlessly, loved scuba diving, and never made a mess. Frank wasn't tidy; he was compact and just didn't dirty anything. Preferring to sleep on the floor, he lived on takeaways. No need to use the kitchen. I'm not sure if he washed.

It was 1989 and, in the UK, another White Paper had been published. This one imaginatively called *Working for Patients*. It stressed efficiency and called for the splitting of care into *providers* and *purchasers*, balanced through an internal market.

I hoped it wouldn't disrupt the concept of health care free at the point of delivery, nor wreck medicine as a career, nor trash the quality of care for patients. I prayed that the NHS might somehow survive. It was a particularly grim year in the UK, including the Hillsborough football tragedy and, on the River Thames, the sinking of the pleasure steamer Marchioness. Meanwhile in Perth accident and emergency, it was plain that many of the accidents were also water related. This wasn't surprising since, being so damned hot, water was integral to Perth social life. Boating accidents were common and there were so many child drownings that pool fences became obligatory. In one incident a teenager had to be intubated directly into his trachea, his airway, on the back seat of his parents' car, in the hospital car park. Charlie had been water skiing and, hit by a speedboat propeller, been driven to hospital, choking and bleeding profusely through a jagged gash in his neck. The propeller had sliced through Charlie's airway, just missing all his major neck vessels. He was fit and lucky. His thick sternocleidomastoid and sternohyoid muscles had shielded both his common carotid arteries and his internal and external jugular veins, as well as his delicate thyroid gland. Charlie survived. Luck plays a significant role in outcome.

By now I was finding the Aussie culture difficult. The Australians seemed interested in what happened locally but in little else in the world. Their work ethic was also a shock. It was regarded as normal to plan a "sickie" a week in advance, to take a day off work and go fishing. I doubted they pondered much the significance of the fall of the Berlin wall. Why worry when you're working in T-shirts and shorts and swimming daily? The racism was shocking. At the WACA cricket ground Pakistan soundly beat Australia, much to my and, I suspect, most of the rest of world's delight. The Australians, however, seemed oddly upbeat, singing "I'd rather be a Paki than a Pom." Why? Then I saw a T-shirt in the market with a lorry running over a rabbit, "20 points", squashing a kangaroo, "50 points", and flattening an Aborigine, "100 points". I'm ashamed I was too timid to challenge any of this, but it was not my type of culture, if that's the right word for such uncultured behaviour. Any attempt to discuss the bigotry was either ignored or rebuffed with hostility, when I'd be reminded that I was a Pom and therefore it wasn't my business.

The growing itch to pack it in and leave was temporarily abated by a stint working in paediatric intensive care and for the Royal Flying Doctor Service. Most of the trips involved collecting sick children from the north of the state, doing little apart from inserting a drip in to a small vein in the child's arm and then sitting by the child, listening to the pilot's stories of disasters.

test dangers the patients faced came from the
vas pleased to have a pilot who was confident,
t covering the inside of the windscreen with
newspapers and flying "blind" seemed a step too far. I was
worried and asked, "Mate, is flying with no visibility and
no radar difficult?" "Nah, mate, nah problem, mate," he
replied.

It wasn't just a dispensable Pom at risk, we also had a
newborn baby girl, Isla, on a ventilator and a paediatric
nurse to worry about. Complicating the situation, the tube
into Isla's lungs dislodged mid-flight and I had to lie her on
a seat and re-intubate her. It was messy and bloody, but
she didn't crash. Neither did we. The tube went in and Isla
survived. I thanked God for my earlier practice on the dead
baby in Sussex.

The end of my time in Perth came quite abruptly as a
result of a job advertisement on the wall of the doctors'
mess:

Wanted

an experienced paediatrician to replace a
consultant returning to Australia. Duration
three months. Basic salary and supplementary
Australian national scholarship paid.
Venue Mt Hagen, Papua New Guini.

They couldn't even spell Papua New Guinea, the lazy
buggers. Where was Mt Hagen? Ah, the Western Highlands
Province. I read that Mt Hagen had a population of
around 80,000. A good proportion of these, however, were
children, since the average age was twenty. I didn't know
much about Papua New Guinea but I understood that the
bird life was interesting and I was vaguely aware of stories
of headhunting.

102

I made enquiries and was given the details of an Australian doctor, a previous incumbent who happened to be a friend of my current consultant in Perth intensive care. "Phone him, mate," my consultant said. His friend, Frank, a senior paediatric consultant in Melbourne, was kind, patient and positive and said "You must go." I'd heard there'd been a previous incident and asked Frank why he'd left PNG.

"I was attacked in outpatients, most unfortunate," he said. I was suspicious and needed more information, as we Poms were always being reminded of Gallipoli, and were widely regarded as cannon fodder. The locals felt we owed them one.

According to the story I'd heard, a disturbed parent had run amok in a paediatric outpatients clinic, had killed Frank's health worker with a machete and had then attacked and disembowelled Frank. Frank's wife, also a doctor, had gone to his aid and resuscitated her husband. The machete blade had lacerated Frank's liver and pancreas, leading to an urgent repatriation to Australia. After a long stay in intensive care Frank recovered then went back to Papua New Guinea to finish his post. Frank confirmed the story and decided it would be an ideal post for a Pom. "I really recommend it to you," he said.

I needed to get some research under my belt, so I read *First Contact* by Connolly and Anderson. Although fifty years out of date, it was an excellent introduction to life in Papua New Guinea. The book focused on the country in the 1930s, when the Europeans first met the New Guinea Highlanders. I doubted that much had changed in six decades. Research completed, I was soon on a flight to Papua New Guinea.

Another glitch. There was a strike in Australia, so although I was going on behalf of the Australian Government, the necessary visa hadn't been stamped in my blue British passport. Since I'd be there for three months, I felt the urge to scour the top shelves and grab some adult reading for when I — well, felt the urge. I was pleased to see that cartoon Carrie had changed into something tastier. I couldn't sleep on the flight.

Too quickly, the plane tilted to land at Port Moresby. Leaflets were handed round by the cabin crew, saying: "If balus go buggerup put head between knees." I guessed "buggerup" was Pidgin for "in trouble" or "going to crash". Where was my guide to Pidgin? I'd scoured the wrong shelves. Then I saw a warning. Never mind the plane, it was me who was in trouble. It was strictly forbidden, it said, to import anything of pornographic content into Papua New Guinea, "punishment by prison". Dismal images of cramped and unsanitary prison cells flashed before my eyes. I guessed this was how an inexperienced drug mule might feel. Sadly, the plane didn't go buggerup and we landed safely. Everyone stared at me at immigration. How did they know I was smuggling girlie mags? Customs came next, where my passport was confiscated. I could see the headline:

Twenty-nine-year-old English paediatrician jailed for smuggling pornography.

An official took me to one side and I was told to wait. Time ticked by. Would my parents fly out to visit me? Was this the end of my career? Five minutes later, John, the Australian paediatric professor in charge of paediatrics in Papua New Guinea, arrived. John told me he had seen an official marching through the airport with a dark blue British passport. He knew that must belong to the new English paediatrician, whom he had come to meet. No tourists came to Mt Hagen so it had to be the English doctor arriving from Perth. John waved customs away and immigration away, he waved away anyone who came near us, and I was in. However, my passport was still with immigration because it didn't have the required stamp. More importantly, the magazines and I were in.

I felt vulnerable, but I was off to Mt Hagen, with John and my 'literature'. No escape now. In the car John gave me a book he had co-written with Frank about paediatrics in Papua New Guinea. He then dropped me at the Mt Hagen Hospital and told me to call him if I had any problems. As I got out of his car he wound down his window, poked his head out and said he had two things to tell me. Both about pigs. "Firstly," he said, "if you run over a pig, leave the country immediately, or they will kill you." Secondly, I needed to read up on a local condition, called *pigbel*. John said this was an important and commonly fatal disease. I'd never heard of pigbel. Until recently, it had been one of the commonest causes of death in the Western Highlands.

Fortunately, a successful vaccination had been introduced, so it was getting less common.

John continued, explaining that pigbel was contracted by eating poorly cooked sweet potato with pig meat. A toxin, made by a bug called Clostridium welchii, became particularly noxious as the neutralising enzyme, trypsin, was not only low in malnourished children, but the sweet potato eaten with the pig also acted as a trypsin enzyme inhibitor. This gave Clostridium welchii free rein to attack. In the Western Highlands, sweet potato was a staple diet and pig meat a special treat. It was literally a recipe for disaster.

John continued with the clinical details; a child with pigbel suffered from severe abdominal pain, diarrhoea, vomiting and gross distension of the tummy and could die within hours.

I knew I was out of my depth. But it was too late to turn back.

10

PAPUA NEW GUINEA

Isolated and in charge I had to learn fast. Forget the girlie mags; I took Frank's book and worked on filling the yawning gaps in my western medical education. The book's index alone terrified me. Twenty-three pages on poisoning. Lima beans, trumpet flowers, physic nuts and wild cassava that could kill. The beans sounded particularly nasty, although the book stated they could be eaten if repeatedly boiled with frequent water changes. Why would anyone do that? Dangerous bites from centipedes, death adders and taipan snakes. Botulism and rust tablet poisoning. This was worse than medical school. I was supposed to be in charge of the sick children of Mt Hagen and I hadn't a clue about any of their common diseases. It clearly wasn't me that was cannon fodder. It was the local children.

The hospital accommodation was disgusting. I called it Cockroach Cabin. Having to enter the kitchen with insect spray in hand, I carved a path through the cockroaches to get to the kettle. I am not fussy about cockroaches but dislike them when they reach plague proportions. The cupboards and ceilings were crawling. I couldn't work out what the thousands of cockroaches were living on. Possibly each other. Some locals used a traditional method to rid themselves of these much loathed six-legged, hard-to-kill pests, introducing the unmatey Australian cockroach variety, Periplaneta australasiae, to prey on the native cockroach. I found a mixture of the spray and a hard bash from a rolled-up girlie mag did the job. Personal hygiene had never been a priority of mine, but there were no washing or drying facilities and only a small, barely-functional shower. I was miserable. There was no way out. I couldn't go home, so the only alternative was to "man-up" and introduce myself to the medical and nursing staff in the hospital. I walked towards the children's ward, to be greeted outside by the guard, armed with a machete. He was half asleep, sitting on a stool.

The gate behind him was chained and padlocked. "Problems with parents," he said.

Between the guard's feet was an enlarging pool of bright red fluid. He spat repeatedly into this puddle and I saw his lips and teeth were red from chewing betel nut. Betel, the seed from a local palm tree, is a stimulant widely used throughout the Western Highlands. It tastes bitter and turns saliva the colour of blood.

The senior nurse seemed surprised by my arrival but was welcoming. I was the only paediatric consultant for the area, but had two local paediatric registrars, Thomas and Peter, to help me. No induction, timetable or rota. That was it. On the plus side, there was no paperwork to complete, nor pager to collect. Peter disappeared soon after my arrival. I never saw him again.

When called at night, a security van collected me from Cockroach Cabin, and drove me the twenty yards to the ward. Too dangerous to walk.

Inside the padlocked hospital gates was an outpatient waiting area, with space for a hundred parents and their children to squeeze into, a small sick-baby area, a typhoid ward, a measles isolation ward, and the general paediatric ward. If there was a labour ward, I never found it. As the only white man I stood out like a single stubborn skittle in a bowling alley.

On the first day I was asked to give an opinion on a critically ill adult who had complicated neurological signs. The patient had a high temperature and examination suggested a probable right-sided cerebral abscess. There were no facilities to scan his brain, so I was asked whether a hole should be drilled into his skull. Didn't they realise that I was a paediatrician and not a neurologist? I didn't know whether they should drill or not and was too scared to guess. I left the ward feeling deflated and inadequate. The hardest and bravest words in medicine, when you are supposed to be in charge, really are "I don't know".

At least the paediatrics shouldn't be a worry, as long as there were no local diseases to worry about. After a couple of days I was up and running with nothing exotic seen, or nothing I'd noticed at any rate. A bigger problem was managing the 200 sick children that arrived each day in outpatients. They weren't referred, they just walked in. A light-bulb moment. I wouldn't see any children in outpatients. The paediatric sister could run outpatients by herself and I would see anyone she was worried about. She was brilliant at identifying the sick and, unlike me, she had thirty years' experience of local childhood diseases.

Meanwhile, I was struggling in Cockroach Cabin. I had difficulty washing clothes and cooking, and the insects kept me awake at night, crawling over my bed and face. I dreamt of Amy and her earwig, except that this time it was a cockroach. I'd yet to be paid, had run out of money and still had no passport. I wondered about making a dash for it. I phoned the British Embassy in Port Moresby and heard a reassuring British voice. "Don't worry, we have recorded your presence and we can get you out in twenty-four hours, anytime you want and you won't need your passport," said the official. That was one problem resolved.

Money now. I didn't need much, as there was little to buy, but I couldn't cope with nothing. The bananas were free, but although I did see a baby brought up on an exclusive diet of crushed banana, I doubted that would work for an active 90 kg adult. I walked into the town and found a target. Two expats having a coffee. With great embarrassment, I explained my predicament. I must have looked a sorry state, as they didn't hesitate in lending me one hundred Australian dollars.

The worst problem, however, was the isolation. I'm a social animal. Good news then, that Mt Hagen had a rugby club. As its newest recruit, I turned up for training and discovered two things straight away: rules were non-existent and touch rugby involved spear tackling. Or maybe they just viewed this as the best way to handle a man with a dodgy neck who was two feet taller than anyone else. Still, it was fellowship of a kind, so worth the risk.

The sun set every evening at six o'clock and it was considered folly to go out after dark. I needed other evening entertainment to supplement the magazines, so started a regular poker game. Poker players were recruited from the rugby club and hospital staff. I was careful not to win too much. The Mt Hagen bowls club was another place of escape. Unusually for bowls, the club was surrounded by an eight-foot-high fence, topped with two rows of coiled barbed wire and protected by armed security guards.

I had no interest in bowls, but enjoyed the security. The club even came with a working machine gun behind the bar "just in case". The clubs were a crutch of sorts but I still craved a kindred spirit brought up on TV Westerns, roast beef and Yorkshire pudding. What about the golf club, three miles out of town on the edge of the rainforest? An ambulance driver dropped me there. The colonial style clubhouse was a rickety two-storey building with a balcony and corrugated tin roof, all framed by oppressive skies and forest-clad mountains.

I sat on the steps, dirty, tired, no money, no contacts, no friends and no passport.

I was ignored. I was invisible. I was also pretty isolated. I was lonely and missing Dot, my new girlfriend in Perth. Cockroach Cabin and its stash of imported "literature" seemed a welcoming prospect. But how to get back? It was too dangerous to walk. Tribesmen had been known to attack expats in this area.

I stood at the club car park exit, right thumb up, dreaming about European hitch-hiking trips from my student days. A car stopped, and my saviour, a young bald bloke said, "G'day mate. What's up mate?"

Bill No Grass (Grass means hair, in Pidgin), told me he was an Australian banker, drawn to the area by the mining at OK Tedi. No Grass didn't believe my story and insisted on seeing Cockroach Cabin for himself. On the drive to the hospital he updated me about the mine, telling me that OK Tedi was a massive open-pit, copper, silver and gold mine.

It was by far the greatest generator of wealth in the Western Highlands but also a considerable polluter. Far from OK then. The mine was in a wild, beautiful and remote mountain area that averaged nine metres of rain a year. Not surprisingly, the management of mining waste was difficult in such extreme conditions, said No Grass, and that year there'd been a "helluva" landslide that levelled the dump. On and on he droned, stuff about precious metals and their properties and all the chemicals needed to extract, clean and polish them until they gleamed. I looked at his dome and wondered if he polished that too. I nodded and stroked my chin, affecting an air of studied interest. I had to. He was my only hope. No Grass told me that production at the mine had started five years earlier and was already causing significant environmental damage with the waste tipped around the OK Tedi and Fly rivers. Over two billion tons of this untreated spoil had been jettisoned into the water, destroying livelihoods, wildlife and everything downstream. Genuine interest now. What to make of this man? Was he really my saviour?

We arrived at Cockroach Cabin and Bill was appalled. "Mate, you can't live there. Mate, I'll tell Mick you're moving in with us." What a stroke of good fortune. Not only a relatively insect-free house, but also the opportunity to wash and to talk to people, with a vaguely similar background.

How was I to know that Bill and Mick despised each other? There had to be a catch and this was it. Communication was almost exclusively via me, the go-between. Nonetheless, I was grateful and managed to keep them apart, for most of the time.

Bill introduced me to the Mt Hagen Cricket Club. Maybe I'd talked up my sporting prowess a little too much on our drive. Bill was a good batsman and captain of the Australian team. I was a slogger and, even worse, a "Bloody Pom". The big game approached. Australia versus Papua New Guinea, they called it. I was due to bat at number seven, but I was asked to umpire for a couple of hours at the beginning while Australia racked up a big score. I didn't mind. I'd done this many times. Four years earlier I'd been substituted when umpiring a league game in Lancing, for giving a batsman not out. Then the bowler had spat, screaming in my face, so that had been an easy decision.

No Grass said, "Mate, remember, nah LBWs, mate."

"Mate, fine, I assume this applies to both teams, mate?" I said.

"Nah, mate."

The rules of cricket are complicated with five common ways of getting out: bowled, caught, run out, stumped and leg before wicket (LBW). There are also five unusual ways to get out: handled ball, obstructing the field, hit-ball-twice, timed out, and hit wicket. Leg before wicket is the most impenetrable and misunderstood rule for amateur cricketers. It was added to the rules of cricket in the eighteenth century, and regularly tweaked since, its purpose is to try and stop players from padding the ball away with their legs. Professional umpires, with a full knowledge of the rules and excellent vision, frequently get it wrong. Umpiring is so difficult that ten years later, in important matches, a review system was introduced. This enabled captains to ask for a replay of the action from specially placed cameras.

It confirmed that even the best umpires in the world made frequent errors. For LBW, the ball has to miss the bat, be on track for the stumps and hit another part of the batsman. However, it must not have first hit the ground outside the leg line if the batter plays a shot. To be given out the ball must also hit the batter in line with the stumps. If the batter doesn't play a shot then the rules change. Well, something like that. I can't really remember, it's far too complicated. Put this into real life, add the average speed for a club bowler of seventy mph, similar to that of a cheetah, and the reaction time is barely more than half a second. It's easy to see why umpires get it wrong. Anyway, I was umpiring and it had already been tricky. The cricket ball had been lost in long grass at deep mid-on. The two Australian batsmen, Mitch and No Grass, sprinted the first two runs, jogged the next three and then, looking rather embarrassed, headed off to join the Papua New Guinean fielders. I was lonely standing at the stumps, so I joined them in the hunt. The ball was found and both teams agreed that three runs was a reasonable allowance.

Then a bigger problem arose. No Grass was batting as the Australian opener and was hit on his pads. Right in front of his stumps. The ball had pitched in line, missed his bat, hit him in front and would have hit the middle stump. Clear LBW. Up went my right index finger. "Out!" No Grass refused to walk. I repeated the finger and told him again: "Out!" He couldn't believe it. No Grass stalked off, shaking his head, muttering expletives, liberally sprinkled with the word Pom.

Out came the new batsman, accompanied by a new umpire. My second substitution as an umpire. The consequences were inevitable. I was promoted up the batting order, to number four. The first ball I faced hit me on the pads, nowhere near hitting the stumps. It would have missed them by two feet. "Out!"

11

FLORENCE

Mt Hagen was dangerous. Rapes and murders were common. Locals were friendly or alternatively, they would try and kill or rape you. There was little middle ground, so I never went out at night. Apart from twice.

Once I lost track of time and got caught after dark, dallying too long at a friend's house, and ran the mile home. Another, more sinister event, occurred after rugby training. Eight of us were walking down the main street. Not to be messed with, these men were seriously hard. Ahead we saw a group of five local men. Both clusters stopped and stared at each other. I was the only white man, maybe the unlucky thirteenth. Through clenched teeth, both groups made strange sucking noises, like something out of a Spaghetti Western. I assumed each set was assessing the opposition's strengths, weaknesses and odds of success in conflict. Thankfully both groups turned away.

At that time most of the local violence was tribal. The consultant I'd replaced had to leave because of death threats. He belonged to the "wrong tribe". I was reminded that racism is endemic and not owned by any one ethnic group.

In a PNG tribal war, rival gangs would charge down a hill, throw a handful of spears, hurl a few insults and then break for lunch. Meal complete, a few more spears would be dispatched, then all would go home. These tribal spats were the balancing of wrongs from previous generations. Often nobody could remember how or why it had all started. Beyond the feuds there was plenty of other violence. One weekend I house-sat for a friend who had gone back to Australia for some peace and quiet. I didn't sleep. The main gates were locked and coiled barbed wire topped eight-foot-high security fencing. The front door was bolted and chained, with a peep-hole overlooking an armed guard asleep outside on a doormat. In the bedroom a walkie-talkie and a red cord dangled by my nose. The cord, if pulled, would set off an alarm which would result in a van arriving with four security men, all armed with machetes and truncheons.

Meanwhile I had two death threats. The first was straightforward. A father said that if his son died, he would kill me. Luckily for all of us, the child survived. The second death threat was more sinister. I'd been seen talking to an attractive local girl at the town ball. Although Pidgin was the dialect, most understood English. The two languages were similar. Next morning, the phone in Bill's house rang. A voice said:

"It's Pete here, you messed with my sister. I'm going to kill you."

A bit harsh, I thought. I didn't want to be attacked from behind and decided I'd rather go and confront Pete and give him the opportunity to do it head on. I found Pete's home and knocked on his front door. Pete opened the door and standing by him was the engaging Emmanuella who I'd chatted with at the ball. Pete asked her to leave the room. She smiled at me and left. Pete was furious. Pete was absolutely hopping mad. The curls on his head tightened, his facial musculature tensed and the tribal cut-marks on his cheeks widened. I steeled myself. Hold on a moment, Pete was burning with anger but was it towards me?

"I'm so very, very, sorry," he said. It sounded sincere. I was confused. Pete told me he'd find out who'd phoned me and personally kill him. Pete thought it was probably his cousin. He'd sort this, he said, as his family honour was at stake. So this was how decades of tribal warring started. Pride.

I found out later that I'd been set up by Mick, my new housemate and Bill's despised work colleague. Mick had seen it as a joke. No joke for the cousin, perhaps.

The bankers' house was comfortable, with superb food, but the atmosphere was souring daily. I'd managed to keep Bill and Mick apart up to now but no longer. Mick had been woken by the house dog, Brownie, and Bill had found her hanging on the clothes line. At this time, the hospital's chief executive said he wanted me back on site. I agreed, but with terms — no Cockroach Cabin.

Alone again, I'd need to cook for myself and went into town looking for provisions. In the high street I noticed a man wearing a spectacular hat. He was sturdily built, in full tribal gear, strutting semi-naked about town. Not for me to judge, but his gourd looked a little over elaborate and big enough for a generous packed lunch. Then his hat moved. Entranced, I followed him into the book shop, studying the creature on his head. It was a cuscus, the world's largest possum. A stunning creature with beautiful, sad, big brown eyes, curled up and dozing on his owner's head. I knew a bit about the local fauna. These shy marsupials are hunted in Papua New Guinea for their meat and fur. I didn't want this one to be Big Gourd's dinner. Negotiations were brief and Big Gourd used my borrowed money to buy a book.

I named the cuscus Weston, after the hospital's chief executive, and took him to our new home. He would keep me company in my new house and I was sure we would be very happy together. I hoped he ate cockroaches. Weston proved a less than agreeable housemate. It wasn't his fault and I should have known. He wasn't housetrained and was a noisy nocturnal. Weston didn't snore, he sneezed and hissed. Was this a warning or a sign of friendship? I suspected the former. To cheer him up, knowing he was a tree dweller, I hacked down a small banana tree and leant it up in the sitting room. The other Weston never found out.

The children's ward was busy and depressing. At least one child a week was dying from measles. I couldn't help most of them. It wasn't only a vaccination issue. For some reason, having black skin makes children more vulnerable to dying from measles. At the same time, we had an outbreak of typhoid. To make matters worse the oxygen cylinders started arriving empty. The contents were being stolen en route.

I wondered how one stole oxygen. Ever suspicious of hospital managers, I looked around to see if any had bought a new bicycle. Then, another odd thing happened. Every sample of spinal fluid, sent from lumbar punctures, produced the same unbelievable figures. The sugar level was always forty-three. Ludicrous. A normal sugar level should have been in low single figures. I'd had enough of this nonsense, so banned lumbar punctures. I never found the reason behind this laboratory anomaly, but I doubt any child came to harm because of it.

One weekend, with Christmas approaching, we set off to climb Mt Wilhelm. It was my first mountain and I didn't give it enough respect. It was, after all, only 300 metres lower than Mont Blanc. Half of our group failed to make the summit. Our guide, Peter, ambled up barefoot, past the wreckage of a Japanese WWII aircraft, and on to the summit. I struggled up behind, golf club in hand, naffly ready to play a shot at the top.

Back at work the next day, Thomas, approached. "Sorry, got to go. Tribal war," he said. No forms to fill in, no diary to check, no clinics to cancel, no on call to swap, no records kept, no negotiation, no discussion. Again, one big positive to *no rules* was that there was no paperwork to complete. So Thomas went to tribal war. I didn't know if he went as a fighter or as a doctor. I hoped the latter, but feared it was the former. Maybe he went as both. Well that was a new excuse for Christmas absence and one to which I couldn't object.

On the whole I preferred their system of war — a lot of sound and fury but not many dead. Unlike European wars, a Papua New Guinean war tended to last only a week or two, admittedly once or twice a year and for five or more generations. But, overall, fewer people were harmed. As in everything there were exceptions. Earlier that year at a nearby village, seven villagers had been killed. The following day eighteen bodies were found from the neighbouring village of Karida, having been hacked to death. It was unusual. None of the victims were men. In traditional PNG tribal wars only the men were involved and the body count was small. This butchery was outside the usual rules. I suspected Western interference was to blame. Money was probably at the heart of it.

When Thomas left, I was alone in the paediatric department with no registrar. The locals had heard of my presence and I was starting to receive personal referrals. I had seen some intriguing cases, including a handful of children who were perfectly well, but with severe anaemia and a blood haemoglobin level one sixth of what it should have been. Then a letter arrived, from the local nuns, personally addressed to me. It was to the point and read: "Would you please see Florence, a fifteen-year-old girl, with no anus." Florence entered shyly and sat down. I thought that fifteen years with no anus should at least make her a bit uncomfortable. She was smartly dressed, of normal build, indeed slim for a Papua New Guinean. I examined Florence and found a quite common condition, that of an anterior anus. In this condition the anus opens forward, close to the vagina or scrotum.

In Florence's case it was even more anterior than usual, since her bowels opened directly into her vagina. For fifteen years Florence had been doing poos through her vagina. She was now at an age where, culturally, sexual intercourse was normal and reproduction was imminent. Florence really didn't need a "front bottom", she needed help. But, oddly, this wasn't what interested me most about her. There was something much more intriguing going on. I wondered. Should this child be blue?

I checked the referral letter. There was nothing in this about her colour. I stared at her. She looked away embarrassed. I hoped she didn't think I was making a pass. The nun was now also looking worried. Was I a white predator? How on earth had nobody noticed, for fifteen years, that Florence was blue? She was a deep blue, an almost purple hue visible through her otherwise black skin. Florence also had big ends to her fingers, and a loud murmur just left of her breast bone. I was pretty sure that Florence had a condition called Tetralogy of Fallot. She was too well to be blue and to have any other medical condition. The Papua New Guineans were hardy and stoical but I was still impressed as to how well she had coped for fifteen years undiagnosed and untreated. Tetralogy of Fallot occurs in about one in 2,000 births, so it's really quite common in paediatrics. It was named after a French physician who described the condition over 200 years after it was first recorded by the Danish pioneer in anatomy Niels Stensen.

Tetralogy of Stensen, with apologies to Fallot, has four components: a hole between the two main chambers of the heart, a narrowed exit to the blood flowing to the lungs from the heart, the aorta lying in an unusual position and, finally, an enlarged right side to the heart. Babies born with Fallot's are well, even though blue, but if left untreated complications usually arise within a few years. In developed nations this condition is easily diagnosed and corrected in the first few months of life. Both Florence and I needed help. I phoned the professor. John arranged for Florence to be flown to Brisbane for cardiac and hopefully also gastrointestinal and perineal surgery. I expect she did well and went on to lead a normal life, but I never heard about her case again.

Christmas came and went. New year and my thirtieth birthday approached. Thomas had returned from the tribal war for Christmas, with no new facial scars, and I was leaving soon, so I gave him Weston. Thomas stroked his thick beard and said

"Thank you, my children will love him."

In what way? With sweet potato and carrots? The next day Weston was gone. To a better home or a better place? Best not to enquire too deeply. Besides, I fancied a paddle and for that I needed a canoe and a river. A new idea was germinating.

I persuaded two friends, Beachball from medical school, who flew out to join us, and Frank, my *perfect* flatmate from Perth, to come and explore PNG. Beachball was an athletic but generally rotund individual with a spherical physique and a rounded mop of curly dark hair. Frank, christened Ian, had a wild streak and collected aliases. Aged twenty, Frank had run away from the Royal Australian Navy, going absent without official leave. Like me, he disliked authority. Frank shaved his head, changed his name and went to work in a flower shop in Sydney and later in the Kalgoorlie gold mines, before ending up in IT. I doubted our planned adventure would need any IT expertise, but you never knew and we were two peas in a pod. I was less sure about Beachball. At last immigration had returned my passport and it even had a stamp. I was free to leave Papua New Guinea. First, however, a kayak trip up the Sepik River, which at seven hundred miles long, is Papua New Guinea's longest.

The three of us met at Madang, the river's mouth and looked for a guide prepared to spend three weeks in the rainforest. We found Steven. Quiet and slight, he must have come from a different tribe to Thomas. We visited a string of villages and explored tributaries, sometimes handling baby crocodiles, wondering if mum and dad were nearby. We got eaten by mosquitoes and waded thigh deep, through swamps, taking turns to pull the single dugout when it got grounded. My thirtieth birthday, was celebrated at a New Year party in a village called Govermas. The Chief's son asked me to dance and we did the twist to the village radio cassette, playing "Love Shack" by The B-52's. Frank, the only non-medic, set up a clinic and treated the children's cuts and bruises.

In New Britain we dived on the wrecks of WWII Japanese warships. One of these, the Kanshin Maru, a 2,000-ton

Japanese transport ship, sank in 1944 in Simpson harbour. It sat at sixty-seven metres, in forty-foot visibility. That's a long way down on air, but we felt invincible. No wet suits were needed, just a T-shirt and a pair of shorts.

On the seabed, Frank, Beachball and I pulled crocodile hats out of our trunks, put them on our heads and swam past the guide. He knew we weren't right and smiled. Our timing was fortuitous, four years later the 1994 volcanic eruption made the site no longer diveable. Unbeknownst to me, happy and warm in my liver, unfazed by nearly seventy metres of pressure, was a healthy crop of malarial parasites.

Papua New Guinea was an unforgettable experience. I loved the country and its culture yet still felt relief to fly back to Australia. Two years abroad and I was missing the UK with its unique seasonal variation, barely adequate newspapers, lying politicians and warm beer. I could have stayed in Perth for another three months and sworn allegiance to the kangaroo and the meat pie and, by doing so, gained Australian citizenship. But that wasn't for me. *Nah mate.*

12

XANTHÉ

Back in London, my promotion to the post of UK paediatric registrar arrived with a familiar fanfare, a night of on call after my first day at work. *Beep, beep, beep. Beep, beep, beep.* Three in the morning. Aaaaaaaaaaaaaaaaah "Emergency neonatal surgical ward."

Fuck.

Xanthé, a month-old baby girl, was in surgical intensive care. Her breathing and heart rate were too rapid, with excessive in-drawing of her ribs. Her oxygen levels were worryingly low and my stethoscope did not register any sounds of breathing. I wondered whether the ends of the stethoscope had been turned the wrong way round. I rotated the bell and the diaphragm and listened again. Nothing. Silence. It could only be an "effusion", a collection of fluid lying outside her lungs. I'd need to "tap" her chest.

Xanthé was so small that the usual technique of going above a rib, rather than below a rib, to miss all of her blood vessels, was pointless. The two different target areas for an incision were only one millimetre apart. First time in, I had success. Inserting the needle between Xanthé's ribs and gently pulling back on the syringe, as the needle advanced, I had a syringe full of lovely straw-coloured fluid.

Xanthé's heart rate and breathing rate slowed, her oxygen saturation climbed and she looked much better. But something wasn't right. This fluid was yellow and didn't look like blood or pus or even the liquid one usually found around a pneumonia. It wasn't. The fluid was liquid baby food compound, total parenteral nutrition, known as TPN, driven by a pump, into a vein in Xanthé's arm. The colour was due to the added vitamins.

Every morning, the pharmacist and I carefully made up each sick baby's individual "food" for the day, based upon their blood results and clinical status. But this meal was now compressing Xanthé's lungs, suffocating her. The black bars marking off five-centimetre measures of the feeding tube were poorly designed and confusing.

A medical colleague had inserted the catheter twenty-five centimetres into Xanthé, instead of the correct ten centimetres. The misleading marks meant that staff inspecting baby Xanthé's arm could not see that the tube had been pushed in almost the total length of her body, the equivalent of five feet of cabling inserted into an adult. The excess tube had curled up inside Xanthé's heart, migrated its way through her heart muscle, and into the gap between her lung and her chest wall. Compounding the error, we'd been filling the gap with liquid, stifling the life out of her. This time, unlike Logan, the baby with the plastic in his palate, nobody managed to stop me publishing the case.[5] The manufacturers would need to change their catheter markings so the error couldn't be repeated. I was certain they would. And it would.

---

5. *Page 79.*

A week later, I finally met my new paediatric consult, who proved an instant disappointment.

The sum of my induction was a couple of notebooks he'd written on tests that needed to be performed on children soon to be admitted under his care. Was that it? It was made clear that I was, yet again, here to do and not to think. What a disheartening reversal, having recently returned from single-handedly running a Papua New Guinean paediatric department for a population of 80,000. Even worse, some tests I was told to do seemed peculiar. No explanation, above my pay scale. Why was I asked, or rather told to do lumbar punctures in the dark with just an ultraviolet light to guide me? This was an intricate procedure in full daylight. With only a faint blue hue to aid me, I struggled to find the necessary gaps between the vertebrae to insert the wide bore spinal needle required to squirt in the vitamins.

I was told vitamins injected into the spinal canal fluid could help treat children suffering from seizures. Cutting edge stuff. Not in any text books and, pre-internet, there was no means of checking the validity or sanity of such a procedure. This treatment had been shown to help diabetic neuropathy and it was always possible that my consultant was right. I did what I was told to do.

Fortunately this non-thinking post soon ended and my next role involved being attached to the professor of paediatrics' team. I remembered him from my time, three years earlier, working in the hospital as a senior house officer and he seemed a good egg. I asked the other junior doctors for any tips on what he liked us to know. The professor was a creature of habit, I wanted to create a good impression and prayed he would allow me to think once more. I memorised the answers to his anticipated questions.

nt,

·ight on cue, he leant back, protruded his
·hragm, raised a jowl or two, cleared his
·d.

·liscovered Crohn's disease?"
ɒurrill Bernard Crohn."
"And where did he get his medical degree from?"
"Columbia University."
"What year did he get his degree?"
"1907."

The prof gave me a withering look. No one likes a smart-arse. No further questions.

No time to bask, however, before "The Dragon" put me properly in my place. Maybe I was now a registrar, but they remembered me from when I had worked at the same hospital a few years earlier and they viewed me as too confident for my own good.

I needed bringing down a peg or two. The Dragon, a diminutive but fiery and able senior registrar, had had enough of my perceived misogyny and cockiness. Short-legged, short-haired and short-tempered, I suspected the professor had set her up when she gave me a set of wooden beads.

"You know what these are?" Blank-faced, I feigned ignorance.

"Go to the wards and measure the testicular sizes of all of the children," she said.

She handed me a Prader's orchidometer, designed by Professor Prader from Zurich. Just after WWII, Andrea Prader had become a world expert in growth and pubertal development. Prader made growth parameters for healthy children, including the size of their testicles. I looked The Dragon in the eye.

I wasn't going to be her ball boy. She'd made her point.

126

Despite being trampled by The Dragon, I was still feeling confident. I had coped with all that Australia and Papua New Guinea could throw my way, but new bear traps awaited. Still basking from saving Xanthé, after a routine day of treating constipation and asthma, complicated by an evening of reviewing snuffly babies in accident and emergency, I pottered off to my on-call room and undressed in the hope of getting a few hours' sleep before the day started.

Beep, beep, beep. Beep, beep, beep.

Beep effing beep. Noooooooooooooooooooooo.

It was five in the morning. Sighing loudly, I dressed and went back down to accident and emergency to see a sick teenager. She had severe asthma and required hourly nebulisers, as well as intravenous drugs. The drugs had made her vomit, partly over me. I was a bit dozy from sleep and didn't back off in time.

"Sorry," she said, a good sign as she was now able to speak so must be better. I reassured her, falsely promising I'd be back, truthfully saying I had to go and lie down. I wiped down my only shirt, went back to bed, prayed for a peaceful day ahead, and hoped the stain wouldn't be noticed by The Dragon in three hours' time.

But medicine can be like London buses, coming all at once. In the morning more would come my way. Being a devout pogonophobe, and purely for my personal entertainment, I was questioning the hygiene of the go-to senior registrar's beard. It seemed a diverting way to start the day. I knew I'd lose the argument. I always did with Ciaran, but my pager intervened — as it always did.

Beep, beep, beep. Beep, beep, beep. "Emergency transplant ward."

On the jog to the bone transplant ward, I assumed it

was just another bone marrow leukaemic child, who had developed septicaemia. I was so wrong.

Ruaidhri had recently received a bone marrow transplant, but his blood test results didn't make any sense. He was now five years old and had first seen his GP six months earlier, with repeated chest and ear infections. He'd recovered from these, but his parents had sought a second opinion. They felt something was amiss. Parental intuition is usually right. The second GP noted that Ruaidhri had a large tongue, a coarse looking face and, on examination, found he also had an enlarged liver and spleen. Hospital tests confirmed that Ruaidhri had Hurler syndrome, also known as Mucopolysaccharidosis type 1. Hurler syndrome usually presents in the first year of life, often with a large head, before the other signs become obvious. It is caused by an inherited deficiency of an enzyme called alpha-L-iduronidase, resulting in an accumulation of sulphate and the consequent malfunction of lysosomes. Lysosomes are small enzyme-containing organs that destroy worn-out cells, bacteria and viruses and help a cell that is damaged beyond repair to self-destruct. This deficiency results in a multi-system disease widespread throughout the body, that batters the connective tissue, eyes, cartilage and heart valves.

Before the age of two, development slows and the natural course is one of worsening heart failure and chest infections leading to death, often before a child's tenth birthday. To try to slow down the rate of decay caused by this devastating disease, the hospital was pioneering bone marrow transplants. Transplant trials had just begun, and Ruaidhri was a pioneer. In 1990, a bone marrow transplant was his only hope since enzyme replacement therapy was not yet available.

Ruaidhri looked sick and his test results reflected that. His heart rate and respiratory rate were high, his blood sugar ten times higher than the normal level. His blood was too acidic and his electrolytes made no sense. And all the time he was coughing up frothy pink sputum. What the fuck was happening? Ruaidhri appeared to be in heart failure, with pulmonary oedema. Weirdly, he seemed to have developed a sudden onset of severe diabetes. As Ruaidhri didn't have any prior evidence of diabetes or heart failure, none of this made any sense. I had to pause and think. I explained to the nurses that I was bemused and hadn't a clue as to what was going on, nor what I should do next. I said Ruaidhri looked like a severe diabetic, in heart failure, but I couldn't understand why. Then my antennae picked up something — the nurses were uncharacteristically quiet.

The staff nurse cleared her throat and asked to have a private word with me in the sisters' office.

"I'm afraid I didn't realise that Ruaidhri's intravenous line was set on flush," she said. Ruaidhri had received, in error, a whole day's total parenteral nutrition (TPN), via a catheter into a vein, directly into his heart, in fifteen minutes.

The nurse had earlier cleaned his equipment and appropriately flushed his lines with saline. But, on reconnection, she'd forgotten to reduce the flow rate. Unsure what to do, I decided I would do nothing. Nothing, bar monitor Ruaidhri very closely. Again, doing nothing was difficult, but I thought we should see what his observations and blood tests did, on a half-hourly basis. The staff nurse was in tears, fearful she may have killed Ruaidhri and sure she would lose her job and her career. It made matters worse that I was doing nothing. She feared facing manslaughter charges. She feared jail.

"Do something," she begged.

"It really is best that we do nothing but keep a close eye on him," I said, explaining my reasoning. I hoped she was unaware of my crossed fingers and toes. There are no guidelines for such a mistake. Not everything can fit neatly into a medical pigeon-hole. I considered giving Ruaidhri insulin to get his sugar down, and diuretics to take the fluid off his lungs, but I hoped his body would sort it better than we could. Half-hourly blood tests showed an improvement. Ruaidhri passed a lot of urine, his sugar level came down slowly and he stopped coughing. Ruaidhri was fine. Hallelujah! Doing nothing was often the right plan, and invariably the hardest decision to make. Again, I wanted to write this up as a report, but was told once more: "You will get the hospital closed down."

Back to the mess to bathe in the smug self-satisfaction of having made someone better. Head erect and tail in a frenzy. Ciaran was puffing away, settled in his "smoking" corner. I didn't reopen the beard debate. Ciaran was the only beardie but he wasn't the only smoker in the hospital. One of the consultants smoked a pipe, even in clinic, so the nurses hid his pipe whenever possible. The smoking consultant, Magnum Nasum, known as MN, was regarded as a bit odd.

I found the best way of protecting the children from MN's sometimes whacky approach was to gently lure MN away from his bizarre, slightly loony, treatment plans by talking about our joint love of Test cricket. I was aware that primum non nocere, "First, do no harm," was an important brake on the potential perils of over-treatment and my aim was to distract MN from doing too much harm to his patients. So when MN wanted the serum magnesium measured, four times a day, I would talk about the approaching Ashes series, or move on to the West Indies cricket tour the following year, hoping he'd forget about the magnesium.

One day MN just wouldn't be distracted. He didn't care about Courtney Walsh's five wickets for one run against Sri Lanka. Neither was he interested in Viv Richards's 146 runs at the WACA in Perth. MN wanted me to examine Lyndsey's "fascinating heart". We went to the postnatal ward together. I was full of dread, bound to get this one wrong. How could I get out of this hole? I was now a registrar, so any mistake was more embarrassing. I introduced myself to Lyndsey's mother, Mabel, and carefully examined her daughter's cardiovascular system.

Horror. Lyndsey's examination appeared totally normal. What had I missed? I couldn't even hear an innocent murmur. I tried hard to hear something interesting. Nothing but normal heart sounds. I tried again. Pulses, noises, even head and abdomen were all normal. I strained to hear something. Nothing. I considered guessing that it was something common and saying that I thought Lyndsey had a small ventricular septal defect. That usually wasn't a serious condition and shouldn't upset Mabel or MN too much. The diagnosis was a fair bet and likely to get me off the hook.

MN stared at me and as his bushy eyebrows lifted expectantly, I could taste his tobacco. Dammit. I made my decision and winced.

"I find this baby girl's cardiovascular system totally normal," I said.

I wondered what my next career move would be. Maybe I could set up a locum agency. I was sure I could do something. MN peered over his large nose, and said,

"I agree."

13

LUCY

More coffee in the mess with lots of tutting and ahhing from friends about the game MN had played on me. Winding down, we watched the new comedy *Bottom*, starring Rik Mayall.

On call once more. *Beep, beep, beep. Beep, beep, beep.* Beep bloody effing beep. "Emergency". No information. Just "emergency" and a run to a children's ward, brain firing wildly. At least this time, although wet, I was fully awake. I'd taken a sneaky shower, praying that no emergency would happen mid-lather. Fuelling oneself through a continuous eighty-hour shift of high-octane physical and mental exercise was a battle; washing, a luxury.

On the ward our hirsute two, the neatly moustachioed Paul and the wildly bearded Ciaran, leant over Harriet. They were the two most senior doctors in the hospital. This had to be bad news. Harriet, a beautiful nine-month-old girl, was dying. There were no consultants in sight. Why should there be? The consultants had done their time and were almost never called at night. Consultants were needed for making difficult diagnoses, talking to well-connecte parents and performing on the radio. Occasional additional work was also appreciated, such as meaningful research, writing medico-legal reports, attending case conferences, shortlisting then interviewing candidates and giving references. And bollocking us, the junior doctors.

I looked forward to the day that I might be in charge. It was essential for the junior medical staff to see a light at the end of the tunnel. Also, the more experienced so-called juniors were significantly better at managing the acutely unwell patients. I was sure the safer bet was to let the consultants get their beauty sleep, leaving the frontline in the capable hands of the happy, hairy couple.

Harriet was bleeding to death from her rectum. Harriet was also blue and we didn't know why. We knew that cyanosis, due to a lack of oxygen, is the commonest cause for being blue and this is usually due to either a heart or a lung problem. But Harriet's heart seemed fine, and so did her lungs. What else could it be? Methaemoglobinaemia was a possible cause. A rare condition that happens when the haemoglobin, in a red blood cell, has a lower than normal pulling power towards oxygen molecules usually due to the iron within the blood cell converting from a ferrous to a ferric form. This reduction in attraction is often caused by prescribed medicines. I never got my head fully around this condition, indeed I never saw a case, including this one. Harriet was on no drugs and didn't have methaemoglobinaemia.

So why was Harriet such a deep blue? To balance the blood loss and to arrest her torrential rectal bleeding, we'd already given Harriet four-litres of blood as well as platelets and fresh frozen plasma. We knew Harriet's total blood volume was under a litre, but she was pouring bright red

er anus. The bed sheets were soaked and the
ess. The smell was nauseating and the pools
lip hazard. I prayed no one would vomit.
re filling Harriet up, as she was bleeding to death
before our eyes. Harriet's haemoglobin result came back.

It should have been about twelve, but it was twenty-three.

The level was unexpectedly high. Aaaaaaaah! Suddenly
we knew. We had given Harriet far too much blood. She
was overfilled. At a petrol station, excess fuel just splashes
out of the car, but for Harriet's body there was no escape
for the blood we were pumping into her. It was obvious,
but it had eluded us for over two hours, even the two
smarty-pants had been fooled. Blood carries oxygen, and
other stuff of course. Cyanosis occurs when the body has
five or more grams of blood that is *not* attached to oxygen.
So if your haemoglobin is extremely low, say three, you
cannot be cyanosed. You will never go blue. You won't
even be blue sitting at the top of Mount Everest. Your
body just cannot make the colour blue. However, if the
opposite happens and your haemoglobin is very high, like
Harriet's twenty-three, you will be blue, even if you have
plenty of oxygen. So simple. So straightforward. So easy to
miss. It had stumped us, but thankfully for Harriet, we had
realised. Just in time.

Harriet bled more, but we stopped transfusing, the flow
slowed, her colour slowly improved and the pools on the
floor darkened like drying paint. Harriet survived and in the
morning it was pats on the back all round. The consultants,
fresh and fully rested from their slumbers, congratulated the
senior registrars and off we all went to start the day's work.

Evenings meant serious studying for the fast-approaching
membership exams of the Royal College of Paediatrics. The

exams interfered with what I regarded as more important social events. But there was no get-out. I passed on my second attempt and was immediately told to get a senior registrar post. Like finals, I mused that it might have been better to have failed. I was comfortable where I was. Then, out of the blue, I received a letter saying I had been shortlisted for a senior registrar job.

With the Jimmy Durante of consultants, MN, of all people. Surely a mistake? Firstly, I hadn't applied for the post. Secondly, I would rather have gone to Ford open prison in Sussex than work for two years, as Magnum Nasum's senior registrar. Thirdly, I had used up all of my cricket stories. I couldn't bear the thought. There had to be a way out. Distressed and confused, I sought wise counsel from a senior consultant.

"Oh dear, I fear you will have to go to the interview and just hope you don't get it. I agree it is most unfortunate," he said. Was that the best he could do?

I found interviews stressful enough when I wanted the job, but I felt sick at the idea of being interviewed for a job that I really did not want. How should I prepare for such an interview? Indeed, should I prepare at all? Should I walk in drunk? How could I make myself unappointable? It was frighteningly clear that MN wanted me. The day approached and I fretted over more than a few pints in the pub. I hoped the resulting hangover would help ruin my performance.

My name was called and I walked in and sat in the hot seat at the end of the table.

As expected, MN was there, with none other than the professor, my consultant confidant, and Ciaran, the bearded wonder, who at least refrained from smoking.

Making up the numbers were the head of human resources,

the head nurse, and the chief executive. The questions were all too easy and it was obvious that they wanted to appoint me. I needed to self-destruct; I needed a lysosome. Ciaran saved the day.

"So Charles, you are applying for a senior registrar post in a famous London children's hospital and you seem to have done very little research."

"Yes."

"Can I ask you why?"

I saw my chance, but did I have the brass neck to pull it off? I decided not to mention the long hours of work, the necessary focus on learning essential skills and the passing of the challenging postgraduate examinations, each of which would have been agreeably mitigating. Truthful too, if predictable, but perilously close, I feared, to an acceptable answer. Kamikaze style, I ploughed straight in:

"I think most research is a waste of time. I think it's overrated and to be honest, I don't have any interest in it." There. Said it. Pick the bones out of that. I felt sick. In truth, I agreed with a toned-down version, but this answer was Stalin versus Corbyn, Hitler versus Thatcher. The other panel members had no further questions. I left to silence.

MN was good about it. We talked about Glenn McGrath and a new bowler called Warne who was showing some promise. Then human resources called me down.

"You really didn't interview very well."

"I'm sorry. I did try my best," I lied.

"They didn't like your reasoning for your lack of research. Anybody would think you didn't want the job."

I thanked them and, as I scuttled off, my pager went off. It was the professor, summoning me to his office. He was a proper professor, with gravitas. I liked him. He had a wicked sense of humour and I didn't want us to fall out. He barely fitted on his office throne, but smiled paternalistically.

"Charles, I don't mind you taking the piss out of *us*, but take my advice, don't do it elsewhere," he said.

The prof had seen straight through me, knew what I was doing, may even have respected my predicament, but he couldn't condone it. I sidestepped MN's post and behaved in future interviews.

Meanwhile, management decided to make it clear that *they* were in charge, not the irritating consultants, and I began to realise that perhaps life might not be a bed of roses at the end of training after all. The spoilt doctors needed putting firmly in their place as, inch-by-inch, anything that could be deemed as a doctor's perk would be removed. An early target was the consultants' parking arrangements. Their designated-parking places would be reassigned to management. Who else?

It was like something out of *Animal Farm*. All staff are equal, and some are more equal than others. Thirty years later, the game is over. Management have won. Like the Manor Farm pigs playing cards with the farmers, arguing the odds, the game now is between echelons of management and the politicians. The doctors stand outside, peering from one to another, barely able to distinguish between the two. The doctors have either gone or, disempowered, have given up caring. They have not given up caring for their patients, just for the system. I didn't have a parking space, but I could see it was troubling the consultants and I made it clear what I thought about that to management. So relations were already a touch frosty. I didn't realise the frost would precipitate a full-on freeze.

Malcolm, the fourth of the senior registrars, came to find me. Malcolm liked to keep a low profile, shying away from trouble, so it was out of character that he should seek me out in the mess. Peering around the door, his pained face and anxious voice betrayed his sense of alarm. "Oh dear, Charles. This is bad, really, really bad. You must go and see the hospital chief executive. Now!" he said. Malcolm wouldn't tell me what it was about. He just looked at me and shook his head.

I went down to see Pip, the chief executive. I liked Pip. Sharp-suited and finely manicured as her status dictated, she nevertheless cared about the patients, prioritising them above the bean counters and, believe me, that was exceptional in management. I knew I hadn't done anything that bad, so was confused, but not overly worried. Pip looked stern, before closing the door behind me and pushing over her desk a pornographic fax she had received, personally addressed to me. A woman "pleasuring" a man. I was stunned.

Major, perhaps the most unhinged of my friends from medical school, in a moment of madness, had sent it to me as a rather belated welcome-home-from-Australia present. By my reaction, Pip quickly garnered I knew nothing about it and made sympathetic noises. I was mortified. I promised I would force Major to apologise. We concocted a story, telling Major that the GMC had been informed of the fax, and that I might lose my job and my career. It was good to have the GMC do something useful for a change.

Major was effusively apologetic, writing under a pseudonym.

Dear Madam,
Please accept my profound apologies for the fax received last week.
It was a stupid, senseless act and I had not foreseen the trouble it would cause.

Please extend my apologies to anyone else who has been distressed by this.
Yours Faithfully,
John Mcintyre.

Meanwhile my Australian diving friends wanted Frank and I to join them in the Solomon Islands, for some penetration wreck diving. I flew back to Perth and before catching up with the dive instructors, saw my first Ashes Test at the WACA. It was 1991, and Bryan Adams had just released "Can't Stop This Thing We Started". I didn't realise my trip to the WACA would be the start of something tiresomely repetitive. The England cricket team couldn't stop losing. And, like cricketing Groundhog Day, I would be there each time to share the pain.

But I was excited. Scorching hot, a fast, rock-hard pitch. Should be a cracking game.

It was the last Test of the series and England were already 2–0 down. No matter, we had Gooch, Atherton, Lamb and Gower in the top five and I was confident we would win this one. We lost by nine wickets and I headed back to London to find I'd missed yet another White Paper. This time the catchy title was *The Health of the Nation* and, for the first time, I heard patients being referred to as "customers". I wondered when politicians would understand that the NHS isn't a business. It's more important than that. It's about life and death.

I'd become quite accustomed to death. I'd seen a lot of it during my house jobs, and a consistent trickle afterwards. On the whole it didn't trouble me too much. This wasn't arrogance or lack of caring; I expect most combatants feel this in war zones. It's hard for those not subjected to such appalling events on a regular basis to understand, but I wouldn't have coped if I'd lost sleep over every death. On the medical frontline we needed thick skins to cope with the extraordinary hours and those only too frequent occasions when a combination of medicine and our best endeavours just couldn't help.

And yet, in spite of all this, possibly *because* the nature of hospital death created its own anaesthetic, I discovered that death outside the familiar and comfortable environs of our sanitised wards could be truly shocking.

I'd enjoyed a Sunday lunch with my parents in Sussex and was driving back up the dual carriageway, when two motorbikes overtook us. Half a mile on I saw one of the bikes wedged underneath a milk tanker. I wanted to drive by but couldn't. I shouldn't have even entertained the thought. What was wrong with me? Had I become dehumanised by all the death I'd seen? On the roundabout the other biker fixed his eyes on me, saying, "Don't take his helmet off." I promised not to. The rider was just alive. He squeezed my hand and I squeezed back. "The ambulance is on the way. Hold on," I said.

I expect many people were around, including the police. I don't remember seeing any of them. I only remember the two bikers. The ambulance arrived and almost immediately the rider vomited into his helmet and started to choke. Despite my promise, I had to remove his helmet — he was drowning in vomit. I went in the ambulance with him. My denim jeans were soaked in a pungent brown mixture of his blood and vomit. We were still on the road when he stopped breathing. I asked the ambulance to pull in as I intubated him in a roadside lay-by.

When we arrived at the hospital, a junior doctor poked his head into the ambulance and said cheerfully: "Hi there. Is it worth bringing him in?" I was shocked. More than that, I was shocked that I was shocked. My skin was somewhat thinner than I'd previously thought. The motorcyclist's death felt so raw compared with those I'd witnessed in hospital in the supporting company of colleagues. The motorbiker's lunch was drying on my jeans, while my own lunch was still digesting in my small bowel. I should have tracked down his parents, should have talked to them. It would have been the brave thing, the right thing to do. But I was drained and couldn't face it.

The next week, still shaken by this episode, I shared a lift up to the wards with an angry consultant. His friend's daughter was ill. "Find the bloody fool who told Sophie's parents she has meningitis, and shoot him," he said.

"The bloody fool" of course, was me, and as I was now on edge, after the motorbike accident, I said so. He looked at me wistfully. Silently nodding.

Sophie did have meningitis.

Sophie didn't have meningitis.

The number of white cells in the cerebrospinal fluid was raised, but minimally and nothing grew. We were both right. Medicine isn't always easy.

*

The diary showed 1992, my passport said thirty-two. As *Men Behaving Badly* and Bobby Brown's "Humpin' Around" entertained the nation, I found little time for either, rotating into a harsher environment.

Beep, beep, beep. Beep, beep, beep. "Please go to the special care baby unit."

I liked the word "Please". On arrival I found Lucy, a one-week-old girl, with a dangerously high level of jaundice.

Lucy had a blood type incompatibility and needed her blood exchanged, a hazardous, time-consuming, delicate and technically challenging procedure. Lucy's blood would need flushing out, repeatedly, to wash out the antibodies causing her problem.

Changing her blood would also remove the accumulated bilirubin that could otherwise cross into her brain, putting her at risk of deafness and cerebral palsy. It didn't help that Lucy's tummy button had dried, scabbing over, leaving me no easy access to the big vein and artery in her umbilicus. These tummy vessels were the site where the umbilical cord had recently been attached to Lucy's mother, sharing their joint placental blood supply. This was the route I could use to remove and replace all of Lucy's blood, not once, not twice, but three times. In all, 1.2 litres of Lucy's blood had to be removed and replaced with the same volume of fresh blood, pushing in the new and pulling out the used blood, a tough ordeal for her small and vulnerable body.

Gowned up, with sterile gloves on my hands and catheter trolley at my side, I cursed as I picked at the dark scab on Lucy's umbilicus. I cautiously inserted a narrow-gauge dilator. Too much force would create a false track and a blind-ending passage, resulting in no access to her aorta and her blood, in which case sixty minutes of sweaty work under the lights would have gained nothing. Slim metal dilator withdrawn, I delicately slipped in the tip of the closed forceps and let them open, stretching her fragile blood vessel further. Mustn't damage it.

Tentatively, holding the tip of the clear plastic catheter, I advanced it, hoping this would feed down the umbilical blood vessel, into Lucy's aorta and hence gain access to an endless supply of her blood. A gentle push as it went "round the bend" and in. Success. But no blood. Why? Because I had failed and I had lost access to her central blood supply. Despite patience, effort and care, I'd created a false passage after all. I could have sworn I'd nailed it.

Now I'd have to use Lucy's small bloo⌐
arms and legs instead. This would mean ₁
and many hours hunched, hot, scrubbe
her body. Poor Lucy; poor me. Over a liᴜᴠ
aliquots of no more than fifteen millilitres at a time. ın ᴠ
out, in and out, in and out. Taking five hours, and over a
dozen cannulae.

I didn't feel well afterwards, but I was never ill so,
ignoring it, I left Lucy to recover from her ordeal and went
to the doctors' mess to do likewise. We were both shattered.

I started to feel worse and my hands began to shake.
Interesting. Was I about to have my first seizure? I was on
call, personal illness not an option. Embarrassed, I hid in
the paediatric office. Unsteady on my feet, afraid I might
vomit on the ward, I managed a cursory ward round
before collapsing in the on-call room, sleeping fitfully and
repeatedly vomiting throughout the night.

*

Next morning, my body was screaming at me, as if
somebody else owned it. I'd completed the seventy-two-
hour weekend shift and, if I had the strength, I could go
home. Scrubbing the sink of sick, I phoned a wise friend
asking for help, offering him my arm, saying: "Please take
my blood and look for everything." We both knew there
was no such test. I just wanted an analysis of all my basic
parameters: of bone marrow, kidney and liver function
tests plus an infection screen. I knew I had something badly
wrong with me. But what?

Driving down the dual carriageway, stopping at the car
park close to where the dying biker had been sick on me, I
threw up in the footwell of my car. Reaching home, I took
to bed feeling delirious. I put my hand to my forehead. I

, burning up. It had to be malaria, but I hadn't been ywhere where I could have picked that up for over two years. I phoned the wise friend back for advice and he agreed that despite the lengthy absence, it could indeed be malaria and he promised to chase my bloods. The samples were lost. The tests were repeated and returned significantly abnormal.

Haemoglobin, platelets and white blood cells were all very low. My bone marrow was failing. Could it be leukaemia? I hoped death would be relatively quick and painless, said an emotional goodbye to myself, and started to plan my last few months.

On waking in a damp bed, I decided that as I was going to die soon, I might as well make something good come out of it. At the very least, I could draw attention to the night-time pay, which was not time-and-one-third. Just one-third pay. This derisory remuneration encouraged the exploitation, over long hours, of junior doctors as cheap labour. Then the call came through, confirming the diagnosis was not leukaemia, but malaria, as we'd first thought. The little buggers had been dozing in my liver, biding their time for two years. The ambulance crew lifted me out of bed, strapped me in a chair and carried me downstairs past my already grieving parents to the waiting ambulance with its flashing blue lights.

Within forty-eight hours I was better. On my return, with not a hint of sympathy, a consultant colleague said, "You've been away a while." As junior doctors, we'd become the pond life of the health service. That's how we felt.

*

A morose atmosphere descended on the accident and emergency department after a doctor sent home a child who

144

had had an episode of abdominal pain. The child had died twelve hours later from a gangrenous bowel and low blood pressure caused by an undiagnosed twisted gut, a mistake any doctor could have made. I hoped the parents, the hospital and the GMC would be sympathetic. I doubted it.

In my office I was reflecting on the potential diagnostic pitfalls surrounding us every day in paediatrics, when the door burst open. Dmitri, a hard-working junior colleague, barged in with bulging eyes and a deathly pallor. I couldn't understand his problem. English wasn't his first language and Dmitri was talking too fast for me to follow what had occurred. Sit down, take a deep breath and start again, Dmitri. He told me he'd been doing a baby check and in the process of examining the hips of Maddie, a newborn baby girl, he'd broken her femur, her main leg bone. Broken femurs are very rare in newborns. I hadn't seen one before. Since Maddie's leg had broken during Dmitri's routine examination, it seemed probable that Dmitri had either used too much force or, more likely, that Maddie had a congenital disorder, such as osteogenesis imperfecta.

This is an unusual, but not an exceptionally rare condition with an incidence of around 1 in 15,000 births. We expected to see one every five years in a big district general hospital (DGH). Severe types can usually be diagnosed before birth by ultrasound, whereby the skull, spine, ribs and legs might all look abnormal, showing a significant lack of calcification, and often with multiple bone fractures. Maddie's parents were understandably angry and upset. There was no family history of any bone disease. Maddie's delivery had been normal. As had all her antenatal scans. The parents scowled at Dmitri. They wanted answers and they wanted them from me. Right now. On examination, Maddie looked normal, apart from her broken leg. Her skin and eyes and all other areas of her body, where one might find a relevant abnormality, appeared unremarkable. We arranged a skeletal survey, a series of X-rays of her whole body. I didn't know what I wanted it to show. Obviously, I should have been hoping it would be normal, but I felt sorry for Dmitri and worried that his being non-English meant that the wolves would be more ferocious than normal. Maddie's X-rays were normal. Her bones had healthy mineral levels and there were no deformities or other fractures. Good news for Maddie, dismal news for Dmitri.

The following day it was another junior colleague's' turn to be in the firing line. In the early hours Clare had examined a woman who'd arrived in the accident and emergency department with a vaginal bleed. Clare believed the woman had recently given birth and told her so. The woman protested, insisting she'd never had a baby.

Clare wouldn't take no for an answer. The nurses took the woman's side. "Surely the patient knows best?" they said. Disagreeing with a woman, about whether she had given birth — what was that all about? Brave, or stupid? It must have been an uncomfortable discussion, but Clare's persistence was dogged. I cannot believe a male doctor would have dared be so stubborn, and dread to think what the response would have been. The convenient option would have been to agree with the patient, as always. Often that was the right approach; it was always the easy approach, but not always the *correct* approach. Management beware, the *customer* is not *always* right.

If Clare hadn't persevered, the baby would never have been found by the police, hidden, suffocated, dead, in her mother's bathroom laundry basket. Medicine is like skating on ice. However experienced and careful you are, sooner or later you'll take a tumble. So far, I'd been lucky. So far. I could have missed the twisted gut, and I was sure I would have missed the dead baby in the laundry basket. I doubt I would have persisted in challenging a woman about whether she had delivered a baby. In a man that called for the kind of reckless courage I just didn't possess. I'd been fortunate not to have been on call when these tragic events happened. I came to the end of the rotation relatively unscathed. My number wasn't up. Not yet.

Another interview and I secured a post on a two-year senior registrar rotation on the English South Coast.

14

ICE BUCKET

At last, on the final rung of the junior doctor ladder. The new senior registrar post was just one step below consultant. Now where to live? Although it would offer opportunities, I didn't fancy living in the nurses' block nicknamed Tampax Towers. Don't rush to judgement; the nurses called it that. Instead I could live with John and Maggot in their flat. John, the younger brother of a friend from medical school, was meticulous in manner but dishevelled in appearance, sporting straw hair that sat on his head like a pigeon's nest. His autistic tendencies manifested themselves in a set of draconian house rules, such as the neat arrangement of shoes, the closing of the fridge door *softly*, and the stacking of CDs in alphabetical order. His wife, Maggot, operated as an essential moderator of his idiosyncrasies, enabling John to mix with society outside of their flat. John was barely capable of adapting but, as their lodger, I had no excuse.

Right now, however, John and Maggot were keeping their distance after hearing the news of my latest bowel movement. There's a distinguished medical history in the inspection of bowel contents. Throughout much of English history, at court the Groom of the Stool was one of the monarch's most respected confidants, given the intimate nature of the job, so to speak. Royal physicians were tutored in investigating the monarch's daily movements for signs of ill health or robust health.

The discolouration of King George III's motions was allegedly one of the first indications of his bouts of madness caused by suspected porphyria. That's difficult to explain as purple-coloured urine, not stools, is the classic sign. I'd long been a follower of the science of scatology, believing faeces could help in the making of many diagnoses. Unwelcome stool colours include: green (fast transit), white (bile duct obstruction), yellow (malabsorption), black (upper gut bleeding) and red (lower gut bleeding). I didn't need the Bristol Stool Chart to find something was amiss when peering at my latest deposit.[6] To my surprise I'd discovered a plump white larva. Excitedly, I shared the find with John. Both he and Maggot were disgusted. The offending larva was carefully placed in one of John's empty Vaseline pots and sent to the hospital microbiology department for analysis. I'd previously caught cat fleas and scabies during my paediatric senior house officer job and more recently my body had provided a happy home for jiggers and malaria after trips abroad.[7] I suspected that this larva would be from some exotic Papua New Guinean animal that had come to join the party. A week later, the result: The larva is a Protophormia Terraenovae. Wow!

6. *The Bristol Stool Chart was designed by Ken Heaton at the Bristol Royal Infirmary in 1997. Drawings help classify human faeces into one of seven categories, ranging from severe constipation to severe diarrhoea.*
7. *Jiggers are burrowing parasitic fleas common in tropical and subtropical climates.*

Terraenovae sounded so new world, had to be something extraordinary. I couldn't wait to find out and rushed off to the computer to check. Damn. It was a common bluebottle fly larva.

The South Coast was a world away from London. The parties just couldn't compare, until "Sharon" arrived at the mess ball. The consultants and their wives sat on the top table, looking down upon the juniors and their partners.

Rumour had it that the previous year one of the wives had gone to the ball "commando", mimicking Sharon Stone in *Basic Instinct*. She was here again. You could have sold tickets, such was the scrum for seats nearest the platform. She had a body built for the catwalk and we all craned our necks to peek from the lower level. This was more like it. I was single and sharking around when, in the fug of the party, I found myself in a close embrace with Sharon. We had chemistry and things were looking up. Then something unexpected happened. Painlessly and silently I drifted across the dance floor, before being placed gently at the edge of the room. Her husband was obviously accustomed to performing these manoeuvres and did so with class and aplomb.

Back on the ward, Steve, a child with an inoperable brain tumour, was in pain. I asked what his dose of morphine was and, as he was only on a moderate amount, I said: "Put it up twenty per cent." I knew twenty per cent was a big increase. But I wanted to keep Steve as comfortable as possible. The priority was to keep him out of distress. Medicine could not cure Steve, but it could alleviate his suffering. I would normally have increased the morphine in only ten per cent increments, but in the circumstances twenty per cent seemed reasonable. What circumstances? Was I treating Steve or was I ensuring I wasn't bleeped again in an hour? Possibly both. An hour later, now six in the morning, three hours before a normal day's work started, my foul companion went off again. *Beep, beep, beep. Beep, beep, beep.* Goddamned Beep. Steve had died. Was it the result of my increase? I don't know. Did I regret increasing his pain relief twenty per cent? No. But times had changed since I'd worked as a house officer, when increasing the dose of morphine to help a dying patient on their way was regarded as a virtue.

The nursing staff took a different view and I don't think I was ever fully forgiven. Ten years on, reviews of every child death became routine and we would have analysed Steve's care and the question of his morphine dosage would have been discussed and lessons learnt.

Party time again. The junior doctors wrote their patients up for sleeping tablets as Meat Loaf's "I'd Do Anything For Love (But I Won't Do That)" rocked the mess. Was this consensual? Not at all. It seemed a kindness at the time and it meant the doctors could also play Oasis, Madonna, Blur and Bon Jovi that bit louder with a clear-ish conscience. A great party and little sleep, but we were accustomed to managing with minimal rest. Bed at three, alarm at eight, and one hour to ablute and shave, then off to run the ward round on the special care baby unit. I was used to small babies, shouldn't be too taxing. I'd washed my hands and cleaned my teeth, all that mattered, so I thought, as I stumbled in bleary eyed, at five minutes to nine. I pushed the baby unit's white swinging doors aside and headed for the kettle; I needed a coffee.

The unit was like the Mary Celeste, when a flushed face appeared. "Thank God you're here, we've been waiting for you." I looked around. Was she talking to me?

I wondered how early I would have to be before being exempt from such an angst-laden greeting.

The night team were resuscitating a sick newborn, with a big pneumothorax — air outside her lung. Vicky had been born at twenty-eight weeks gestation, so three months too early. On the ventilator she'd crashed. A collapsed lung had been diagnosed by shining a light through her chest and then been confirmed by taking an X-ray. Vicky's collapse had happened at 07.55, sixty minutes prior to my arrival.

The team hadn't had the confidence to rely on the fibre optic light source to drain her chest. When this light was pressed against a normal baby's chest it created a small halo of light around one centimetre in diameter. In a premature baby with a big pneumothorax, like Vicky, the whole chest would light up like a lantern. In an emergency, the light was an excellent tool and avoided a critical delay.

Unfortunately no one had been brave enough to act on the result of the bright light, prior to seeing the X-ray and then when the X-ray confirmed the diagnosis, there was still nobody prepared to do the procedure. The X-ray had come back at 08.45, fifteen minutes before my anticipated arrival. The staff decided to wait for me and had been bagging Vicky in the interim, a process that risked making her pneumothorax bigger. Bagging was straightforward, pushing oxygen into the lungs via a face-mask and a compressible plastic bag. This wasn't the treatment of choice for her condition. She needed a chest drain, a procedure that isn't inherently difficult, but could be described, nonetheless, as a squeaky-bum experience. I gowned up, put sterile gloves on, and made a small incision between Vicky's ribs.

Did her blood vessels run above or below the ribs? I couldn't remember, still feeling bleary. But the gap between her ribs was so small it seemed an academic question. Thankfully there wasn't much blood, so I thought I'd done it correctly. More likely I was just lucky. As usual the hole I'd made was too small. More blunt dissection was needed through Vicky's intercostal muscles. When the hole looked and felt big enough to admit the tip of my right little finger, I pushed the plastic drain into this gap between her ribs, pushing firmly, but not so hard that when it gave, the tube risked shooting into her dove-like chest cavity, traumatising all in its path. Drain inserted, attached to an underwater seal, stitched up, all done in fifteen minutes. Time for that coffee. Still no reporting mechanism, no post-procedure feedback session. Nothing learnt.

Because this was the last career step before trying to obtain a consultant post, I was allowed a fair amount of freedom and autonomy. Nominally, however, I was still a junior doctor, so stuck in no man's land. Tensions were inevitable and an unnecessary and unpleasant battle had commenced around the rota. I also had another problem, harking back to that unfortunate interview with Magnum Nasum. I hadn't done any meaningful research and had to get some under my belt if I was to progress. My mistake at Oxford in muddling the MAP of *mean arterial pressure*, with the MAP of *mean airway pressure*, had been an inauspicious initiation into this dark art. Fortunately the senior paediatrician had a sparkling idea to use nebulised steroids to help children with croup.[8] A study that would need approval from the ethics committee. Additionally, I needed support from a drug company on producing placebo samples, then agreement for the protocols, with input from a statistician. Finally, I produced a video for parents, explaining the purpose of the study, what it entailed, and why I wanted their child entered into the trial.

---

8. *A common childhood condition, usually caused by a virus, that causes swelling of the upper airway, difficulty in breathing, and a characteristic barking cough.*

The process was time-consuming and took me further away from the ward and clinical work, exacerbating the tensions that had arisen following Steve's death. The week before we were about to start the study I reviewed the video we'd made. I knew its content back to front, but something made me check it for a final time. Instead of seeing a child on a nebuliser, I saw a video of surgeons performing a paediatric liver transplantation. I never discovered how this mix up happened. Was it a sick joke or just a mistake?

A weekend off included a party with long-lasting consequences. H arrived on the scene. I had a sleepless night and, feeling worn out, drove to work from her flat, aiming to arrive at work half an hour early to have a coffee and gather my thoughts before starting on the newborn ward round. I needed to think through the night's activities alone, so sat by myself in the hospital canteen, cradling my cup of coffee.

Beep, beep, beep. Beep, beep, beep. "Emergency Neonates."

I looked at my watch. It was ten minutes to nine. I wanted to ignore the loathsome contraption but thought I probably shouldn't, or did I just not dare to do so because I knew I'd been spotted grasping my coffee? Grudgingly, I left my cup and trotted off thinking, "Not another one." I'd worked out before that a mad sprint, although looking good on US television dramas such as *ER*, was pointless. It just meant arriving out of breath and being unable to think or perform. Besides, George Clooney never ran. I was also feeling queasy, so I just walked over.

Arriving on the unit I saw that Mattie, a four-day-old premature baby girl, had a heart rate of well over 220. Normal is around 150. More worryingly, Mattie also looked extremely unwell. Mattie was pale, matching my face and the bleak sky outside. This had to be a tachyarrhythmia. A fast, abnormal heartbeat, caused by an electrical malfunction in the heart's wiring. It just didn't seem plausible to me that Mattie's heart could go that fast due to an infection, pain, blood loss or some weird hormonal issue. It had to be a short circuit. A quick electrocardiogram (ECG) supported this conclusion. Christ alive! What do I do? Everyone stared at me, expecting immediate answers.

My options included inducing a slowing of her heart by generating a diving reflex, giving a drug in a vein, or giving Mattie's heart an electric shock. That last one scared me. The dive reflex is inherent in all air-breathing vertebrates — whales, dolphins and a whole lot of other beasts, including the platypuses and humans. The reflex is a response to a lack of oxygen, an inevitable consequence of immersion in water for all mammals. The shock of immersion automatically stimulates the parasympathetic nerves making the heart slow, while at the same time stimulating the sympathetic system, constricting the small arteries and keeping the blood pressure up. It is the body's desperate and extremely clever last-ditch attempt to stay alive.

I made my decision, wrapped Mattie up in a towel and asked the nurses to get me a bucket of iced water. We both took a deep breath and, as I immersed her head into the water, I prayed the diving reflex would do it. The parasympathetics kicked in, Mattie's heart trace slowed and then stopped. Not breathing; no heartbeat.

I heard a gasp, sadly not from Mattie, but from Chrissie the physiotherapist, who had just walked in and seen what I'd done. I pulled Mattie out, limp and pale. Mattie's heart trace was flat. She had gone from 220 beats a minute to zero. Fuck. Surrounded by silence. The stares were now glares and I prayed.

I'm not sure whether I prayed for Mattie, or for me. Then a few bumps appeared on the monitor, then her heart spontaneously restarted. I could have kissed her. I thanked the Lord that the heart has its own pacemaker, usually capable of restarting automatically. Usually. Mattie was fine, but I felt sick.

*

Another NHS reorganisation. With increasing seniority, I was grudgingly starting to pay attention to the relentless fiddling with the system. Regional Health Authorities (RHAs) were to be reduced from twelve to eight. I wondered, if there had been eight RHAs, whether they would have increased them to twelve? Couldn't we just be left alone to do our work?

*

It was a difficult time in my life. Father had been diagnosed with cancer of the pancreas and the atmosphere at work was sullen, depressed by the recent massacre in Tiananmen Square. The sense of disquiet deepened when I looked at some retinal haemorrhages in an irritable baby. Having left a graphic child protection teaching session, I'd peered through the ward's ophthalmoscope to examine Tim, a two-month-old boy, admitted with irritability.

Tim's infection screen, including a lumbar puncture, had been negative. He had no temperature and no visible bruises but something was clearly wrong. Tim was in a foul mood. At least I now had company. Looking at the backs of his eyes I was shocked to see numerous bilateral and extensive retinal haemorrhages; shocked, because I was pretty inept at this skill, but also because I knew the far-reaching consequences of my finding. With such widespread bleeds at the backs of both eyes it was almost certain that Tim had been abused.

The machinery of safeguarding kicked in with a skeletal survey, case conferences and court proceedings. I would never find out the conclusion as, still being a junior doctor, I would move on from the trust before any judgement.

The senior registrar post was a four-year rotation, but I'd done two years and wasn't sure about rotating to Southampton. I'd had enough of being a junior doctor. Twelve years of tough rotas with hundreds of disturbed nights, was just about enough. I was tired of being a dogsbody but wasn't sure where I wanted to settle down as a consultant.

I needed to clear my head. Cricket, anyone? It was 1995, Bill Clinton was the president of the US, and the scruffy Pom was back at the WACA, for his second Ashes Test. As usual, Perth was scorching hot with a concrete-hard pitch. It had to be better than in 1991. This time, although we still had Gooch, Atherton and Thorpe, Gatting had joined the party. The opposition had the Waugh brothers and Warne. The Waugh brothers were particularly irritating — too good and too cocky. Warne was unbearable and unbearably good. It was the fifth Test and we were 2–1 down. I was sure we would win this Test and level the series. We lost by over 300 runs and I returned home.

Back at work, the atmosphere on the unit had deteriorated from sullen to morose.

A tragic nursing drug error had resulted in the death of a baby. I'd been lucky in Oxford with my prescription mistake but again I was reminded that, however careful one is, mistakes can and will happen. Everything was stacking up for an early exit.

I started scanning the *British Medical Journal* for job adverts and saw one for a consultant post in an area I knew well. I didn't think I'd get the job, didn't think I wanted it, but I saw the interview process as useful practice for another consultant job I had my eye on, this one on the South Coast. Far too quickly the day of the interview arrived and I found an ironed shirt.

*

The panel asked the expected questions and then the chief executive said:

"If I gave you £1 million for the paediatric department what would you spend it on?"

I hadn't a clue, so I said I'd put it in an account to earn interest. That seemed to go down well. I suspected that the other candidates had tried to be too clever with their answers, but when I closed the door behind me, all I could hear was laughter. What had I said that was so funny? It was my request for my own secretary and my own office. I sat down outside, chatting with the other candidates. They all appeared smarter and more experienced than me. Time went slowly, then out came the human resources manager and, to my surprise, I was called in and offered the post.

Didn't they know that this was only supposed to be a practice session for another post? I wasn't sure that I wanted it. What could I do? My current consultants knew I'd applied, but I'd told nobody else. I drove home, alone and confused, my mind in turmoil. What had I done?

I had completed eleven years of intensive training in paediatrics, an exhausting but generally enjoyable romp. As I left, I said to one of the consultants, "Thank God that's over".

"No," she said. "It's just begun."

How did I get here?

COFFEE BREAK

When Do They Grow Ears?

Families are like fudge – mostly sweet, with a few nuts.

Les Dawson

15

ARTICHOKE SOUP

It was 1960. *The Royal Commission on Doctors' and Dentists' Remuneration* was published, and I heard my first words. "When do they grow ears?" Uncle Walter had seen me, his godson, for the first time. Walter was intrigued. I had a cap on. He also had a cap, but he wasn't wearing his. His was a Scottish rugby union full international cap, but, more importantly, Walter hadn't seen a baby with a cap on. In truth, he'd never seen a newborn baby. As my ears were bound tightly to my head, he quite reasonably thought I hadn't yet grown any.

Father, meanwhile, was particularly irritated. A week earlier, on Christmas Day, he'd come back from Cornwall, as Mother was having labour pains. A mining executive and part-time farmer, born in the early 1920s, Father had been troubled by the horrors of war when fighting in the trenches at Anzio, witnessing death close up. Father was sixteen and still at school when WWII broke out. When he was eligible, he joined the East Kents as a schoolboy cadet. Applying for a commission meant transferring to the

Middlesex regiment before, aged nineteen, he joined his unit stationed with the 1st Army in Africa.

The Germans had invaded Italy, when his regiment was sent to reinforce the beachhead at Anzio during some of the heaviest fighting of WWII. He'd spent February 1944, the month before his twenty-first birthday, at the infamous flyover at Campo di Carne, (the field of meat) in charge of a mortar platoon, trying to hold off a formidable German effort to repel the invading allies. Thousands died on both sides and the desperate conditions resembled those on the Western Front in World War I. The corpse of an American soldier lay rotting outside Father's trench, unreachable to those alive who were taking what little cover there was. The memory of that dead GI haunted Father for the rest of his life. Burial was impossible under dense German fire. One mortar burst killed his communications officer who, only two minutes earlier, had been sharing a cup of tea with Father.

Tea had the benefits of improved alertness from caffeine, rehydration from water, comfort from warmth and was a reminder of the taste of a previous normal life back home. But it didn't help Father much in the recurring memories that troubled him when the war was over.

In fact, the end of war in Europe was not the end of Father's war. The following year, aged twenty-two, he was seconded as an intelligence officer to the Guards Brigade in Palestine, before his final release from Army service in February 1947. He then achieved a law degree from Cambridge, but he'd seen and done too much to appreciate university and found student life difficult. Keen to stay in England, he turned down a posting with the Foreign Office and seemed to be somewhat footloose, abandoning law to study as a chartered surveyor. At this time, he found both my Mother, at a hunt ball, and a career within the family phosphate mining firm. His grandfather, John, had been a Cornish mining engineer and, aged twenty, in 1870, John had been sent prospecting for minerals in the Caribbean. John returned there a year later, with the backing of his father, my great-great-grandfather William, and his ship put in to the Dutch Antilles for repairs. Going ashore, John identified the sandy material under his feet as guano, sea bird droppings, highly prized because of their rich phosphate content. So began the family mine. Phosphate was shipped to Europe, and Cornish granite returned as ballast for colourful new buildings in Newtown, Curaçao. It would be a hundred years until the phosphate ran out. Father's connection to the company ended when it was taken over by a Dutch business that continues to mine there, mainly for limestone these days.

Mother insists that Father worked hard after the war. But it seemed to his offspring that he spent his days drinking tea, tidying his desk, smoking Piccadilly King Size cigarettes, and serving time on the magistrates' bench before falling asleep during the nine o'clock news. He'd seen enough action. He had done his bit.

Forward to 1960, and the source of Father's irritation. Mother's labour pains were the gastrointestinal consequences of her having consumed an excess of artichoke soup.

I wasn't ready and hung on for a week, before arriving at just past midnight on New Year's Day. I was told that with my arrival, the cheers from Trafalgar Square, celebrating the arrival of the new decade, ceased.

Mother herself had been a difficult home delivery. At the time, her parents, Eric and Betty, had been living in Berlin where Eric was employed as a solicitor. They came back to England for the birth of my mother. As her mother, Betty, slipped into unconsciousness, she heard the specialist say, "Put the baby down in the corner nurse, it cannot possibly be alive, and come and help me." Mother came from a colourful background, boasting both Saint John Kemble and the celebrated actress Sarah Siddons in her family tree. More complicated still, Betty's mother, my great-grandmother Lillian, was godmother to Baldur von Schirach who founded and led the Hitler Youth. After the war at Nuremburg, Schirach was sentenced to twenty years for crimes against humanity. Great-grandmother Lillian said afterwards she wished she'd dropped him at birth.

Mother's parents returned to the UK permanently, prior to the birth of my aunt Sally, Mother's sister. They knew that if they'd had a baby boy in Berlin, he would have faced military service in the German army. My grandfather Eric was a colonel in the Eighth Army, who organised El Alamein reunions after the War, and became friends with Field Marshal Bernard Montgomery. One day Grandfather took me to meet the ageing Monty at his home.

"Get a haircut boy," said Monty.

"I had one yesterday, sir," I squeaked back.

The first three years of my life were spent in Surrey suburbia, before our escape to the country when we moved to West Sussex and a newly built, six-bedroom, three-bathroom brick house designed by Father. With the house came a small farm of just over one hundred acres including two ponds, a couple of woods and a spectacular sixteenth-century oak Sussex barn on stone staddles.

At four I went by bus to my first school, a prep school for four to seven-year-olds.

The bus driver had his hands full managing us brats. My hands were also full, of a fellow child's hair. Lucy pulled mine first. I'd had enough of aggressive girls after fighting my two elder sisters. I disliked and distrusted girls and I wasn't going to stand down. The bus driver saw it all in his mirror. All the children were called to an emergency school assembly. Sixty boys and girls sat pensively in their green school uniforms as the headmistress glowered and bellowed: "There is to be no bullying at my school." I was called to the front, taken up onto the stage and spun by my hair and off my feet, 360 degrees. I wonder if she ever understood the irony. It really hurt and I made a note to never tolerate bullying.

By the age of seven, I was getting bored. The lessons weren't interesting and the headmistress was worried. I was also missing my friend Zandy, who'd been expelled after a fellow pupil had snitched that they had broken the heads off three boxes of England's Glory, Bryant and May matches, and were planning on blowing up the school. Full marks to Zandy, but I suspect it would have taken rather more than a few match heads. The punishment seemed extreme. Then I discovered that I too was in the firing line. I had to leave. But who would have me? Margo and Caroline, my two sisters, certainly didn't want me around, branding their younger brother an obnoxious brat. The feeling was mutual. Why didn't they share my interests in exploring the farm and shooting anything that moved? In fact, the three of us barely met during childhood, apart from Sunday lunches, Christmas present opening, quarterly family attendance at church, and a rare family holiday. It was better that way.

There was plenty of fun to be had at home, but neighbours started to complain.

I pushed a fellow seven year old in an apple box down a slide, which he survived, just. More seriously, I'd driven a pitchfork into a friend's scalp, requiring ten stitches.

The final straw for my exasperated parents was when a friend of my sister's came round and I opened the door shouting: "Mother, a girl's here, she's got even more spots than Margo." I was unmanageable. My parents discussed sending me to a child psychiatrist but chose boarding school instead.

The school was good but I was only eight and it felt constricting. I wanted to be on the farm, running wild as I'd always done. However, it wasn't long before two girls caught my eye. Strange, I'd never had any interest in them before. Sarah, swimming naked in the school pool, and Susan, who I met on a family holiday in Corfu. Susan took me to her bedroom and asked me to strip.

"Everything?" I said.

"Everything," she replied.

"What? Pants as well?"

"Yes, everything." It was Susan's fault. She came from Norwich. Susan's brother Timmy was already there and he stripped off too. We all had a look. I'm still not sure what the point of this exercise was. Probably just normal childhood inquisitiveness, though such episodes never made Enid Blyton's *Famous Five* books.

Apart from Sarah and Susan, I avoided girls, especially my sisters. One evening there was a commotion and much wailing. Father had banished Margo to her bedroom for arriving late for lunch. Margo was going to miss *Top of the Pops*. I disliked this programme, had an intuitive suspicion of the creepy straw-blond long-haired presenter that Margo fancied and preferred the new series called *Star Trek*. Margo, however, was distraught as her lifelong ambition was to join the all-female dance troupe Pan's People and this was the most important 45 minutes of her week. In a hormonal hurricane she leant over the bannisters shouting,

"Beat me, Daddy. Beat me, Daddy." I went to see whether I could negotiate on my sister's behalf. Father relented and she saw the second half and, as a sign of gratitude for pleading her case, Margo gave me my first job: tickling her feet for a penny an hour.

Like many war veterans of the time who had seen so much violence, Father had nightmares for years. And a temper. To handle the latter, we used both defensive and attacking tactics. He had, of course, seen all these techniques deployed at Anzio and was better equipped to deal with them. Defence involved books down trousers. Attack carried much more risk but, just once, I felt it was merited to redress the balance.

Father was having car problems. Firstly, his three children had hosed his lovingly waxed and polished motor. Then he damaged the car door when reversing out of the garage. His response was to give the car a good kicking, denting a few more panels. The damage was fixed permanently shortly afterwards when he crashed the car, writing it off. After the accident Father was on crutches and I enjoyed playing with their adjustable lengths. This just made him even more cross. My revenge was to hide a row of sewing needles pointing upwards out of his favourite dozing chair.

School holidays were full of adventure, driving an old Ford Popular around the farm.

Zandy, Julian and I drove flat out around a circuit, through a wood and up and down a pylon lane. Although both Sussex farmers' sons, my two friends couldn't have been more different. Zandy was stocky, big nosed and Hispanic and Julian skinny, pale and ginger. I soon began to love the thrill of risk-taking. That's probably how it started. We towed each other on a sledge, attached to the car with binder twine, breaking forty mph before we were

167

aged fourteen. The driver focused on hitting cow pats with the car's back wheels to splatter the sledge passenger behind. An even better thrill was to jump onto the car roof and to hang on, as the driver tried their best to shake you off. Seeking yet more danger, we practiced handbrake turns, rolling the car over. Feeling invincible, we jammed the accelerator down with a brick, and jumped out. Somewhat belatedly, our parents became concerned and we were ordered to start wearing riding hats. For something else to do, once the car was wrecked, I started climbing up the farm pylon. Spotted, and banned from extreme sports, I dipped into quick science, but my multiple random potions failed to stop the grass growing. A change of tack, and I decided to make a fur coat.

My disgusting bloodlust thankfully faded over the years but at that time I would shoot or trap squirrels, rabbits and moles, before curing their skins and stitching them together. Skinning squirrels was the hardest. The plan was to make a fur coat to sell to sister Margo. It turned out a messy disaster but the dissection had been good practice. It certainly cured me of any latent squeamishness and may have helped later life choices.

Biennial holidays abroad were planned meticulously by Father, months in advance. We flew to Yugoslavia, with Zandy invited to join us. Father leant back in his airline seat, smoking his Piccadilly cigarettes, craving a peace that was denied him as Zandy pestered him for the whole flight for his WWII experiences. Nobody else asked. It was kind of the parents to bring my friend. It wasn't long before Zandy and I began to explore the nudist beach. For two pubescent boys, it was fascinating swimming in snorkels and masks, studying the naked bodies. We noticed that my sister Caroline had hair in different areas to us. Indeed, quite a thick thatch. We wondered what the point of it was and asked Father.

Father patiently explained that head hair protected one from the sun, he was unsure about armpit hair and refused to answer any questions about pubic hair.

Human bodies were starting to become interesting.

16

WELLINGTON

Prep school had ended and, at the age of thirteen, as Elton John's "Don't Shoot Me I'm Only the Piano Player" and Slade's "Merry Xmas Everybody" rocked the charts, I was packed off to my new boarding school, Wellington College. The college was proposed as a fitting memorial to Arthur Wellesley, Duke of Wellington, victor over Napoleon at the Battle of Waterloo. Designed by John Shaw, it was founded in 1859 with rules that hadn't changed much in a hundred years. I was still in infancy when Wellington was chosen as my future place of education. The family had connections with Repton School in Derbyshire, but my paternal grandfather William fell out with the then Master of Repton, Geoffrey Fisher, later ninety-ninth Archbishop of Canterbury, about the treatment meted out to my uncle John. I never met either of my paternal grandparents; Marjorie died in childbirth, thirty years before my birth, and William died eleven days after I was born.

Wellington had quite a reputation, being one of the founding twenty-one clubs of the rugby union and boasting a colourful alumni, including: Field Marshal Sir Claude Auchinleck, Sir Christopher Lee and James Hunt. I hoped I wouldn't metamorphose into a bloodthirsty military playboy.

I was just thirteen, a full boarder and the youngest child in the school house. But, even though I was the baby of the house, I wasn't classified as the most junior boy. In the archaic UK public school system this was something that mattered. That ignominy fell on Mark. He was six months older, but he hadn't been put down on the Wellington College list till he was five, whereas I'd had my name down in infancy. You can imagine how this must have grated when Mark found that I, not he, was regarded as the senior new boy, so I got the pick of the worst two fagging options left.[9] Mark had no choice at all. I chose "Toast Fag" which meant that Mark was left with the fag end of fags, "Call Fag". He never forgave me. Toast fag was fine. You just had to make the toast every morning for the prefects. The perk was that I could also make some for my chosen friends. Leverage, boy, another new lesson in life. Mark, on the other hand, had to get up early and call the time every ten minutes in his high-pitched unbroken voice, making sure all the "prisoners" were awake and at breakfast promptly. If any child failed to surface, the blame was Mark's and his fine, five pence, would be inscribed with all the other offenders, on the weekly house-fines list of shame, pinned on the wall for all to ponder. Where did the fines go? I wish I knew.

---

9. *Fagging was a practice in British public schools whereby younger pupils acted as servants to older boys. Tasks included making toast, serving tea, cleaning shoes, making beds and warming toilet seats. Probably established in the sixteenth century, fagging became obsolete at the end of twentieth century.*

A tough system? For sure. Wellington was rough, but it had moments of enjoyment.

I had a good housemaster, charming Portuguese kitchen staff, and great sport. Sadly, however, bullying was relentless. It was mainly verbal, but also physical.

It didn't do to stand out. Too tall, too short, too fat, too thin, too pretty, too spotty, too stupid, too intelligent, too anything. Doing well in lessons was particularly punishable. To make matters worse, the locals also liked to fight. I wasn't small, but I had been anti-violence from the age of six, ever since that headmistress had humiliated me with her sadistic hair pulling. My passivity seemed to egg them on.

Every day I would run the mile back from the main school buildings, to the school house, hoping to avoid ambushes from the locals, only to meet more violence when I reached the house. Why was everyone so aggressive? I knew adults were brutish, but it seemed children were equally bad. Even the house rules were cruel. It was institutional bullying. Prefects could and would fine other boys, for anything. I was fined for offences ranging from tardiness, through scruffiness, to pyromaniac tendencies. My pocket money was two shillings a week and each fine was one shilling. No appeals were allowed.

One December, aged fifteen, I'd managed three fines in a week, exceeding my pocket money. For this unavoidable oversight I was "gated". Gating was a cruel punishment involving getting up in the dark and running, petrified, a mile to the Porters' Lodge to sign a book, before six in the morning, and then sprinting back, still in the dark. It was 1975 and two-thirds of the public had just voted for the UK to join the European Economic Community. What about the European Court of Human Rights? Were public school boys excluded?

No dormitories at Wellington. That had to be a good thing. I started out sharing a room with Mark, then, after a year, moved with my treasured tuck box into a *tish*, the nickname we gave to small, partitioned rooms off a corridor. The partitioned room, tish for short, measured just ten feet by five feet and the partition itself was made of wooden boarding that stopped three feet short of the ceiling. My worldly possessions were locked away in my tuck box. Pencils, comics, the odd Mars bar and girlie mag. For most public schoolboys the tuck box was kind of sacrosanct, a special place of your own. It was a little bit of home to which we became emotionally attached. Someone defecated in Jeremy Clarkson's tuckbox at Repton – probably explains quite a lot.

I'm not sure how I would have coped with such animalistic behaviour. If the tuck box was our most treasured possession, the tish was almost equally valued, something of a civilised oasis, a retreat to which we could return to lick our wounds. Yet, even here, safety was relative. One day I was minding my own business in my room when, unprovoked, three boys burst through the door to rough me up. At first, they just pushed me around. No big deal, I was used to it. Then one of the three made a mistake. Pushed hard in the face, I got a bloody nose. A switch went in my head. WHACK. That was the first and last time I really hit someone. Oh it was so sweet.

It was beautiful. It made a lovely noise. Yes it may have broken a bone in my right hand but that punch stopped it all. It was worth it. There was no further trouble.

With that out of the way there was just the money worry. I didn't have enough. I was fifteen, averaging four fines a month and short on petty cash. Time, then, to set up my second business. The first one — making and selling sister Margo a fur coat — was abandoned before it got off the ground. Mid-teens brought acne and other stirrings. Hormones were kicking in hard, so it seemed natural to start a business in pornography, supplemented by phoning Father weekly to bet on the horses. Once a month, I would sneak off to the village newsagent and buy either a Mayfair or a Penthouse girlie magazine. I found Carrie, in the cartoon section, particularly erotic. Having checked out the latest monthly edition, I would then rent out these magazines, as nearly new, for one shilling a week. Is that what "second hand" means? Demand was high and all proceeds, beyond the cover price, were pure profit, with no national insurance nor income tax to declare.

Rumours abounded about a sexually predatory prefect, but I was never pestered. Maybe I was too spotty to be attractive, or perhaps word had got around about my punch — such deeds tended to assume a life of their own. Something, however, was clearly going on behind the scenes, as one morning the housemaster called us to an urgent assembly. He cleared his throat and in the broadest Yorkshire accent said, "Boys, I have only one thing to say. I don't mind mutual masturbation, but there's to be no buggery."

What about our legendary flexible student, Robin, who could perform auto-fellatio? What an achievement! Was that act banned as well? Who cared? The big news was that girls had just been introduced to the school. Soon one girl was caught swimming, in the dark. The teachers were going to the pool for the same, only possibly less innocent, version of entertainment. The first girl in, therefore, was also the first out, expelled. Another lesson for later life: one can't beat the establishment.

The appearance of girls meant exciting times ahead. It seemed to me that a younger son would need the wise counsel, advice, even protection of his sisters. Running to Mother was a no-no in any matters of the teenage heart. I thought I'd check Caroline out first. But could I trust her with my closest secrets? I'd developed a vivid imagination and used it to concoct a story to test her.

"Caroline, tell nobody," I said. "Julian had sex on the back seat of Father's car."

"Yuk," she said. "How disgusting. I thought it smelt bad."

A week later Mother announced that she wasn't amused by what had happened in Father's car and she was going to raise it with Julian's parents. Poor Father. Poor Julian. Untrustworthy Caroline. Right. At least I knew that one sister couldn't be counted on.

*

During school holidays, Sunday lunches provided a rare opportunity for the family to meet as a whole, and attendance was a three-line whip. But beforehand, on most Sunday mornings, I would be collected by Rog, the elder brother of a girl in whom I had a one-sided interest. Rog would drive me to the pub and I would return a few pints later, somehow escaping censure. My two older sisters had never enjoyed such freedom and it understandably irked. I was grateful for the lift and the beer but I did wonder why Rog was so invested in my friendship? Was there some as yet hidden agenda? I was right to be concerned. With his wavy long blond hair, Rog looked like the US tennis star, Vitas Gerulaitis. Or at least how Vitas Gerulaitis might have looked after spending a seedy night in the corrupting company of Jimmy Savile. Altogether dodgy, then. I doubted Rog's interest in me was sexual. How wrong I was.

It was entirely sexual — in an oblique way. His motives only became clear a year later. By then Rog had "acquired" the majority of my new girlfriends. They felt safe talking to me, while he lurked menacingly, in rampant anticipation in the background. Rog offered more excitement than I could and they happily hopped into his low-slung sports car. I seemed the perfect aperitif. Rog was the finisher.

Too soon A levels were looming. Why was everyone taking it all so seriously? Couldn't we just continue as we were? I much preferred watching *Kojak* or the *Six Million Dollar Man* on TV. Or, even better, blasting out Queen's latest release: "Bohemian Rhapsody". Studying was deathly boring. To escape, a group of us borrowed a car and drove to Ascot for the races, an event that would influence my future more than I could have predicted. We arranged to meet up with four fellow absconders, from a different school, the one where they grow prime ministers.

One of these characters was Scaf, a long-haired scruff. Scaf had already gambled away his pocket money and was in need of a loan. He promised to repay me. I believed him. I must have been so gullible. Sister Caroline had taught me awareness of broken promises, but nobody had taught me yet about stealing. I hadn't learnt about such dishonesty at this stage in life. I handed Scaf a fiver — a year's pocket money. Scaf went to the tic-tac men, lost my money and disappeared.

A-levels were taken and decisions had to be made. What next? I knew I couldn't muck about on the farm, trading pornography and betting on the horses for ever. But what could I study? What on earth did I want to do? Really, in honesty, probably nothing. In the boys' public schools there was an expectation that the investment made by parents in their sons' education would lead to something more. The majority achieved a place at university. The brighter boys chose pure subjects, such as English, history or mathematics. Those unable to achieve the necessary grades tended towards a life of service in the military, or a life of self-service in the City. But where did I sit in this matrix? A reluctance to go to university combined forces with the inertia of deciding what to study, and the apathy of where to go. I was paralysed. My parents raised the idea of medicine. They said there would always be a need for doctors. But I had no burning desire to be a doctor. It sounded too much like work, too smelly, too dangerous and too serious.

By chance it was at this exact time, that I discovered a lump on my anus. I crouched over a mirror, pulled my pants aside and cautiously peered between my legs, and gasped. I had cancer.

Wasn't that what everyone got? Horrified by what I saw, I went in search of the school house Encyclopaedia Britannica and looked up cancer of the anus. I couldn't tell anyone about this, nor could I ask anyone to look at it or treat me. I came to the conclusion that I would have no choice but to treat this terrible condition myself.

I hoped death would be swift. Maybe being a doctor would help my exit. My reflections were interrupted by a knock on the door. I quickly hid the mirror. My exasperated housemaster had hunted me down. The university applications had to go in *that day*. My mind had been distracted by my impending demise and, as I was clearly not going to last long, I'd forgotten about my future education. I reluctantly filled in the UCCA (Universities Central Council on Admissions) form, ticking medicine.

My problems weren't over yet. I was now forced to choose and rank five universities. Haphazardly I chose two regarded as "national top choices" and then randomly, three others. The next day the haemorrhoid popped back in. My first choice was Cambridge. Wellington said they could get me into Oxford, but Father had studied law at Cambridge, so I stubbornly stuck with his alma mater, then fluffed the exam.

My second choice was Southampton, but we had an instant, deep and enduring mutual dislike. When I visited their medical school, I was shown a bucket with a lid on it. The lid was lifted. There was a human head in it. Yes, a real head, recently attached to a real live body. A real human being, now with grieving family and friends. Incredible. Who could be so disrespectful, thoughtless and crass?

For my third choice I squeezed a few of my worst spots, had a shave, dabbed the blood off my face, put on a suit and headed off to London. Back to the same hospital where I'd been born seventeen years earlier. The Middlesex. The interview didn't go to plan. Again I wouldn't budge. Having two elder sisters had made me stubborn. The panel feared my interests of hunting and shooting were incompatible with my applying to train as a doctor. Maybe I should have been more honest and included my trading in girlie mags and gambling? When challenged on my hobbies, knowing I had no chance, my cockiness surfaced and I said, "It's different in the countryside."

I must have made some kind of impression as I was accepted by both my fourth choice, The London, and by Charing Cross Hospital Medical School (CXHMS), my fifth and final choice. I decided that if the one I listed last really wanted me, then that was my safest bet. My fate was now sealed. But I needed to grow up and grow up fast. I was seventeen and about to hit university, medicine and London all at once. I knew nothing about any of them. I had spots, a few facial hairs, and a haemorrhoid. That was about it. Then I found I could arrange a deferment to study history of art, in Grenoble, France. That seemed a wheeze. The concept of a gap year was in its infancy. What a great idea.

Domestic complications with my sisters arose at the same time. Margo had just embarked on her first marriage and now Caroline was determined to marry. That was bad enough, but to compound the shock, Caroline had chosen a French Roman Catholic. Mother was devastated. I too was heading for France.

On arrival at Grenoble University, the professor, speaking French, asked:

"How many years have you studied the language?"

"Ten years," I replied in my best French.

An easy start to the process of being placed in the right class. Except the professor then said in English, "If you have studied Le French for ten years, why ees it so bad?" I guessed they were unaware of how it worked, or rather, didn't work, in England.

Sorting the course had been simple. I had friends studying in Grenoble who helped arrange the necessary paperwork and found me some digs to live in. They'd also organised a trip, to the ski resort of Chamrousse.

At the entrance hall, my eyes roamed. Aged eighteen, it was time. The Bee Gees "Stayin' Alive" was top of the charts and although I was a "late starter", I felt very alive. I needed to get a metaphorical monkey off my back, my sisters had been "at it" for years, I was falling behind and France would be the perfect location. Damn. Nothing tempting. But who was this, slouched against the wall? It couldn't be, but it was. Scaf. The rogue who hadn't repaid the five pounds I'd lent him the previous year. It seems that he too was on the pull. But was he trying too hard? With his curly brown locks, quilted green jacket and oversized pink collar, he looked quite the dandy. Along with flared pale blue jeans, held up with a mock snakeskin belt, and with brown leather winklepicker boots, the only question was: who was he trying to pull? Never mind, if we couldn't crack it here, we couldn't crack it anywhere. We shook hands in manly fashion and agreed to share a flat.

Our leaving party approached too soon, it was there that a Lebanese friend, Carl, told us that Land Rovers were valuable in Saudi Arabia. Another light-bulb moment. I hatched a plan. We'd buy a Land Rover and sell it for a healthy profit in Saudi after driving overland. Scaf would come so long as I did all the planning and all the work. At least he offered to share the driving. There was one flaw, Saudi Arabia didn't allow tourists to visit. No worries, we would go as caterers working for a friend's company. Concerns were raised by my parents about our driving through Turkey, Syria and Saudi Arabia and being mistakenly identified as Jewish, so the M&S labels were removed from our shirts and underpants. You can't be too careful.

Scaf had been given one job. One single responsibility. He was asked to get a tool box. He forgot. Mother drove off to get one from Halfords. As we got in the car and said our goodbyes, Mother was standing in the drive, weeping. Father turned to her and said, "Don't worry, it's just a crusade." The trip went well, until we reached Kent, when the water pump blew. Then, crossing from Syria to Jordan, the Jordanian army stopped us. What were two eighteen-year-olds doing driving, at three in the morning in an ex-military long-wheel-base Land Rover? Caterers going to Saudi Arabia? A likely story! The Jordanian army officer asked us once more why we were doing this trip. We repeated we weren't sure why we were doing it.

Not sure that went down too well, but they did like the story about Lebanese Carl's idea. Maybe they knew what we were to find out later. We laughed, and that broke the ice. Through the night we drank sweet coffee and played cards. We left the next morning after hugs and a handshake and headed for Saudi Arabia and the Tapline. The Trans-Arabian Pipeline was the sole, but reassuring, feature for the 1,000-mile drive. The Tapline is only 700 miles long, but it seemed to be there for all of the 1,000 miles. The pipe is over two feet wide and designed to carry up to 500,000 barrels of oil a day. Sand, pipeline, camel, jeep, sand, pipeline, mirage, sand, pipeline. We stuttered to a halt 200 miles from Dammam. Damn Dammam.

It was only our second breakdown. I had to hitch. The jeep ride was welcome but uncomfortable, shared with four bearded locals too friendly for my liking. On arrival in Dammam I sought the manager of the catering company and explained that I'd left Scaf and the Land Rover in the desert and needed to rescue him. Back at the Land Rover we found Scaf supine, with flies on his face and his eyes open. My God, Scaf was dead. At least the Land Rover wasn't obviously missing any parts. That meant Scaf hadn't died too long ago. I sniffed. I sniffed again. No particularly bad smells. Scaf blinked. He had a disconcerting habit of sleeping with his eyes open.

We had to sell the Land Rover, leave Saudi Arabia and divvy up our profits. We'd borrowed £2,500 for this adventure, a serious amount of money. From earlier discussions with Carl, we'd hoped to double it. I was heading for the big time. This was my golden egg. Except we were only offered £900, upped to £1,000 and nothing more. Land Rovers were significantly cheaper in Saudi Arabia than in England. We'd driven the wrong way.

A month later we heard that the Land Rover had been sold. An American businessman had heard of our story and couldn't believe how brave, naive and stupid we were and bought the car for our original outlay of £2,500.

Father had always said we should be nicer to the Americans. Maybe he was right. This was my fourth business adventure, after my sister's fur coat, the trading in pornography and gambling. Aged eighteen, as childhood ended and the adventure of medical school beckoned, I was relieved to be still ahead.

17

FIONA

The summer of 1978. Louise Brown was born, the first birth from *in vitro* fertilisation (IVF). Newspapers called her "the test tube baby" though in fact she was conceived in a Petri dish. The Bond film *The Spy Who Loved Me* went on general release and I entered medical school in London, a city I didn't know and doubted I'd like. Freshers' week gave a taste of the lunacy that would define the next five years. Drink a pint of baked beans, eat a tin of Pedigree Chum, oh, the competitions. What fun. More importantly, we got to meet the nurses, as we danced semi-naked in the university bar.

Medical school proved quite different to the privileged life I'd spent growing up on the farm. There were days out on farm shoots to think about, for a start, so I brought along my shotgun to the university digs and tucked it under my bed. I suppose I was one of the posher ones, but our year's intake of one hundred students, from a broad mixture of social backgrounds, gelled remarkably well. It wasn't all roses, but the good times outweighed the bad.

Easy access to our Sussex farm's home-grown turkeys provided a welcome change to sausages and baked beans in the student halls.

I would have to adapt nonetheless. In fact, apart from *MASH* on the TV, I had no real interest in medicine. I don't think I was exceptionally lazy, but I didn't fancy doing much studying.

Lectures disrupted my supplemental source of income — playing poker. I teamed up with a fellow medical student, Major, and we started the West London Gaming Club (WLGC). Major was short, stocky and lived on the edge; another anarchist who disliked regulations and authority. The WLGC was a decadent and disgusting men's club and I loved it. A game of cards involved eight hours of poker and too much to drink. The drink of choice, called armpit, was a random mixture of cheap supermarket spirits doled out as a fine, for anything from a misdeal, to winning a big hand. One evening, Skiddy, another medical student, misdealt and refused to take his penalty. Skiddy said he'd drunk enough. Such insubordination was unthinkable. What should we do? As an alternative, Skiddy accepted a half measure of armpit, a thirty millilitres measure of mixed spirits injected via a catheter, inserted rectally. Skiddy rapidly lost consciousness and the game had to be suspended for a couple of hours while we checked his pupillary reactions to light. I suppose he shouldn't have misdealt, but we could have ended up in jail.

Blouse, a further miscreant medical student, so called because of his flowery shirts, was also living on the edge. He felt that he was missing out and requested the same.

Unfortunately, the catheter wasn't inserted far enough and when the balloon was blown up, it was sitting in his anal canal. Most uncomfortable. Blouse, however, was beyond sympathy. He'd illegally imported a police .38 Special revolver from the US. When things weren't going his way, Blouse would use his .38 to perform frighteningly realistic mock executions, with the trembling victim pushed up against the wall, loaded pistol pressed hard against the temple. Loaded with blanks? We never knew for sure. Maybe Blouse had an excuse. Equipped with oversize testicles, Blouse had sought the help of a consultant urologist.

Testicles come in many sizes but can be enlarged due to fluid collections within the scrotal sac, or due to a chromosomal abnormality, called Fragile X. Fragile X is associated with a narrow face, large ears, big testicles and mild intellectual disability. Thinking about it, Blouse ticked most of those boxes. He wasn't complaining. His super-sized scrotum proved a steady earner, netting him £8 a shot at the sperm bank. With beer at thirty pence a pint, this was a handy student income. In the clinic, the consultant weighed Blouse's specimens up doubtfully, like a snooker player looking at two pinks in the top pocket, then, sucking through his teeth, he shook his head. "No", he said, "They're just big. Congratulations."

A rule was introduced forbidding anyone from leaving the poker table for eight hours. With stretched bladders initially we used "the penis extension", a plastic tube designed as a cover for golf club shafts, with the lower end inserted into a plastic bucket on the floor. As our medical knowledge expanded, we advanced to using peniflows filched from ward supplies. These were condom-style attachments connected by a tube to a bag strapped to the lower leg. At last, no poker player had any excuse to leave the table. Chasing more extreme behaviour, we experimented with a nasogastric tube, before a cannula was produced which Major inserted into a vein, filling a glass with his own blood, which he drank. We had lost all boundaries.

Girlfriends tended to stay clear of these poker events, but Gill was made of sterner stuff. On one memorable evening, she came downstairs as Major was refusing to go to bed. Major wanted to play on until four in the morning. Gill was a free spirit and well known to a few of us. Not amused, Gill left the room before coming back down and standing in front of us, lifting her dark blue dress, revealing a shapely, naked body "Are you coming now?" she said. There was a rush for the stairs.

Not too soon, the moment arrived when medicine moved from theory to practice, and for me, changed from dull to interesting. We moved out of the lecture theatre, to be given our first taste of what really happened as practicing doctors. Swabbing the insides of our mouths, we spread white cotton tips over a red culture medium, before returning a couple of days later to inspect our oral flora. My plate looked different to the others. Was this a rare Sussex colony I was incubating? In the middle of my dish was a slightly off-white, raised growth, surrounded by concentric rings. It looked rather attractive. The other students' bacterial growths looked sparse by comparison. The microbiologist sought me out, whispering, "I think you need to clean your teeth better. A heavy growth of Escherichia coli. Lives in the lower bowel of mammals."

I heard a noise behind me and saw Elliot giggling. Medical school attracts strange characters, as I've probably made clear, and few came stranger than Elliot, a student from London. Bright, but not half as bright as he thought he was, with thick black curly hair and large black rimmed glasses, Elliot was both a lot smaller, a lot younger and a lot more trouble than most. He confessed to rubbing a swab between his buttocks, then smearing his "sample" onto my culture dish.

Another intriguing individual, Rod, then arrived on the scene. He was a bright trainee accountant and ought to have realised that tagging on to barely sane medical students might be dangerous as well as fun. Village People had released "In The Navy" and camp was becoming cool. Rod was a straight, but rather pretty, boy and had developed an annoying cough. I offered to help and went to hospital with him. The pneumonia on his chest X-ray looked like pneumocystis, a fungus, that was the talk of the town, amid the current AIDS epidemic.

Rod was asked by the specialist whether he took drugs but before he could answer, I interjected "I doubt it, but I'm not so sure about his sex life." This puerile comment led to the unfortunate Rod having an HIV test. Despite being negative, Rod discovered later that, because there was such a stigma and fear of HIV/Aids at the time, he had to declare this investigation, and he was marked as an insurance risk.

Medical school had given us a ridiculous amount of freedom, something we were unaccustomed to and sought to enjoy to the limit. But we'd lost sight of the limit and we needed to rediscover boundaries and control before we got into serious trouble.

But first, more study was required and histopathology came next. This was based around Fiona, who'd died a couple of years earlier, having previously generously donated her body to medical science. Fiona's corpse had been drained of blood, embalmed, and stored in the hospital's rack of fridges, so the smell was minimal.

Over the years, I'd dissected sparrows, rabbits, moles and squirrels, so I was confident this would give me an advantage over the other medical students. Six of us worked around Fiona's body. Bit by bit we slowly dissected and carefully and respectfully put her body parts into her individual metal bin. Then, horror of horrors, we realised that tables six and nine had muddled their lids. Fiona's breasts would have to be incinerated with James's organs in a transgender cocktail.

I hoped neither minded.

18

DARIÉN

The five-year course at medical school consisted of two pre-clinical years, followed by three clinical years, during which time we would start to see real patients. Having scraped through the first year, there was only one more year before we'd be let loose on the public. Finally, if the exams were passed, employment had to be sought, working as a junior doctor.

The morning routine started with jumping out of bed, turning on the three-bar electric fire, throwing damp clothes over it, then back to bed, watching the steam rising, waiting for the telltale smell of burnt cotton. The timing had to be perfect before anything singed. Then a cup of tea, two grilled sausages, wrapped in sliced buttered white bread, and smeared with tomato ketchup. The sandwich would be bagged, stuffed in a pocket, and eaten on the drive to medical school. Five pence petrol money per passenger. Most students took their studies seriously; I struggled to understand why. Perhaps I'd made it this far, not through being smarter, but through the edge lent by a private education at public school. Any perceived advantage, however, was mixed as the public-school types stood out like sore thumbs. That said, unlike my school experience, there was no unpleasantness.

However, there was unhappiness in the ranks. The dean called a meeting of all of our year. In future, he said, nobody would fail the internal exams. Students would instead be graded from one to five. That was a stroke of good luck, as one particular lecturer had taken a dislike to me. He'd failed me the week before, on the dissection of Fiona's face. My dissection retake had been booked for that very afternoon. I left with a smile on my face and walked in for my retake viva on hers.

*

We used mnemonics to recall medical terminology. Some were easy to remember.

Such as this well-established one, covering the twelve cranial nerves: olfactory, optic, oculomotor, trochlear, trigeminal, abducens, facial, auditory, glossopharyngeal, vagus, accessory and hypoglossal. No sexism intended in the mnemonic: Oh Oh Oh To Touch And Feel A Girl's Vagina And Hymen. I wondered what the women felt, but I suppose I should have thought of that beforehand.

Most mnemonics were harder to remember and the one for the facial nerve that I needed now, in my renewed acquaintance with Fiona, escaped me. The viva didn't go well. How many branches of the facial nerve were there? Was it four, five, or six?

I remembered the temporal, buccal and cervical segments but was pretty sure there was another one, or was it another two? I didn't care that much, it really didn't matter now, as my pass was assured. The lecturers, called demonstrators in this area of work, were all wannabe surgeons full of their own importance.

"Fail," he said.

"Students can't fail any more," I said, with more than a hint of cockiness. But he had an ace up his sleeve.

"Charles, you are so bad, that whatever the new rules are, I don't care and I'm still failing you and I will see you again next week."

So I failed, but I couldn't fail, so there'd be no retake, as I hadn't failed. The demonstrator was caught in a sublime catch-22 not of his making. Most of Fiona was now safely in her bin and I decided I wouldn't attend the second retake. I'd take my chances.

Restlessness was setting in; it was time to escape, but first a game of football. This was pre-political correctness, the medical school was wonderfully socially integrated and race was no issue. We noticed, but we didn't notice. It was as irrelevant as we were irreverent. A "Blacks versus Circumcised" football match was arranged. Incredible, beautiful. I can't remember who won and nobody cared.

Between studies, I spent most of my time browsing travel books. On the last few pages of a South American handbook I found a section on the Darién Gap that set my spine tingling. Every year, it said, a few people, maybe half a dozen, crossed this way overland from Panama to Colombia. But where was Darién? And, why was it a gap?

I'd never heard of it. I found it — a one-hundred-mile-long strip of untamed rainforest. The guidebook said it wasn't recommended. Ideal then; I had to do it. Even better, the best season for undertaking the crossing was between January and April. The end of pre-clinical training at medical school would be in August. Perfect, the adventure would be out of season.

There was another problem. Who would be stupid enough to go with me? Bruce perhaps? Bruce was a farmer's son, so hardy, and he was on for an adventure. That I barely knew him and that he'd never hitch-hiked before were minor concerns. He was Scottish, but nobody's perfect and I was sure it would work out fine. Hitching south after our flight to Mexico, Bruce's preferred position was lying down on top of his backpack, hat covering his face, leaving me to try all the tricks I could to get a lift.

Bruce never rushed. Bruce wasn't languorous, he just liked doing nothing, apart from sleeping and drinking tequila. We headed on to Belize then Guatemala. Relations between Guatemala and Britain were not good. The border had a sign up saying *Belice Es Guatemala*. A quick lift at the border, in a van driven by a middle-aged Guatemalan businessman, was an encouraging start. The driver seemed friendly and I looked forward to making good progress on my Spanish and to reaching the next set of Mayan ruins before sunset. I slipped into the front, while Bruce slid the back door open and clambered in with both of our backpacks. Two miles later, the army stopped us. It was dark and raining. Two soldiers got into the back and, standing over Bruce, they started rifling through his luggage. Popping his pills onto the floor. The antimalarials, the antibiotics, the painkillers, the water sterilisers, indeed everything we needed for the jungle and the adventure that lay ahead. Bruce was distressed, crying out, "Please help me Charles." Foolishly, I leaned back and gently pushed one soldier on the shoulder.

"Dejalo en paz," I said.[10]

In seconds, Bruce and I were out of the car and lying face

10. *Spanish for "Leave him alone."*

down, handcuffed together in a ditch, with pistols pressed into the back of our heads. I'd never seen Bruce move or be moved so fast. He was a broad-shouldered farmer's boy, weighing over 100 kg, and they threw him down like a rag doll. So this was how it would end.

Would it hurt? Would our bodies be found? Would wild animals eat our remains?

Would our killers be caught and punished? Would our parents find out how we'd died? Would Major continue running the West London Gaming Club? I soon heard other Guatemalan soldiers rushing over. Maybe they would pour petrol over us and set us alight? A heated debate was held in Spanish. It was impossible to resist or to follow the argument raging over our bodies. This time the good guys won and we were uncuffed, returned to the van, and driven off. The driver didn't need this.

He looked at me with disgust. Attempts at an apology were rebuffed. A mile down the road he told us to get out.

"Vete a la mierda."[11]

Aged twenty, abandoned in the rain, in darkness, in the middle of nowhere, we were learning the Latin way.

Surely El Salvador would be more welcoming, though this was 1980 and a friend back home had raised his eyebrows, asking, "Why are you planning to hitch through a war zone?" Fair point, I suppose. Some might believe it stupid to hitch-hike on holiday through a war zone and the local Salvadorians were astonished to see us doing so. This was the era of banana republics. The El Salvadorian civil war had started that year and was to rage for the next twelve years, often targeting the clergy. Archbishop Romero had been murdered four months before we arrived. The war

---

11. *Spanish profanity. Equivalent of "Fuck off."*

was between the military-led government, the junta, and a coalition of left-wing groups. Like most administrations, the junta had done little to improve the living standards of the poor. We were lucky. We swam in Lake Llopango, then heard that five people had been killed there that week. A year later, a village we passed by, El Mozote, was wiped out with a thousand people killed.

The next country, Honduras, was bland in comparison. No war there and the capital Tegucigalpa offered some respite. It didn't last. In war-torn Nicaragua, there was widespread destruction. The Sandinistas had taken over from the Somoza dynasty the year before, but they still hadn't achieved total control. The US-backed Contras didn't join in until the year after we left. Bruce and I hitched with rifle-cradling Sandinista soldiers in an armoured combat vehicle, as Blondie's "Call Me" blared out from a cassette deck. It was a great way to brush up on our Spanish and the Sandinistas were supportive, not suspicious, and genuinely interested in our plan to walk through Darién. They were fascinated by our lives back in Europe, and showed no anxiety or doubts about our motives. The jeep dropped us off at the cathedral in Managua, the Nicaraguan capital.

The Catedral de Santiago had been shattered eight years previously by an earthquake and was now open to the elements. A giant billboard of a Sandinista fighter had been screwed to its neoclassical facade. Earth's convulsions had collapsed most of the roof and removed one of the crosses on the cathedral's twin towers. A lone statue remained, looking down benevolently. Two giant wooden lighting poles had been placed incongruously like football stadia floodlights on either side of the pale grey frontage. We found the entrance atop a flight of concrete steps from the road, between a couple of straggly palm trees. Inside was silence, as if even the birds were muted in respect of a holy place. No respect outside, with cars honking and traders shouting their wares. We made our way through the bustle to the nearby waterfront.

An event-free hitch-hike through Costa Rica proved too comfortable for my liking. Then on to Panama City, with the wonder of Darién beyond. We'd been travelling for a month on a budget of five dollars a day, sleeping in the cheapest rooms and eating street food. Bruce was getting tetchy about the hitching, preferring the bus option. I hadn't told Bruce that in Darién there was no public transport, nor indeed any road. One hundred miles on foot didn't sound far. I knew about the drug cartels but hadn't read up on the terrain or the local fauna. This lack of preparation meant we didn't need to worry about the poison dart frogs, black scorpions, venomous snakes or awaiting jaguars.

Also waiting for us in Colombia were another lot of revolutionaries, this time the Revolutionary Armed Forces of Colombia, better known by their catchy title of FARC. We had got on so well with the Sandinistas that I reassured Bruce we would do likewise with FARC. That was my coping strategy — denial. It would prove useful later, dealing with the distressing parts of clinical medicine. Colombia's own civil war, La Violencia, raged between 1948 and 1958 and killed 250,000 people. Life for the downtrodden had not improved, so along came FARC, modelled on Cuba's revolutionaries, fighting for the peasants against inequalities. The cause was depressingly similar to the Sandinistas. I promised the somnolescent Bruce that I would behave. Bruce was smart. He never really trusted me. At the time FARC had up to 20,000 fighters, and made money from cocaine, protection taxes, and its specialty — kidnapping. It was twenty years before Tom Hart Dyke and

Paul Winder, while hunting a rare species of orchid, were ambushed here by FARC. Kept hostage for nine months, their ordeal is described in *The Cloud Garden*.

We paused for a couple of days to gather our thoughts in a crowded, chaotic and noisy Panama City. Finding a rudimentary map and compass, I feigned shock that there appeared to be no roads. No matter, we bought dried beans, replacement sterilising tablets, camera film, machetes, ponchos and insect repellent before heading to the docks. We miscalculated on the food. Without soaking for twenty-four hours, the beans were inedible. We had no way to do that on the move, in the forest. So we'd have nothing to eat, apart from whatever we could find in the jungle or beg from the local population.

We cadged a lift on the Don Basilio banana boat from the main docks in Panama to La Palma, then up the river to Yaviza and on to Boca de Cupé for a swim in the silty brown Tuira River. Bruce still had no real idea of where we were going. A local farmer gave us a lift upstream in a compact dugout canoe with an outboard, pushing us on to Púcuro, a village of about three hundred people. This was our first night on the trail. The next morning we used our machetes to make our way to a village in the *corregimiento* of Paya, where we were welcomed by a mixture of African Americans and indigenous, semi-nomadic, Emberá-Wounaan families. From below shocks of thick, straight black hair with central partings, confident faces assessed their recently arrived and unexpected guests. We pitched our small blue tent on the edge of the village's central dirt square. As bare-chested teenagers in shorts played football, Bruce drew on a cigarette and munched on a banana.

The next stage to the Colombian border and Palo de Las Letras was more difficult.

The locals insisted we took an armed guard, Muchero, who, bemused by our plans, escorted us to a spot in the middle of nowhere, marked by a metre-high lonely lump of concrete, similar to a trig point in the UK. This was the Panama Colombia Darién border. That night we weren't alone. We fancied we heard jaguars in the undergrowth, probably howler monkeys on reflection.

Our first day in Colombia was spent wading down streams, munching on bananas we found on the trail, and cutting through the undergrowth. We had two litres of water each. I rationed mine carefully. Three hours into the hack, I discovered that I'd lost my second bottle. Fearing parasites, I was determined not to drink from the watercourses, not knowing then that a multitude of different parasites and I would later become associated. On arrival at camp, while Bruce boiled water, I celebrated by smoking one of his cigarettes.

We walked past cocaine-producing fields, bypassed the cartels and FARC and glimpsed workers in the coca plantations. After a week in the jungle, we'd run out of money. For the price of my camera, a Colombian farmer/drug dealer — how could you tell? — took us downriver. The boatman, bare from the waist upwards, wore rust-coloured trousers held up by a white belt. In the shallows he cut the engine and skilfully manoeuvred his dugout with a stout wooden pole. His eyes remained fixed upon us. He stared shiftily beneath his pudding bowl haircut, like Peter Lorre in every film that Peter Lorre made. For the first time since Guatemala, I sensed real hostility. I prodded Bruce awake, giving him a warning look. We pushed out our twenty-year-old chests, sat upright and stared back. The staring competition continued as we motored down the Atrato River to Turbo, the end of Darién, and a final ceremonial burning of our shirts.

Bruce got his way; we cashed a traveller's cheque and bussed it to Bogota, before a brief trip to the Galapagos, with the prospect of a flight home and of seeing real patients at last.

At Miami airport, after twelve weeks of no shaving and minimal washing, I bumped into my cricket idol, Clive Lloyd. As captain of the West Indies cricket team, Sir Clive had just scored a century in the Old Trafford Test match against England, before suffering an injury. He'd been recuperating at home and was on his way back to England. I had a new wind-on camera and, with just one photo of the allotted dozen left to take, I approached him.

"Excuse me Mr Lloyd, do you mind if I take a photo of you?"

"No problem," he replied.

I thanked him, took a last picture and went to sit and reflect alone in departures. After a few minutes a tap on my shoulder.

"Excuse me, do you mind if I join you?" Mr Lloyd said.

What a wonderful moment. What a great man.

19

PARASITES

After two pre-clinical years in laboratories and lecture theatres, I was looking forward to seeing real patients. But Darién had a sting in its tail — well, more of an itch. It started when I found an ulcer on my left ankle. It wasn't healing. The occupational health team peered and prodded at the pale depression around a small central black dot just above my ankle bone, before deciding it was jiggers. I knew nothing about jiggers and felt sick on reading an article about it. Female chigoe fleas, *tunga penetrans*, lay hundreds of eggs under the victim's skin and then die, it said. The baby fleas hatch and feed on the host, before burrowing and popping out through multiple tiny exit holes. Tungiasis, native to the Caribbean, was first described in crewmen sailing with Christopher Columbus. The entry hole could be up to a centimetre wide, with a black central spot, made up from the back legs, sex organs and breathing apparatus of the female flea. Peering at my ankle I could see the central black spot and was tempted to start digging it out. But I never liked the sight of blood, and definitely not my own blood. I was shipped off to the hospital for tropical diseases.

There I shared a ward with the victims of various other intriguing diseases, most of which I'd never heard of before, nor seen since. Pete, occupying the bed to my left, had sleeping sickness, caught from tsetse flies, and wasn't great company. Pete had fallen sick after returning from Uganda.

It was clear the nurses had missed their training on patient confidentiality. They knew I was a medical student and informed me that Pete was thought to have the East African, not West African, type. The East African variety was often fatal if left untreated, but the nurses thought that Pete was lucky and would make a good recovery. On my other side was Sophie, from Oxford, who had been living in Mexico and travelling in Central America as I had. Sophie had caught chagas disease, spread by insects called "kissing bugs". That one would go down well in the pub, I thought. The disease was labelled after the Brazilian physician, Carlos Justiniano Ribeiro Chagas, who first described it in 1909. The majority of patients only suffered from mild flu-like symptoms. However, in a third of sufferers, including Sophie, it lay dormant for up to thirty years, before causing multiple problems, including heart failure and stroke. Quite a few patients had malaria — something that, unbeknown to me, lay in wait twelve years in the future. I enjoyed the rest. Nothing had to be done since the fleas had already dined and fled.

Out of the hospital and back to the medical school to study. Exams approached but beforehand we had stints learning medicine in the provinces. Prior to engaging in general practice in Scotland, I learnt how to take blood from patients in our university hospital. Medical students were paired up, hesitantly jabbing at each other's veins. In trying to be kind, we pushed the needles in through the skin too gently, causing much more pain than necessary. Then in the excitement of hitting a vein, we advanced the needle, penetrating the far wall of the vein, causing large, tender, blue bruises. It was an effective but unpleasant way to learn. Blooded, in every sense of the word, I went to the ward to take blood from a patient for the first time. I was hungover and nervous. Pale and trembling, with needle and syringe in hand I approached Simon, a muscular forty-year-old. He had bulging veins in his arms. Surely I couldn't miss those. Simon looked at me.

"Are you OK doctor?" he asked.

"Fine, thanks," I said, and immediately stuck the needle in my thumb. No matter, not that much blood. A quick dab to the tip of the needle, to get what I could see of my own blood off it and then I shoved the same needle straight back into Simon's vein. He didn't seem fussed and I was delighted to have hit the target. I suppose I must have missed, or paid little heed, to the infection control team's warning of the potential dangers of blood-borne transmission of diseases. Forty years later I cringe, recalling our lack of medical knowledge, common sense and, most of all, lack of respect we showed to the patients.

To Perthshire, Scotland, and my first exposure to general practice. A problem arose with Gary, a thirty-year-old, twenty-three-stone scaffolder, who had been suffering black and sticky excretions. Gary wasn't the first oversized Scottish specimen I'd met on the wards. The previous day I'd struggled to pass a tube down the penis and into the bladder of Jason. Jason had so much fat on his pubic mound that his penis had retreated and only the lonely tip of its head was visible, a button mushroom with a smiley face. To catheterise Jason I had to compress this fat pad, while holding the end of his penis, stretching the shaft and feeding the catheter down. Difficult with only two hands, like grappling with a shy tortoise that didn't want its lettuce. Gary's problem was more interesting. I reckoned his dark poos meant that he either ate charcoal, gorged on black pudding or, more likely, had bled into his gut. If Gary had bled from his intestines, then, as the blood was now black, it was probably from the upper half of his gut, rather than the lower half. My guess was an ulcer due to his drinking ten pints of lager a day. Well, Gary admitted to ten pints, so he probably drank twelve or more a day, excluding his Captain Morgan rum sharpeners and snakebite top-ups. Nonetheless, as the lecturers said, "If you don't put your finger in it, you'll put your foot in it." This would be my first rectal examination. What could possibly go wrong? I asked Gary to roll onto his left side and pull his knees up to his chin. Rubber gloves on, Vaseline onto my right index fingertip, deep breath. I prayed the glove wouldn't split and that he'd recently had his weekly bath. Parting Gary's massive hairy buttocks and peering between them I couldn't see my target. Had to be there somewhere. Rolls of fat, a pimply excoriated thrush-type rash and a thick forest of ginger hair. A visible smear, but no hole. Five minutes later Gary was getting worried and I was getting frantic. I just couldn't find Gary's anus. Surely he had one? How far should I prod and probe? I'm a doctor not an explorer. And this was an anus, not the source of the Nile. I'd tried everything short of assembling a task force, so called off the search. Gary was my first experience of the human with no hole. I truthfully told Gary that I hadn't found anything abnormal and semi-truthfully put in the notes "NAD". Conventionally, NAD means Nothing Abnormal Detected. But, your honour, for this one and only case it meant "Not Actually Done".

Gary came to no harm from this abandoned procedure. Patients rarely did. To cover both our arses, I arranged a faecal occult blood test. This looks for blood in poo. Unsurprisingly Gary's test was strongly positive and black pudding was innocent. Alcohol and an ulcer were to blame.

Crunch time was nearing and the medical school decided I needed to learn some medicine fast, and preferably a long way away from the capital. Elliot and I were sent to Derby. It was a clinical attachment to learn about paediatrics. I had no interest in paediatrics. I didn't even like children. In fact I found them bloody irritating.

Mock finals followed and the embarrassment of zero per cent in surgery. It was a fair score. I suppose I shouldn't have answered the question: "Describe the anal canal in under five hundred words," as "Short, dark and smelly". I tried harder in pathology.

In our notepads we had to draw and label parts of tissue, fixed on a slide under a microscope. In a flash, I recognised it as a fetal penis. It was the right size and shape and, critically, the different structures were clear to see. Two sections of tissue to collect the blood, and one section for the urethra to pass through. That was the clincher. I gave myself a pat on the back. I suspected the other students wouldn't get this right and marked up the sketch with growing confidence. The end of the organ as the glans, the two corpus cavernosum which fill with blood to stiffen the penis and, finally, the corpus spongiosum. This section doesn't harden, allowing seminal fluid to shoot up the urethra, unobstructed, to the tip. My sister, Margo, had always insisted to the contrary, but here was the proof – there is no bone. Exam over, we discussed the slides in the corridor. Sadly my fetal penis turned out to be heart muscle and my urethra, a coronary artery. A summons to the long-suffering, but well meaning, dean.

Retakes again. My alarm didn't go off, or maybe I forgot to set it. This was serious.

I was facing the premature end of my fledgling career. The shame, the ignominy, the disgrace it would bring to my family. A few students had already been thrown out and others, like myself, were sailing perilously close to the wind. The jolt was almost physical. I realised that I cared and, for the first time, I understood that I wanted to qualify as a doctor. Or was it just that I didn't want to fail? The university secretary was standing outside the examination hall. He didn't look pleased, but his face softened when he saw the fear etched into every line of my face.

"Don't worry, Charles. Calm down. I'll give you fifteen minutes to get your breath back," he said.

20

AFRICA

Medical school was almost over, and time was up for the area health authorities (AHAs). The Government decreed that the AHAs' responsibilities would be transferred to smaller district health authorities (DHAs). So what? As a final year medical student, I couldn't give a toss. However, my sabbatical attachment, in KwaZulu, would be a refreshing challenge. The hospital, a largely charitable institution, run with Canadian support, was sited near Mkuze, north of Durban, on the border of South Africa and Mozambique. I was relieved that, for a change, I would be trying to do something useful. Combined with this sense of purpose, there was the thrill of danger. A month before, a bomb had blown up the local Mobil storage depot. The South African defence forces were raiding the African National Congress and explosions had recently struck the Cape Town nuclear power station.

On arrival I was told there was only one rule — not to mess with the pilot's daughter. My role was to run the minor ops unit and manage the Zulus' teeth. The staff weren't worried that I had no dental training, and the patients didn't know. I didn't even know how many teeth one should have. No matter. Aristotle was equally ignorant, believing women had fewer teeth than men and underestimating the number of teeth in horses by four. It didn't hamper him.

Confronting the dental armoury, I'd never seen such instruments. Ancient steel tools designed for getting in between teeth, then levering them loose and out of their snug sockets. Teeth were the one area of Fiona's body that we hadn't dissected. But who was objecting? I was in charge. I found pulling teeth all day gory, but also boring, although only through ignorance. The Zulus were brave, uncomplaining and grateful. They could teach us a lot.

The hospital was well placed — for those of the staff who had cars. Situated at the top of a steep hill, there was an impressive view over the plains, and patients, below. This was medical triage, African-style. The sickest people couldn't get there.

It started to get hairy when I was promoted to running a minor operations clinic. A Zulu cattle herder needed a cyst removed from his neck. Local anaesthetic supplies hadn't yet run out, a source of comfort for both of us. He was a muscular chap. He lay face down on the table, as I studied my instruments, looking for something that might do the job. I doubted they were sterile. The herder had a couple of inches of thick neck muscle to cut through and he lay still, as I hacked away like Sweeney Todd on mescaline. I'd carved stuffed neck of lamb before, but had never cut into a human neck. Well not a live one, nor one that bled like this. He trusted me and I was determined to not let him down. Aged twenty-two, with minimal training, I just had to do my best.

Slicing deeper through his trapezius muscle, I noticed his blood was trickling ever quicker onto the floor, producing enlarging, sticky, dark red puddles. The herder wasn't complaining. I could now see the glistening off-white fascia over his neck bones. To my great relief, the cyst popped out, before either of us passed out. If only he could have been given a general anaesthetic. As if on cue, an opportunity to learn this dark art presented itself.

We'd had no anaesthetic training at medical school. Rumour had it that more time was spent by consultant anaesthetists at solving crosswords, than in treating patients.

I was crap at crosswords. Room for improvement then, and an opportunity arose to learn more. The hospital tomcat, Andy, was going to be destroyed since the hospital management was fed up with the number of kittens he sired. I negotiated an alternative and it was agreed that Andy would be pardoned if I could catch and castrate him. Catching Andy was easy — we were friends; the second part, less so. What could I use to anaesthetise him? I tried ketamine because the name had a "catty" ring to it, sounded ideal for cats. There was no dosage guidance, so I gave Andy a quarter of the usual adult dose and it sent him to sleep — for a while. Andy woke up halfway through the procedure and escaped, with one ball. Andy had joined the formidable but dubious company of Napoleon Bonaparte, Adolf Hitler and General Franco, all of whom reputedly ended up with having only one testicle, monorchism. Remembering an earlier examination of a man with a prosthetic testicle, a hard implant in his scrotum, I recalled that millions of normal men, this infamous trio excepted, functioned perfectly well with one testicle. I hoped Andy wouldn't mind too much, nor develop aspirations for global dominance. The Zulu nation was hardly ready for that.

A rare day off and a trip to the beach. Apartheid still ruled in South Africa. Queen's "Another One Bites the

Dust" had been adopted by the military who played it whenever a terrorist/freedom fighter was killed. On the beach at Sodwana, near Durban, I had to be restrained. We had a black medical student, Thomas, with us. Who cared? A boar-like Boer did. At that time, obtaining a place in a South African medical school, as a black student, was an outstanding achievement. Thomas was a pioneer, but the Boer didn't care. We were on the beach, in the "International Section", meaning that "Blacks" and "Coloureds" were also allowed on that part of the beach. "Whites" were not banned from this section, but the "Whites" also had their own private section, where the "Blacks" and "Coloureds" were forbidden. Six of us lay on our beach towels, hoping for a sunny relaxing day by the sea. Four men, two women, five white, one black, two over six foot, four under six foot, five with pets at home, one with no pet at home. You get the drift. Having always pushed against regulations, I suggested we ignore the rules and settle in the "Whites only" section. Thomas said he would be more comfortable in the "International" section, so we placed our towels there.

The Boer had driven his white four-wheel drive vehicle up the beach, into the "International" area and was rolling around with his family. Like a pig in shit. Fair enough, I supposed. Appearances can deceive and, after all, he had every right to be there. But it didn't *feel* right. The wife dressed for a wedding, the boar bearded and big bellied. The rest of his family all had stocky short legs squeezed into tight shorts. I didn't like the look of any of them. Next to us, on the beach, was a family of five black South Africans. One of their children, aged about six, ran a few yards in front of the Boer's vehicle, just where the waves were gently breaking.

The big man jumped up, brandishing a heavy leather whip, a sjambok, and chased the child. I stood up to challenge him, but Thomas pulled me back, saying "You will be shot." Thomas may have been right, but my switch had gone. Chastened, and humiliated, we got back in our car before driving off through the village. Another Boer, on seeing a black man with a group of whites in the car, spat through the open window. I was in the front passenger seat and his gob landed on my shirt. Imagine, that was a single day on a single beach. We sped away before matters escalated further. Disgusted, and downright depressed by the apartheid system, Elliot and I decided to explore the country further.

We went south, hoping it would be better integrated. With no transport, we decided to hitch-hike to Cape Town. South Africa was tinder dry and ready to explode, but this felt safer than Darién. At least the parasites weren't likely to get us. We stood by the roadside on the outskirts of Johannesburg, thumbs up, frying in the African sun. A blue BMW estate driven by a single white male, stopped. We ran up, but he waived us away. Was this the police, were we in trouble? Then another car stopped, driven by a woman. The male driver got out and walked to her car, and they both stared at us as they exchanged words. It turned out they were man and wife and she felt like a break. "Can you drive?' he asked.

Arriving in Cape Town refreshed and with renewed confidence in humanity, we decided to test our luck further and hitch-hike five hundred miles north, back up Route Two, the east coast road, to Port Elizabeth. Within minutes a car, with four black men, stopped and Elliot and I hopped in. I felt uncomfortable. Not only were six of us jammed into a small car, but racial tensions were high at the time.

To my dismay, the car stopped. One of the men retrieved an empty glass bottle from the footwell and smashed it on the tarmac. This was now serious. The boot was opened and a small package removed. I exchanged unsettled glances with Elliot. The top of the broken bottle was stuffed with dope from the package, lit and handed around as we sped up the east coast. Damn, it appeared we would have to sit medical finals after all.

Being a medical student was such fun that I couldn't bear the prospect of work and career. I'd been slothful for much of university. Now I had to cram. The poor dean was fed up with telling me how disappointed he was with my performance. I needed to make a significant effort.

Elliot and Major noticed the change in their friend. I avoided parties. I was wedded to the books. I focused on study. After an hour or two of studying, we would break for five minutes of corridor cricket and then go back to work. A few days into this new routine, I noticed Major being uncharacteristically kind in the early evenings, making me coffee, to help keep me alert, he said.

Finals went in a blur. We waited in the flat for the results. We were told that the names of those that passed would be posted on the wall, by the students' bar. The plan was for another friend, one more confident of passing, to go to the results board, check the list, phone our flat and say the word "Doctor" before our names. But only if we'd qualified. Otherwise we would be addressed by our Christian names alone. More corridor cricket, waiting for the phone call.

Ring ring, ring ring. Ring, ring, ring ring.

Somehow Elliot, Major and I had all qualified. Shocked, we went down to the bar to celebrate. Gill, now Major's ex-girlfriend, gave me a hug and kiss. "I'm so pleased you qualified," she said. I didn't know Gill cared so much. Soon after I was swamped by other delighted women. What was going on? Was it the aftershave?

"We've been so worried about you Charles. We couldn't believe the drugging they gave you and thought that filling your stethoscope with cotton wool was so unfair." So that was why I'd been so tired — Major's broth. Later I found out I'd been the victim of my flatmates' pharmacological experiments. Parents' medications had been raided and, while attempting to study, I'd been fed a cocktail of stolen drugs. The usual dose I received was four 10 mg temazepam tablets. The dose of temazepam, to help an adult get to sleep, is 10 mg or 20 mg in "exceptional circumstances". The maximum dose recommended by the British National Formulary, prior to surgery, is 40 mg. My dose. The temazepam had been squeezed out of capsules and added as a slightly greasy film to mugs of black coffee. The small yellow capsules were too firm and presented a problem, but the higher dose, 20 mg green ones, were softer. My flatmates preferred these, referring to them as "oilers". The oilers mixed well with my black coffee.

On other days I received 110 mg of furosemide, ground between two teaspoons in the kitchen, that or lormetazepam. Furosemide is a diuretic, so it makes one pee. The drug works by blocking the absorption of salt and water from the kidneys. This usually kicks in within an hour and the effects can last up to eight hours. Astonishingly I didn't wet my bed. Worse, lormetazepam is a hypnotic, that causes drowsiness for up to twenty-four hours, confusion, and even dependence. The drug interferes with the brain's chemicals that help transmit messages. Not helpful when trying to study for medical finals. I was on the heavy stuff. No wonder I felt tired, I was a walking pharmacy. How did I manage to pass? Then Gill said, "That's not all they did." My stethoscope had been tampered with, stuffed with cotton wool. I made a note to identify the ring leader. I would redress the balance later.

I suspected Elliot was the Mr Big behind the drugging and the cotton wool, so he was firmly in the cross hairs. I invited him to join me on a trip back home. If I was wrong, no matter. I would work through the flat, one by one. Blanket retribution was the best way to manage these fellow ferals. On the drive to my parents' house, I pulled into a lay-by. "Elliot, can you please check the rear right, I think it might be flat," I said. It was dark and cold and we were three miles from home. Back in bed I felt sooo comfortable, basking in a job well done. Two hours later I heard Polly, the dog, barking frantically. I was tired, rolled over and ignored the commotion going on in the house. Next morning, Mother was angry, but Father was intrigued. Later, I gave Father a sanitised version of the truth, and he agreed Elliot had had his just desserts.

But Elliot was unstoppable. On the coronary care unit there was a sister he had his sights on. Quite literally. After a good lunch, as he settled down in the doctors' mess, Elliot was excited to see a colleague walk in with an air gun, complete with telescopic sights. Elliot poked the muzzle out of the mess window and, as the sister prepared the cardiac medicines in the drugs cubicle, he fired from thirty yards at her buttocks.

Ping.

She spun around. The glass hadn't broken, but she saw the end of a rifle pointing at her. The police interviewed the occupants of the doctors' mess. The gun had already been secreted in a safe hiding place and all denied any knowledge.

Next morning Elliot had a rare flash of contrition and decided both to confess and apologise to the ward sister. I suspect that this was less of a sincere apology, and more of a strategy to get around her defences. She was mortified. "I am so sorry Elliot. If I'd known it was you, I wouldn't have called the police," she said.

*

The noose was tightening. Student life had ended and we would now have the dreaded General Medical Council chastening us, on everything and anything. It was decided to do a final sting operation on the police.

A couple of students approached some workmen, who were digging up the road.

"Just to warn you that two medical students, dressed as policemen, are going to come and tell you to stop," one said.

At the same time a different pair of students went up to two nearby policemen.

"We thought we should let you know, that some students are digging up the road, pretending to be workmen."

Time for house jobs.

Middlesex 2nd/7th Battalion The Middlesex Regiment.
Father seated in the middle row, fourth from right.

With Mother and my sisters Margo (Liz) left and Caroline, right.
1962.

With Father on holiday in Corfu, 1968.

Hitching with the Sandinistas in Nicaragua, 1980.

Hiking in the Darién Gap,
1980.

Poling upstream in Darién,
1980.

On the Darién Colombia-Panama border,
1980.

The phosphate mine in Curaçao,
1980.

Bethesda hospital KwaZulu, Natal,
South Africa, 1982.

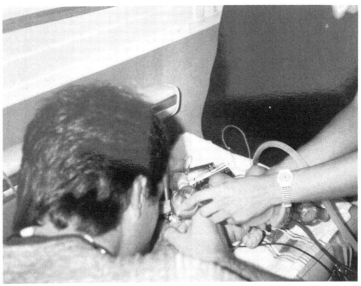

The pilot's photo of my emergency intubation of a critical newborn, on
an aircraft seat, over Western Australia, 1989.

Cockroach Cabin, Mount Hagen,
Papua New Guinea, 1989.

Christmas ward round, Mount Hagen children's ward,
1989.

PART II

Should This Baby Be Yellow?

He who knows all the answers has not been asked all the questions.

Confucius

21

CAROL

On my consultant appointment, I'd no idea I'd outlast seven Secretaries of State for Health. The magnificent seven were Stephen Dorrell, Frank Dobson, Alan Milburn, John Reid, Patricia Hewitt, Alan Johnson, Andy Burnham and Andrew Lansley.

OK, that makes eight. Well counted. Worse still, there was a ninth, dear Jeremy Hunt.

Neither did I have any idea that in twenty-one years' time I would suffer a clinical event pushing me into early retirement, when abandoned by a medical colleague as we tried to resuscitate the newborn baby, Grace. My registrar's desertion to catch a train back to Watford had shaken me to the core. We all have our tipping points and that was mine.

I reflected back on how I'd reached this point in life. Childhood on a farm in Sussex, boarding school from the age of eight, freedom again ten years later, followed by five chaotic years at a London medical school, a reckless hitch-hike through Central America, capped off with a walk across the Darién Gap.

The medical training to reach this new consultant post involved house jobs in Yorkshire and London, a stint in the Channel Islands and a general practice rotation in Sussex, before paediatric specialty training back in London. Then care of the newborn in Oxford, work in Australia and a locum consultant post in an untamed Papua New Guinea. Returning, aged thirty, to paediatrics in the UK, before, to widespread surprise, being appointed five years later, to this new respiratory consultant paediatric post. It's 1995, Oasis have released "Wonderwall", and the Conservatives are in power with Stephen Dorrell as the Secretary of State for Health. On election to Westminster, Dorrell had been the youngest member of Parliament, like me twenty years earlier at Wellington, the baby of the House. Fourteen years later he is Secretary of State for Health. It's taken me a similar time to get this far.

I turn up for my first day as an NHS consultant quietly overconfident. I assume I've seen most paediatric conditions and have all the bases covered. Clean-shaven, with a newly ironed shirt, pristine blue chinos and a borrowed silk tie, I strut up to the children's ward, see one of my three new consultant colleagues and address him by the wrong name. I only have to memorise three Christian names and I've failed at the first hurdle. Two are men, Laurel and Hardy. One of these has a moustache, so it isn't much of a challenge telling them apart, but I've always been useless with names.

I'm not expecting this post to be too difficult. The pay is better and, having only once woken a consultant in my previous twelve years as a junior doctor, I don't expect to be disturbed on my first night of on-call. Whenever that will be. The first day passes with only a single bleep from my pager, almost comforting, like a baby snuffling in its sleep. It's Laurel, the senior consultant: was I OK and did I want a coffee?

With so little to do, the hours drag before home time and an opportunity to celebrate the end of my initiation with a takeaway curry and a cheap bottle of Rioja, maybe more, who knows? Ambling to the car, I wonder if I really need a pager. It goes off. It's Hardy. There's been an administrative cock-up, he says.

"Sorry Charles, I'm afraid that means we need you on call tonight." Never mind. I pat the pager: sleep little baby, sleep.

The takeaway is shut on Mondays, so H prepares a spicy fish curry instead, as I settle in front of the TV with a glass of wine, just one to be on the safe side. This will be a doddle and I thank God that consultants have it so cushy. After more than 4,000 days as a junior, longer than the reign of King Edward VII, I reckon this is payback time and well overdue. H and I toss and turn in bed for a couple of hours, too excited to sleep. I can barely believe I am on call and being paid for doing absolutely nothing. Bloody marvellous!

Beep, beep, beep. Beep, beep, beep. Noooooooooooooooo.

Two in the morning and the junior doctors are struggling to get an intravenous line into Tess, a sick newborn on the special care baby unit. FUCK.

Clothes on, in the car and off.

Tess has fragile veins. Every time I try to slide the small plastic catheter into a vein, it buckles and an enlarging, dark blue bruise grows under her skin. Not the ideal start.

Unable to site the cannula, I decide we will speed up her feeding in the hope that Tess will tolerate the milk without it damaging her guts.

Back home at 6 a.m., still dark, H asleep, ablutions, toast and marmalade, change of clothes and back in to work for the nine o'clock round. Jaded, I grab a coffee, climb the stairs to the baby unit and poke my head in. Tess is behaving; seems like luck is on my side. She's managing the accelerated feeding plan without any difficulty. Phew! I make my way to the handover.

Handovers are an integral part of the day's work, when outgoing and incoming clinicians sit together and discuss patients before doing the round, examining the children, and making care plans. This system is so much better than piling in uninformed and unprepared. The handover provides a confidential place to talk through clinical problems. It's an opportunity to kick-start the brain where issues are complicated, a forum to mull over and consider alternative diagnoses, and a chance to teach and to learn, as well as allowing the night staff to leave at a sensible time. The reception I receive for my first consultant ward round is polite, but neutral. I sense that the junior doctors are assessing me, both professionally and socially. I suppose we are all testing the water, but it's unnerving to feel the scrutiny of a dozen pairs of inquisitive eyes. I'm sitting with an empty chair on either side, and I understand; I have crossed the line, forever onwards to be regarded as "one of them", no longer "one of the lads".

The registrar outlines the cases. No interesting patients, unless one includes a case of pyloric stenosis, where an abnormal thickening of the muscle at the exit of the stomach stops the food from travelling southwards and the baby forcefully vomits and can't gain weight. I listen carefully, something isn't right. I'm not convinced. Carol is only five days old. That she is female is also significant.

Pyloric stenosis is usually found in baby boys at around four weeks after birth. Babies with the condition tend to look like wizened old men. Everyone knows that, it's something we all learn about at medical school. Yet there are exceptions. My eldest sister, Margo, had the condition in the late 1950s and nearly died after her doctor declared: 'Girls can't get pyloric stenosis'. I really didn't need this on my first consultant handover. The earlier struggle with the intravenous line had already put me on the back foot. Now this, with a jury of medics looking for the faintest flaw. I'm desperate to show confidence and competence. Making bizarre, alternative diagnoses to common conditions won't impress. I recall Margo's case. The first doctor's pronouncement was nonsense, a second doctor agreed with Mother's intuition that Margo was seriously ill, but he was appalled that she hadn't been christened. She was saved, like many before and many after, by medicine's most important attribute, common sense. Practices had changed over the subsequent forty years. In the UK babies are no longer given brandy as an anaesthetic and pyloric stenosis is no longer a matter of life and death, but a deathly boring condition, giving me no chance to prove my mettle.

Working through the first six patients in the main bay and then on to the babies' cubicles, there seems nothing medically interesting, no chance to show off. I'm getting the hang of this, smoothly in the groove already. The night has been an unexpected jolt but at least the day work is straightforward. Pyloric stenosis masses tend to only be palpable during a feed. I hope Carol will be hungry, enabling me to confirm the diagnosis. She should latch onto her mother's breast, suck greedily, then vomit. That's the pattern. I'd feel a mass in her abdomen and observe visible waves of peristalsis, as her stomach tries to push the milk through the obstruction. Better wear an apron, I don't want my ironed shirt and borrowed tie splashed.

But Carol has already had a recent breastfeed — opportunity missed — so as I lay my hand on her, as I am expected to do,

I know there will be nothing of note to feel. I place my hand gently on her soft skin. Hold on, what's this? To my surprise there is a lump, the size and firmness of a golf ball. Taking into account her sex and age, I am pretty sure this is not a case of pyloric stenosis. But what? I stall as Carol's parents, the junior doctors and two fresh-faced medical students stare at me. What are they thinking? Duffer?

I'll trust my convictions and risk the ridicule that might follow. I explain to Carol's parents that I am, as yet, unsure of the diagnosis, but that I will get an urgent ultrasound scan. In the mid-nineties, it's not usual practice to get an ultrasound scan for a pyloric stenosis. It shows a lack of confidence, a clinical weakness, and is considered a waste of resources. Twenty years later, scanning for this condition had become routine. Indeed, a failure to do so would raise eyebrows. Times change, but I was at the wrong end of this particular piece of medical evolution; nonetheless, I request the test. The scan comes back as a congenital hepatoblastoma. Carol has been born with cancer of her liver. Ridiculous. I've never seen nor heard of a congenital hepatoblastoma. After ten years working exclusively with sick children, I have never even seen a baby born with any cancer, of any type. Not one. My first day. I couldn't survive thirty years of this. Obviously Theo, the radiologist, is incompetent and has screwed up. I will have to challenge the diagnosis and put him right. Theo is slight in stature and at first I mistake him for a medical student on attachment. At his height he has to be out of his depth. He isn't; I am. Theo has seen similar ultrasound pictures before and shares these with me on his screen. He is bang on the button.

Carol's parents are awaiting my return. I haven't a clue what to say. In need of help, I call London's King's

Hospital. King's are all too aware I'm new in post and are as sceptical as I have been about the diagnosis. Reluctantly, they agree to see Carol the next day. Armed with a plan, I can now face Carol's parents. We sit down and I explain that their daughter is going to have to be transferred to London and that initial tests have shown that there is something, presumably malignant, but hopefully treatable, in her liver. They ask me how many cases I've seen, and how certain I am of the diagnosis? What treatment would Carol be given and what are her chances of survival? What can I say? I pale, say I know nothing about the condition, but that King's are world experts.

About one in a million four-year-olds have a diagnosis of a hepatoblastoma in the UK, that's less than one diagnosis per year. I didn't have the figures for newborns, but they will be even lower. King's, it turned out, also needed help. They liaised with cancer specialists at Great Ormond Street Hospital, who, in turn, asked for expert advice from Germany. Such a simple initial provisional diagnosis, on my first consultant ward round, had ended up as a Europe-wide medical mystery. Although I had three supportive consultant colleagues, I couldn't help but feel alone. Carol's case was the hardest of all growing pains, a mule kick to the head: it's not about you, stupid. It never was about you. It's about the patients.[12]

Then "mad cow" disease panic hit the UK. First raised as a concern eleven years previously, the number of cases rose sharply and a new variant was identified and blamed. The first death from this type had occurred when Stephen Churchill, a nineteen-year-old man studying for his A

---

12. *I followed Carol's progress throughout her childhood and, when she was discharged to adult routine follow-up eighteen years later, Carol was in perfect health and disease-free.*

levels, died four months prior to the start of my consultant post. The public was split between a terror of all beef products on one side and disdain of doom-mongers on the other. I verged towards the latter. I had never bonded with authority. Our local Sussex landlord made his views clear with a sign outside the pub, saying: "The only mad cow here is my missus".

The introduction to consultant-on-call and consultant ward rounds had been more difficult than I'd anticipated. Outpatient clinics seemed straightforward in comparison. It helped that, being a new consultant appointment, I had no patient "baggage" and, for my first clinic, I had only three patients. Lots of upsides: no awkward sods, no frustrated or angry parents, no need to seek help from anyone, no professional disagreements with colleagues, and no mistakes (or not knowingly). Easy-peasy, child's play, you could say, as my patient lists slowly built. Then a patient arrived who once more reminded me that I still had so much to learn. Mirriam, a fourteen-year-old girl experiencing tiredness and muscle ache, had been diagnosed with systemic lupus erythematosus (SLE), a condition that provokes the body's immune system to attack healthy tissue. When Mirriam was first examined, another doctor had been alert enough to organise the appropriate tests, confirming a high auto-antibody level and a low level of complement. Complement is a complex system of over twenty proteins that help boost (or complement, as the name suggests) the antibacterial activity of antibodies. Complement marks invading cells for destruction, then removal, thus protecting us from infections. Combining these results with the analysis of Mirriam's urine, revealing a significant protein leak from her kidneys, enabled the diagnosis. Juvenile SLE — another rare condition I had never encountered. At this rate I worried I'd be getting an unwelcome reputation in London for collecting rare diagnoses — a paediatric Jonah. It proved disturbingly unimportant that I couldn't fully understand the rationale behind Mirriam's treatment. I was adequate at making tables of her blood results and liaising with the family and Guy's Hospital, and Mirriam's parents were experts in their understanding of the blood readings, the condition itself, and the treatment options. They were sympathetic, rather than critical of my lack of knowledge. It didn't matter that I knew so little about SLE.

Away from work I couldn't find a house to buy so hung on to the rented flat in town, with an occasional commute from H's house in Dorset. Early one morning I was in my car, listening to reports of car crashes in the fog, pondering why some drivers were so bloody careless. Suddenly, everyone was breaking ahead and I was breaking too. Cars behind me were travelling at speed and the inevitable impact was severe enough to break the key in my ignition.

An ambulance took me to the very hospital where I happened to work. After a quick check over and inspection of my sore neck, I made it to my nine o'clock clinic with five minutes to spare.

Back home, feeling rather stiff and sore and struggling to edit down a fast-approaching first lecture as a consultant, titled *What gets up my nose*, I wondered if I would receive a letter of appreciation for fulfilling my clinical duties. The following week I did get a letter.

I was touched.

What?

It was a bill!

There was a charge from the hospital for my being scooped up off the road. The funds raised helped the trust run the accident and emergency department, I could claim this back from my insurers if I wished.

That would be going into the lecture, for sure, alongside my frustration with the Government's recent "standing order of three per cent efficiency savings". I worked out that twenty years of these so-called savings would reduce hospital running costs by half, enabling the Government to truthfully claim it had *increased funding by fifty per cent* over twenty years, while costing them absolutely nothing.

As careers go, I'd barely begun, but my senior consultant colleague, Laurel, decided he'd had enough. In his mid-fifties, frustrated by the relentless bureaucracy grinding down even the most resilient clinical staff within the NHS, he opted to take early retirement.

I was saddened. His resignation seemed premature. How little I knew.

22

GEORGE

The first chief executive I worked with was neither self-serving, nor duplicitous. Jim cared for the NHS and displayed none of the dark arts of management I would encounter later. Nevertheless, my first step into this murky area of hospital politics proved both uncomfortable and disorientating.

Short, stocky, suited and sincere, Jim could be blunt, rude and demanding. However, he was intelligent, willing to listen, capable, and he didn't hate doctors. That was refreshing. In his forties, in a career where musical chairs was the norm, Jim mistakenly thought this wouldn't be his last management post. He surprised me one day, asking if I would be the new consultant spokesperson representing the junior doctors. Meetings focused on attempts to resolve issues that arose around the junior doctors' working environment. Junior doctors' pay was based on diaries of hours worked. The hours cards were a potential source of conflict between the trust, under pressure from the Government to minimise staff pay, and the junior doctors who wanted to be fairly remunerated for their work. My role was to scrutinise these cards and decide which bands the doctors qualified for, effectively deciding their salaries. In a sense I was a kind of shop steward with one foot in the management camp.

I was surprised to discover that chief executives weren't really in charge. The Government was the bully boy, badgering, hounding, harassing and nagging the Trust Executive. The Executive passed the demands to a minor manager, in this case me, to pass them on to the workforce, usually the clinical staff. The problem for me was that I wouldn't pass the buck on. In fairness, Jim didn't put me under unreasonable pressure, so I was free to grade the junior doctors as I thought fit. The diary cards became a genuine snapshot of working conditions, instead of an exercise in fiddling the books.

Twenty-four hours after the results of this process were published, the recriminations started. Jim called me down to his office. He was hopping mad. I'd never seen his little face so red and hoped he'd had his blood pressure checked recently. Those beetroot cheeks were a warning sign. Jim's greying-badger, bushy eyebrows met at the radix, where his forehead joined his nose. Was that steam puffing forth from his nose? He demanded an answer: "Why have we been mentioned in the bloody House of Commons as having the highest band-three percentage of junior doctor posts in the United Kingdom?" he said. Band three the group of doctors deemed as non-compliant with the European working hours directive, thereby attracting the highest salaries, double basic pay. So this was all about money. How dare we? More precisely, how had I dared? I soon understood the real issue.

It turned out that the neighbouring trust had an ambitious,

high-flying, goody-two-shoes of a chief executive, the new darling of hospital management, climbing the greasy pole in a hurry. The junior doctors in his trust had racked up far fewer hours. Poor Jim was stuck on his own pole, slithering nowhere, while GTS greased up his.

"I want answers," said Jim. I gave him one.

"Theirs are wrong," I said.

Both trusts were asked to repeat their exercises. This time, although our returns hadn't changed significantly, those compiled by the neighbouring trust had remarkably lost their shine and were matching ours. Their original returns had been fudged, or an error had occurred in collation.

As always, patients came to my rescue when a couple of complicated social problems arose ahead of a much-needed break. Managing the non-medical part of a sick child's care was often more time-consuming and demanding than the clinical part, which in most cases was moderately straightforward. First up, a heated debate was raging on the baby unit. The ward was uncharacteristically quiet, with only three babies, but each was interesting from a different social perspective and one was causing a rumpus. One of the babies was the firstborn to a fifty-five-year-old mother who'd been refused IVF within the UK because of her age. To get around this policy, she'd gone to Italy for private treatment. Then she'd returned to the UK with her newborn so that the NHS would manage her new arrival, and foot the bill. It's called playing the system.

The second mother was fifteen and social services were involved since she was below the age of consent. Another anomaly, within different nations. In Italy, Austria and Portugal, for example, the age of consent was fourteen. I wondered what would have happened had she been admitted to the Mangiagalli Hospital in Milan.

The trickiest problem was with the third mother, the wife of a local army officer.

Tracy, the mother of Finn, a three-day-old girl, wanted to go home. Tracy insisted that Finn had been born at term, meaning after forty weeks *in utero* gestation. The nurses and doctors, however, estimated that Finn was a baby of about thirty-two weeks maturity. She'd been born two months early. Their estimate looked right. The nurses were better at assessing this than me and agreeing with them was by far the easiest option. Besides, Finn appeared and behaved like she'd been born eight weeks early. There was nothing wrong with Finn, she'd just been born too early.

How did we know that Finn was born two months before term? We look for certain indicators. Finn didn't have the red transparent skin, similar to that of a skinned rabbit, or the fused eyes of the extremely premature, but she had the size, shape and handling characteristics of a premature baby. She also had the *lanugo*, the fine downy pale hair that usually develops around twenty weeks and sheds after thirty-four weeks. I know it is impossible to be exact in medicine, but nothing about Finn suggested she was fully baked. If I was to allow Tracy to take Finn home, I would risk her daughter being unable to maintain her temperature, feed adequately and keep her blood sugar levels safe. Finn had to stay. But there was a snag. We knew what it was, and so did Tracy. Her husband, Jamie, was a captain in the army who'd been stationed in Hong Kong for three months, coming home twenty-eight weeks prior to Finn's delivery. If only Finn could have been a term baby or one of twenty-eight weeks gestation, then Tracy's dilemma would have been solved, as conception at Jamie's leaving party, or on the day of his return from service, would have settled any potential doubt over paternity. The last thing Tracy needed was Jamie to start counting his fingers.

We did a Ballard score. The score was devised by Dr Jeanne Ballard, Professor Emeritus of Pediatrics, Obstetrics and Gynaecology at the University of Cincinnati, sometime during my second year at medical school, and refined two years later. Using a series of observations, the scoring offers a moderately accurate estimate of the maturity of babies born with a gestation between twenty-six and forty-four weeks. The test involves six neurological assessments: posture, wrist flexion, arm recoil, flexion of the knee, making a scarf with the baby's arm and moving the heel to the ear. The scores on these are added to a further six physical recordings: appearance of the skin, ears/eyes, soles of the feet, presence/absence of breast buds, fine lanugo skin hair and, finally, the appearance of the baby's external genitalia. Each of these twelve separate assessments and observations is scored between zero and five, making a maximum total of sixty. The lower the score, the more premature the baby. I could remember that *term*, meaning forty weeks in the uterus, conveniently scored forty. Finn recorded twenty-three. That was awkward news for Tracy. Referring to the published charts, I saw that the score corresponded with a gestation of around thirty-three weeks.

What is sometimes referred to as "misattributed paternity" or "extra-pair copulation" is not an unusual event and, of course, although maternity is a matter of fact, paternity can be a matter of opinion. It was one of those tooth-sucking issues that needed some thought. Fortunately, it was lunchtime, so I could run it past my colleagues. Returning refreshed, I decided we were a baby unit, not marriage guidance counsellors.

I explained the Ballard score to Tracy and, not completely untruthfully, the inaccuracy and unreliability of some of the tests, allowing her some wriggle room. Tracy didn't push further and Finn went home a month later, when safe to do so. With luck, Jamie would be none the wiser and there'd be no need to cancel the milk round.

The second problem arose due to the clash of the conflicting forces of parental expectations of healthcare provision and of those offered by NHS paediatrics. Prune's mother was tanned, coiffured and French and she was now kicking up a stink in outpatients. She was angry and adamant that we must act, claiming that this English care was *épouvantable*.[13] The confrontation was unsettling and my mind started to wander to other fruity children's names: Peaches, Clementine, Olive, Cherry — any more? Her beautiful, healthy nine-month-old girl, Prune, had been an uneventful birth, had had no illnesses, but had been referred to NHS outpatients three months earlier, as her head was flat at the back.

The GP's referral letter was apologetic, and it was easy to read between the lines. Our registrar had previously reassured Prune's mother. Now she was back to see me, seeking answers, and she wanted them this instant. I ran my fingers through Prune's thick thatch and carefully measured her head. The skull has two holes at birth, maybe three if you have Down's syndrome or a low level of thyroid hormone. The front hole, commonly referred to as the *soft spot*, is the biggest and usually closes between nine and eighteen months. Prune's soft spot was open, supporting the earlier finding that her "box wasn't closed". I could feel no ridges on Prune, which, if present, might have suggested premature fusion of the skull bones, and her head growing at the expected rate. All was normal. Damn!

---

13. *French word for appalling.*

An angry mother, with nothing abnormal to find, is like a tiger with toothache after eating the dentist. Prune was perfect, apart from having the frequently seen and innocent condition of brachycephaly, or occipital plagiocephaly, where the back of her head is rather flat. It's more common today following the success of the Back to Sleep campaign, which slashed the frequency of cot deaths.

The advice, nowadays, is to lay babies on their backs when they are put down to sleep. Six years earlier, in 1991, studies published in the UK, Australia and New Zealand showed an unexpected and significant association between sleeping position and sudden infant death syndrome (SIDS), better known as cot death. Public health campaigns recommended babies slept on their backs or sides and a year later the US followed suit. At the time of my discussion with Prune's mother the advice had just been altered to recommend babies slept on their backs exclusively. There were rare exemptions for the tiny proportion of babies with specific medical conditions, but for the vast majority, babies were now to be placed fully on their backs. This simple advice reduced the incidence of SIDS by about three quarters, saving over 1,000 babies' lives, in the UK alone, every year.

The problem was that Prune's mother didn't believe that her daughter's head would remodel into an acceptable shape in later life, which it would, and she demanded treatment. Helmets claiming to cure this condition could be bought privately, but Prune's mother wanted one free on the NHS. Since there was no clinical need for one, I turned her down, telling her she could seek one out privately if she wished. Apart from the unnecessary cost, I warned her that Prune might be harmed if a helmet was not made and fitted with skill and care. Whether she took the advice or not, I have no idea, she never came back.

Meanwhile the Labour Party was returned to power with Frank Dobson, the new Health Secretary. Dobson had *cojones* and, on appointment, told Prime Minister Blair: "If you want a first-class service, you have to pay a first-class fare — and we're not doing it."[14] As I sifted through my work boxes, full of notes to review, letters to sign, results to chase and parents to phone, I mulled over the coming week, wondering how the workload would pan out.

There was a consistent pattern to admissions during the week, with Mondays usually the busiest, as many patients tried to hang on at home over the weekend. Midweek was pretty standard, while Fridays and Saturdays risked the additional consequences of teenage partying — admissions with alcohol poisoning and sports injuries. But Sundays were by far the worst. Sundays were a social commentary on marriage in modern Britain, and the residual conflicts in those that foundered. A disproportionate number of allegations of child abuse came to our attention on a Sunday, when children were returned to one parent from the short-term care of the other parent.

It was a quiet Friday evening, the start of my weekend on call that would end eighty hours later on Monday evening. All had gone well and I was home by seven, playing with my duck in the bath.

Beep, beep, beep. Beep, beep, beep. Shitting beep. Noooooooooo. I'm a consultant now. Stop bloody bleeping me. I looked at the duck. The duck looked at me. It was smiling.

H popped her head round the bathroom door. The landline had gone at the same time.

14. *Testicles in Spanish.*

"Social services on the phone, a sixteen-year-old girl claims she has been raped," she said.

The police doctor wanted a paediatrician. I wanted my supper. Food would have to wait. No matter that I'd received no training in sexual violence or in perineal sexual assault trauma. There was a rape suite and I was needed on site, in thirty minutes. My role was that of a chaperone to ensure that the examination was conducted in a child-friendly manner. The room was seedy and bare, degrading for the girl and unpleasant for the staff. It reminded me of my cabin in Mt Hagen, Papua New Guinea. Was I imagining, or was that a smart suburban cockroach scuttling by? The police agreed that their so-called suite was woefully subpar and I decided Frank Dobson was right, if you want a good service, you have to pay for it.

Crystal told us she had been sexually active for over two years, with regular boyfriends from the age of fourteen. She already knew the alleged assailant intimately. The examination was unremarkable. Swabs were taken from every relevant orifice and I was back home for a reheated microwave supper and an attempt to sleep. I dreamt of cockroaches, crawling over female genitalia. Pick the bones out of that one, Sigmund Freud.

Next morning, being a Saturday, both the roads and the hospital were quiet and, with fewer distractions, I found work more efficient and enjoyable. Overnight a teenage boy called George had been admitted. Like the majority of parents who try not to have favourite children, I tried not to have favourite patients. George was an exception. George had cystic fibrosis. Badly. There are about three million healthy cystic fibrosis carriers in the United Kingdom unaware of their condition. One in 500 couples both carry the gene mutation and a quarter of their children will have a diagnosis of cystic fibrosis. Knowing he had a shortened life expectancy, George was fiercely independent and impressively mischievous, determined to make the most of his poor luck. His lungs and pancreas were clogged up with thick secretions and didn't function properly. The demands placed upon George and his family were enormous, with an hour or more of physiotherapy every day, essential to keep his airways as free from secretions and as open as possible. The physiotherapy was followed by an hour of nebulisers — either antibiotics penetrating deep into the lungs or drugs to open up his airways. Combining this with his daily need to take vitamins, pancreatic enzymes and prophylactic antibiotics, even ignoring the frequent outpatient attendances and hospital admissions, George's day was three hours shorter than yours or mine.

And that was just the routine maintenance when he was perfectly well, or as well as he could be. With no other alternative, George would take the bus in to outpatients.

It meant a round trip of three hours for a thirty-minute review of his medication and a listen to his chest. His notes were packed with pages stamped: DNA (Did Not Attend). His time was more precious than ours. We both understood.

Ten years earlier the discovery of the cystic fibrosis gene had led a few optimists to predict a cure within a short time, but although life expectancy had increased significantly, it remained then, as now, a catastrophic diagnosis. It adds up to hundreds of different genetic defects, all under the one label, each needing individualised treatment plans, for every child. Although it seemed probable a cure would be found one day, it would not be in the foreseeable future and not soon enough to save George.

George was a character. I'd had to admonish him the previous month, for putting salt in the ward kettle and for smacking the nurses on the bottom as they passed, while cheekily shouting, "Slappers". I had to reprimand him; I was jealous. I wanted to do that, but we both knew I couldn't and we both agreed the salt game wasn't a clever thing to do either. A pact was agreed and George kindly promised to behave that weekend. He recognised I was under par. He didn't know that it was Crystal who was still troubling me.

George was a fanatical Manchester United fan so I had a running book with him, betting Mars bars on football results. I was on a reluctant winning streak. George was quieter than usual on this particular Sunday and we agreed to wager a Mars bar on the outcome of the home game to Leicester City. I'm bound to lose that, I thought.

Leaving the cubicle, I was concerned to see the hospital radio team looking for some action and steered the presenters away from George's bed. They were a pushy lot, however, saying they wanted George's views on the service. I relented.

"So George, what are you in for?" one asked.

"Chest infection."

"What do you think of the care you're receiving?" the DJ persisted.

I stared at George as he focused a few yards beyond me. He'd promised to behave.

But our pact hadn't included radio interviews. George puckered his lips and paused.

"Crap," he said.

Then Leicester City let me down, beating Manchester United 1–0.

I wrote to Old Trafford to complain. David Beckham replied to George, including a signed figurine of himself with two VIP match tickets for Old Trafford. That was real class. Thank you, Becks.

George died not long after. He'd made the most of the hand he'd been dealt. I didn't go to patients' funerals as a rule, but neither George nor I played by the rules.

I couldn't let George down.

23

KILIMANJARO

My eldest sister Margo's second wedding was approaching. I was giving her away but she was late. Second thoughts perhaps? The celebrant looked at his watch. He had another wedding to churn out in thirty minutes. This was beyond a joke. Where was my damnedest, eldest, biggest, loudest and most difficult sister? Margo flounced in, looking stern and flushed.

"Bloody cheek," she said.

"What's the matter?" I said.

"Nowhere to park, so I put my car outside and the bloody warden gave me a ticket."

"That's his job Margo."

"Yes. But he laughed when I said I was getting married."

"Why?"

"The bugger said, 'Likely story at your age darling.' "

Back to outpatients, memories of the wedding fading fast, and a couple of interesting, but *probably* straightforward, paediatric problems. I stress *probably*, as I'd come to realise that definitive clinical diagnoses were easier in hindsight.

What starts out as an uncomplicated problem can quickly become complex.

Two babies, one a six-week-old girl with a birthmark and the other, a one-month-old boy with vomiting. Juliette's parents had noticed a few tiny red dots on her back at birth. These had now enlarged and were causing concern. Of more interest to me, her cry was unusual and Juliette had an enlarging, pea-sized, strawberry-like growth protruding from her lower lip.

I expected that the birthmarks on her back would get bigger then fade and disappear.

If it continued to expand, the one on her lip might need treatment with propranolol, a drug that had recently obtained a licence for use with birthmarks (haemangiomas). Propranolol works by blocking receptors in blood vessels, thereby reducing the size, colour and firmness of birthmarks. But Juliette's croaky voice was most interesting and puzzling. It might be something, or nothing. It needed to be monitored, however, in case Juliette was cultivating a hidden growth on her vocal cords. Better to watch and wait, than dive in too early and interfere in a vulnerable and difficult to access area, risking significant and unnecessary harm.

The second patient, Maxime, was a month-old-boy, struggling to gain weight. His mother had been unable to breastfeed, so Maxime was now established on a standard formula. Yet he was still unsettled and faltering on his growth chart. The history didn't support a diagnosis of pyloric stenosis — possible, but unlikely — and an examination proved unremarkable. Management was more complicated since the drug we had used for decades for treating reflux had been withdrawn because of a possible association with cot death. We agreed a trial of a cow's milk-free formula and I warned his mother that Maxime might later need medication. I hoped the new milk would settle him, but, if not, further investigation might be warranted. I explained we could insert a probe down Maxime's gullet to measure the acid levels, or even carry out a barium X-ray study of his upper gastrointestinal tract. Again, my preference was to hold back. I told Maxime's mother that I would do my best to resolve his issues before resorting to drugs. Like so many, Maxime improved with a change of diet. Just how much this improvement was down to his reflux fading with age, or how much was down to the exclusion of cow's milk, I cannot say. What mattered was the outcome – he got better.

I soon discovered I wasn't beyond reproach. Consultants weren't free spirits any more. My setbacks had only just begun. I'd been ticked off over the care of a two-year-old girl in whom I'd recently diagnosed labial adhesions after she'd been referred in with "too small a vagina". I'd requested an ultrasound of her pelvis and fielded a phone call from a consultant gynaecologist who'd informed me that "The ultrasound is inappropriate since, as you had no doubt learnt at *medical school*, the embryological pathways of the renal tract and female external genitalia are totally different."

It hadn't helped that I'd missed most of embryology at medical school. The telling off was harder to bear when the ultrasound found unexpected abnormalities within the drainage system of the girl's kidneys. This presented a common dilemma: of how much to make from a coincidental finding to an investigation? It was a quandary that kept recurring throughout my career.

While chewing over this issue, I found myself under the scrutiny of the hospital's ethics committee, a self-appointed smarty-pants busybody outfit that intervened to block approval of a new procedure I wished to introduce.

A scientist had asked for my help in trialling a device measuring the electrical impedance in the oesophagus in order to estimate the amount of reflux up the gullet. The existing method of doing this was complicated and unpleasant. A tube would be inserted up the child's nose and threaded into the lower oesophagus, enabling measurement and recording of the acidity every fifteen minutes. The proposed new method seemed altogether cleverer and kinder. The committee wanted proof that the approach was safe. We couldn't give them that because the technique was new. The rejection hurt, and appeared harsh, but maybe it was my just desserts.

The previous week I'd called to a halt a study on a fragile child with weak veins. She was undergoing painful weekly blood tests to measure obscure trace elements. I decided the investigations were hurting, not helping, her and stopped them. Was it a case of two can play at that game? I hope not. More likely the committee were too cautious and declining our study was the easy and lazy option. Oesophageal impedance studies would soon be accepted as a useful and safe method of assessing gastric reflux. A pity the smarty-pants were so wary.

The games people play. It just wasn't cricket. I had to go to Perth for that and the arrival of the England team for another assault on the sacred Ashes. England had drawn in Brisbane and were set for victory, the best position I'd seen. They lost.

*

Meanwhile the Government fiddled, as Nero to Rome. Alan Milburn succeeded Dobson, saying: "When there is a limited amount of public-sector capital available, as there is, it's PFI or bust." Private Finance Initiative (PFI) developments flourished. Designed as a way to fund the NHS, they were later exposed as a drain on NHS resources, not a supplement. PFI undermined already creaky foundations. The idea was that the upfront costs of the design, build and maintenance of big hospital projects would be funded privately. The medical profession raised concerns that private investors would, quite reasonably, want a handsome return for their money.

But the Government, by rote, disagreed with the clinicians and saw it as a cheap way of funding projects. It was cheap in the short term, but in the long term, which few seemed to care about, it proved an egregious waste of public money. Contracts extended twenty years, and early terminations were restricted by an expensive spider's web of impenetrable constraints. The Government, both Labour and Conservative, held a jaundiced view of those in the public sector. It appeared both parties believed in the Thatcherite doctrine, that the private sector was the best option for service delivery. I feared an irreversible wedge had been driven between the public and private sectors. Slowly it dawned that, by working as a consultant, the dirty world of politics had become unavoidable.

Time sped by. I celebrated my fortieth birthday on the first day of the millennium, sitting in a flight simulator in France. My plane crashed. But as the hour struck, real aircraft didn't fall out of the sky. The so-called millennium bug, expected to send computer software haywire, proved something of a damp squib.

Going on holiday, however, is never a good idea for those whose names might crop up in committee meetings. I did, and mine did. *While the cat's away*, they say. On my return I was asked by the paediatric department, and the chief executive, to be the new lead clinician for paediatrics.

Truly, a hospital pass. There were only four of us and I was the lone winger at the end of the line. It was like my being asked to be a prefect at Wellington — Buggins's turn. I agreed to take over the role but feared the interface with colleagues would change if they perceived I'd acquired some supposed importance. It wasn't really importance, or even seniority. It was more subtle, more divisive, more unpleasant than that; it was influence.

As my tenure of lead clinician commenced, let's list the changes over the previous two years, with those bullet points, beloved of management. Seems appropriate somehow:

- The Bristol Royal Infirmary enquiry was launched to investigate an excess of deaths of babies undergoing heart surgery.

- NHS Direct was created — a nurse-led telephone service accessible twenty-four hours a day for basic healthcare advice.

- GP fundholding was abolished — previously created by Prime Minister Thatcher to give GPs budgetary control over their patients' care in hospital.

- Primary Care Groups were established — with GPs now placed at the heart of commissioning hospital services.

- Another White Paper was produced: *Saving Lives: Our Healthier Nation*, intended to encourage patients to take more responsibility for their own health.

God help us all. I wondered how the managers were supposed to keep up. No wonder we had so many. The clinicians had no chance, the NHS was being wound up in a ball of red tape. As lead, I would be expected to get involved and promote this nonsense, extolling the virtues to blank faces and vacant stares from colleagues. Bollocks to that. There was no option but to think outside of my comfort zone. Fortunately, there was one useful project on which to focus that would keep me away from volumes of orders. Our paediatric facilities were luxurious compared with those in some places around the world, but were basic by European standards. Despite all the efficiency savings and previous promises, there was no money returned to the paediatric department to re-invest. Thus, the wards were scruffy and cramped, with no overnight accommodation for parents. The trust agreed that we could fundraise to improve the children's ward.

Chris, our glamorous fundraising chief, suggested we identified some equally glamorous project to kick-start the campaign. Helped by a previous career as a model, and aided by long legs and flowing platinum blond hair, Chris knew how to work the system. We just needed an idea. The seed was sown by Beachball, who'd recovered enough from the ordeals of Papua New Guinea to climb Mt Kenya. We agreed this would be a great idea for a trust fundraising adventure. A team of twelve formed. But I'd muddled Mt Kenya with Mt Kilimanjaro. Not that it mattered. They were both high. Researching the walk, we discovered that about 100,000 people a year climbed Kilimanjaro and on average only five a year died. Not bad odds, I guess, unless you are one of the five. We'd do it as a fundraiser with a target of £100,000, a tenth of our one million pounds project cost.

Meanwhile clinical work continued. It never stopped. The ward was quiet, but a problem had arisen between a consultant colleague and an angry father. Neither wanted to continue their professional relationship and I was asked if I'd take over the medical care of the boy. I didn't want this on my plate, but how could I say no? As lead clinician it was my job to absorb anything thrown my way. "It would be a pleasure," I lied. I was still a relatively new consultant and unsure how to handle the situation. A loving and intelligent but medically maverick father was at loggerheads with an equally caring but conventional and competent consultant medic. The two could not agree the correct or safe approach for the management of the young boy. This fractured doctor/parent relationship risked putting the care of the child in danger. Divorce was the only sensible solution. The consequences of that casual corridor conversation between my colleague and I were significant.

My reflex acceptance was followed by frequent conferences involving the trust's legal team, the chief executive, the head of nursing and Muggins myself. There were fears that meetings with the father could turn ugly, so seats were carefully arranged with hot coffee containers strategically placed, allowing a safe and quick exit if things kicked off. Get-togethers remained civil, but the atmosphere was threatening, and security were on standby, only a call away. I was learning fast. The role of the consultant stretched way beyond treating sick patients.

In contrast to these complex behind-the-scenes discussions, outpatients itself seemed pretty straightforward. I enjoyed resolving the simple problems. Frustration, monotony and tedium lay years in the future. Anything and everything was refreshing and interesting.

Well, most of it. Surgical outpatients was dull. The two surgical consultants were charming characters who enlivened the clinics. But their lists were a parade of hernias, testicles, hydroceles and lymph nodes with only an occasionally interesting bottom or penis thrown in. Abnormal vaginas were referred to a different department.

So apart from that small detail, it was like my first job in obstetrics; like most of life I suppose — boring if you don't have a feel for the nuances. My role was keeping the clinic running smoothly and resolving administrative issues for the visiting surgeons. A medical air steward, I suppose.

The first patient needed a rectal biopsy to exclude Hirschsprung's disease, a condition which causes severe constipation due to a lack of nerves to the lower gut. Richard had a different tail-end problem, a recurring rectal prolapse, where weakness of the muscles and ligaments supporting the rectum fail. Causes predisposing to this condition include chronic constipation, diarrhoea, Hirschsprung's disease and malnutrition, including cystic fibrosis. Aged three, Richard had experienced nearly a dozen episodes of his rectum extruding through his anus. His family had become accustomed to the sudden appearance of the red, jelly-like blob, like a sea anemone, poking its head out of a rock pool as the tide receded. By covering this delicate structure with moist gauze and gently compressing and pushing upwards, his rectal prolapses had been managed effectively by his parents. But this couldn't continue. Something had to be done. No one wants an inside-out bum. Richard and the majority of the cases we saw had none of the aforementioned causes. Their rectums dropped out for no discernible or identifiable reason. Just bad luck. Fortunately, all Richard needed was the injection of some "glue" to fix his rectum permanently in the right place. A simple day case operation with a high chance of success.

Undescended testes were the bread and butter of the list. Most could be gently coaxed into the scrotum and needed no surgery. Bang on time, the penultimate patient, Marty, arrived with swollen testicles — a likely misnomer as, Blouse excepted, genuinely enlarged testicles are rare, whereas relatively big ones are common.[15] More probable, Marty's marbles were either bilateral hydroceles or inguinal herniae.

In the womb both ovaries and testes grow within the abdominal cavity. Testes start their development in the lower back, then move to the inguinal region before making a final descent in the last month of gestation. Normally it's as smooth a process as the first moon landing, one small step for an unborn boy, one crucial leap for mankind. As the testicles ease themselves into the scrotum, they drag with them the so-called vaginal process. This protrusion of the lining of the abdominal cavity joins them in their travels south, before self-sealing, like a vegetable polybag. If the tract remains fully open, then the bowel can extend into the scrotum, creating a potentially life-risking inguinal hernia. More commonly, the vaginal tract remains partly open, in which case only sterile fluid can descend, creating hydrocoeles. Differentiating between a hydrocoele and a hernia is generally straightforward. If one can get above the swelling, with ball in hand, a hydrocoele is a fair bet. Marty's mass was limited to his scrotum. Bilateral hydrocoeles: a simple operation, in the right hands.

The final patient, Freddie, had been referred to the clinic following a parental request for the oldest known surgical procedure to man, circumcision. The unkindest cut of all? Boys and men throughout history have faced persecution due to the presence or absence of their foreskin. From first century discrimination between Jews and Greeks, the Moorish and Ottoman empires, Nazi Germany, Indian partition and the more recent genocide in Bosnia, this hooded ruffle of skin has proved a bizarre source of arbitration, sometimes between life and death.

---

15. Page 185.

The tradition may have originated in eastern Africa before recorded history. In the Bible, circumcision is recorded in Genesis, when God says to Abraham: "This is my covenant which you shall keep between me and you and thy seed after you – every male child among you shall be circumcised."[16] The commandment included Abraham himself, who'd made it to the age of ninety-nine before saying goodbye to the shrivelled skin bunched at the end, so not the full hood.

Traditionally there were two types of male circumcision – the full monty, and a partial cut beyond the head of the penis. Just why God should be so concerned about this flap of skin is neither explained in the Bible nor by religious scholars, but the practice appears to have emerged independently in scattered tribal societies, embodied along the way into religious observance. In the first century, reticence to be circumcised emerged among Christians. To settle further argument, Paul decreed: "For in Christ Jesus neither circumcision nor uncircumcision has any value."[17]

Some 2,000 years later, in the late nineteenth century, British doctors recommended the procedure as a deterrent to masturbation. In Europe and the US circumcision is less common today, though most baby boys in ultra-orthodox Jewish communities, such as New York City's Hasidic society, are still circumcised in a 5,000-year-old practice known as bris, or brit milah. In this ceremony a trained practitioner called a mohel removes the foreskin, and with his mouth performs Metzitzah, sucking blood from the baby's penile wound to cleanse the incision. Unfortunate, then, that human mouths, like those of all animals, are a breeding ground for bacteria and viruses. In particular, it's not unusual for humans to carry oral herpes, without any

16. *The Bible, Genesis 17:11.*
17. *The Bible, Galatians 5:6.*

255

symptoms, and newly circumcised baby boys have died from disseminated herpetic infection as a result of this practice.[18]

At the time we saw Freddie, circumcision could only be performed in the UK on the NHS for a medical reason. Fifty years earlier, parental preference sufficed. Then it was considered posh to be circumcised, reinforcing the UK's social class structure.

Over the following decades the operation became less common, "roundheads" rarer. The consequences in the UK was that the number, experience and skill set of the operators dwindled. On examination, Freddie had a tight foreskin, but he was only six months old. It was supposed to be tight. But, hey-ho, his father and grandfather had been circumcised and they wanted Freddie done. Now. What's the fuss? What's the matter with bloody doctors these days?

Cue discussion on the unique and complex life of a foreskin. We explained that at birth the tissue is attached to the head of the penis (glans). Over the first few months of life and up to six years of age, this normal physiological attachment breaks down. The foreskin has to be fully free from the glans before sexual activity begins. Otherwise, an erection would prove both difficult and painful. Freddie's parents shifted uncomfortably. Parents' knowledge of medicine, and of surgical procedures, had been much improved by the internet, so one had to be prepared.

No questions arose, so no need to explain the circumstances where circumcision may be advisable: a tight foreskin (phimosis) and recurrent urinary tract infection, for example. Or the rare circumstances where the procedure

18. *Clinical Pediatrics (Phila) Nov 2016;55(13):1245-7.*

is essential: balanitis xerotica obliterans, when the foreskin is tight and the head of the penis risks becoming scarred and inflamed, or recurrent paraphimosis, a condition that occurs during an erection, when the foreskin becomes trapped below the head of the penis and unable to return to its resting place. No need to describe my experiences as a junior doctor, treating paraphimoses with cold compresses, ice wrapped in gauze, pressed around the head of the engorged organ. When the penis cooled, the foreskin could be slid back, once more wrapping the penile head, usually followed by a slit in the foreskin or a full circumcision.

On examination, Freddie's pee-hole was in the centre of his glans, so he didn't have hypospadias (when the urethral opening is not where it should be). The further any abnormal exit from the penis is from its bull's-eye location, the more drastic the necessary surgery. For some boys, hypospadias is just a matter of not being able to pee in a straight line, but when the urethral opening is at the base of the penis the consequences extend to an inability to pass urine standing up, and difficulty in fathering a child. The relevance here is that in such circumstances proceeding with a circumcision risks complicating later corrective penile surgery and must not be permitted. Where is the line drawn in providing all relevant information to aid a decision? No point lauding the advantages of circumcision if the aim was to save Freddie from the chop. Best not to discuss that over a period of years, a newly circumcised penile head becomes keratinised and less susceptible to the transmission of virus particles, reducing the rate of transmission of HIV by nearly fifty per cent.[19] Other benefits of circumcision include an almost total removal of the risk of cancer of the

19. *Sexually Transmitted Infections 2011; 87: 88-93 Hallett TB et al.*

penis and a significant decrease in the chance of developing prostate cancer.[20]

Freddie's parents seemed likely to agree to leave him intact and unlikely to search out an alternative practitioner to operate on their son. Unnecessary to mention that in the US over a hundred male circumcision-related deaths occur every year. Rarely, the baby boy has an undiagnosed clotting abnormality and bleeds to death, more commonly an inept and barbaric hacking at the external genitalia results in significant blood loss, infection and a lifelong damaged penis.

In 2009, one UK hospital reported treating over one hundred boys with complications from circumcision, classifying one of these boys every month as suffering life-threatening injuries. Three years later, *The Guardian* reported the death of baby Goodluck Caubergs after a botched private circumcision by an incompetent midwife, who'd charged £100 to do the job with a pair of scissors. Following a brief discussion of the benefits and risks, Freddie's parents agreed to leave him as nature intended.

Freddie's father's face paled as he cradled his son and left the consulting room. This was all news to him and he wasn't going to allow anyone near his son's penis.

I much preferred the medical clinic lists. These produced more intrigue. Six-year-old Ava had been diagnosed in infancy as having sickle-cell disease (SCD). Her symptoms started early, with swelling of her hands and feet, irritability and lethargy.

Treatment and management had improved since my days as a junior doctor. No longer was there a rush to transfuse a child with SCD who suffered from a marginally

---

20. *Advances in Urology* 2011;2011: BJ Morris et al.

low haemoglobin. The risks of iron overload from an excess of transfused red blood cells and the inadvertent introduction of viruses, such as HIV and hepatitis, had become better understood. It changed the discussion over a blood transfusion, from one where little debate was called for, to one where resorting to the procedure was only approved after careful consideration of the associated risks and benefits.

Sickle-cell disease involves abnormally hard and sticky red blood cells clumping together, blocking blood vessels, causing pain, organ damage, and a potential for clotting resulting in strokes. One striking feature of being a carrier is that it offers some protection against malaria. The patient's abnormal red blood cells adopt a crescent-shaped deformity (hence the sickle) when invaded by the parasite and are then removed by the immune system before they can be released to invade other red blood cells. For this reason, in some malaria-prone communities in Africa and the Caribbean, nearly half of all people are carriers. Darwinism in action.

The spleen plays a significant role in producing and maintaining immunity, and in the filtering out of abnormal cells. In SCD the spleen works like an ant community repairing a damaged nest, but in doing so, it risks burn-out, increasing the likelihood of serious bacterial infections. The cornerstones of SCD care, therefore, are a close attention to immunisation, and a relaxed attitude to the use of antibiotics. Care in the UK has improved markedly over the years. Ava's case, for example, was under shared management between myself and a paediatric haematologist based at a London tertiary hospital. In developing countries with limited medical resources, the consequences of a diagnosis are far more serious. In Africa around a thousand children are born with SCD every day. Most will die before they reach their fifth birthday.

In spite of her management regime, Ava's symptoms had been troubling for her, her parents, and the medical teams involved in her care. The possibility of a future stem cell transplant had been raised and, while this offered Ava hope of an outright cure, the procedure was rarely performed as it carried significant risks. Her existing symptoms didn't warrant such a potentially hazardous treatment.

I was pleased to hear from her mother that Ava had settled in to her new school. On examination, she had no signs of jaundice nor pallor, both of which could be caused by an increase in the breakdown of her abnormal red blood cells. Her hands and feet weren't swollen and her growth and development were perfect. Her mother knew all this but had a specific reason for seeing me this day, a family dilemma. Could she take Ava skiing? I advised caution as cold and altitude are both triggers for creating a SCD crisis. If she were my daughter, I said, I'd book a warmer holiday, and one at sea level. I suggested she talked to her haematologist about the added risks of flying, where the ambient oxygen percentage is reduced from the twenty-one per cent we breathe at sea level, to fifteen per cent. This mild hypoxia is another potential cause for the precipitation of a SCD crisis. Her parents agreed to talk to the London specialist. I was aware of "fit to fly" tests, performed for patients with conditions such as cystic fibrosis. In this hypoxic challenge test the patient breathes fifteen per cent oxygen, via a mouthpiece and bag, while their oxygen saturations and heart rate are monitored. This gives a simulation of the air quality in an aircraft. However, I considered such a test was neither appropriate nor safe for Ava. Why would one risk this? But this was beyond

my expertise and maybe the specialis...
recommend Ava flying with supplement...
know, and although striving to keep up
one never really is.

Over the next twelve years, prior ...
adult care, Ava managed well. She was twice admitted
to the hospital in a SCD crisis, requiring three blood
transfusions. In comparison to many other sufferers, she
had been relatively lucky to be born at a time when the
care and management of this crippling condition was better
understood. Moreover, she was surrounded by a supportive
and caring family, one well informed and agreeable to
consider all the help medicine could offer.

Tommy was next. A waxen eleven-month-old boy whose
weight had faltered and his bowels had changed after the
introduction of cereals. He was referred in with a possible
diagnosis of coeliac disease. Tommy had dropped off his
growth chart, from the fiftieth to the fifth percentile. It was
obvious that something significant had happened. Tommy
sat on his mother's lap as I inserted a needle into a small
vein on the back of his hand. Tommy's face went white.
He went limp and started fitting. His mother screamed. I
reassured her and put Tommy flat on the couch as his four
limbs jerked rhythmically.[21] Responding to the pain of the
needle, Tommy's vagus nerve had kicked in, slowing and
then stopping his heart and Tommy had had a reflex anoxic
seizure (RAS). It's a similar response to the diving reflex
that kicks in when your face is submerged in cold water.
Sometimes mistaken for breath-holding, or epilepsy, these
episodes appear alarming but they are an exaggeration of

---

21. *A rare potential complication of taking blood from children. Time does not allow for explanation of every possible side-effect.*

261

...ural physiological response. Terrifying to witness, but ...ey do no harm.

It was no surprise when Tommy's blood tests returned, supporting the clinical impression of gluten intolerance (coeliac disease). Management of the condition had advanced since the days of using biopsy capsules fed down the gullet. Blood tests alone now sufficed. A gluten-free diet with an occasional outpatient review was all Tommy needed.

*

The Kilimanjaro team also looked pasty, with some members lardy and in need of exercise, so we headed to Scafell Pike in the Lake District. At 3,200 feet it was an easy test that the team failed. Too puffed to conquer England's highest peak, we turned back when only halfway to the top. Then Cadwr, the chairman of the trust, decided to join us. I knew Cadwr quite well. This canny Welshman was rightly suspicious of me, having recently had the indignity of losing his tie in a bet we had together on the outcome of a rugby game between our respective nations. Cadwr had never camped, never used a sleeping bag, never shared a room with others (bar his family) and had shaved every morning since puberty, always before breakfast. I told Cadwr he would be fine, without believing my own assurances. As the team doctor, should I discourage him? Losing the trust's chairman on a charity walk would be careless and bad publicity, on a par with Mr Worthing losing both his parents.

I fabricated a story that the prostate gland expanded at altitude and, as he was the senior member of the team, we would need to be ready. I told Cadwr we would be taking a urinary catheter to be on the safe side. The hospital consultant urologist agreed to back up my deception. Just

262

as well, as the wary Cadwr went to seek advice, to be told that I was indeed telling the truth.

The pharmacy provided a medical bag, or team "goody bag" as some viewed it.

This contained Cadwr's catheter, assorted bandages and plasters, suture equipment and all the emergency drugs I fancied taking, including Diamox, dexamethasone, nifedipine, PC4, and a small, striped, silvery, rubber snake for Cadwr's sleeping bag.

The hardest to explain was PC4, the so-called morning after pill — one can never be too careful. Acetazolamide next. Also known as Diamox. Taken a day or two before reaching altitude, it works by inhibiting an enzyme and helping the excretion of alkali in the urine, resulting in increased urine production and reduced swelling inside the body. Diamox regularly causes tingling in the toes and fingers and makes fizzy drinks unpalatable. We were all planning on taking this, but I worried about what it would do to the taste of beer.

Dexamethasone was added. An emergency-only drug, routinely used to reduce brain swelling after head injuries, post brain surgery, and in the treatment of brain tumours. Dexamethasone also decreases the similar brain swelling caused by high altitude cerebral oedema (HACE) that starts with headaches and confusion, visual problems, hallucinations and fits; it can end in death. I doubted we would use this. I was wrong. Nifedipine was another emergency-only drug. Used to treat high altitude pulmonary oedema (HAPE). HAPE causes a cough, shortness of breath, followed by the production of pink frothy sputum and, potentially, death. In an emergency nifedipine can reduce blood pressure and thus shortness of breath.

I knew Sammy the snake would have his moment, but wondered if we would need the PC4. We chose the

Marangu, or "Coca-Cola" route, so called as its huts served drinks such as Coca-Cola. It's also by far the easiest route and, having failed to manage Scafell Pike, it seemed the only sensible option. If the weather was kind and nobody got altitude or morning sickness, I was optimistic the walk wouldn't be too tough.

Now in Tanzania, the thirteen of us set off on the 45-mile trek from Marangu Gate. Porters carried our heavy bags and, although we only bore day packs, we were aware that altitude sickness was more likely with too rapid an ascent, so we snaked slowly up the mountain escarpment. The first nights were spent in bunk beds at Mandara and Horombo huts, before an acclimatisation day-walk to Zebra rocks. Cadwr was unsettled, he wasn't used to so many sweaty bodies packed together in a cabin or accustomed to "rats" scurrying past. As white-necked ravens scavenged the campsite and our eyes roamed for a glimpse of an imaginary honey badger, aardvark or porcupine, Cadwr squealed as his toes touched Sammy the snake, nestled in the foot of his sleeping bag.

Leaving Horombo we made comfortable progress to Kibo, the final hut, aware that the early morning push to the summit would be our biggest challenge yet. On the summit day one of the team sensibly stayed put in her sleeping bag, as the remaining twelve of us set off. The youngest, Ellie, collapsed on the way up but was revived to rise like a mountain goat and we reached the summit greeted by the first warming rays of dawn. Standing on ice at the top of Africa, peering down to the plains, watching elephant and giraffe grazing below, I kissed Cadwr.

24

AGATHA

Within days, the euphoria of climbing Mt Kilimanjaro, and of receiving confirmation that we'd exceeded our financial target, had given way to the relentless demands of the wards. Despite this success, as lead clinician, I was caught in an ever-tightening financial squeeze, with no way out.

Prior to the start of this unwanted responsibility, I'd sat propped up in bed, worrying, watching the clock tick to midnight, wondering what dramas lay in store, whether I'd get time off for good conduct, and whether the paediatric team would stick together. I didn't feel up to the task. After a couple of months, the role felt less onerous. It helped that the post did not carry seniority. My management style was to avoid confrontation and to bumble along instead. Soft hands over firm grip. It was impossible not to notice that, in spite of the recent appointment of a fifth consultant, the department was getting stretched, with too many clinical incidents occurring, exposing a dangerous lack of continuity of care. The week had become chocka with handovers. In the space of one admission of a single child, as many as six different juniors and five different consultants might voice multiple differing sets of opinions. Treatment plans were changed daily, sometimes twice a day, often with no discussion, explanation or handover.

It was no way to run a hospital department. However hard one tried, it was inefficient and failed to provide good care. Care was becoming piecemeal, disjointed and, in some cases, quite arbitrary. It was each consultant to their own, but I was not immune from such practices. Latest college guidelines stated that children under the age of two years who had a urinary tract infection, would require a micturating cystourethrogram (MCUG). The procedure involves prophylactic antibiotics, catheterisation, filling the bladder with dye and the taking of multiple X-rays, while the child passes urine. An invaluable test for some, but over-interpretation of borderline urine tests had resulted in the radiology department being swamped with our demands. There were risks to consider as well, including exposure to radiation and the introduction of infection. My view was that we were being too aggressive in our investigations and I decided to interpret "under two years" as "under one year", unless there were other factors supporting such an invasive test. The department was split between those who followed the letter of the law and those who used their clinical judgement to decide best personal practice. As lead clinician, should I have been flouting the party line with this variation in policy? With time, guidance changed and fewer MCUGs were done. But was my approach reasonable?

The problems providing safe ward cover continued, patients were suffering and the children's ward had become an uncomfortable environment to work in. But I had a plan. The NHS was touting a new plan too. Theirs was grandly titled "The ten years NHS Plan". Cue bells, whistles and fireworks; cue loss of clangers, silence and damp squibs. I was looking at a shorter time frame with a not-so-sexy name: "The-duration-of-my-lead-clinician-tenure-plan". It won points for sheer, brazen, sneakiness.

I wondered whether, with the addition of two new paediatric consultant posts, we would be able to start a *consultant of the week* rota, with seven of us, so that each consultant in turn would be in charge of all of the children in the hospital for an entire week, for, with holidays, one week in six. This way no consultant could avoid responsibility and we'd share the role of clinician-in-charge, passing it between us like a baton. I felt confident this would improve care and make our work more enjoyable and satisfying. Not to mention or, at least, not to shout about, the gain of a couple of senior staff tucked inside the bowels of my Trojan horse. Would anyone notice that?

The biggest issue was in getting financial approval, but I would also need agreement from my fellow colleagues and from Jim, our hard-pressed chief executive. It called for some softening up. I started booking weekly one-on-one meetings with Jim. Every Monday morning, Jim and I discussed the previous week's ten worst paediatric failings. Usually they were the result of poor communication, leading to periods when no consultant was available on the wards. No consultant, Jim. Did you hear that?

Do you like the horse?

The model of hospital inpatient care had changed. Backed by political promises, the public now expected consultant input throughout the day, seven days a week. After four of these meetings and four depressing lists, Jim told me he'd had enough.

"I've had enough," he said. "Either you solve this or we will have to close the children's ward."

I trundled in the horse, metaphorically, and parked it, metaphorically, in front of his desk. Metaphorically it took a huge dump on the carpet. Look at the horse, Jim. Give him a sugar lump. Jim was no fool and knew my game, but listened to my idea and agreed in principle. So long as my colleagues concurred. I didn't mention that I had yet to work out the finer details, wanting the concept agreed with Jim before I started on any leg work. No matter, I had the green light. The horse was through the gates and victory was in sight. A three-day neonatal study course in London proved the perfect opportunity to do the spadework. Bored witless, unable to comprehend what the academic doctors were harping on about, I had hours to explore new rotas and design different work streams, until finally I found a mathematical solution. The only remaining hurdles now were Amanda, the finance director, the local negotiating committee (LNC), and my fellow paediatric consultant colleagues. I already had Jim's word, which I trusted. Amanda was sceptical, but not too fussed. Like Jim, Amanda was the last of her kind and, although supportive of my efforts, I suspect she had doubts I would clear the third and fourth hurdles. Wait a minute, this was a wooden horse. I hadn't counted on hurdles and this was shaping up like the Canal Turn at Aintree.

The third hurdle, the LNC, proved surprisingly obstructive. They disapproved, said no ambitious junior doctor would apply, and it would create a two-tier consultant system.

That threw me, from my metaphorical horse you might say, as most departments, apart from ours, already had senior and junior consultants. Not in name, admittedly, but a hierarchy of sorts existed, evident in rotas, work patterns and the accepted amount of private practice.

The last hurdle looked like Becher's Brook. My paediatric colleagues. Were they with me or against me? They agreed with the LNC's objections. Out powered and outnumbered, I flogged my failing horse for a final effort.

"What's the harm in advertising the posts and proving yourselves right?" I said. "If it doesn't work and you can come up with any other scheme, I'll support it. We can't continue to work as at present."

Four green lights and the hatch burst open in the belly of the beast. Go, Go, Go.

I suspect my colleagues relented out of kindness to me and in acknowledgement of the fruitless hours I'd expended. None of us expected the new system to work.

It's hard to explain but, in a way, achieving acceptance and attempting to resolve the problem mattered as much to me as to whether or not it worked. If my new model failed, no matter, I was sure another scheme would arise. The seed was sown. I just needed an acronym. The horse had served its purpose. What else had four legs and a tail? COW. That would do. The work pattern involved seven days continuity with one consultant in charge — Consultant Of the Week — COW.

A quick lunch in the canteen and a much-needed opportunity to discuss patients, football and, occasionally, mothers. The mother discussions had moved from our leery junior doctor debates, to bitching over awkward parents or, even worse, awkward colleagues. Nipples arose. I was intrigued as to the frequency of children with triple nipples, boys and girls. I spotted one, or rather three, most months. The extra nipple was often no more than a small raised nubbin, barely noticeable. These accessory nipples cause no harm but can become more prominent, and even produce milk during breastfeeding.

Darwin addressed this topic in *The Descent of Man*, speculating that both males and females among our ancestors could have breastfed. We now understand that nipples arise from a mammary ridge that develops in the womb from a month of age. The line starts in the armpit, travels down "the milk line" through the breast area, down to the inner thigh and groin area. The mind boggles. We'd all seen many in our paediatric patients. But I stood alone in having previously been intimately acquainted with an adult triple-nipple. "It was like this," I said, with the room all ears.

Beep, beep, beep. Beep, beep, beep. "Emergency Baby Unit."

Goodbye nipples. Agatha, a three-week-old baby on a ventilator had crashed. Agatha didn't appear septic and the tests didn't suggest that infection was a likely cause. She hadn't blown a pneumothorax. The lungs on her chest X-ray were both normal, her chest was moving well, didn't transilluminate with the ward "bright light" and she appeared to have good air entry on both sides of her chest. Her head scan was also normal, so Agatha hadn't bled into her brain. Agatha's heart rate was getting slower, her blood pressure lower. Fuck, Fuck, Fuck. She was not one we expected to lose.

Agatha was dying and I hadn't a clue why. Fortunately, I had Jenny, an excellent, experienced junior doctor, with me and together we repeated one-by-one all of the potential causes of sudden collapse. Still, we were flummoxed and time was running out. Agatha was going to die. Mmmm. Maybe worth trying? What was there to lose?

Neither Jenny nor I were trained at scanning hearts, but thought we might as well have a look with the machine that scanned the babies' heads. We put the probe over Agatha's heart. It looked odd. Just odd. No other word could describe it. It just didn't look like we had expected. But what looked different? We didn't know, apart from seeing that Agatha's heart wasn't contracting well. There was also something peculiar around it. We hadn't any inkling what it meant, and there was no one available to ask. Agatha would be cold before my coffee in the canteen. It was now or never, feeling sick, time to go for it.

"I think I have to tap her heart," I said.

"Yes, I agree," Jenny replied.

Jenny looked at me. She knew I had little idea of what I was doing. I stuck the needle in, just to the left of Agatha's breast bone. Agatha, Jenny and I felt clammy.

I had previously accidentally punctured a heart in Australia, while draining a pneumothorax, when bright red blood had come rushing, pumping up the tube, straight out of the baby's heart. I dreaded a similar experience for Agatha. With a burning pain in my chest, I wished I hadn't eaten the canteen curry so quickly. Forget the GMC – no support there. The barristers would shake their bewigged heads. Would colleagues? Surely they'd appreciate we'd tried our best. And what of Agatha's parents? How would they respond to their daughter's death? Would grief turn to anger? Would someone have to pay? Me? Or would they nod in understanding that we'd done our damnedest in an unforgiving situation that demanded the fastest reaction we could muster, acting beyond all the algorithms, guidelines, protocols, experience and textbooks? Because that's how it is in medicine sometimes. In fact, that's *often* how it is. That's the pressure under which we work, day in, day out. I didn't have the luxury to debate these questions. It didn't matter any more; the automatic pilot had kicked in, decision made, out of my hands now.

Back in my hands, our respective heart rates were reversed; mine was now over one hundred beats per minute, and Agatha's had dropped to under sixty bpm. I stuck the needle through Agatha's delicate chest skin, through the muscles between her ribs, through her pericardial sac, where her heart was contracting weakly, and deeper downwards, towards her inner heart. The puncture wound didn't ooze blood. Agatha's cardiac output was too weak for that to occur. Withdrawing on the plunger, and praying hard, I pushed the needle further and remembered I must go to church.

Please, please, no bright red blood. Please.

Hallelujah, Hallelujah, Hallelujah! A syringe full of yellow fluid, not red, but yellow, cloudy, beautiful fluid. Jenny and I couldn't believe it. We could have screamed with relief. As I withdrew the straw-coloured fluid from her heart sac, Agatha instantly looked better and I thanked the Lord that her puncture wound started to ooze dark blue blood. I thought I might vomit. Agatha's heart rate rose, her skin colour improved and within ten seconds Agatha was back to normal.

Agatha had been receiving total parenteral nutrition (TPN), liquid food given into a vein. The feeding catheter had been fed up her arm into the collecting chamber in her heart, where all the body's blue blood pools, prior to being pumped into the lungs and its conversion to red blood, to return to replenish her body.

This tube had somehow migrated through Agatha's heart muscle and into her heart sac, similar to my experience in London when the feeding tube had migrated into the lining around Xanthé's lung.[22] Agatha's heart had been strangled by the food we were pumping into her. Agatha had a TPN cardiac tamponade.

---

22. *Page 124.*

I had never done a procedure like that. I'd had no training, had no confidence and had been terrified at the prospect. I had never even seen one being done, apart from on medical TV dramas.

Back to my still-warm cup of coffee, where colleagues had moved from nipples to discussing the previous weekend's football scores and Steve Job's announcement of a new music library, called iTunes.

They'd not even noticed my absence.

25

NEVILLE

A death always felt like failure, and harder to accept the more senior I became. Death extends beyond work. Of course it does, and sometimes we forget. H's father, Keith, was seriously ill and nearing the end. Keith had fought in WWII, at Anzio, at the same time as my father was there defending the flyover at Campo di Carni, the field of meat. To cheer Keith up I listed all the parasitic diseases from which I'd suffered. Jiggers, cat fleas, scabies, intestinal bluebottle fly infestation and malaria had to be a winning combination. Like a poker player Keith turned over his cards one by one: amoebic dysentery, human fleas and crabs caught at Anzio. I'd had more, but I think Keith had the better hand. A straight flush beats a run and Italian crabs sounded classy. Keith died on a hospital ward, where half of UK adult deaths occur. Most of the paediatric deaths I saw occurred in the hospital accident and emergency department, but of the six I remember clearest, most did not. For different reasons, they will each stay with me for as long as I live.

Before death in hospital, there is usually an attempt at resuscitation. It's what we do when the car conks out, turning the ignition, turning the motor, praying for a spark. Death is final. Neatly compartmentalising our existence. Resuscitation sits in an ethical twilight zone.

We've all seen the films, might even have learnt a few things on heart massage as paramedics, police, best friends, fathers — though rarely priests — beat the chests of lifeless bodies until miraculously — because miracles always happen in films — the victim splutters to life, dusts himself down, marries his sweetheart, has kids and lives happily ever after. It isn't like that. In real life, resuscitation is messy. It's fraught with the conflicts of unproven medical advances, differing ethical beliefs and disparate religions. Clinical staff attend resuscitation courses that outline the ratio of heart compressions to breaths, the drugs to give in specific circumstances and the electric shocks needed to treat arrhythmias. These bits are easy. Little is discussed about the thornier issue, the very tricky one, of who to resuscitate and who not to. It is just too difficult. Real life. Real death.

Three teenagers, a toddler and a pair of newborn twins.

Jane, a fifteen-year-old girl, left on the trolley in accident and emergency, as everyone departed the scene. Jane had died from meningococcal septicaemia. The team had simply walked away, leaving her naked, exposed on the white sheets, her pale body desecrated by the obscene purple patches caused by this pitiless, corrosive disease.

Four hours earlier Jane had been in perfect health. That was before the cytokine storm resulting from invasive bacterial toxins. This self-destructive defence mechanism, where the immune response goes into overdrive, gave Jane little chance. It's the clinical equivalent of turning your gun on yourself. Jane would have had a better chance of survival if she'd caught meningococcal meningitis, rather than sepsis.

I demanded Jane be shown some respect, her body needed covering. It didn't matter that she was dead, Jane still deserved some dignity. A sheet was placed over her, the area tidied, and the curtains drawn.

Two-year-old Dylan died after a road traffic accident. One of 300 similar childhood deaths a year in the UK, a toll comparable to all of the deaths from childhood cancers. After making no progress, despite twenty minutes resuscitation, I turned Dylan over. If I'd done this earlier, we wouldn't have started. A basic, medical school lesson, examine both sides of the patient. Dylan's skull was caved in at the back. His brain was visible through shattered bone, catastrophic and unsurvivable injuries. You see these crushed and fractured skulls in archaeological digs at battle sites where dispassionate historians ponder over the injury — broadsword or bill hook? Sanitised deliberations over sanitised carnage, muffled by time, shorn of flesh, blood and sinew, the tangled butchery of violent death. Why had none of us looked earlier? How could I have been so stupid? I was in charge and, like the captain of a boat, whatever goes wrong, it is the skipper's responsibility. My fault. After what's termed a "failed resuscitation" we aren't supposed to remove tubes and intravenous lines. Coroners insist that all pieces of medical equipment remain affixed to the body, so they can investigate whether clinicians have put them in the wrong place. I was not alone in disagreeing with this edict. We removed Dylan's tubes and attachments and returned him, unfettered by medical debris, to be held by his grieving parents. This was not an attempt at covering up a possible medical mistake; it was about compassion and common sense overriding insensitive bureaucracy and protocols. I'd take my chances.

Some deaths are too raw, still. Twenty years after the event, it's painful to recall Teddy. Teddy was an active thirteen-year-old boy, whose sudden collapse, playing football, was caused by a rapid irregular heartbeat, preventing his heart from pumping blood efficiently around his body. Contracting so quickly, Teddy's heart couldn't fill properly, depriving his brain and other essential organs of oxygen. Frantic, but calm, phone calls to London cardiologists drew me away at five-minute intervals as we went through the list of antiarrhythmic drugs, before starting on the electric shocks, as Teddy's parents and brother sat helpless at his side. Nothing worked, a complete and total miserable and abject failure. You do your best and sometimes it just isn't good enough. Teddy had been born with abnormal electrical wiring to his heart. This lay hidden, causing no symptoms, until his first and final arrhythmia. Such is the suddenness of sudden death.

Nameless stillborn twins. Born on Christmas Day. With no heartbeat, four months early at twenty-two weeks gestation, they each weighed 350 grams, the weight of a can of Campbell's cream of chicken soup. I remembered when extremely premature babies were routinely placed on scales, immediately after delivery. Decisions on resuscitation were based around their weight. The "viability cut off" was 500 grams; "Under this, don't bother," said our seniors in a less enlightened era. The consensus changed with technical, procedural and educational improvements. It was accepted now that weight alone was insufficient to make such a life-and-death judgement. Nonetheless, twins, each weighing 350 grams, born at twenty-two weeks gestation had almost no chance. It didn't help that it was Christmas, when staffing was light. For once I wasn't working that Christmas, but my Christmas curse had still come to bite, as returning to work a couple of days later, I was bleeped by an unfamiliar phone extension.

"Come down urgently," said the mortuary attendant.

A rude start to the day's work. How could I be needed urgently in the mortuary?

It was just possible, I supposed, a physician could be needed to resuscitate a collapsed porter. But a paediatrician? The immediacy, it turned out, was the need for paperwork to be completed before the babies' bodies could be released for burial. On arrival I was informed that the twins had died three days earlier. Their death certificates were needed, and I had to sign them on the spot. I'd neither seen, nor heard any details of their own unique story, but was told it didn't matter. "Just put extreme prematurity on the certificate," said the technician. I insisted on seeing them. As the tray was pulled out and the white linen peeled back to reveal the tiny, frail white bodies, I heard someone utter, "Well if they weren't dead when they went in, they are now."

It was incidents such as this that set me thinking about the possibilities of organ salvage and transplant to save the lives of critical newborns. Was it possible?

Clinically, yes. Would it be useful? Undoubtedly. Babies who would have otherwise died could be saved. How would it work? As far as I could see, there was no existing service for rescuing organs from babies who had recently died. The national focus on organ transplantation seemed to bypass this sector of the population. There were good reasons for this. The criteria for brain death were based upon the physiological processes behind adult death, not that of the newborn. Maybe it was too difficult a topic, but exploring the idea further, I found a promising development, an unheralded regional neonatal transplant service with senior nurses on call to discuss potential donors. The numbers were small, however, and this departmental development never took off. It could have saved lives but there was insufficient will, it seemed, to confront the grief of distraught parents with medical logic that might seem heartless, however well intended.

The last death that will remain with me, was that of Pamela, a severely disabled teenager who died after suffering a perilously high temperature. By far the commonest cause of a high temperature, or hyperthermia, is an infection: viral, bacterial or parasitic. But there are other rare causes, including environmental — being left in a hot car, brain dysfunction — hypothalamic disease or status epilepticus, hormonal — thyrotoxicosis, and drugs — neuroleptic malignant syndrome or malignant hyperthermia (usually during anaesthesia). The post-mortem was inconclusive. We will never know the cause of Pamela's death.

Moving on, or perhaps backwards, from death to ethics. The system of consultant of the week (COW, remember? The one that started as a horse) was installed and my on-call week began with the usual round of seeing non-thriving babies, asthmatics and self-harming teenagers. But one patient's condition was beyond the textbooks. Neville, aged nine, had a severe chromosomal abnormality and had been admitted to the ward with a hard-to-shift pneumonia. Humans should have forty-six chromosomes, each with a central centromere, two short p arms, and two long q arms. The naming of the short arm involved a three-way stand-off between a German proposing k, the abbreviation for *kurz*, meaning short; a Frenchman proposing p for petite; and an Englishman proposing *s*. It's self-evident what that stood for, and who won. The long arm, classified as q, fell into alphabetical place after the *p*. Two of these chromosomes decide our sex and the other forty-four comprise the rest of us.

Neville had significant abnormalities of chromosome one, the largest, containing almost ten per cent of the total DNA in the body. The consequences for Neville were catastrophic. Neville had severe developmental delay. He suffered seizures and could neither see nor hear, but he could express pleasure with human contact, by a subtle muscle relaxation and a slowing of his heart rate. He was much loved by his family. Admitted with a severe pneumonia, Neville was on intravenous fluids and antibiotics. Deteriorating fast, Neville was likely to die soon. Nevertheless, if his condition worsened, his parents wanted him fully resuscitated and ventilated. The medical and nursing staff explained, as sensitively as they could, that this might not be the right thing to do for Neville. His parents, however, were clear and adamant.

"We want everything done," they said.

It was my turn to be responsible for Neville. I spelled out the gravity of his condition, but his doting parents wouldn't budge. That evening, before I left the ward, I was planning a bedside conversation with his parents if he arrested. I took the registrar and ward sister aside and told them to call me if Neville stopped breathing and to give him some puffs from the resuscitation bag until I came in to assess him. I asked the staff not to call the hospital crash team, and not to have Neville intubated prior to my arrival. This fell some way short, I knew, from doing "everything we could". I was unsure whether my instructions were legal, but decided I'd take the risk, and if it ended in court, so be it.

But should it have been my decision? Probably not. In theory, doctors cannot be forced to resuscitate against their will, but in this case I was ignoring the clear wish of Neville's parents. In such circumstances, textbooks and protocols would have recommended Neville's transfer to another hospital, where a different consultant would be found to comply with his parents' request. The alternative was a legal application to have Neville made a ward of court. A judge would then become the arbiter of life and death. I went to bed tossing and turning, knowing I should have taken legal advice, wondering whether I'd been brave or stupid. Maybe both? In my heart I was certain it was the right decision for Neville. Bugger the consequences, I thought.

Next morning Neville had improved. Or, at least he was as well as he could be. At lunch I shared my stance — my dirty secret, if that's what it was — with my colleagues. Who all nodded in agreement. It was easy to agree after the event. Neville left the ward and went to respite care. On hearing of his departure I took a deep breath and headed off to my office to hide. This had just been moved, as management had claimed ours for their expansive ambitions. Like the Germans in WWII, management wanted *Lebensraum*.[23] They'd turf you out before you blinked, to use your space for a new bean counter or two. Three desks now squeezed into a square three-by-three metre room, with minimal ventilation. To remind us of life outside, photos of children, dogs, ducks, sporting heroes, mountains, and photocopied letters of complaint adorned the walls.

A loud knock and the office door opened, revealing a cheery face asking for help with yet another difficult ethical problem on the ward. Lauren had been born the

_____

23. *A concept promoting settler colonialism between the 1890s and 1940s.*

ınder my care, with a fatal condition. Lauren
e issue was, how soon? Prior to conception,
e of Lauren's parents' chromosomes to split,
ion, had resulted in Lauren being conceived
with an extra chromosome, trisomy 18. Unlike Neville, her
standard forty-six chromosomes were normal, but she had
one too many. Lauren had forty-seven chromosomes and
the result was equally catastrophic. Like Neville, Lauren's
parents wanted everything done for their child. What parent
wouldn't? It's a common and completely understandable
parental response. However, the question arises: where
does "everything done" end? So often the debate turns
on the future quality of life when even deeper questions
emerge such as: what is life?

How logical can a parent be when so emotionally
entwined?[24] As they sit by their child, lost in despair and
hopelessness, how can parents possibly judge the way
forward? All the time, issues such as residual guilt, loss
and the torture of letting go, are gnawing away. If not the
parents, who should decide? As a paediatrician I believed
decisions should be made primarily in the interest of the
child. But it was often hard to know what was best for the
patient. Those who knew the child best were, of course, the
parents. If agreement was impossible to reach, the courts
could be called upon, but that was a last-ditch option
that no one but the most ethically challenged wanted to
explore. Lauren had most of the hallmarks of trisomy 18,
or Edwards' syndrome: a small head, overlapping fingers,
a loud murmur and a cleft palate. Chromosomal analysis
confirmed the diagnosis. Lauren would die very soon. But

---

24. *Throughout this book, but particularly relevant in this chapter, the
word "parent" can be replaced with the "child's carer", where the child
is adopted or fostered.*

when? Predicting death, or rather, duration of life, is not easy. Edwards' syndrome babies have an average lifespan of just over a week, but it's more complex than that, as one in twenty babies might survive to live ten years. Therein lay the problem. Nobody could predict with certainty that Lauren would die soon. Every hour of Lauren's life was precious for her already grieving parents.

Lauren needed respiratory support. Respiratory support comes in many different guises. It had moved on significantly since the original iron lung, first used in 1928, when a critically ill child with polio made an unexpected recovery. Poliomyelitis was then a terrifying "new" disease causing sudden paralysis. In fact, polio was not new.

Polio had plagued the human race for thousands of years but had become increasingly rare, before returning in epidemic proportions in the early 1900s.

Most of those afflicted made a full recovery, but some survivors, like US President Franklin D. Roosevelt, were left with permanent limb deformities, in braces or wheelchairs. In severe cases the respiratory muscles were paralysed and patients died of suffocation. The iron lung offered some relief until, in the 1950s, a new vaccine promised the chance of worldwide eradication. In the iron lung, patients lay in a chamber while negative pressure, like that of a hoover, made the chest expand. As the pressure equalised, the lungs could then release the used air. This brilliant concept had first been suggested by an English scientist, John Mayow, as far back as 1670, but machines were only made from his idea over 150 years later. A further century passed before a girl at Boston Children's Hospital in the US became the first patient to benefit. Some patients spent decades encased in the machine. Dianne Odell spent fifty-eight years enclosed in one, after contracting polio at the age of three, before dying during a power cut caused by a fallen tree.

Respiratory support had improved, and recently at pace. Headbox oxygen therapy had been replaced by oxygen supplied directly up the nose, which was then refined to nasal high-flow oxygen, warmed, with humidification added. Not only does this work more effectively, but it's better tolerated by patients who are now fully visible, not stuck in a metal cylinder, or half hidden inside a plastic box. When respiratory support needs to be increased further, continuous positive airway pressure (CPAP) is given via two tubes, again up the nose. The CPAP machine also helps breathing out, by reversing the flow at the right moment. This fluidic flip reduces the effort of breathing by over fifty per cent. Less effort usually means a better outcome. If this level of non-invasive support fails to keep the patient safe, then invasive treatment is needed. The least aggressive is bilevel positive airway pressure (BiPAP), but it can be quite fiddly and is therefore seldom used. Finally, there is the most invasive form of ventilation, where a tube is inserted through the vocal cords to deliver oxygen and remove carbon dioxide, the toxic waste of breathing. This breathing tube reaches its target by being inserted through the mouth — endotracheal, or through the nose — nasotracheal. I preferred nasotracheal intubation, as it's less likely to dislodge, but following a reported case of inadvertent brain penetration of a newborn during such a procedure, I was in a minority as usual.

Lauren couldn't breathe adequately for herself. She was intubated through her mouth and her vocal cords and put on a ventilator, with no prospect of ever coming off the machine. We fiddled with the knobs. Lauren fought, and we fiddled. Peak inspiratory pressure, peak end expiratory pressure, inspiratory time, rate of ventilation, flow rate and percentage of oxygen administered. All of these variables meant a lot of twiddling. What life was that? Was it acceptable? Was the cost of this care to the NHS and the country justified? Should her parents be allowed to be the decision makers? Who should decide what to do with Lauren? Lauren had pretty normal lungs and so she didn't need much respiratory support. Her breathing issue was neurological, her brain wasn't working properly. Her ventilation pressures were low and she only required twenty-five per cent oxygen, not much more than you are breathing now. The low pressures we were using minimalised the chances of a collapsed lung, a pneumothorax. They also reduced the frequent hangover of later chronic lung disease created by ventilation. But all this was academic. Lauren wouldn't live that long.

Team consensus was that we were prolonging Lauren's suffering by continuing her ventilation, but no one wanted to go against her parents' wishes, so advice was sought from the regional centre. Supportive, yes, but no real help. We sought legal advice. Sympathetic, yes, but again of no practical help. Compromises were made and Lauren survived a few months at home. We all did our best.

It was extraordinary to have so many depressing and complex patients at the same time, when usually the ward was full of simple and easy-to-treat children. Then along came Tyler, a readmission. Tyler was a twelve-year-old boy dying from a brain tumour. As I reviewed Tyler on the children's ward, the antagonism I'd faced previously, after Steve's death during my senior registrar post five years earlier, was still fresh in my mind. Although I knew that predicting duration of life was nearly impossible, Tyler's breathing had become irregular and laboured, a sure sign that the end was imminent.

We'd previously agreed a hospital-based treatment plan with his parents, who were caring people, devoted to their son and devastated. Then Tyler's parents changed their minds and said they wanted to take their son home to die.

They had every right to do so.

It's entirely understandable to choose the confines of home over a hospital ward when it's clear that a loved one is beyond medical help. But the timing of the decision was fraught, as I was sure Tyler would die in a matter of hours, if not minutes. I was worried Tyler would die on the way to the car, or on the drive home. Tyler's parents were brave people and willing to take that risk.

My anxiety was misplaced. Tyler lived another week before dying peacefully, with his parents at his side, in his own bed, at home.

26

HENRY

The Blair Government introduced a new game, one with league tables and star ratings for hospitals. It was like going back to school. Hands up everyone who wants to play. What? Nobody? The truth is that we were never asked. Hospitals would now be rated between zero and three stars and placed in leagues like football clubs, only we, the medical staff, were the ones being kicked around. The idea was to stimulate competition and drive up standards. The carrot was a promise of more financial freedom, and the stick, humiliation in published charts naming and shaming hospitals with poor performance. It betrayed a fundamental lack of understanding of the principles that underpinned the public sector. We weren't selling cars. We weren't playing football. Medicine is not commerce and it's certainly not a game. Prime Minister Blair believed we should reward success stories and punish those struggling. I wondered whether the money should be distributed the other way round. On reflection, maybe both those at the top and those at the bottom should have received more support. Oh, and those in the middle too.

Meanwhile H and I embarked on another challenge. Off to Corsica to walk the GR20 trail. A week in we entered a bar. People sat in silence, eyes fixed on the TVs attached to the four walls. It was Wednesday September 12th 2001.

Two days later a different storm hit – thunder, lightning and rain. We left the track, both emotionally and physically drained, with the holiday and the rest of the walk now irrelevant. Back at work, the atmosphere was understandably subdued. What would the US response be? Patients offered a respite, but I was soon rendered speechless, when a junior doctor turned to me with a grin.

"Did you have a good holiday, Charles? Of course, the Americans deserved it," he said. Incensed at his comment, but aware of the anti-bullying regulations and all the accompanying red tape, I kept my counsel and left the room. It was the cowardly option that I took. My junior colleague shouldn't have been allowed to get away with it.

In our absence, management had been up to its tricks, decreeing that it was now inappropriate for staff to be treated differently to patients and visitors, so the small staff section of the canteen had been closed; a seemingly harmless move, but not without consequences. Removal of our private lunch area destroyed any opportunity for doctors, and all the other hospital staff, to talk shop confidentially, so that mealtime conversations became less useful, and the cold macaroni cheese tasted less attractive. At the same time, we were confronted with a new recruitment process.

Few departments are seduced by trends as much as human resources and, under pressure from deaneries and colleges, HR had instructed us to come up with a scoring system to replace our existing method which was perceived to be haphazard and open to prejudice. Previously, when faced with over one hundred applications for one post, most were sifted out on the grounds of poor writing, wrong-coloured envelope, bad spelling, or our own sheer boredom. Anything that reduced the pile seemed acceptable. Perhaps routinely rejecting every third curriculum vitae was taking it a bit far. To save us from ourselves, HR insisted on a competency-based system, asking us to design a departmental list of competencies we expected from aspiring junior doctors. Competencies included the ability to intubate, perform lumbar punctures and carry out routine baby checks. They did not include the ability to stay awake for twenty-four hours, independent thinking, excellence at stud poker, and standing one's round at the bar. Instead, each application was scored against this list of bland attributes, and what did we get as a result? A bland, homogenous collection of potential new colleagues. I wondered whether we could be a little more imaginative and flexible in our scoring. Others insisted we stuck rigidly to our new egalitarian structure. I needed a distraction. Coming up.

Beep, beep, beep. Beep, beep, beep. "Emergency special care." Well, that was brief and to the point, three words seemed the norm now. No information, no priming.

Little bloody use.

Henry had been born too early, with unexpected malformations. In pregnancy his mother had been confirmed with polyhydramnios, too much fluid in the womb, so some problems were anticipated. But Henry's abnormalities were worse than feared. In cases of polyhydramnios, it was usual practice to check the patency of the newborn baby's gullet, the oesophagus, at birth. Put simply, did this feeding tube reach the stomach or did it end prematurely, with an obstruction and a "blind-ending pouch"? If so, the stomach was cut off from the gullet, with a complete break in the digestive tube. In that event, any ingested food would be unable to enter the gastrointestinal tract and would be either vomited back or would pool at the end.

Henry was also frothy, another warning sign that his secretions might not be able to reach his stomach, but were instead building up in this pouch, before spilling out of his mouth. Adding to this complication, Henry had a previously undiagnosed, deformed and rotated right arm. We put Henry on the ventilator, and after some debate about the potential benefits and risks, agreed to give him surfactant. Since the 1980s surfactant had been used in the UK to help mature the lungs of babies born too early. The drug had been quicker to take off than the iron lung, but it had still taken fifty years to move from what seemed like a good idea to a life-saving treatment. There weren't many contraindications to using surfactant. We realised, however, that severe congenital malformations should make one reflect, before committing to squirting the cloudy liquid down the tube and into the baby's lungs.

In 1929 a German-born physiologist, Kurt von Neergaard discovered surfactant reduced the surface tension in the lung and, by doing so, the air sacs within the lung were able to open more easily. Surface tension makes rain come down as droplets, and is useful if you are a pond skater, but not if you are a premature infant, as it prevents your lung air sacs from opening and being allowed to do their normal business of gas exchange. Twenty years after von Neergaard made his revelation, surfactant was tested on stillborn infants and shown to offer potential advantages in the treatment of babies born with premature lung disease. Then over a decade later, in 1963, the US President John F. Kennedy lost a child at two days of age. The baby had been born just five weeks prematurely, and was unfortunate to have died from this condition. It took the publicity around this single, tragic and high-profile death to at last bring the problem to the attention of the world's media. Worldwide, millions of babies whose lives could have been saved had died in the three decades after von Neergaard's discovery. The world woke up, trials began, and twenty years later surfactant became the first drug made solely for the newborn.

Although Henry's obvious abnormality was his "blind" gullet, we knew this usually went hand-in-hand with another hidden deformity, an abnormal tube connecting the gullet to the airway, a so-called tracheoesophageal fistula, or TOF for short. Within six hours, Henry was sedated, intubated and stabilised. Phone calls had been made, letters written and he'd been transferred to London for surgery, all neat and straightforward. Clever us. Except, we weren't. My brain wasn't functioning sharply. I was still fretting about the junior doctor's unforgivable comment. I hadn't fully examined Henry. I'd focused on his top end, sorting his ventilation requirements and his cardiac output and hadn't checked Henry's anus. Henry didn't have one. Henry had a condition called VACTERL, a syndrome, with abnormalities of the vertebrae, anus, cardiac, trachea, esophagus, renal (kidneys) and limbs. Well, he clearly had AEL, and almost certainly T. You don't need the full monty to qualify. The condition occurs in around 1 in 10,000 babies. Most have abnormal anuses, so having known Henry had a TOF and a limb abnormality, I should have checked Henry's tail end. But I hadn't. Bad medicine. No longer smug; now sheepish.

It's always easy to criticise, and I realised I was now in no position to do so. Had I lost my balance, ordering unnecessary tests and making incomplete examinations? Was I at risk of losing any gravitas I had accumulated?

After all, I'd reached the stage, with sufficient experience under my belt, when it would be reasonable to explore the world of private medicine. If I wanted to. I had nothing against the principle of doctors earning a fair wage for their skills and experience by undertaking private medicine. But was I interested? Different specialties in health care have a different allure to the private pound. For example, popping out cataracts is a quick and easy area of care that can be managed almost as a production line, benefitting both the patient and the surgeon, with minimal risk. Two half days a week on cataracts, and a consultant's NHS salary is doubled. Printing money. On the other hand, intensive care is extremely expensive to provide and has to be adequately provided for by the Government. No waiting lists are permitted. Too much risk of losing votes.

Private medicine presents an opportunity to take some of the heat out of NHS waiting lists and fulfils a useful and necessary role. But unless performed with care and sensitivity, I feared it risked having a deleterious effect on the NHS. There was much unseen work in hospitals that didn't include "measurable outcomes". Management seemed unaware that there was more to the role of a consultant than churning through outpatient and operating lists. Some consultants shared this lack of awareness too, happy enough to scuttle off to their private clinics, ignoring the value of being seen in and about their departments when they might have been available for mentoring, committee work or, heaven forbid, giving advice. Isn't that what consulting is?

A sociologist called William Bruce Cameron once wrote: "Not everything that can be counted counts and not everything that counts can be counted". The system would fail without consultant time for shortlisting, interviewing, appraising, mentoring, teaching, supervising, supporting troubled colleagues, sitting on and chairing committees, writing guidelines and offering emergency cover for absent colleagues. And, most important of all, just being there – being around as a sounding board, support or consoling shoulder. If consultants spend every spare hour off site performing private practice, who will be left to fulfil these critical roles?

My view is that senior medical staff should be paid a good enough salary so there is no need for moonlighting. It's a scenario comparable with members of parliament supplementing their salaries with consultancy. These public service employees should have enough on their plates resolving issues with the public without having to delve into the private sector. For a few there was another issue. Some consultants' chief executives denied them the opportunity to do procedures within the NHS, such as IVF, leaving little option for such specialists other than private practice. I was confused. I ran through my anxieties with a consultant orthopaedic surgeon who had accumulated a significant private practice. He cautioned me that private practice could prove a trap. Having become accustomed to a higher income, stepping back is difficult, he said. However, he stressed that the advantages of practicing privately included having a direct relationship with the patient and having the ability to see and treat a patient without any of the usual NHS waiting list constraints or management interference. One could provide suitable follow-up without being ticked off for not passing the patient's care straight back to the GP. On the down side, take-home pay, after the costs of secretarial services, private room hire and taxes was only about one third of the charges, he said. I could barely hold back the tears. Oh well, I was probably too lazy to do it anyway. Convenient, too, that paediatrics wasn't a big private earner. Satisfied I had adequate excuses, I decided to side step this option and focus on the role of an NHS consultant. Plenty to do there.

Having missed Henry's anus, almost immediately two other very different babies, Jess and Jan, presented. Neither had passed meconium, a black and sticky substance comprising of cells from the lining of the bowels, bile, amniotic fluid and lanugo, the baby's fine hair. After a few days of ingesting milk, meconium transforms to the paler, softer, yellow baby stools, rather like piccalilli. Six years into my consultant post, I'd seen a handful of babies readmitted, at a few days of age, with grossly distended abdomens and vomiting, who on re-examination were found to have no anus. In each case, on reviewing the notes, the baby check had a tick marked on the examination sheet, confirming that the anus was where it should have been. An apparently simple and unforgiveable mistake. Similar to the one I'd made, but if the nappy was full of meconium, it could be regarded as a reasonable guess that it had emerged from a properly functioning anus. However, in one patient of mine, it had been squeezing out of a hole in the scrotum — far from ideal — a lesson for all those who examine the newborn. Everyone counts fingers and toes. Holes should be counted too.

Both Jess and Jan were about a week old and I agreed with the juniors' newborn baby examinations that, despite the lack of meconium, both had normal anuses. Jess, an exclusively breastfed, ten-day-old baby, had been sent to the ward for an urgent review. Her parents were distraught. She was their first child. They had waited nine months for her first poo and nothing had happened. Their concern extended beyond the welfare of their daughter since they were also missing out on the long-anticipated "baby poo" chat with relatives and friends. You know: my piccalilli, your piccalilli. Everyone likes to compare. Oddly, we rarely compare our motions as adults, but what comes out of a baby's bum seems different somehow.

The examination revealed a healthy baby girl, with a normal-looking abdomen and anus and normal growth. Jess was perfect, nothing was amiss. The poo-less nappy was a result of the purity of her mother's breast milk. So pure there was no waste to excrete. Only reassurance was needed. If only all we ate was so good.

Jan was seven days old and, likewise, she had not opened her bowels. She was her parents' third child. They weren't that fussed and had sat tight for a week.

Examination revealed a normal anus but a distended abdomen, with visible thin blue streaks of small veins, spreading out from her tummy button like an exploding azure starfish. Something was up; so was my finger. The gentle withdrawal of the tip of my right little finger was followed by a gush of Jan's sticky faeces. A referral for biopsy confirmed Hirschsprung's disease. Jan had been born with a short section of her large bowel devoid of any nerve supply. She would be cured by what had recently become a routine operation.

Back on the neonatal unit with no critically unwell babies, there was more time to teach and an opportunity to think deeper than allowed when rushing from patient to patient. Lottie was progressing well. She'd been born eight weeks early and had needed little support apart from assistance with her feeding and some supplemental oxygen. Reviewing her blood results, I noted her blood calcium was low. I explained to her mother that the blood tests were fine, but we would repeat the one for calcium, adding that it wasn't surprising to have a test falling outside the usual ranges. While giving this assurance, I found I was struggling to feel the pulses in Lottie's feet. Again, not usually significant. I moved on to the remainder of the examination; all normal, so back to those feet. I smiled inwardly, remembering Perth airport a decade earlier, and the send-off from an Australian friend saying, "Mate, I've just realised that you look after children, not feet." He'd confused my role of a paediatrician with that of a podiatrist.

Feet. I was irked by the lack of any pulses in Lottie's feet and it must have showed. As I mulled whether to come back in the afternoon to check them again, her mother piped up.

"Is there a problem?" she said.

"I can't feel her foot pulses but that's often the case. I'm not worried," I said.

"Could it be related to the blood test you're repeating?" she asked. The question niggled. Could it? Tricky one, this. Yes, two abnormalities can, in theory, be connected, but they seldom are. What should I say?

"I suppose it's possible, but neither finding concerns me, so I suggest we repeat Lottie's calcium and I come back later and examine her feet," I said.

I returned a couple of hours later to find her feet stubbornly pulseless. Her mother adjusted her sights, pausing this time, then fixed me with a maternal look.

"What could it be, if her blood test and feet are connected?" she said.

Similar question, subtly reframed, less wriggle room. Cornered. No opportunity to dither now.

"Well, there is a rare condition called DiGeorge," I said. The response was loaded with caution and I spared her all the details. Why alarm her unduly? DiGeorge is a syndrome, occurring in 1 in 4000 live births, caused by a micro-deletion on chromosome 22. Associated problems can include characteristic facial features, a cleft palate, poor tone, delayed development, heart defects and a low level of calcium.

"I will ask the technician if she can arrange an ultrasound of Lottie's heart," I said.

Next morning, nothing had changed. Lottie's observations, including blood pressure, were normal. However, her calcium remained low and the pulses in her feet were still missing. I'd boned up on DiGeorge the previous evening. I rechecked her palate and tone, and still couldn't find any other pointers towards the condition.

The cardiac ultrasound department was busy as ever, but they slotted her in all the same. Out of my hands now, I headed off with the nurses for a post-ward-round cup of coffee and some chit-chat.

Beep beep beep, Beep beep beep.

The technician is on the phone. Can we call Great Ormond Street Hospital urgently to arrange Lottie's transfer? In the scanning room she's collapsed, needing immediate intravenous medication for an interrupted aortic arch, then urgent transfer to a paediatric surgical cardiac unit. She's being sent straight back to the neonatal ward for stabilisation before transfer.

On the ward Lottie is pale. Her heart is racing and blood tests show she's acidic. She's intubated, put on a ventilator and given intravenous medication to keep her duct open. Transfer is uneventful, surgery successful, and she makes a full recovery.

Would I have diagnosed DiGeorge without the intervention of Lottie's mother? I really don't know. I do know, though, that it's generally unwise to ignore the instincts of a mother, however inconvenient they may seem.

Lottie was always in perfect health when I reviewed her afterwards in outpatients. Instead of adjudging me a dithering fool, her mother thought I'd done well. I thought she'd done well, so mutual backslapping all round. What of the future? With her chromosomal micro-deletion, it's possible Lottie could have some later behavioural issues, but she should live a normal and active life.

*

Meanwhile the Government gave another shuffle to the pack, in the belief that the funding problems of the NHS would be eased if District Health Authorities were replaced by new Strategic Health Authorities (SHAs) and Primary Care Trusts (PCTs). I doubted many clinicians understood the change. Even fewer cared.

I didn't; my COW (consultant of the week, remember?) was almost over but, as so often, there was a final sting. The police called, requesting I accompany them on a visit to a house on a local estate, "About a dead baby", they said, giving no other details. It was news to me but it was hard to refuse the officers of the law. That was a mistake; I should have asked a more experienced paediatrician for advice. I met the two plain-clothed policemen at the address.

A terraced, two-up, two-down, no front garden, etched, glazed, white plastic front door, vinyl flooring, small electric cooker, copies of the *Daily Mail* on the floor, nobody-at-home type of house. It felt wrong. I wondered what had happened and whether the occupants were now "helping police with their enquiries".

The three of us looked at the family wedding photos on the mantelpiece, went through the cupboards in the kitchen, then upstairs to examine the contents of the drawers in the main bedroom, before turning left and entering the dead baby's bedroom and coming across a box of soft toys. "Doctor, do these look dirty to you?" the detective inspector asked. Back downstairs, to be quizzed about the state of cleanliness and suitability of the contents of the larder. Hold on. What was I doing? What was I looking for?

I discovered later that neglect had been raised as a possible contributing factor to the baby's death and that my role was to assess the suitability and safety of the home environment for bringing up a newborn baby. The intentions may have been right, but my presence wasn't. The last thing this still relatively wet behind the ears, eager to please, recently chastened, consultant paediatrician needed, was a bit part in *Silent Witness*. Discussions followed between the hospital management and police top brass.

It didn't happen again.

27

ACONCAGUA

Sheryl Crow's "Soak Up the Sun" and the new James Bond, *Die Another Day* were released, and I booked a flight to Perth as England prepared for another assault on the Ashes, my fourth visit to the WACA. England had already lost the first Test in Brisbane. Surely I couldn't witness four England losses on the trot?

First, Twickenham, and a rugby union Jonny Wilkinson masterclass, as England beat Australia by one point. The omens looked good, the planets were lining up. I sensed fortunes were changing and fancied a bet on England winning the next four Ashes Tests. OK, unlikely, but surely possible, definitely possible after all those beers.

Shocked into semi-sobriety, after reviewing the odds, I emailed *The Times*.

Sir,
I have been a loyal follower of English cricket since childhood but need advice. I have a bookmaker account and prior to flying to Australia at the weekend thought I might place £5 on England to

win the series 4–1. To my astonishment the odds of this happening are exactly the same (500–1) as Elvis being found alive. Shall I go for the double at a quarter of a million to one or be safe and just back Elvis?

By the time I'd arrived in Perth we'd lost at Adelaide, so England were 2–0 down, and I was five pounds worse off. The WACA ground was roasting hot, the pitch marble hard and the lager dreadful. Nothing had changed in the past four years.

Well, almost nothing. This time stewards were spraying the English spectators with water, maybe containing Roundup. Sitting in the stands was bad enough, but surely hell for the English players in the field, who weren't used to playing cricket in such searing heat.

The Australians well understood the increased risk of malignancy from exposure to an excess of sunlight, so the shade was reserved for the locals. The Australian Cricket Board had put the visiting Poms out to fry. Sautéed Poms. There were a few new faces in this England team, but the Aussies still had McGrath, Lee, the irritating Ponting, much-feared Warne and hopefully uncomfortable Hayden, who was recovering from a recent haemorrhoid operation. We would fight and this time I really thought I would see a win. We lost by an innings and forty-eight runs.

Sorting out the mail back home, I gasped. My grandfather Eric had helped secure my membership of the Marylebone Cricket Club (MCC) over twenty years previously.

I knew the members had a reputation for being a bunch of stiffs but, surely, they weren't that stuffy? My letter to *The Times* had been published. I'd received a handful of supporting and sympathetic letters, but also a threatening note from the MCC complaining about my "Elvis Letter".

I felt nauseated and my chest pain returned as I collapsed onto the sofa.

Dear Sir,

Contravention of M.C.C. Rule 32 (iii) b: Your letter to the Editor of The Times Newspaper of 16th November has been brought to my attention, and discussed this day by a Disciplinary Select Committee of the M.C.C. The Select Committee considers that the views expressed in your correspondence to The Times Newspaper are disrespectful and undermining of the morale of the Senior England cricketing party, currently touring Australia. It is my duty to inform you that such disloyalty is in flagrant contravention of M.C.C rule 32(iii) b. Accordingly, I have no option other than to propose your name be struck from the list of full members at the next AGM. You are at liberty to defend your status on this occasion and may wish to name four Senior Members willing to vouch for your erstwhile good character.

H burst into tears. It didn't help that she'd just reversed her car into a bollard. Again. Slowly, I smelt a rat. Like making clinical diagnoses, there was something amiss with the scene. But, what? I examined the envelope. Ah ha. Without moving house the Royal Mail had recently allocated me a different postcode. Strange, but true, and this envelope had the new numbers on it. I was sure that I hadn't got round to informing the MCC of this. So, the letter wasn't from the MCC. I texted the only two people who I thought might be capable of pulling such a fast one: Slimes, my old landlord from Oxford, and my dentist friend, Terry the Tooth. Slimes confessed and I marked him down for later retribution.

On return to hospital Jim, the chief executive, called me down. What could it be? Not the cricket, surely he hadn't read *The Times*? He looked like the lecturer in *Educating Rita*, same manner, a typical Guardian reader, the lived-in suit and tie, laid-back, almost placid appearance, which wasn't Jim at all. Jim and I had a good relationship and maybe even respected each other so, knowing this could prove an interesting discussion, I started to prepare my defence. His opening sentence shook me to the core.

"I'd like you to become the new director of medical education, a five-year post."

Had Jim lost his marbles?

I enjoyed teaching, but knew little about postgraduate education. Jim suggested I discuss the proposal with my colleagues. Cornered again, I agreed to take on the role, but only if I could first hand over my current post of paediatric lead clinician. I was certain I couldn't do both management positions at the same time, as well as my clinical duties. What had I let myself in for? The longest bluff of my life. Within days of this meeting, a good friend, a fellow consultant, died while at work. I was shocked. I'd previously assumed only patients died in hospital. I sat silently on the sofa, handkerchief in hands, not sure what to do. His contribution to the hospital had to be celebrated, he'd been such an integral part, an essential cog, a voice of reason, a perma-smile. Nobody is irreplaceable, but it was inconceivable to let this tragedy pass unrecognised, his name rapidly forgotten. With agreement from his widow and Vicky, the boss of the education centre, we established an annual memorial lecture. For the first, we approached Terry Waite. Waite shared his experiences of being held in solitary confinement for over four years, with no clock or light to tell day from night. Chained to a wall, Waite's only clue to the passing of the days was the morning beating of the rugs, echoing down to his cellar from the balconies of the nearby flats. It put life into perspective. On call wasn't that tough and I should stop whingeing. Bloody Pom.

It wasn't long before the Government fiddled again, and I really had something to whinge about. We were instructed that the junior doctor rotations needed rewriting and these would now change every four months, rather than after the current six months. With three posts per year, rather than two, the idea was the juniors would be exposed to a greater variety of specialties. The training would be broader, but shallower. This should make later career choices easier. I didn't approve. I remembered the thrill in my first paediatric job, of realising for the first time that at last I'd some idea of knowing what I was doing. That had taken me four months.

I might have been a slow learner, but I found the warm glow of competency was only felt in the last two months in post, when the confusion started to clear and work became productive and enjoyable. Starting within any new specialty was tough, with days spent exhausted and muddled, and now it had been decided that all junior doctor rotations would end at the very point where proficiency was taking root.

These shortened rotations didn't go down well with my consultant colleagues either.

They'd had decades of developing and carefully refining their own medical team structures within an excellent junior doctor training system. And, as director of medical education, I was seen as the one responsible for wrecking it. Barking was particularly furious. His eyes were spinning. A fearsome colleague, Barking was having a good day and made a very good point. Why were we proposing to trash a safe and well-established educational framework, for little or no gain? Why indeed? Midge, the new chief executive, was also in a tizzy. Jim had given himself a birthday present by resigning and Midge, his replacement, was far from happy. Midge was used to having his own way and wouldn't tolerate anyone challenging his authority, let alone a fucking doctor.

Midge couldn't bear the cheeky buggers and called me down to his large office to read an extensive charge sheet. I think he hoped I'd stand to attention. My offences were, firstly, that I'd written to the Department of Health identifying thirty-five typing errors in their document (nobody likes a smart-arse) and, secondly, that I was resisting his attempt to grab two rooms in the education centre. I pleaded guilty as charged. Neither accusation could be denied. The official health department document, explaining the new national junior doctor training system, was so shoddy and so appallingly produced, I couldn't let it go without comment. Quite apart from the principles behind the concept, the document's grammar, spelling and general syntax were that of an average ten-year-old child. It could have been written by a doctor. Midge pinched his eyes in a sergeant majorly way. How dare I draw attention to his paymasters' tawdry work? My job was curing sick children, not making waves.

I didn't blink. There was clearly no love lost nor ground to be given between us.

Impasse, then, was saved by news of a developing crisis with one of the trainee doctors. Midge would just have to wait to get his revenge.

Consultant colleagues alerted me that Tom, one of the new junior doctors, was repeatedly making dangerous mistakes, exposing a lack of basic medical knowledge.

I phoned the dean for advice. "You must suspend him immediately," he said. Medical checks were conducted on Tom, a brain scan and IQ tests performed. Four months later a hearing was scheduled at the GMC.

I felt sorry for Tom. It's always been in my nature to side with the underdog, maybe just to be awkward and *contraire*, or maybe as a consequence of my prior humiliation at prep school. I guessed Tom had been forced down the wrong career pathway and suspected his exam results had been fudged, maybe sat by a friend, or simply forged.

Tom's GMC hearing resembled a Victorian melodrama. I was used to supporting doctors, not attacking them and their mistakes. We all make mistakes. The GMC might not be able to grasp that, but I did. Twelve of us sat around a long and imposing table, like that in Leonardo da Vinci's *Last Supper*. Indeed, it was for Tom, and I felt like Judas Iscariot. Tom sat close by and gave me a friendly smile. I couldn't hold his gaze as I answered the questions about why Tom's lack of medical knowledge warranted such a hearing. The result was announced after my return to the hospital. The GMC had agreed. Patients first. Tom would lose his licence to practice, the end of his career as a doctor. No victory. No winners. I heard no more of Tom. All those years of study, wasted. It must have been devastating. I hoped Tom would reflect on the decision and come to accept this was the best outcome possible for him. To continue would have been miserable. The support and sympathy he received as a junior for making errors would have faded with increasing seniority. Tom may not have realised at the time, but I hoped that in later years he would thank me and thank his lucky stars he'd escaped so lightly.

I needed an adventure to clear my head. I'd read somewhere about the highest peak in the Andes, the biggest mountain outside of Asia, tallest in the Western Hemisphere,

Aconcagua. Approaching 7,000 metres this was one of the world's Seven Summits — the highest mountains on each continent. A British expedition, led by Edward Fitzgerald, made eight unsuccessful attempts before their Swiss guide, Matthias Zurbriggen, reached the summit in January 1897. I knew this would be a different ball game to ambling up Kilimanjaro. Over a thousand metres of extra height is a lot at that altitude. And no oxygen here to "bring down the height" as it does for those who pay to climb Everest. I needed a team, but first I needed a guide.

I called Baptiste, my friend from Chamonix, and he agreed. Chamonix guides are a special breed. Of Baptiste's initial group of forty-four trainees on the exacting course, fourteen had since died in the mountains. What could go wrong? Then I phoned four friends, each of whom had previously reached the summit of Kilimanjaro, and they all agreed, but they wanted more details. Details? I didn't have any. Baptiste was methodical and professional, many people had died doing this ascent he said, two already that year. However, I was confident; I knew we would have luck on our side, as I'd be taking along a "good luck" present: a house brick. Terry the Tooth, my affable Australian friend (there are no absolutes), had handed me the brick in a local pub.

"This may help you, mate," he said. I'd expected a dental emergency first aid kit, a water sterilising syphon, or maybe some crampons. But no, it was a standard house brick. On our kitchen scales the brick weighed 2.265 kg. I was getting quite attached to it. So the brick joined me on the flight to Buenos Aires. Our party comprised:

Baptiste: quiet, fit, charming, with a dangerous twinkle. Hard to assess.

John: taciturn, stocky, powerful builder with a worrying liking for concrete. Hard to read.

Dick: overweight, blonde, unfit, hypochondriac, journalist, Yorkshireman. Hard to share a tent with.

Jane: Ab Fab, lighthouse owner, long brown hair, try anything. Hard to understand.

The Vicar: something in the Church, irreverent, uncontrollable. Hard to dislike.

The Brick: standard issue red clay and lime. Hard.

In Buenos Aires I slipped the brick into John's bag. John sniffed it out pretty quickly, signed the brick in Tipp-Ex and surreptitiously placed it into The Vicar's bag for the short flight to Mendoza. The brick was discovered on arrival at Puente del Inca, inscribed again and slipped into Jane's bag. No discussions on any of this. As each victim found the brick, they secretly passed it on. The serious trekking started, but Baptiste was confused. Our bags weighed 2 kg too much, and he'd been so pernickety about the weight. We had pre-weighed everything so carefully. As I squeezed into a tent with Dick, for the first night at Camp Confluencia, Baptiste informed us that we would have to leave the biscuits behind. We awoke at seven in the morning, the fly zip was undone and Baptiste's flushed French face appeared.

"I am not amused," he said.

"What?" I said.

"I have found Le Brick," he said.

"The" is a tricky word, for Le French. Baptiste hurled our lucky charm into the river and we spent the rest of the day in silence. And the following two days. We trekked in the Parque Provincial, an acclimatisation hike that would take us to the base of Aconcagua. As the mountain reared up, majestic and massive, three vertical kilometres above, silence was at last appropriate and comfortable. The mountain was a beautiful and awesome sight.

The Vicar buzzed around. We should have taken a lead for his collar. Baptiste was irritated by this unnecessary expenditure of energy and everything else. With the boredom of rest, interspersed with extreme exercise, and maybe because of the lack of oxygen, genitalia started to feature prominently. Dick liked having ailments. With his thinning blond hair and fading Yorkshire accent, Dick was a nightmare for any general practitioner or wife, and insisted he had now developed a new medical condition called *Cock au Nègre*.

Realising mild cyanosis was affecting one of Dick's multiple peripheries, four of us anxiously peered at our own, but Jane felt left out, so I drew a female perineum and we played a mountain version of "pin the tail on the donkey". Confusion reigned about the relative positions of the female anus, urethra, vagina and clitoris with nobody certain, not even Jane, and she had a head start. Baptiste won the competition, and broke the tension, drawing a flower over the whole area.

It became clear that The Vicar was suffering. Even with God on his side, he was pale, continuously coughing, a tinge dusky and frothy. The Vicar had developed pulmonary oedema. This can be fatal and he was ordered to return home, by mule. It was almost biblical. Two down, including Le Brick, leaving just the four of us, and Baptiste. As we headed off higher, to Camp Berlin, a miserable area marked by a wooden hut surrounded by a few deserted tents, Baptiste hinted that summit day was fast approaching. Feeling mortal, Dick produced an indelible pen, writing "This leg and other bits belongs to Dick". To be helpful, he then inscribed his home telephone number on his calf. I didn't tell him that it should have been "belong", not "belongs".

Soon another problem — well, two, in fact. Dick and Jane. Dick's marching uphill, stuck in first gear, unstoppable in bright yellow thermals, was unsettling Baptiste. Clash of colours, clash of personalities and clash of cultures. Irritated further by Dick's celebration at the end of one of our exercises, mimicking a Silverstone race pit tyre change, Baptiste finally lost the plot on discovering we'd been emptying our night- time urine bottles, under our tent.

"I 'ate le Engleesh, you are sooo dégueulasse," he said.

We awaited a weather window. Then, just as the clouds cleared, I had a case of the runs. Going every thirty minutes, my energy and enthusiasm drained. "Ve vill leave for le summit at three, now sleep," Baptiste said as night fell. We stuffed our boots into our sleeping bags, as everything outside the bags was frozen solid. I asked to be left behind. Jane's back had also given in. I thought only two of us should go for it, Dick and John.

Unknown to all of us, Baptiste believed that with her bad back, Jane wouldn't be able to make the final climb to the summit and, to underline his conclusion, he had left Jane's crampons behind at base camp without mentioning it to any of the group. Baptiste insisted, however, I should go to the summit. I wished he hadn't. Curled up tight in my sleeping bag, eyes screwed shut, I ignored the howling gale battering the tent, pretended to be asleep, and prayed time would stop. "Three o'clock, le time to go," said Baptiste.

I was roped to John and Dick; all of us wore crampons now, making painfully slow progress over the ice and fresh snow. We were still tied together when I opened my bowels. Who cared? At that altitude there is no privacy. No energy for such refinement. Five hundred feet from the top we spotted two exhausted climbers sitting alone, staring into space. It didn't trouble me.

I felt like I was dying and in a way I was. If these two men also died, then so be it.

A crawl over the last boulder and on to the flat, rocky, freezing, howling top. Looking down at South America below was glorious, apart from feeling like death.

At nearly 23,000 feet, we were only 3,000 feet below the "death zone", where the body cannot acclimatize any further, but still 6,000 feet below the summit of Everest. Our blood oxygen saturations would have been around seventy per cent, as opposed to a normal level above ninety-four per cent. A few photos, sitting on a rock, with blue lips and clenched hands, Baptiste at last accepted I was unwell and spoke for the first time in four hours. "Le time to go. Ve are only half vay." I made rapid progress down the mountain alone, feeling better every metre of descent, before lying down in the snow and vomiting blood. I crawled into our tent and cuddled up to Jane.

Back home I found out why Dick had been collecting receipts for our ice creams, our sun lotion and anything else we'd bought. He needed to claim expenses for the article he was writing on our trip.

In Dick's own words:

'The tests were clear, said the doctor. I did not have diabetes, my heart was fine, pulse healthy, cholesterol low and blood pressure perfect. I left the surgery feeling dejected. I knew there was something wrong with me. My wife knew too. "You want your head testing," she said when I told her I planned to climb a 23,000-foot mountain in the Andes. She had a point.

For the price of this mountain adventure I could have a week of pampering on a private island in Mauritius. Why would anyone want to spend good money risking their life and health, surviving on poor food, numb with cold, and struggling to sleep on a windswept rocky mountainside?'

28

MADISON

The trip had taken its toll: returning to work was hard. I just had to get on with it.

Mr Blair was still in power, more reorganisation. No sooner had *The Health and Social Care Act 2001* been passed, than the Government was publishing another piece of NHS legislation.[25] How many changes of direction was that in the past eight years?

John Reid had taken over from Alan Milburn as Health Secretary. Rumour had it that on appointment, Reid had said, "Oh fuck, not Health." Reid introduced private companies to run treatment centres for orthopaedic procedures, gave GPs a significant pay increase and, for the first time, allowed delighted GPs to opt out of the responsibility for the provision of out-of-hours care. Many GPs had already made arrangements for cover for these periods but, for the first time, this was no longer their duty. They were cock-a-hoop. Few in Whitehall understood or

25. *Health and Social Care (Community Health and Standards) Act 2003.*

respected the drain on personal health and the strain on normal life that out-of-hours work caused.

Then something happened that would change UK hospitals permanently. Since 1998 consultants had been contracted under European Working Time Directive (EWTD) protection for their working weeks, entitling seniors to eleven hours continuous rest a day and a day off every week. This protection had been ignored by both management and the consultant body.

Then, six years later, it was extended to cover junior doctors. Unlike the consultants, the junior doctors demanded that the protection was fully implemented and stringently monitored. Over the next five years the maximum working week for junior doctors was reduced to forty-eight hours. They were no longer permitted to work for more than twenty-four hours consecutively and, for the first time, they were entitled to eleven hours uninterrupted rest every twenty-four hours. A limit set at twenty-five hours continuous work, to allow for patient handovers, might have been manageable. But a twenty-four-hour limit, leaving no time for handovers, was nigh on impossible.

The juniors needed some relief from their workload, that was clear, but suddenly they'd achieved a level of protection never demanded by their senior colleagues, nor dreamt of by their predecessors. Analysis of work diary cards was now significantly more complex as the issue shifted from one of pay to one that also incorporated legality, causing most trusts within the country significant woe. Among consultants there was a sense of "We had to do it so why couldn't they?" Sour grapes? No.

The insane hours worked by the junior doctors in the eighties and nineties had long since gone. Good riddance too. They were inhumane. A sensible balance was needed between abusing juniors with punishing hours on the one hand, and making shift work regulations too tight to enable safe care for patients on the other. The change boomeranged too far and too fast, endangering patients and the ability to run hospital departments safely.

More Government meddling. The anticipated first wave of NHS foundation trusts arrived. Ten hospitals were initially earmarked, supposedly granting them more autonomy. Trusts were described as halfway between the private and public sectors. Managers were seduced and extolled their virtues, naively believing this would give them a new freedom to decide on local spending and clinical priorities. Management informed us it was Hobson's choice — foundation trust or die.

I sought solace in a paediatric asthma clinic, anticipating spending the morning reassuring the worried well. Silly to anticipate anything in this job; there never was any room for complacency. Sam, aged eight, needed a review of her medication.

Her asthma was under control and I expected to be able to discharge her back to the care of her GP. As Sam clambered onto the couch, I noticed her gait was unusual. I wondered whether to start exploring something unrelated to her referral, or to just ignore this possibly new clinical finding. I was running late, it was coming up to lunch and I was hungry, but I couldn't ignore it. Maybe I was imagining things. I hoped so; time was not limitless. It may be for Einstein, but not for us. On the couch it was clear that Sam had signs of spasticity in her right leg. It was stiff, three centimetres shorter than her left leg and her right leg reflexes were abnormally brisk.

A glance at the soles of her shoes confirmed the diagnosis. One had no grooves left. No lukewarm macaroni cheese for me today. To my surprise, Sam appeared to have an unusual form of cerebral palsy, she seemed to have only *one* stiff leg, a spastic monoplegia.

Cerebral palsy is a permanent, non-progressive disorder of posture and movement caused by damage to the developing brain. For some children this is a catastrophic diagnosis but for others the disability is so minor that it's barely noticeable and doesn't disturb their daily lives. By dividing the condition into four different categories, I found I could more easily remember its typical causes. The commonest class was spastic, meaning increased tone. Then there was ataxic, meaning poorly coordinated, and choreoathetoid, with large brisk abnormal movements, and finally mixed cerebral palsy.

Sam's true spastic monoplegia was surprising. Classic spastic cerebral palsy is either a quadriplegia, meaning all four limbs are affected, or a diplegia, where both the legs are worse affected than the arms. This is most commonly found in children born prematurely. Sam had been perfectly healthy from birth, apart from moderate asthma, and had sailed through her first eight years of life with nobody spotting her uneven shoe wear. Her parents must have been shell-shocked, having come to see a consultant for a routine respiratory review, now leaving hospital with their daughter having been diagnosed with a significant and permanent neurological issue. Was this good medicine or should I have stayed out of it? Sam would have managed undiagnosed for many more years, but over time her imbalance would have put extra strain on her spine and hips. All things considered, I felt it *was* worth the distress I caused in making this diagnosis, as in the long term it reduced the likelihood of Sam needing corrective orthopaedic surgery in the years ahead.

Another general election, another win for Labour and Mr Blair. Blair appointed his fourth Health Secretary, Patricia Hewitt. Budget deficits, bed closures and cuts, combined with comments made about "The NHS's best year ever" weren't well received by the hospital staff. The British Medical Association said that rather than the best year ever, the reality was conversely very bleak, with hospital closures and training budgets slashed. Who was fooling who?

*

It's Sunday September 11th 2005. Four years after the atrocities in the US, the Israeli flag is lowered for the last time in Gaza, as the last of the occupying troops depart. At The Oval cricket ground in London the English and Australian flags are raised over a different battle. Australia are losing the series 2–1 and this is the fourth day of five in the final Test. I am with Rog, my old Sussex friend, best known for stealing my girlfriends. Randy Rog, with his Brian May mop, was always in the wings, waiting to pounce.

We both dislike watching Australia bat. They are just too damned good and, combined with their abrasiveness, it isn't entertaining. This is Australia's last chance. We have Strauss and KP. They have the terrifying trio of McGrath, Lee and Warne. McGrath, while warming up at Edgbaston, ahead of the third Test, had trodden on a cricket ball, tearing his ankle ligaments, putting him out of the third and fourth Tests. Now he's back. England start well and bowl Australia out, six runs shy. England must avoid a second innings collapse, facing one of the best bowling attacks ever. Strauss scores a century in the first innings, but in the second innings he's out with only two on the board. The fourth day ends with everything poised. This is building into a five-day classic, with so much at stake. Somehow, I have to get a final day ticket. But the Oval is a sell-out, so the ticket office at the ground is my last chance. Approaching the open window in the small white hut, I clear my throat, "I am sorry, but my Uncle Rog is very ill and this will be his last Test," I say. "If you get a return ticket, please could you let me know?" Management has taught me life skills, dastardly, dishonest, but effective behaviour. I get two tickets and we reserve a table for lunch in The Oval pavilion dining room.

Next day, when the lunch interval arrives, England are collapsing. England are one hundred runs ahead, with five wickets left. History is repeating itself. Rog and I feel sick. I regret fibbing at the Oval ticket office. This is just returns for my dishonesty. We don't leave our seats. We don't eat lunch and England bat to safety. We draw the test and win the series.

After the weekend I return, nursing a sore head, to the special care baby unit to find that a ventilated baby has been given ten times the prescribed dose of morphine. The baby is fine, but her parents have yet to be informed. Compounding the situation, the nurses plead with me to cover it up. I'm not going to share the blame and I'm not going to conceal anything, however sympathetic I feel. Nurses, as a group, are more vulnerable than doctors to criticism and are rightly scared of the professional consequences of making mistakes. Although no harm has been done, the nurses are rightfully fearful of the trust's response. I explain that since I've been made aware of the problem, I will need to inform the parents and offer a transfer of their baby to another hospital.

I don't mention the attempted cover up. What good will that do? Like the vast majority of parents, they are charming and sympathetic. They are understandably angry, but grateful that we've come clean with them and opt to stay with our unit. Would they have done so had they known the nurses had sought to sweep it all under the carpet? This was the only attempted concealment of a medical error that I came across in my career and I found it depressing. Not because of what the nurses did, but that their fear of excessive punishment was such that it overrode their usually dependable common sense and good practice. Where did this culture of fear originate? How did it come about? The Government should have realised; ruling by fear doesn't work.

But it just couldn't stop fiddling around with the NHS. Another shuffle of the pack, and more instructions for managers in the new White Paper: *Our Health, Our Care, Our Say*. Hitherto I'd worn my cynicism like a robust pair of Y-fronts — restrained and concealed. Now it was more of a high-viz vest, draped around my shoulders.

It was dawning on me that politicians were keen to light up their departments with a sense of dynamism, but less interested in the outcomes as, down the line, it was often a different party in charge and almost always a different minister. Reluctantly, I had to start paying attention to this destructive cycle of change and chaos, as my patients' lives were at stake.

The cricket was like the London buses. Time again for the Ashes in Australia. I needed a wingman for the trip, someone able to handle the hostility from our sporting hosts; someone to share the pain and draw the enemy flak. There could only be one candidate, my larger-than-life friend, PV.

He'd earned his nickname after overindulging at a dinner in London. Rolling out of a taxi he'd vomited with such ferocity, he was forever afterwards nicknamed Power Vomit, or PV for short. PV was outstandingly resilient and gloriously unflappable. Ten years earlier, driving by the River Arun on his way home from the pub, he'd spun his car, splash-landing, to find it sinking. Unable to push open the door due to the pressure of water, he remembered the survival manuals explaining the need to wait until the forces equalised. The water had risen to nipple height and PV was still trapped. Heaving against the door, it jammed, leaving the car window his last chance of escape. With some effort he squeezed his bulk through the window and clambered onto the bank, only to find himself in a garden pond, in the company of a donsy of gnomes.

With PV on my side what could possibly go wrong? Leaving more in hope than expectation, PV and I flew out to Brisbane, with Adelaide, and a fifth trip to the WACA on our itinerary. Wedged into my meagre slice of seat, I wondered how many more years of COW I had left in me. A full seat was a luxury I knew I'd have to abandon alongside PV who weighed nearly 150 kg. Most of his bulk hung over his tight MCC eggs-and-bacon-coloured belt, making his legs look tapered and his head shrunken, an inflated *Despicable Me*. If that wasn't hard enough to bear, PV also had greedy elbows. Uncomfortable in the plane and worrying about work, I curled up in my restricted space in the hope that I might, at last, see England cricket win abroad. After all, we had Strauss, Cook and KP, as well as Harmison and Anderson.

Admittedly the old enemy had Hayden, Ponting, Gilchrist, Lee, McGrath and, OMG, Warne. Both teams were packed with world class cricket stars and if England didn't win, I knew they'd at least put up a good fight.

It was bad enough travelling with PV, even worse when we got there. This was a man who, with his thinning blond hair, couldn't avoid the sun's attention, unlike the hippo, which cannot get sunburn. I anticipated a fry up Down Under. At the Brisbane GABA ground cameras were collected and confiscated. "Mate. Could be a missile, mate," the official said. The Australians, jealous of our better songs and stronger spirit, if not our better cricket, had decided to split up and dry out the English supporters, christened the "Barmy Army" by the Australian media. On the stadium screen flashed a warning, directed at the Poms: "Text us on 13579 if you spot anyone drinking alcohol. We will have them evicted." Ponting, the architect behind this segregation, won the toss. First ball, Harmison bowled so wide the ball went to Captain Flintoff, picking his nose at second slip.

Howls of derision descended from around, as the locals smelled blood, the Poms turned a brighter shade of pink, and PV started to crackle. I closed my eyes, shut out the baying, and recalled David Gower's alleged response when he'd arrived at Brisbane as the England Ashes captain a few years earlier.

"Do you have a criminal record?" asked the man at immigration.

"Is that still necessary?" said Gower.

This warmed me inside, but I was too hot outside and, on opening my eyes, reality sank in. PV and England were melting in the sun, the fans had been hung out to dry, and Australia went on to win by nearly 300 runs. But not before the breakout of a sole, slow hand clap a few rows behind our seats. Soon the numbers swelled and the sound increased, before being interspersed with rhythmic chants of "Kazakhstan". On turning my head, yes, it was Sacha Baron Cohen, AKA Borat, as our ringleader, distracting the English cricket faithful from their impending humiliation.

On to Adelaide, where Collingwood scored a double century, putting on 300 runs with KP. With a loss now impossible, Flintoff declared. In sight of a rare victory, England froze and fell apart. Warne the wizard cast his spell and we lost again, this time by six wickets.

Our luck had to change in Perth, my fifth trip to the WACA. With four thrashings under my belt, I was the seasoned whipping boy, yet something in my bones told me this would be the moment. Australia batted first and lost six cheap wickets. PV had left the ground before lunch to doze in the shade of a eucalyptus tree. I sensed the Englishman seated beside me needed some advice.

"Don't get too excited, you must realise that there's really no hope," I said.

"Why not, they've collapsed," he replied.

You had to have been there so many times to understand my pessimism.

The English respected the Aussie wicketkeeper/batsman Gilchrist and Gilly paid the tourists back by scoring a brilliant century off fifty-seven balls. With defeat for England inevitable, we sang to the pale blue skies: "Only rain can save Australia now." Put to the sword again, we drowned our sorrows in weak lager and songs about Brett Lee's pretty blond hair and Glen McGrath's ageing body. A finale was reserved for our bête noir, Warne, as we sang repeatedly, to the tune of "My old man's a dustman":

Shane Warne's an Aussie, he likes to play around,
he's got a different Sheila in every Aussie town.

He's always in trouble, he's always in strife,
but when he lost his hair...

...he also lost his wife.

On my return to the UK, I started receiving abusive phone calls to my landline. "Tosser." Nothing more. Number withheld. "Tosser." Had Warney tracked me down? I finally identified the culprit. It was my oversized travelling companion, PV. I'd forgotten, that prior to leaving England, I'd had another ethical problem. Trivial, compared to anything on the wards, but troubling nevertheless. Flying with PV, I was worried about the space that would be left for me. I knew I was being selfish, but I didn't want to sit next to PV. Who would? I wasn't sure how to handle this problem.

Conveniently, at this time, *The Times* newspaper was running a regular advice column by Joe Joseph, titled "Modern Morals", that aimed to help readers solve personal ethical quandaries, like fancying your wife's sister or preferring your neighbour's dog to your own. Propped up in bed, reading his daily paper, eating his usual full English breakfast of two fried eggs, three sausages, four portions of fried bread, five hash browns and six rashers of bacon, PV felt a burning pain in his chest and choked on the pork sausage that he was trying to swallow whole. There, nestling in the Joseph column was this reader quandary:

In November I am flying to Brisbane to watch the Ashes campaign. Being more than 6ft tall, I am considering booking two seats that are apart, rather than adjacent, because my travelling companion weighs 146 kg and I'd rather not sit in three quarters of a seat for such a long flight. Would it be wrong to do this, and tell him that there are no adjacent seats left?

Readers' contributions ranged from rants at my intolerance to sympathy with my predicament. Sympathy had more votes.

Yet another NHS reorganisation. Strategic Health Authorities were to be reduced from twenty-eight to ten. Primary Care Trusts would be pruned from 303 to 152. One thing was clear – the Government preferred even numbers. Closer to home, and impossible for me to ignore after fifteen years had lapsed since the previous legislation on the care of children, the *Children's Act 2004* belatedly came into force. This stated that the interests of the child were paramount and, for the first time, clarified a critically important point, that safeguarding (child protection) was everyone's responsibility. A children's commissioner was to be appointed and each local authority had to appoint a director of children's services.

Next, the Government put in place the Medical Training Application System. This online computerised system introducing a more arbitrary selection and placement of junior doctors was roundly despised. Many doctors have partners who are also medical. Who else would understand the pressures and problems of life as a junior doctor? Now medical couples risked being placed hundreds of miles apart. Twelve thousand doctors marched in London in protest, joined by the leader of the opposition, David Cameron.

As a further slap in the face, in a breathtaking breach of security, the personal data of 30,000 junior doctors, including their addresses, telephone numbers, previous convictions, religion and sexual orientation, was leaked and became widely available.

Few doctors were surprised, as NHS information technology services were regarded by most clinicians as a depressing and expensive shambles. Staff were becoming increasingly disillusioned with the political football the NHS had become and, although clinical decisions were not always right, at least our plans were made carefully and were open to challenge and scrutiny.

Back in outpatients, a welcome break from politics, and two new problems. First, one of my patients, Madison, a teenage girl, had a rare condition called Cantu. The syndrome could be confirmed by genetic testing and was supposed to be extremely scarce, with under one hundred cases reported in the world literature. Apart from being hairy — the most obvious characteristic of Cantu — patients also risked having significant heart and spine problems, with abnormally thin and weak bones and muscles. Coming from a hairy family, I knew a bit about abnormal hair growth.

Hirsutism is usually familial, but there are a few other rare conditions that result in abnormally hairy humans. These include the mucopolysaccharidoses, porphyria, polycystic ovary syndrome and a multitude of other genetic abnormalities, the most extreme of which is Ambras syndrome, where thick hair can cover the whole of the patient's face. But, in twenty years clinical practice, I'd seen no more than a handful of hirsute children with a relevant, underlying diagnosis. More perplexing still, only one hundred of the world's population were reported as having Cantu, and the UK's population was under one per cent of this. But Madison wasn't my only case of Cantu. I now had three cases. Three! All unrelated. What was that all about?

Madison was uncharacteristically subdued. On my enquiring, she told me that some boys at her school had been bullying her, making insulting remarks and monkey noises. Furious, I wrote to her headmaster warning that, were it repeated, I would call the police. This worked. But why was there an over representation of Cantu patients in my outpatients? Was the prevalence wrong, with many undiagnosed hairy children and adults with Cantu, going about their business unfettered by such a label? Was there a Cantu gene in the region? Or were my diagnoses wrong? It just didn't add up. Any answer would do. At lunch I asked "The Disappointment", one of the medical, rather than surgical, consultants. The Disappointment was one of those people who is always ready with an opinion, whether or not they know the topic. His answers helped, as just talking about the problem with him over coffee assisted me in formulating a strategy, not so much about what to do, but about what *not* to do.

The Disappointment enjoyed taking risks, but never with his patients. In the canteen he was something of a strategist. He'd taken to pressing the large cup button on the Costa machine, allowing two shots of caffeine to shoot into his medium sized cup. By pushing the cup aside, as the extra hot water was dispensed, he gained a large dose of caffeine, while saving himself twenty pence each time. I agreed it tasted better. The wheeze soon caught on, but there were risks for his disciples. I doubted that the omniscient Disappointment had heard about Mr Hope, a senior examiner for the Royal College of Surgeons, and a national expert in blood vessels in the brain. Hope had recently been suspended from Queen's Medical Centre in Nottingham for taking extra soup and croutons at lunch. Predictably, the Disappointment proved disappointingly short of ideas on Cantu. Curry and coffee consumed, I encountered my second problem, called Alex.

Alex, a newborn baby of an HIV positive mother, was withdrawing from methadone on the baby unit. Alex's mother had been taking antiretroviral drugs in pregnancy. The drugs, combined with an elective Caesarian section at thirty-nine weeks, and the avoidance of breastfeeding, meant that the likelihood of Alex remaining HIV positive would be decreased from twenty-five per cent, to under one per cent. As expected, the maternal antibodies had crossed the placenta and Alex tested HIV positive at birth. But being HIV positive at birth did not mean Alex was necessarily infected with the virus. The antibodies present in such cases were usually those obtained from the mother, not from the baby. So the antibodies, and not the virus, had crossed the placenta during pregnancy. Later blood tests, we believed, would most likely confirm that Alex had not been infected.

Alex's mother was a heroin addict and, throughout her pregnancy, had been on methadone. Alex had been bathed in methadone for nine months and, with his birth, this supply had been rudely and abruptly removed. If Alex's mother had been HIV negative, then breastfeeding would have been encouraged, and would have proved a useful source of medication, via her milk, to lessen his withdrawal symptoms. But she wasn't, and Alex was showing the classic signs of neonatal abstinence syndrome (NNAS) — cold turkey for newborns. This hangover could last up to six months. Alex was irritable, twitchy and sneezing — in a foul mood, like a bear with a headache. Alex wanted his drugs. More. Now.

Looking at the withdrawal chart at the foot of his bed, our local modified Finnegan score had been increasing.[26] Every four hours, an hour after a feed, the nurses assessed Alex's sleep, pitch of cry, degree of tremor, sneezing, yawning and vital signs. No fits, yet. But Alex's score was too high, sitting stubbornly at nine. His morphine would need increasing.

---

26. *A system, first described in 1975, to quantify and diagnose withdrawal from maternal drugs that have crossed the placenta and entered the baby in the womb.*

Alex was in for the long haul. It would be a month before his symptoms settled, allowing him to go home. Responsibility would then be transferred to social services to provide monitoring of the care his parents provided, and to assess the safety of Alex's home environment. The HIV test could stay positive for up to eighteen months, in an uninfected newborn, but Alex was lucky. His three-month antibody test was negative and he'd avoided contracting HIV.

29

CLOT

My role as director of education was a useful foil to the paediatric clinical work.

Clinical work could be somewhat workaday with sudden, unexpected, razor-sharp moments of terror thrown in. A peculiar irony was that the more senior I became, the more I realised it was wise to ask for advice. My sanity and safety were maintained by nursing and medical colleagues, so, on the frequent occasions when I didn't know what to do, I could always find someone with whom to discuss a problem.

Two-year foundation programmes were the new Government fad. Central diktat demanded that, rather than having to apply for jobs every six months, junior doctors would now be appointed to two-year rotations and then move on to a "Run-through programme". Depending on the specialty, these lasted between three and seven years, before the junior doctor was able to exit the scheme and apply for a consultant post. This training process would only involve two successful interviews post qualification, compared with the eight or so hoops my cohort of trainee doctors had been put through. I was not alone in disliking this concept. I worried that it was too quick and took away the useful regular challenges to career progression.

People mature and do so at different rates, and an excellent doctor aged twenty-eight, might not have been so three years earlier. Objections aside, new rotas had to be developed and the latest system explained to consultant colleagues and put in place, all overseen by me.

While work progressed in selling this concept to a sceptical consultant body, the time had come around for the annual Clinical Excellence Awards (CEAs). Nationwide, each year, consultants were invited to fill in a form, selling their own worthiness. Points towards these awards were allocated for research, teaching, innovation, management, clinical work and brown-nosing. The awards were funded by money removed from the negotiated consultant pay package and then, once a year, a panel of peers met to decide which consultants were worthy of an award. It was a sort of selective bonus for which one had to compete. Each award was worth about £2,500 and, more importantly, they were pensionable, so each was worth over a thousand pounds a year after retirement, for life. In other words, a tidy sum.

For some doctors, the kudos of an award was more important than the money. For others, it was the reverse. Some didn't apply, regarding the process as too much hassle or the disappointment of not being awarded too dispiriting. A few financially comfortable consultants ignored the system, feeling they were well enough remunerated in the private sector, thus allowing other colleagues, in specialties with limited access to private income, a clear run. Each consultant had a different view so, sadly, these awards were the source of much rancour and discord, causing dissatisfaction between departments and discontent within departments.

A perfect instrument for divide and rule. Even management claimed to dislike the system, disingenuously implying that consultants were the only set of employees to be given bonuses. That year management had five per cent of their salary held back, though most went on to get this portion of their pay returned and many managers got a further pay uplift of two-and-a-half per cent. Surely this was a bonus? Not so, said HR, exhibiting their best efforts at sophistry. It was not a bonus, but an uplift.

However hard an award panel strived to be fair, it was an unenviable and near impossible task. How could one compare the role of an average consultant obstetrician, woken at night every week, paid next to nothing for doing stressful on-call work, with a consultant dermatologist, with no on call, no weekends away from home, no bank holidays spent in the hospital, but who advised the Government on the management of eczema? The latter invariably ticked the necessary boxes and was more likely to be awarded. Nearing the end of my five-year tenure as director of medical education, I'd received just one award, while both of my two predecessors had each received five. It was clear that I was either bad at the job or disliked, or possibly both. I suppose I didn't doff my cap to management as much as they would have liked. I suppose I should have allowed the robotic Midge to reclaim at least one room, and I suppose I shouldn't have identified all of the thirty-five typos in the Government propaganda.

Embarrassingly for me, and the trust, a member of staff on the awards panel was furious with the treatment I'd received. Unsolicited, he sought me out. "You must appeal.

It's ridiculous. Please, please appeal," he said. I declined, but he was persistent, trusting, too, perhaps even foolhardy. Management would never have forgiven him for this breach in confidentiality. I didn't want to hear this news.

It was upsetting and I found the whole process humiliating and distasteful. There would have been other consultants just as deserving, maybe more so, who'd been treated equally shabbily. However, having been cornered, I felt obliged to go ahead and lodge an appeal.

The trust used stalling tactics for months. Data was "unavailable" or "confidential". The more they obstructed, the more determined I became. The British Medical Association stepped in, supporting and encouraging me to persevere. I felt like Oliver Twist with his empty bowl, or a teenager asking for his exam results to be regraded because he'd had hay fever on the day of the exam. The appeals hearing convened and I was asked to attend. Pending the arrival of the chairman, we made small talk about the origins of our surnames. Any distraction was welcome. The paperwork was slid over the polished board table towards me and, for the first time, I saw how the panel had scored each of the successful applicants. The scores were anonymised, with Doctor A getting the top score and me, as Doctor F, coming sixth. The scores went all the way down to Doctor W, the twenty-third and last consultant, of the forty-two that applied, to be given an award. Doctors A, B, C, D, E, G and H had all been given three awards. Doctors I, J, K and T were each awarded two and the others, including yours truly, Doctor F, got a single award. I wondered what the letters stood for, maybe:

A for Agree with anything management want
B for Believe everything management say

C for Compliant with all that management request
D for Deferential to management
E for Employer's stooge
F for... well, you can work that one out.

It was clearly unreasonable and I should have felt elated at having exposed their unfairness and the power this gave to my appeal. But I didn't. I couldn't understand why I was being treated like this. Why did they hate me so much? Did management only want "yes men"? Did they not like constructive challenge? I didn't believe the scores should be followed slavishly. They were, after all, only a guide, but this looked bad. I started to feel sorry for the appeal panel members, paling at this indefensible victimisation. It wasn't the *appeal* panel's fault. It was clear that the *awards* panel had singled me out for special treatment. It went quieter than the grave. The odd high-pitched cough, eyes lifted ceilingward, a roll of a pencil, hair flicks, nose scratching. The British at their most unbearable.

I had to break the silence, so I asked the chairman of the trust, "What score would I have needed to obtain another award?"

Her answer surprised me. "You must realise Charles, that we need to encourage the younger consultants."

Suddenly I understood the treatment meted out to Admiral Byng *pour encourager les autres*, with apologies to Voltaire.[27] This tradition went way back. It wasn't funny. I shouldn't have laughed. But it was a nervous reaction to my first taste of ageism. If this was happening in my mid-forties, what would it be like in ten years' time?

We settled on a fudge, and I received a further award

27. *Explanation of the 1757 execution of Admiral Byng for not killing enough French at the battle of Minorca. From Candide by Voltaire.*

on the agreement that I would not appeal to the higher London board. There was no apology. Doctors and nurses were told repeatedly that they must apologise, and they did so frequently. I had no problems apologising, but management never apologised, whatever they had done. Never. Management regarded an apology as a sign of weakness, a chink in their armour. As H said afterwards, their mantra was "Never explain, never apologise". Award secured, point made, little gained, faith lost. I would have preferred an apology, and an explanation, to the damned award.

We needed to finish off the Corsican GR20. H and I were six years older and found it significantly tougher than before. Exhausted but mentally refreshed and back at work, more intense training was needed, as I'd decided to ski the Haute Route, from Chamonix to Zermatt. Planning to undertake this challenge and being by far the worst skier in the party, I needed to compensate by being super fit. I trained hard with the lyrics from Queen's "We Will Rock You".

Then one night I awoke with severe chest pain. I felt better on sitting up and H told me to get a glass of milk. I stumbled down the staircase, but on climbing back in to bed I couldn't bear the crushing pain any more and phoned the accident and emergency department. A consultant answered and, before I explained, she said: "Have you got chest pain?" By coincidence, the next morning I had an appointment with a senior manager about this very consultant. I wanted to warn the manager that he'd upset her with some unwise comments and that he should consider his next steps with care.

It was an uncomfortable drive in to work, hunched over the steering wheel. I struggled to reverse into a space. The pain was manageable but I felt giddy and sweaty as I told the manager how upset the consultant was. The manager was worried for a different reason. He was concerned that I looked like death. He knew it wasn't yet hospital policy to kill off consultants in managers' offices, and a dead doctor on the carpet would be bad form. Even if it was the notorious Doctor F.

Climbing the fifteen steps up from the management offices, I stopped twice to gather breath. One, two, three, four, stop. One, two, three, four, stop. I should have used the lift. They were waiting for me. Whisked into a cubicle, X-rays taken, electrocardiogram (ECG) of heart trace, venous blood tests, arterial stabs ... ouch!

This was role reversal in spades. I was only one cubicle away from the paediatric resuscitation area. The tables were well and truly turned. It was unnerving, being a patient in my own hospital. Everyone was professional, but understandably uncomfortable in having to treat me. The same female consultant came in to see me, calm and charming, and I was informed that I'd go to the cardiac care unit as my blood tests showed my blood oxygen level was worryingly low. Thirty seconds later the doors flew open and in crashed the crash team complete with crash trolley — a cupboard on wheels, packed with tubes, fluids, drills, drugs and masks for resuscitating the dead and the dying. I knew this meant that my chances of survival were now well under fifty per cent. Oh well, I'd faced death a couple of times before. So be it.

In the wake of the trolley was a pale-looking H, who had fed the dog, had her porridge, had her two cups of tea, one cup of coffee and driven to accident and emergency to see when I was going home. I raised my arms. "I'm fine," I said. Like most people who say this, I wasn't. But neither was I keen on anyone jumping on me, compressing my chest, and trying to intubate me. Unnoticed by all, as the emergency consultant had left my cubicle, her fulsome derrière had brushed against the emergency button and an automatic *Arrest* call had gone out across the hospital. Off I was trolleyed to the cardiac care unit (CCU) where, outnumbered, outpowered and defenceless, I became both a medical and social nuisance. The charge nurse was in a tizzy. He treated his charges like a mother duck treats her ducklings and wanted to protect me from predators. Visiting consultants — colleagues and friends, maybe some enemies — were clogging up his ward, rubbernecking, checking out the colour of my pyjamas, winking and making faces. No managers, though. Perhaps they were praying in the chapel of rest. As in Noah's Ark, visitors arrived in pairs. Two consultant oncologists brushed my feet aside, sat on the end of the bed, and had a blazing row. An orthopaedic consultant and his sidekick walked in, looked at each other, stared at me, said "This is ridiculous" and walked out. Two non-medical friends peered at me through the ward glass, like zoo visitors checking out the penguin compound. On seeing the machines and wires, they got cold feet and ran.

Two computerised tomograms of my heart and lungs, and many more tests were performed before the problem was identified. A couple of sizeable blood clots were partially blocking both of the major lung arteries coming out of my heart. This was serious, likely to be the end and probably also meant that I had a hidden cancer, making my platelets sticky and my blood thick, gooey and clot-friendly. Goodbye Doctor F, thank God that clot has gone. The medical team suggested thinning my blood with powerful drugs to stop the clots travelling deeper into my lungs and finishing me off. I said I'd take my chances, preferring that the clots moved and I died, rather than have a bleed into the brain and stroke out due to my colleagues' hospital treatment. Typical, bloody doctor.

I was bored lying there. It was disconcertingly similar to work — dull and frightening in equal measures. My heart was ticking along nicely at around sixty beats a minute, wired up so that alarms would go off in the nurses' observation station if the rate fell below fifty or went over 110. I wondered. No, I mustn't. I knew I shouldn't. Custer's last stand? It was a unique and probably final opportunity and it was dreary being stuck in bed. One eye on the monitor and the other on the nurses' station. Bugger. Heart rate going up way too fast. Stop!

Next morning Theo, the radiologist, came and reassured me that he would find whatever there was hiding within my body. He'd been spot on with Carol, my first patient, fifteen years earlier and I felt safe in his hands.[28] He scanned my legs for clots. None. He scanned my abdomen for cancer. None. He reviewed the films of my lungs and heart. No sign of cancer. Cancer could not be found. How irritating. A ventilation perfusion scan was ordered, a CT scan of my lungs after breathing radioactive krypton gas and being injected with radioactive-labelled albumin. To give them credit, they were hunting hard. Still bloody normal. No clots had embolised.

Nothing had broken off and spread into the depth of the blood vessels within the periphery of my respiratory tree. The consultants were perplexed. It didn't make sense. Doctor F was continuing to be effing irritating. Barking was now in overall charge and in a good mood. I was relieved that I'd almost been forgiven for fiddling with his doctors' rotation. Or was he basking in my demise?

_____

28. *Page 226.*

"Charles, what do you think you've got then?" he barked.

"That's a good question. Well, the pain is much better on sitting up, so I'd guess it could be pericarditis?" I whimpered back. Even though the tests showed clots, I wondered whether I had this alternative diagnosis, an inflammation of the heart. Barking agreed, despite the tests showing something different. Clots! As if!

It turned out Doctor F was a time waster, a bloody nuisance, a bed blocker, clogging up CCU. What a ludicrous diagnosis, clots in his arteries with no clots in the veins, cancer, but none to find, what the hell! I took a deep breath, not too painful, for my last chance of a roll of the die and said, "I'm often perplexed by difficult patients. Perhaps we should consider sending my films to London? I find that sometimes helps." Barking grunted in agreement. The images of my heart and lungs were dispatched and a different diagnosis returned. London confirmed that there weren't any clots but that the compression of my lung arteries was from the *outside*, from enlarged lymph nodes, not from within the arteries.

So, what was the final diagnosis and the cause of my admission? After some deliberation Barking and I agreed that as a result of an unidentified viral infection, my heart had become inflamed and the resulting swollen nodes had compressed the arteries within my lungs. The cardiologist disagreed, but what the heck? We'd never reach a consensus and both Barking and I had had enough, and it was as good a diagnosis as any.

Good news indeed, but I'd now been in cardiac care for four days and was getting increasingly worried. Bowels. They'd always been a priority, right across the family throughout my upbringing. Regularity was sacrosanct, privacy inviolable. Where and when I went was ritualised. It mattered. A lot. I knew that my bowels would have to start soon and I wasn't going to crouch over a standard-issue grey cardboard bedpan or be lifted onto a commode. Not at any price.

Theo had scanned my whole body, assiduously hunting the elusive cancer, and he knew more than I could possibly know.

"Theo, when will I do a poo?" I asked.

"Definitely not today, probably tomorrow afternoon, maybe around a quarter to four," he replied.

Right. Before my self-discharge, I had to self-discharge, at the very latest the following lunchtime. I was not sitting on a bedpan in my own hospital. My colleagues had had enough time exploring my body.

I was going home to take my chances.

30

JONNO

On return to the hospital from sick leave, the atmosphere was poisonous. Management was running riot. The purchase of charity-funded cooling equipment for sick babies was being challenged. Worse, a consultant friend had been suspended under adult safeguarding regulations for holding the arm of an elderly patient "too forcefully" while taking blood. The trust now classified such suspension as a "neutral act". What? I'm sure his consequential distress and public humiliation didn't feel neutral, more like abandonment. The know-nothings had taken over the asylum. I was not immune. Not everyone was pleased to see my recovery. Paediatric job planning was being undertaken in an incompetent, hostile, confrontational and counterproductive manner. I wrote to HR identifying reasons why I felt it was being handled badly and the negative effect this was having upon me personally. This resulted in the common trust sanction of my being sent off for an outpatient psychiatric assessment. I kid you not. Like something out of *Catch-22*. Was I perceived as another

Yossarian? Given all the legal fears and risk, any consultant working on call in paediatrics must be crazy. But seeing a psychiatrist proved you were sane. Any sane person would raise concerns, wouldn't they?

I wasn't the first of my consultant colleagues to be shipped off for such an assessment, but I was still rather surprised, maybe even disappointed, that nothing abnormal was found. The psychiatrist's report stated:

> 'Behaviour is professional, eye contact is good, mood appropriate and cognitive function is normal. Insight and judgement are intact. There is no abnormality of thought or perception.'

Surely I wasn't *normal*? But I was and that was the catch-22. This worrying diagnosis gave the trust free rein to twist the knife in further. As my time as director of medical education headed to its natural conclusion, Beyoncé released "Irreplaceable" and I received a letter informing me that I would not be allowed to return to work as a full-time paediatrician. Shocked, but not surprised, I had forecast that the dark side would bide their time. I had expected management to be a little more subtle and intelligent. Maybe even to talk to me. It was tough enough rebooting my paediatric clinical skills, without this unwelcome and unreasonable interference. For some time our work had resembled a game of chess, clinicians versus management, and my pieces were getting hemmed in by some aggressive play.

Although I felt physically weak still, my memory remained sharp and I could recall accepting the educational role, in the full prior agreement, that when my tenure as director of medical education ended, I could return to my previous full-time paediatric consultant job. But Midge wouldn't budge.

Maybe it wasn't personal. Most unpleasantness wasn't, even if it felt so. Perhaps it was just another clumsy opportunity for the trust to save money. By returning me to a seven-tenths consultant contract, the trust could save around £30,000 each year. Enough to fund the annual management uplifts, or put air conditioning in their offices. But it seemed downright wrong and I wasn't going to accept it.

Midge didn't like to be challenged by anyone. It was just this kind of management hubris that would later be identified as an issue in the Mid Staffs hospital enquiry.

Anyway, Midge had picked the wrong adversary. I asked for advice from Jim, the previous chief executive, who wrote, correcting "the misunderstanding" and made it clear that there was no option but to reinstate me in my full-time role. Grudgingly, Midge folded. He had no choice. A week later, at the local negotiating committee, the two of us avoided eye contact. Then, reviewing the trust's finances, Midge cleared his throat and said: "Let me make it clear. I will balance the books, whatever it takes." Money ruled now. I feared Midge's grip was too tight, to the detriment of our health care. Hospitals didn't need tin-pot dictators. Care had become of secondary importance to finance, not a healthy situation for a hospital and its patients. In my five years in the educational role, I'd become a significant irritant to him. Nobody was irreplaceable and, moreover, there was a strong replacement on hand in the form of my deputy. With support from a consultant colleague with balls, I left the post in education, the clouds parted and all obstacles disappeared. Why all the fuss?

Mr Blair, meanwhile, had been replaced by Gordon Brown. The new Health Secretary Alan Johnson introduced a new policy, *Bare below the elbows*. Johnson was all for germ-free forearms.

"This is a clear signal to patients that doctors, nurses and other clinic staff are taking their safety seriously," he said.

I hadn't appreciated we hadn't been doing that.

Johnson's diktat was a godsend to me, as I never wore a jacket and disliked ties, but I also had a reason to break this latest commandment. I was suffering from excruciating burning pain down my right arm, the consequences of a damaged neck suffered twenty years earlier on the ski slopes. I'd tried painkillers and nerve-numbing antiepileptics, all to no avail. It felt as if a cigarette was being stubbed out on my skin and I was struggling to focus. In desperation, I borrowed a TENS machine, strapped the unit to my waist, and stuck the electrodes to my forearm. TENS stands for transcutaneous electrical nerve stimulation. It works by causing a distraction, diverting the pain from its troubling source to an easy-to-identify area, where the electrical shock discharges. It's a bit like hitting your head against the wall to cancel out the pain in your big toe. By turning the knob to maximum power, I found the shocks, though unpleasant, did offer some relief. I didn't want to scare the children, so ignored the Johnson edict and examined the patients with shirt sleeves down, while every two seconds a sharp jolt fired through my arm.

The new guidance meant that all hospitals had to adopt a new dress code of short sleeves, no watches, and no jewellery — apart from a simple wedding ring. White coats were banned. The consultant staff committee took a dim view, especially the surgeons who were wedded to sharp suits and stiff collars and regarded this a politically motivated manoeuvre to undermine their gravitas with the patients. Doctors didn't like the Government telling them how to dress. One colleague queried whether bare midriffs should be allowed, another if pierced belly buttons would be tolerated, while a third asked how much leg the juniors were allowed to show. The Government said the policy would slash hospital infection rates and gave all trusts three months' notice to remove their consultants' jackets.

Political disquiet then arose about the thorny issue of patients obtaining treatment privately, while also being treated by the NHS. Discussions, discussions, discussions, no solutions. Johnson recognised the rockiness of the private/public marriage, arguing that private treatment undermined the very principles of the NHS.

Then Lehman Brothers went bust and world markets dived. A short while after the collapse, the Government honours system and the unsuitability of recent recipients became a hot topic. I knew someone who deserved recognition so I began exploring the nominations procedures. I wanted to put forward an internationally renowned paediatric cardiologist for a gong. Here was someone who hadn't feathered his own nest but who had made a real difference in the world. A trip to London confirmed that his colleagues agreed in principle and wished me well, so long as I did all the leg work. They warned me that the Government was unlikely to give recognition to any doctor for brilliance alone. It would help overcome the Government's natural distrust of medicine if the doctor in the spotlight had done something for the politicians, rather than for the patients. For national recognition, patient care came well down the list of priorities. Eighty national experts from around the world wrote supporting my application. Letters from Toronto, Ireland, Brisbane, Denmark, Sydney, Greece and Malta. Letters flooded in from parents, patients, relatives, nurses, physiotherapists, pharmacists, ward clerks and doctors. After thirty years as a consultant and over forty years of service, exclusively within the NHS, it was clear this man was a legend.

Parents wrote describing him as the kindest doctor they had ever met, repeatedly describing him as an unsung hero. Parents who had lost their children to heart disease wrote, saying how they treasured his care and had kept his letters of condolence.

He was widely described as self-effacing, shy of personal limelight, with a stellar career marked by generosity, showing profound compassion and kindness, a clinical pioneer, inspiring and authoritative. When our member of parliament wrote in support of my application, I started to feel optimistic.

He was even referred to as someone akin to the doctor described by Hippocrates 2,500 years ago. His approach to work was compared to that of President Theodore Roosevelt when he declared: "Do what you can, with what you have, where you are". Another consultant wrote: "If a poll was taken today on the person who has contributed the most to paediatric cardiology in the NHS, he would lead by a very large margin".

Glowing testimonials don't glow much more than these. With the political support I had, I was sure he would get the recognition he deserved and my hopes soared further as I saw his name listed among the official nominees. In fact, he was so good, it seems, that his name was listed twice. But I should have listened to the professor who had cautioned me, saying, "Charles, I agree with your effort totally, but sadly you and he have no chance." I noticed that the two individuals with identical names to my applicant were not doctors. One was a school-crossing lollipop man and the other worked in a museum. It was a common name. Both may have been worthy of a national award, but neither worked in medicine. As the cardiologist's colleagues had predicted, the application failed. Such is the British honours system.

Gordon Brown appointed Andy Burnham to replace Alan Johnson as the new Health Secretary and a month after starting, Burnham launched an enquiry into the high death rates at Mid Staffs. To cap that, quite separately, Lord Darzi published another *Ten Year Plan*. Then something unexpected happened. Panic set in as the Government and a significant number of clinicians began to show concern that a pandemic was just around the corner. Inevitably a pandemic would emerge again in the world at some time. But it needn't be catastrophic, decimating populations. The problem was that people cried wolf so often.

We were told that swine flu was on the way, and this would be really bad. *Really bad* was an annual event in the NHS. Every winter the pressure on the wards became really bad. Cynically, I suspected that with the NHS stretched taut, any extra work might bring the system crashing down. Politically, that too would be *really bad*.

It didn't help that the 390,000 beds allocated to the NHS in 1948 had dwindled to half that figure. The slack had gone. Endless cries of impending disaster had diluted our concerns, but the panic this time was of a different order. In the doom-mongers defence, this was only the second recorded outbreak of the H1N1 virus and the first one had killed between fifty and one hundred million people worldwide. Estimates varied. That pandemic came in three waves in 1918/19, targeting toddlers, young adults and the elderly. Most of those infected in the first wave were protected from the ravaging second and third waves. The first outbreak, inappropriately labelled "Spanish flu", originated elsewhere, maybe in the US or China. The epithet

Spanish was inaccurate as during and just after WWI, most newspapers in Europe were censored of alarming news to keep up morale. Neutral Spain was the only country accurately reporting the pandemic, hence it became the Spanish flu that infected a quarter of the world's population, killing ten per cent of those with the virus. When the new variant of swine flu broke out, each hospital doctor in the UK had to be fitted with a snuggly fitting individualised facemask. We were told to be prepared for hundreds of thousands of deaths and warned that there would be so many sick children, that paediatricians were only going to look after those aged under five. As a respiratory man, I didn't believe a word of this. The scientific data didn't support such an impending catastrophe, but I hoped it would be good practice for when something more significant did finally happen. It wasn't, and little was learnt.

A consultant geriatrician approached me, terrified. He believed the Government stance and wanted tutorials on how to look after sick children. Specialising in patients in their eighties, he admitted to knowing little about managing sick children. I told him not to worry and to go to the golf driving range instead, reassuring him that, however busy we were, we would not be sending him any children. All of a sudden, any child admitted with a temperature triggered the response: "This is swine flu" or "This may be swine flu". As a result, hundreds of thousands of patients in the UK received ineffective medication, and few clinicians dared challenge the treatment.

The prescribed drug resulted in significant financial reward for some, but was of insignificant benefit for most. Psychologically it may have assisted, but minimally on a biological level. In the United Kingdom, on an average day, 1,500 people die. Yet, fewer than 500 people died in total in the UK from this outbreak of swine flu. Five times that number died in car accidents that year. Over £1bn was spent in response to the outbreak.

*

A week of on call was fast approaching which meant endless debates about swine flu. A group of us managed the hysteria by marking the back of our name badges with a little blue dot. A childish, anarchic, anti-establishment clique was born. The dot was barely noticeable, and was never picked up by management, but we knew the meaning. It was the mark of silent disbelievers. It helped us cope.

Stephen, an eight-year-old boy, was admitted with pneumonia. An ultrasound confirmed a collection of pus around his lung. Stephen needed transferring to a major hospital for surgery to drain this pus. Previously, this would have been done locally and Theo, the radiologist, would have managed the procedure with no difficulties. But times had changed. The London team arrived. They looked at Stephen. They looked at his blood tests. They looked at his X-rays. They frowned. They looked at me. It was clear to me that Stephen had a bog standard, probably pneumococcal, pneumonia with an empyema, pus around his lung. I had seen and treated dozens of these over the years and the vast majority were easy to manage and nearly all made an excellent and full recovery. The London retrieval registrar, with twenty years less experience than me, said, "Clear the six-bay ward. Full protective measures, this is a classic case of swine flu."

I couldn't believe it. Where was the *classic* bit? I'd seen fifty or more similar paediatric cases and none had a diagnosis of swine flu. As Stephen's parents paled, the nurses glanced over their shoulders, giving me dirty looks.

My credibility as a respiratory paediatrician was in tatters and I wondered if anyone would spot my blue dot. I accepted that this would result in the case being referred to a serious untoward incident review and my having to attend a panel to explain my incompetence. I hoped that those chosen to analyse my care would have some understanding about childhood respiratory diseases. I'd probably have to be retrained or re-educated, more like, as happens to dissenters in China. It was going to be humiliating. Too late, I wished I'd been a yes-man. Much easier and less dangerous when mistakes are made.

Personal protective equipment (PPE) was donned. The ward was emptied. The whole atmosphere spelled *drama*. Cue a gowned and masked George Clooney. Shunned, I sat alone in the nursing office, cradling a cold comfort coffee. Stephen was wheeled out in full protective measures and transported to London, flashing blue lights, hazmat suits, maybe a Dalek or two for good measure. Once there, the ambulance would be put out of service, just as our ward was, while every surface and piece of equipment was sterilised.

On his return, seventy-two hours later, I noticed that Stephen's swine flu tests were negative. This was, after all, just a classic case of a pneumonia and empyema. Decades of paediatric experience had taught me what humble pie tasted like. Have a slice of that, Mr London registrar.

Forty-eight hours later I'd almost forgotten Stephen; I'd blocked him out. My attention was focused on another teenage boy, Jonno, recently back from South Africa, who also had a tricky pneumonia. I still wasn't prepared to allow swine flu into the differential diagnosis. A few eyebrows were raised when I said I had no concerns that Jonno had the trendy condition of H1N1.

Jonno was fourteen and had returned to the UK from Cape Town a month earlier.

He'd already visited two other hospitals in England and had been treated twice for pneumonia, with oral antibiotics. On examination, Jonno was breathing fast, with right-sided chest pain, a grotty looking chest X-ray and with blood tests that supported a serious infection. Jonno was unwell, but not as sick as Stephen. Without being blasé, this was a pretty standard situation for me and I didn't think Jonno warranted intensive care or transfer to a tertiary hospital.

However, his story was far from standard. Jonno told me he thought that he might have inhaled something. In South Africa, using his blue asthma inhaler, Jonno said he'd felt something hit the back of his throat, he had choked, lost his breath, coughed violently for five minutes and a week later had become unwell. I suspected a foreign body was to blame.

Foreign bodies in babies tend to be inhaled peanuts or bits of apple and can be fatal, though most babies make a rapid recovery. Older children can choke on lumps of meat or biro tops. So many children choked on Bic plastic tops in the early days of pen manufacture, that the pen makers put holes in the tops so that children could still breath, should they inhale one. An international safety standard was generated to protect children up to the age of fourteen.[29] That said, inhaling pen tops still causes over one hundred deaths a year in the US, but before this minor alteration in design, it used to be many more. Foreign bodies left in the lung can cause later tissue damage, with recurrent infections in the area that can't clear properly, resulting in lifelong lung scarring. The affected part of the

---

29. *ISO11540.*

lung can then become dilated and ineffective, unable to absorb oxygen and dispose of carbon dioxide. If the story is suggestive of a foreign body inhalation, it's good practice to look down into the lung to see if there is anything that needs fishing out. The chest X-ray is usually unhelpful and often normal.

Jonno's X-ray confirmed a pneumonia, but didn't show any evidence of a foreign body. But it's often possible to learn more from the patient's history. I asked Jonno to repeat his story. It was impressive and consistent. Even if I'd become deaf to management, I'd learnt to listen to the patients. Jonno was anaesthetised. Barking inserted a tube into his main airway and then, where the airway divided, slid it further down, deep into his right main bronchus. There, nestling in the recesses of Jonno's lung, was a Chappies fruit sweet wrapper.

Jonno went home twenty-four hours later. As he walked off the ward I asked him why he hadn't told the other doctors his story.

"I did," he said, "They just didn't listen to me."

31

THE GOOD, THE BAD AND THE UGLY

It was satisfying that the system of COW was established and safer for the patients.

But there were downsides and chief among them was the need for "acting down". The practice of acting down involves a senior colleague covering for an absent junior post. So you're going back to a job you used to do — that of a registrar if you're a consultant. This was due to many causes: the introduction of COW, which included a shift working as a registrar; difficulty in filling junior doctors' posts; consultants' increased visibility and therefore perceived availability on the wards; and the consequences of reduced working hours under the European Working Time Directive. Acceptance of the directive and a closely marshalled working hours culture changed the mindset of many a junior doctor. Why should they do extras? Why indeed? Ten years previously a registrar would never have dreamt of asking a consultant to act down. But this was today and things had changed. No one was listening to the senior consultant muttering "Not in my day." My loathing of the evening four-hour stretch, of working once more as a registrar, was made worse by my having no one else to blame. There was the occasional oddball pretending to enjoy the experience, but they were the vocal minority. I understood that getting one's hands dirty could be exciting and satisfying, but I struggled to do that and simultaneously to be in overall command. It wasn't the equivalent of being too posh to push, more a case of an essential requirement to remain alert to whatever minefields lay ahead.

By this stage of my career, the making of diagnoses and decisions on management plans had become semi-automatic. Fruitless searching in drawers for clerking paper and the taking of a full history and examination of a child with a heavy cold were skill sets I'd left behind. Maybe it shouldn't have done, but it grated. As a junior doctor, this had been my bread and butter, but those days had long since gone, together with my night-time bladder control and hearing.

The week kicked off with the normal eighty-hour weekend stint, in charge of the babies and children on the children's ward, the neonatal ward, in accident and emergency, on the postnatal wards, on the labour ward, and anywhere else where a child might stray. I was tetchy. In truth, I would start every week in charge worried about what lay ahead. This week I began in a darker mood than normal. On my previous on-call night I had been woken from a deep sleep by a concerned grandfather about a child in Dorset with a high temperature. It didn't seem to trouble him, or the hospital switchboard, that I had no connection with his family or his health district and was tucked up in bed more than one hundred miles away.

Friday, the first day of COW, was a critically important day. If Friday went well, the week would usually go well too. If problems arose at the start of the week, then it would be tough to get to the end. That seemed to be the pattern. Tricky clinical cases were part of the package, troublesome parents likewise. But when issues with management cropped up, it invariably became unpleasant. A frequent problem was persuading tertiary hospitals — those that provide highly specialised equipment and expertise beyond that of a district general hospital — to accept the transfer of a sick child to their unit. Attitudes between hospitals and even between departments within the same hospital varied enormously. I suspected that this was a reflection of the style of leadership in each different location and specialty. It wasn't supposed to be like this, hospital pitted against hospital, department against department. Where was our joined-up health service, our Emerald City? Somewhere over the rainbow?

Five weeks earlier, during my last COW, Phoebe had been the biggest challenge. Phoebe suffered from Lennox-Gastaut syndrome. After her fifth birthday she'd started to have seizures and her development had regressed so that she was losing skills she'd previously gained. Now aged ten, Phoebe was averaging over thirty fits a day. Phoebe was on a cocktail of five different anticonvulsant medications and her care was beyond my expertise. I struggled to spell some of these drugs, let alone know how they worked. Her tertiary hospital had, unsurprisingly, again been unable to find Phoebe a bed and we were left to sort the mess. Flying without a pilot's licence. A second child was now fitting on the ward. Complicated neurology, like metabolic conditions, was a weak area of mine. Jasper was nine-months-old and seriously ill, with a stiff neck and high temperature.

Jasper's sodium was dangerously low and he'd already had a couple of short, focal, right-sided fits. The diagnosis of meningitis and the need to prescribe antibiotics was not in doubt. But many urgent clinical decisions remained to be made, including the possible need for an immediate brain scan, an electroencephalogram (EEG) — to measure his brain electrical activity, anticonvulsants, endotracheal ventilation — for the building pressure in his head, steroids — to diminish the likelihood of future hearing loss, fluid restriction — for his possible inappropriate anti-diuretic hormone production, antiviral medication to add to his antibiotics, and a lumbar puncture — or was he too unwell and that procedure unsafe? And, finally, the question of whether he should be transferred to a tertiary hospital when the tertiary hospital was already pushing back. These ten critical areas needed to be resolved within the "golden hour", or in reality, in the most important first fifteen minutes of Jasper entering our care. What could we tell his parents? Fortunately I wasn't acting down so I didn't have to add to the already long and complex list, these five administrative queries: where was the note paper? Who had hidden the ophthalmoscope? Where were the spare blood forms kept? Which colour bottle did we send to the laboratory for kidney function tests? And where was the nearest parent toilet? A wrong decision in the crucial first few minutes of diagnosing and planning was often hard to reverse and might have serious repercussions for Jasper, his family and, later for us.

Jasper's sodium level was probably the most difficult to resolve. It was most likely that his blood was diluted as a result of his body producing an inappropriate excess of the hormone that usually, and appropriately, cuts off urine production when water is scarce. On the other hand, it was also possible that Jasper had excreted and lost too much sodium via his kidneys.

Kidneys naturally allow some sodium to leave the body but if they are diseased, more can be lost. This was another possible cause for Jasper's condition. It was probable that Jasper had bacterial meningitis and likely that he would be left with significant, disabling and lifelong consequences. So it was critical to decide which was the correct treatment, as the approach for these two contrasting sodium scenarios differed markedly. Being *almost* certain about what to do was fine when it worked out, but indefensible when it didn't.

It's not to dramatize to say that getting the treatment right was a matter of life and death. What Sir Alex Ferguson called "squeaky bum time", when manager of Manchester United, is a constant companion when making clinical diagnoses. It mattered most for the patient, of course, but in an increasingly litigious society, it mattered also to us. Reputations were at stake, millions of pounds were at stake.

Indeed, cumulatively, we're looking at billions of pounds, all of which have an impact on NHS service delivery.[30] Litigation is a modern sword of Damocles that can hang over a single clinical decision for decades. The UK legislation regarding medical malpractice states that mothers have three years from delivery, or from when they become aware of their injuries, in which to make a claim. Children are given an eighteen-year starting window, followed by these three years. Twenty-one years in total, therefore, to submit any medical negligence claim concerning possible errors in their care *in utero*, during delivery, or afterwards.

It was probable that at some stage in the next twenty-

---

30. *In 2021 The Academy of Medical Royal Colleges, The Hospital Consultants and Specialists Association, and the Medical Defence Union called for reform of the clinical negligence system in England, describing the £84bn estimated bill for outstanding claims as unsustainable.*

one years a lawyer would be poring over Jasper's case notes, dissecting my decisions, looking for some flaw in his care. I hoped my wheelchair and catheter bag would fit in the dock. Inappropriate management of sodium levels was one of those dream causes for the hospital litigators, and a nightmare for clinicians. The handling of a high sodium, due to a lack of water, was even more problematical than that of treating for a low sodium, as in Jasper's case. The temptation to reduce a high sodium level too quickly had to be resisted. To help protect us from this error, dilute intravenous fluids had been banned from the children's ward. But clinical need, not fear of legal action, should underpin such decisions. With experience, it became increasingly clear that in most corrections of abnormal levels of sodium, sugar or acid, a softly-softly, slowly-slowly approach was best. What would I be doing, when or if Jasper reached the age of twenty-one?

Would I remember the case? Would I remember what normal clinical care had been so long ago? Would I still be alive?

Jasper's sickness kept the meddling managers away. I knew they would bide their time. There was currently an uneasy truce, like that between Blondie and Tuco in Sergio Leone's 1966 classic film, *The Good, the Bad and the Ugly*. Both sides needed each other, neither side trusted the other. During that week of COW, we came across all three of Leone's characters.

The Good

Leah, a four-week-old girl was admitted to the children's ward unsettled and unwell. Leah's mother was worried as her daughter had been irritable for a couple of days. Leah had a high temperature and a fine rash, but apart from being well and truly miserable, her examination was otherwise unremarkable. I didn't think she had measles or meningitis, but we had to check. A needle was inserted between two lower back vertebrae and gin-clear fluid dripped out. Analysis was normal and the fluid bathing Leah's spinal cord had no significant cells, nor later growth of any bugs. Her urine, chest X-ray and blood tests were unhelpful. There were no other findings. Leah was just so miserable. It entered my mind that she might have been abused and either have a hidden bleed on her brain, or a fractured bone that we had missed. There was no evidence of either. But I knew we were missing something. Despite having no diagnosis, with nothing growing from any sample we'd collected, I worried we would regret inaction later so took the unusual step of starting her on a course of powerful antibiotics. But what was I treating? I didn't know. If the antibiotics hid an undiagnosed but important diagnosis such as osteomyelitis, so be it. I couldn't hold off treatment any longer.

Twenty-four hours later there was still no improvement in Leah's condition. She was exhausting herself, crying, desperately trying to tell us something. Leah's cultures remained negative and further tests, including echo-cardiography of her heart and ultrasound of her abdomen, were normal. I wished Leah had been a few months older and had a few lymph nodes in her neck and conjunctivitis as then she could have been treated for Kawasaki disease. But she didn't and she wasn't.

Regrettably there is no single test to confirm Kawasaki disease, a condition first described in 1961, by Dr Tomisaku Kawasaki when writing up a child's clinical notes. Unable to make a diagnosis, Kawasaki labelled the new condition as "God only knows". Still with no known cause, it is characterised by an inflammation of blood vessels, and diagnosed by a collection of symptoms and signs. Early treatment of Kawasaki with intravenous immunoglobulin and high dose aspirin has been shown to result in a reduction in the likelihood of dilation of the coronary arteries, the vessels that feed blood and oxygen to the heart muscle. I was aware of the professional pitfalls of this condition. Tareq, a friend in London, had been sacrificed by a senior colleague for not treating a case in a one-year-old boy. On the ward Tareq had suggested Kawasaki disease as a possible diagnosis. His consultant had said "no need to treat". Six weeks later, in outpatients, Tareq had requested an ultrasound of the boy's heart, which had shown dilated coronary arteries, confirming the diagnosis. Later still, in court, Tareq was fed to the wolves.

I remained worried about Leah. She'd now been in hospital for forty-eight hours, had been raising a temperature for nearly four days and, despite antibiotics, was not improving. Although she didn't satisfy the criteria, I decided to share my discomfort and phoned the experts in London. They informed me that "This is not a case of Kawasaki and you should not treat". I had to agree. This was reasonable advice, as treatment is not without its own dangers. Both immunoglobulin and high dose aspirin can cause harm.

A week later Leah seemed fine and everyone was happy. Bar me. I was worried we had missed something. Following Tareq's lead, I ordered a repeat echocardiogram of Leah's heart. This showed significant dilatation of both of her coronary arteries, confirming Kawasaki disease as the diagnosis. Leah was at risk of a heart attack and would need years, maybe a lifetime, of blood-thinning treatment and possible later cardiac surgery. Despite knowing the full story, Leah's mother was delighted with her daughter's care and full of praise. I wasn't, because mine was the name at the end of the bed. I was depressed and felt that I had let Leah down. I wondered what errant thought process had led to Leah being saddled with these complications and trawled through the common patterns when medical mistakes are made.

Had I made an *anchoring heuristic*? This refers to hubris in a clinician who just will not change their mind, even though contrary information later becomes available. Brigitte Bardot and the English economist John Maynard Keynes were united in their understanding of the pitfalls in such stubbornness. "Only idiots refuse to change their minds", said Bardot, while Keynes is often quoted as saying: "When facts change, I change my mind. What do you do, sir?"

Or was the error an *availability heuristic*, when the recollection of a similar case means the diagnosis is accepted without thorough challenge? Both of these are natural human faults, but even in this analysis, Leah wasn't that simple, and neither applied. There may appear little *good* about this case, but Leah's mother showed extraordinary understanding and compassion, knowing we'd tried our best.

As often happened, "The Bad" followed, too soon after "The Good", but not before a chance for me to respond to my Aconcagua good luck present, the house brick. I printed headed notepaper from the National Institute for Clinical Excellence (NICE), and acquired a specimen semen sample pot. A pre-franked stamp steamed off nicely. Job done, package addressed, then hand delivered to Terry's house early in the morning.

Dear Sir, please do not worry. Due to a few unexpected pregnancies in your location we have been carrying out free quality checks on semen samples. If you would like confirmation that your sterilisation was a success, please produce a sample of sperm and send it back to us at The National Institute for Clinical Excellence in the enclosed receptacle. We will be in contact with the results within a week of receiving your sample.

Terry already had at least three children and didn't want any more. Flicking through his green and gold diary he realised he might have dozens. Moving to the map of the world, pasted onto his bedroom wall, he noted, with delayed alarm, how many different countries he'd inked in. Shuffling to his bedroom, the doorbell rang. Red faced, he zipped up his flies and opened the door, to be greeted by an Aussie friend. "Look at this, mate, this is bad news, mate. I can't afford any more."

The Bad

Only two days after "The Good". For reasons that befuddled many paediatricians, we were significantly better than most surgeons at diagnosing acute appendicitis in children. This mattered, as healthy children were being kept in hospital unnecessarily, pointlessly observed for days on end, with ultrasounds contributing little or nothing to their care, only deferring decision-making and their discharge home. Of more concern were the children where we diagnosed appendicitis but where the surgeons disagreed. I never saw a case where the surgeons diagnosed acute appendicitis correctly, where we disagreed.

Beep, beep, beep. Beep, beep, beep. Aaaaaaaaaaah. Not too bad. I recognised that number. The paediatric registrar answered my call. At least I would be able to have a professional discussion with her and not a panicky blind race into the hospital.

"Please can you help me with a difference of opinion on a diagnosis of a twelve-year-old girl with abdominal pain?" she said.

The registrar continued by explaining that she suspected acute appendicitis, but that the *male* surgical registrar disagreed. I drove in, fearing a battle of the sexes, but hoping to sort the problem, one way or another, without too much collateral damage.

Chloe, a previously healthy girl, was on the bed, not moving an inch. She was slightly pale, had a fast heartbeat, normal temperature, but her blood inflammatory markers were significantly raised. Distracting Chloe, I pressed on her abdomen, and she flinched. It was clear that Chloe had abdominal sepsis. Somewhere. There was no longer any need to do the old-fashioned rectal examination. Acute appendicitis was by far the most likely diagnosis, but a twisted ovary was also possible. Although there is usually one ovary on each side, the pain nearly always localises in the right lower quadrant, similar to most cases of acute appendicitis. Differentiating between the two conditions in girls is fraught with difficulties. But in a way, it makes little difference. Both conditions can result in reduced fertility, though ovarian pathology is more urgent.

Straining to make my handwriting legible, I recorded the reasons why I was confident that this was indeed an acute appendicitis. Chloe's parents seemed relieved, but confused. Why the debate, they wondered, when the diagnosis is so obvious?

Ninety minutes later, examination, notes and discussions with parents completed, I called the consultant surgeon, expecting Chloe would be prepared for theatre.

Mr Reeves, the consultant surgeon, arrived. No acknowledgement, hand on Chloe's abdomen, scanned the notes, wrote something, said nothing and walked out.

Intrigued, and concerned about his lack of manners, I found the notes trolley to discover his wise verdict and reasoning. Below my page of considerations and the reasons for my conclusion, Mr Reeves had written, "There are no signs at all of acute appendicitis." Arrogant bastard. My opinion had been dismissed without discussion or explanation. The nurses agreed to ignore the surgeon's opinion and prepared Chloe for theatre the next morning. Chloe's parents were now grey with worry and any residual confidence in our clinical care of their daughter was ebbing fast. Part of me hoped I was wrong. It would have been better for Chloe and a useful learning experience for me. In the meantime, I asked the opinion of a different surgeon.

Next morning, before the handover, I popped into the ward to see what had happened and was surprised to see Chloe sitting up, complaining she hadn't been allowed any breakfast. My confidence drained. I had been wrong. Chloe's symptoms had disappeared and she no longer had any pain or clinical signs. I had overreacted and made a mistake. There were no signs of sepsis. I was unaware that the second surgeon had already carefully reviewed Chloe, concurred with my earlier findings, and was about to take Chloe to theatre. There, he discovered a ruptured appendix with widespread inflammation of her insides. Chloe had only appeared so much better in the morning because her swollen pus-filled appendix had burst in the night. The cavalier and arrogant treatment doled out to Chloe had been shameful. Livid, I prayed she wouldn't develop fibrous bands and lose her fertility. I wrote the only letter of disquiet about a colleague's clinical practice in over twenty years as a consultant. Three carefully constructed pages sent to the surgeon concerned, listing my reservations about his attitude, clinical decision-making skills and, in particular, his lack of communication. I never received a reply. QED.

In spite of my frustration with Chloe's treatment, I was feeling chipper as Jasper had made a good recovery from his meningitis and low sodium. Then I was asked to see an agitated parent, the mother of a child called Claire, who had cystic fibrosis. Claire's parents wanted to have a second child and had requested an NHS pre-implantation diagnosis (PID), so they could be certain that their second child wouldn't also be born with cystic fibrosis. Prior to the introduction of this test, there would have been an unavoidable one-in-four chance that any further child of theirs would have the condition. This is halfway between the chances of calling heads correctly on the toss of a coin, and scoring a one on the roll of a die.

The odds of having an affected child don't change according to the outcome of previous pregnancies. One in four newborns will have the diagnosis and one in two will be carriers of cystic fibrosis. For the vast majority, being a carrier doesn't matter. One in twenty of us are carriers of the faulty gene, but it's only a concern if, in later life, a carrier has a child with another carrier, when a quarter of their children will have cystic fibrosis. As Chloe's parents already had one child, they had been informed that neither a PID nor IVF would be funded on the NHS, so they could take their chances or pay. I disagreed with this policy, for both moral and economic reasons. I believed it would be better for the mother, the family, the child and also the NHS and the country as a whole to pay a little to remove this risk. Without doing so, should their next child also have cystic fibrosis, its lifetime care would cost the NHS about

£250,000. I agreed to take up the fight. With perseverance, her parents got their wish. The NHS paid for the PID and the IVF, and they had a healthy second child.

The Ugly

Thursday afternoon, 4 p.m., the handover of my residual patients just sixty minutes away, when Tim, a six-month-old baby boy, arrived in accident and emergency with a broken arm and no explanation as to the possible cause. A skeletal survey confirmed three old healing rib fractures beyond the broken arm. Immediate suspicions. Tim had normal-shaped and calcified bones, normal eyes and skin. Was the injury accidental? It looked unlikely.

Tim was admitted to a place of safety, the ward, before being allowed, under supervision, to be cared for by his aunt and uncle at their home. It would be up to a court to decide whether Tim had been unlucky at different stages of his young life, suffering multiple unwitnessed accidents resulting in fractures, whether doctors had missed an underlying diagnosis, or whether somebody had deliberately hurt him. The court would also have to decide if Tim's parents should be allowed to continue to care for him, or if he should be fostered. The court case approached. I was sent a list of eighty-five questions to answer, supplemental to my earlier six-page statement.

The first question was easy. *Which year were you appointed as a consultant?* Aware that we run an adversarial system in this country, I was uneasy about the battle ahead, anticipating aggressive cross-questioning from a cunning barrister whose tactic would be to make witnesses and experts lose their temper, and hence their credibility.

The dreaded day arrived and I put on a suit and tie for the first time in ten years.

As I entered the witness box, my fears were confirmed. The defending barrister was a smart-arse. I doubted she needed her large, yellow-framed glasses, but suspected she thought it made her look more intelligent, or perhaps more intimidating. Looking more closely, I pondered over whether her specs were clear glass, with no lenses. Ms Yellow-Specs was winning, winding me up with deliberately confrontational questioning. I hit my coping button and imagined her sitting on the loo.

"So, doctor, do you make mistakes?" she said.

"Yes. Of course. Everyone makes mistakes, but I try to make as few as possible," I said.

Of course, I shouldn't have said *of course*, it showed I was rattled, an opportunity. There was no going back now.

"Doctor, I asked you eighty-five questions."

"Yes," I said.

"Doctor. Shall we start with the first one?"

"OK," I replied.

Her repeatedly calling me *Doctor* was winding me up. It was meant to do so.

She paused, as barristers do, then continued.

"Doctor. You stated that you were appointed as a consultant in 1996?" She smiled that barrister's smile that says "think again".

I thought again and replied, "Actually, no, I think it was 1995."

"So, doctor, we have already established that your first answer was incorrect."

And so it went on for two hours. I left not knowing the outcome. Is this the best way to protect the nation's children? Why put yourself through the mill when it's so easy to turn a blind eye? Little wonder that so much child abuse is unacknowledged. It's the system that's at fault.

The latest Bond film was under a year old and I left seeking a quantum of solace, when I saw Ms Yellow-Specs tottering over to her car. It was a miserable grey day, with enlarging brown puddles on the tarmac mirroring my mood. I settled in my own car, listening to Madonna's "Give it 2 Me", as my right foot hovered over the pedal. What would Bond have done? Probably seduced her.

Ms Yellow-Specs may have enjoyed making my day miserable. She might have even considered it a job well done, ridiculing my answers and nitpicking over trivial, inconsequential mistakes.

But the judge didn't waver, and Tim went into the care of his aunt and uncle. Two years later, filling up my car with petrol, I spotted the aunt and uncle. I averted eye contact, kept my head down and considered doing a runner. They caught sight of me and approached, smiling, in pincer formation. Was this to be another death threat?

Tim's aunt pursed her lips, "Thank you, doctor. We now realise you did the right thing."

32

KORA

Disillusioned medical staff had resorted to playing "management bingo" in meetings with their bean-counting masters. Bingo helped us relax and, although we found it no challenge to build a grid of management nonsense words, concerns were raised as to how the winner should alert competitors of a full house. Fearing the consequences of shouting "Bingo" in the middle of a consultant staff committee meeting, we resorted to using a loud cough. The first half of the alphabet sufficed. *Agenda for change, blue-sky thinking, cascading, clinical governance, conversate, cradle to grave, customers, dashboard, disinvestment, efficiency savings, going forward, heads-up, incentivise.* The same game could have been played with abbreviations or acronyms instead, but when dozing off, we suspected that these would be harder to hear. Much to my frustration I realised I'd started to use the term *heads-up*, but thankfully I still didn't know what *conversate* or *disinvestment* meant. I still don't.

Midge, the chief executive, suspicious of our lack of

involvement, wanted to remind us who was boss and informed the hospital that *all* staff must attend a lecture that would transform the health care given by clinical staff. All the problems could be solved by being pleasant to patients. Sorry, I mean customers. The entire hospital staff had to attend a presentation titled "Give him a pickle". Had I read this right? What did pickles have to do with anything, apart from the fact that we were in one?

Apparently, it had something to do with showing we cared by being polite. Being courteous to patients was natural to most clinicians. It also had significant self-interest attached. Those choosing to live their lives by being confrontational rarely had an easy ride. Midge should have known his onions, pickled or not. Pickle jars were needed for the managers, to hand pickles to the staff, not pickles for the clinicians to hand to the patients. The poor pickle presenter had found himself in a pickle of his own making. He tried valiantly, but he had the wrong audience. At the end of the presentation the chief executive walked across the stage and said he wanted to make a very important statement. I was intrigued. He looked rather stiff, like a pallbearer.

Why didn't Midge move his arms while walking? Was he a robot, as we'd suspected all along? "We are all equal in this trust, and every one of us is worth the same. We are all essential and all valued equally," he squealed. I could see his snout growing and his twin pointed ears budding from behind his two small insincere pink eyes. I suspected he'd read George Orwell's *Animal Farm* and was about to proclaim: "All staff are equal, but some staff are more equal than others."

Winter approached, a stressful time to be a doctor, child or parent. Viruses returned from their summer holidays, and the children's ward heaved with coughing babies, commonly with a diagnosis of bronchiolitis, a respiratory condition, often caused by respiratory syncytial virus (RSV). Together with rhinovirus (the cause of most common colds), adenovirus and coronavirus, RSV is one of the four most prevalent UK viruses causing cold-like symptoms. Up to the beginning of 2020 there'd been little interest in coronavirus. Then a new, rogue form of the virus, Covid-19, strangled the world and changed how we viewed such a previously innocuous germ.

Of the other types, adenovirus generally leads to mild symptoms, but infection can result in permanent lung scarring, a so-called bronchiolitis obliterans. RSV likewise *usually* causes a mild cold in adults but, in babies, it can be devastating. At the time no vaccinations were available for these various cold viruses, so the rapid production of the coronavirus vaccines in 2020 was a world first. Although a vaccine was not yet possible against RSV, what we called *passive immunisation* could be achieved through a course of monthly injections, costing around £3,000 per baby. Because of the cost, these were rationed to the most vulnerable. As the respiratory consultant, I was required to complete a separate form, with clinical details and reasons for consideration, for every baby who might qualify for this treatment. Once we'd been the sole arbiters. Now we had to justify our actions in the name of budgetary restraint.

Cubicles were packed with babies having difficulty in breathing. The winter ward was almost exclusively respiratory. To take pressure off other hospitals, we'd started giving continuous positive airway pressure, to the more unwell babies. Air and oxygen was blown up the babies' nostrils, to help keep their airways open. Managing sicker children than it was used to, the ward needed careful juggling of staff, scarce cubicles and the appropriate transfer of babies out to tertiary, better-staffed and equipped hospitals, when the need arose. This was part of the package, a core responsibility of the job.

I had another problem, one that I never resolved and one I knew little about — children, sex and the law. A fourteen-year-old girl with pneumonia had opened up to the nurses who had reported the details back to me. The issue involved the age of consent, sixteen in the UK.

Since many fourteen-year-old girls are sexually active, whenever this came to my attention, I would fret about whether to alert social services. If we overlooked a fourteen-year-old school girl having sex with her fifteen-year-old boyfriend, did we do the same if the boyfriend was eighteen or twenty or ninety-nine? Surely the age differences mattered. I didn't like inconsistency, but this was one area I knew I wouldn't solve. My deliberations on this awkward issue were gratifyingly eclipsed by the relative comforts of paediatric outpatients. The first patient, Susannah, was packed, bunged up, chocka. Constipation blocked clinics and tore families apart. It was unusual to find any underlying medical problem, and although conditions did exist, such as Hirschsprung's, coeliac disease or a low level of thyroid hormone, hunting rare conditions tended to be unfruitful. I suspected that many of the cases were related to poor diet. As Susannah's parents walked in, holding her hand, I immediately realised what this poor four-year-old girl must have been going through. The smell made me gag. She was obviously heavily soiled. Opening the window, I tried to breathe solely through my mouth, while Susannah's family explained that they'd lost their patience. The nursery was refusing to take Susannah until she was clean and her condition finally sorted.

On the examination couch I felt a hard, compressible, abdominal mass, and on inspection of her tail end, all I could see was a sea of soft, brown, pungent faeces. I explained that this was overflow, whereby soft stools seep around a blockage higher up the bowel, but was met with blank stares.

"How can she be constipated when she goes eight times a day?" said her father.

"We know she's just being a naughty little girl, because she dislikes school," said her mother.

Exploring Susannah's diet and drawing a diagram explaining the physics of the problem didn't help, so, for the sake of Susannah, I told a white lie. Filling in the abdominal X-ray form, I wrote a fib: "Abdominal pain – cause?" We weren't supposed to do X-rays for constipation. The radiation dose was regarded as too high, around three-months background exposure. But this was a worrying family drama, and had to be resolved fast. My duty to Susannah was paramount, and overrode any hospital protocol. Assuming no underlying conditions were found, the first line of treatment for Susannah would be improving her diet and giving her oral medication; if this failed, then enemas had to be considered. The final, most extreme, and highly unusual step, was the surgical advancing of the tip of the child's appendix out through her abdominal skin. This procedure made a neat access point from the lower bowel to the outside world, like a drainage rodding point. The track could then be flushed daily, with fluid injected via a fine catheter, inserted through this new orifice, shifting the faecal blockages, and pushing them southwards. With Susannah's constipation out of my hands, so to speak, I could move on to Sara, whose problem was puzzling.

Sara had a prominent blood vessel on the left side of her head. It looked like a juicy earthworm. I would need to investigate this further. Magnetic resonance imaging (MRI) angiography showed that Sara had an inoperable congenital deformity deep within her brain. A unique and bizarre connection between her veins and arteries, making the superficial rogue vein tortuous and enlarged.

There was nothing we could do to repair the abnormality or treat the resulting disfigurement. We would just have to hope that it behaved. In a way I wished I'd just reassured her mother and not investigated further. Was I helping Sara and her family, or was I again generating needless anxiety?

I thought back to Sam's monoplegia and wondered whether there was any point in my diagnosing something untreatable. A suitable topic for a lunchtime discussion, if we were permitted any privacy. I appeared to be causing trouble rather than solving problems and I found this frustrating. It was becoming apparent that despite fifteen years' experience as a consultant, the more I knew, the more I realised I didn't know. I'd hoped that, with time, paediatrics would become a walk in the park. But in reality, the early confidence of youth was giving way to experience-fuelled anxiety, as increasing knowledge exposed a world of paediatric uncertainties. Worse lay ahead.

Lunchtime, and all was calm; too calm, as they say in the war films. Sitting staring out of the window, luxuriating in the boredom, I could have been a Battle of Britain pilot languishing in my deckchair, waiting for the balloon to go up.

Beep, beep, beep. Beep, beep beep. Aaaaaaaaaaaaah.

Why did the bloody pager go off at lunch more than any other time? Legal services wanted to see me *urgently*. I understood urgent as having to stop eating lunch, aborting opening one's bowels, or getting out of bed in the middle of the night to see a sick child or an angry parent. Not this, whatever *this* might be. This was pager abuse.

Arriving in the bowels of the hospital, I opened the door and saw Janet, the legal services facilitator, looking tired. In Janet's hand a white bread, cheese and pickle sandwich, on her desk, stacks of notes; on the worn mauve carpet under her chair, more records of affliction. Pickles? She must have taken that lecture to heart.

Janet looked up and smiled sadly. I knew each set of these medical records would contain details of a family tragedy, past and pending medical misery and, with certainty, that I was to become a reluctant member of this unhappy gang. Janet told me that a parent had made a claim against the hospital, for the care given to her daughter seven years previously. Having attempted legal action against other hospital departments, the parents, or rather, their lawyers, had fixed their sights on us.

Surprisingly I still remembered the patient well. Kora should have died.

Born prematurely, Kora had spent eight weeks on a ventilator, suffered dangerously low blood pressure, sepsis, a bleed into her brain and haemorrhage into her lungs. She was one of non-identical twins. Her brother, Henry, had died on the unit aged two days. I'd expected Kora would die as well, but somehow, she didn't. That's just how it is. Luck plays a massive part. It helped that Kora was a girl. Premature girls fare significantly better than premature boys. Also, Kora was black and black girls tend to have better outcomes than white girls. It's a simple undeniable fact, not accounted for by other variables such as smoking or socio-economic background. Too bad for ginger males then, since this group does worst of all. What price racial equality in the light of such considerations?

I wonder whether in future resuscitation guidelines will be drawn up to reflect these differences, guiding clinicians about what they should do when faced with an extremely premature black girl or, alternatively, an extremely premature ginger white boy. The outcomes for these two groups will differ and although there may be some logic to different guidelines, I doubt society is ready to accept such an uncomfortable debate, and hope it never is. Better to pretend the differences don't exist. Surely we'll never engage in triage based on sex and ethnic background? We triage for gestation however, so it could happen. There has to be a cut-off somewhere. Could it happen on predicted outcomes? Could it happen as a result of financial restraints? Yes, it could.

Leaving aside sex and race, deciding which babies to resuscitate and which to allow to die is fraught with difficulty and there is no perfect answer, no "one size fits all".

Parents' views are important, but cannot be absolute and protocols have to change, not only to keep up with emerging evidence but also to reflect current attitudes within society.

At the time differences existed between health care settings within Europe. In Sweden neonatologists resuscitated babies born beyond twenty-two weeks gestation. In the UK it was beyond twenty-three weeks and in Holland beyond twenty-four weeks. This two-week difference was significant — and still is — affecting thousands of births every year. I was more surprised to learn that in Sweden, one in twenty paediatricians would resuscitate a newborn baby at twenty-one weeks gestation and, one third of doctors would resuscitate a baby no matter how low the chances of a good outcome. Vikings had always shown strong independence of mind.

If I'd tried to resuscitate a "nonviable" baby against the UK guidelines, I would have met immediate forceful resistance and been reported, suspended, investigated and called to attend a *serious incident panel*, before being retrained or, more likely, sacked. The British public might be surprised at this lack of discretion afforded to consultants in the resuscitation of newborn babies.

Kora had been critically unwell from birth but after careful stabilisation, she'd remained on the unit for over one hundred days. One morning, around the middle of her stay in our care, after a night of on call, I went to the ward and was surprised to see that the whites of Kora's eyes were yellow — not slightly yellow, but yellow as the mustard on a fairground hotdog. Why had nobody noticed? Why wasn't Kora already under the phototherapy units?

"Should this baby be yellow?" I said. "Put the lights on her."

Phototherapy helps reduce the level of jaundice by aiding the excretion of bilirubin and is quicker, easier, cheaper and safer than an exchange transfusion. It transforms bilirubin into a water-soluble isomer that can then be naturally removed, without going through the complicated journey of conjugation in the patient's liver. The life-span of red blood cells in adults is around 120 days, but in premature babies only about a month. Bilirubin is generated by the breakdown, haemolysis, of these cells. The newborn baby's bone marrow has to work hard to keep up an adequate production of blood, hampered by various conditions that make red blood cells fragment and fail much quicker.

With the recent improvements in phototherapy techniques and equipment, exchange transfusions are rarely needed today. A good thing too, as they are unpleasant, perilous, expensive and time-consuming. But they are still needed on rare occasions, when a situation is out of control. I believed we were in *exactly* that position.

We would have to remove and replace all of Kora's blood the standard three times, to wash out the jaundice and the accumulated, threatening antibodies. Setting up the equipment for the exchange and obtaining the necessary packs of blood from the transfusion department would take over an hour, so we started the lights.

To my delight and surprise, Kora responded beautifully, didn't need an exchange and survived this and her many other life-threatening conditions. Unfortunately, but not unexpectedly after such a torrid time, Kora was left with cerebral palsy, and seven years later, despite no complaint about her care before, nor even about the cake H made for her one-hundredth-day birthday, the hospital was being sued. With so many serious conditions occurring at once, was it possible to pick them apart and point the finger of blame, with confidence, at one single issue being the cause of *all* of her disabilities? In my view, no chance. The hospital admitted liability and paid out an eight-figure sum. No testing the claim in court, no arbitration, no attempt at apportionment. We'd become easy pickings for contingency lawyers and they knew it.[31]

The specifics of this case aside, I struggle to comprehend a system where parents who have a disabled child, despite no identified fault in care, receive no financial support or recompense from the Government. However, those who have a child with disabilities, involving a judgement that a medical error has occurred, can receive millions. I know this is how the system works, but it just doesn't sit right.

However hard the medical profession strives, despite detailed protocols, excellent training and supervision, mistakes will always happen. In the previous decade medico-legal claims had trebled. Payouts to claimants, from the NHS purse had increased by fourfold, to nearly

---

31. *A contingent fee is a fee that is only payable if a lawsuit is successful.*

£2bn. Ten years later the potential liability has risen to over £80bn, second only to the money set-aside for nuclear decommissioning.[32]

Imagine all the waiting lists that sum could reduce, the beds and staffing it could supply. All that money was so often secured by contingency lawyers, ambulance chasers in every respect, working on a no-win-no-fee basis. Such profligacy. I had barely gathered breath before another writ landed, triggering more medico-legal madness.

James came in to our unit with a significant problem, already diagnosed. Delivered prematurely in Africa, he'd suffered from a turbulent start. His family were British, lived in England, but had decided to take a holiday when his mother was twenty-four weeks pregnant. James's mother lived locally but had received no antenatal care with us, no member of staff had ever met her, she'd never visited the hospital, not even for a cup of Costa from our newly restructured entrance hall, now so packed with shops and stalls it looked more like Namche Bazaar than a hospital.

But after his birth James had developed meningitis and, as a complication of this, had a problem draining the fluid that his brain sat in. This cerebral juice is made by the choroid plexuses in the brain's ventricles and drains by absorption into veins and lymphatics which, when damaged, cause the system to fail, as more fluid is produced than absorbed and the pressure builds relentlessly.

A baby's head is not the same as the closed box of an adult. It compensates by expanding, causing hydrocephalus. James's fluid recycling system had malfunctioned. He had an excess of fluid, and his head was enlarging at an alarming rate. James needed a drain, what we call a shunt. A tube

---

32. *BMJ 2020;368:m552.*

needed to be inserted into James's brain to allow the fluid to escape into his heart, abdomen, or the sterile space between his ribs and lungs. Unfortunately, the London centre of excellence couldn't do this straight away. Triage came into play and other patients were deemed more pressing than James. Therein lay the problem, and the opportunity for later legal recourse. It's a weakness in the system, with rich pickings for lawyers.

Nobody was more important to his parents than James, but the neurosurgical centre covered a population of millions and they had the facts and they had priorities. James was otherwise well and went home awaiting his turn, while we awaited another summons. Six weeks passed. *Beep, beep, beep. Beep, beep, beep.* No message, just the ward number 3786. Why do pagers go off at such inconvenient times? I wiped, flushed, and phoned the ward.

"Please come immediately to see James on the ward," the registrar said.

I put the phone down and pottered off. Did I remember to wash my hands? Why no information? Nice to hear that rare word "please". Makes such a difference.

James was now aged six months. He hadn't attended hospital for a couple of months. He was struggling to breathe with a markedly raised respiratory rate, pulling in of his ribs and pauses in his breathing. Aware James was still waiting for his brain drain, I noted with alarm that his head circumference had enlarged by over a centimetre in the past five days. Far too fast.

The stop-start nature of James's respiration was concerning. This could have been due to either a lung infection or the raised pressure within his skull interfering with his brain's messages to his lungs. Or both. I phoned the London specialists for urgent advice.

"You have to drain James's head. Now," they said.

I hadn't done this procedure for over twenty years and didn't fancy doing it now. But there was nobody else who could do, or would even entertain doing this operation within the hospital, and no one available to do so sitting at home on call. I explained my lack of current expertise and asked the London team whether we could delay this intervention until they arrived. I suggested that, in the interim, I could focus on stabilising James and treating his chest.

"No. You have to do it now," they said, "we can talk you through it, down the phone."

I'd never before asked for consent for something that I didn't feel comfortable with. Was I really going to do a hazardous procedure in the full knowledge that I wasn't safe to do so? This wasn't in the consultants' manual. Sadly, neither was most of the important stuff. Guidelines and protocols can't cover every eventuality.

James's parents were patient and sympathetic, bemused, but understanding of my predicament. They trusted me to do the necessary. Feeling sick, I thanked them for their confidence and prepared for the operation, took a deep breath, washed my hands, twice, while the nursing staff vanished. It seemed the paediatric nurses had less faith in me than James's parents.

I shaved James's head and, after swabbing his scalp, I cautiously inserted the cannula. It needed to go into his soft spot at an angle of forty-five degrees. James's scalp was thick and difficult to puncture. The first cannula buckled. I was more forceful with the second one and, after a firm push through the outer scalp skin, I felt it give way. The wide-bore needle started its journey through James's brain tissue, hopefully on the way to the enlarged fluid-filled cavities within his brain. I prayed I wasn't doing James too much damage. I pushed forward and deeper into his soft brain. Towards the bridge of his nose, all the time praying I wouldn't puncture any of James's critical brain structures or blood vessels. I withdrew gently on the plunger as I advanced the needle. This was full-on brain surgery. Yes! Clear fluid appeared. I had reached the ventricles.

I was surprised that the pauses in James's breathing stopped. London had been right.

Later, the trust agreed millions of pounds in compensation because of the delay caused by the unavoidable queue in the system within the NHS.

As the Government appreciated a decade later, when drawing up a vaccination programme for the UK to protect the public against Covid-19, not everyone can be inoculated on the same day. There has to be planning and those in the greatest need must be prioritised on a graded scale.

Should you be able to sue if you're not in the first rank to benefit? Surely not.

Yet it's such arguments that are sapping the NHS every day through legal claims.

Maybe the British aren't so good at queuing after all.

33

PARENTS

Outpatients was subdued. Our clinic sister, after thirty years' service was retiring.

Going through my paperwork, feeling rather glum, I found an unopened letter.

It was personally addressed to me, from a local general practitioner, about a patient, who'd had to wait an inordinately long time for an ultrasound. The letter made some valid points:

> *I fully understand who is responsible for the current lamentable state of the system and I have long ceased to kick against the self-important preening little pricks in question. I fear I let my impotent rage at the lunacy of the whole thing contaminate the works. I know you are still in your prime of youthful vigour but once you get to my age you lose your appetite in engaging in what may well prove to be futile campaigns. My wife tells me that I must guard against*

*the Victor Meldrew tendency in my behaviour and I
fear, once again, she has been proved right.
Kind regards.*

I was quite chuffed. I didn't feel in youthful vigour any
more but I hadn't yet given up chasing futile campaigns
and, if that moment came, I knew I would either have to
join the dark side or click the heels of my ruby slippers and
resign. Surely, I wouldn't join the dark side?

Another weekend of on call followed, starting with a
repeat Friday night visit to the rape suite. After my earlier
complaint to the police, the premises had been moved to
more suitable accommodation. I still wasn't comfortable
with my level of expertise, since there was minimal training
offered in this field and I knew I was out of my depth. But
I had no option but to be there. The patient was a sexually
active teenager who claimed her partner had forced her to
have sex and, as she was aged fifteen, she fell under the care
of the paediatric department. This wasn't medical however.
She wasn't unwell. This was social. I was there fulfilling
the merged role of a social worker and an independent
witness while the police surgeon documented the history
and clinical findings. Nothing abnormal to see. Not even a
cockroach on the floor this time. I wondered what would
happen, and hoped I wouldn't be exposed once more to
the misery of the adversarial court system. I feared another
clash with Ms Yellow-Specs, in the knowledge that, this
time, I would make easier pickings for her.

More tampering. The calendar said 2009, enter the
Care Quality Commission (CQC), a body designed to give
joined-up regulation for health and social care. At the same
time the focus on *efficiency savings* was accelerated and we
were informed that NHS savings of £20bn were needed

urgently. Repeated messages that "There is no magic money tree, there is no more money" just didn't make sense. Martin, our much-loved and scruffy medical director (MD), could have done with some cash spent on a new suit. His repeated pleas for better funding for patient care fell on deaf ears. Martin knew that where to spend money was a political decision, as we discovered when coronavirus struck eleven years later and hundreds of billions of pounds became instantly available, backed by cheap borrowing. Back in 2009 however, the politicians just didn't want to spend money on healthcare. That was their prerogative. They got the votes. It was their job to make that call, but, make no mistake, money was there if it was needed. These efficiency savings occurred at just the time that the post-war baby bulge was causing a demographic time bomb, as increasing numbers of baby boomers — those born in the two decades after WWII — were entering retirement. In the past fifty years, the proportion of senior citizens aged sixty-five or over in the UK population had swollen from twelve per cent to eighteen per cent, and now stood at over eleven million. Two-thirds of the annual NHS budget was spent on this cohort. The success of keeping patients alive, and the resulting increase in the numbers of pensioners, came at a price. Current healthcare spending is high in the first year of life, at around £1,500 per child, then decreases until early adulthood, when it starts to climb to a staggering £7,000 a year, for each patient aged over eighty-five. Combine this with an increasing overall population (five per cent in the past decade), better educated and more demanding citizens, and unstoppable advances in healthcare; the sums didn't — couldn't — add up.

Too soon it was my turn to be COW again. Although the ward round was going according to plan, I was worried. I'd been tipped off and knew there was trouble in store. Mrs Jones, whose daughter Tallulah was significantly unwell with some as yet undiagnosed illness, stood in wait, keen to lecture me about the dangers of immunisation. Dealing with mothers is an essential part of the package of being a paediatrician.

Mathematics would suggest that fathers are half of the package, but they tend to take a back seat, rarely questioning their offspring's clinical care plans, leaving that part to the mothers. Nearly all parents are well-meaning, even the minority who can be difficult, obstructive or rude. Even those who inadvertently risk the health of their own child usually act in the best interests of their progeny. It's also an uncomfortable and undeniable fact that deliberate causing of harm can happen, but it's far less frequent than the indirect harm resulting from misplaced love. It took us months to diagnose that the frequent readmissions of one child were due to the factitious disorder of a mother repeatedly mixing her own drugs into her daughter's food. Munchausen syndrome by proxy (MSBP). When the evidence was incontrovertible, the mother admitted her actions. This poisoning had occurred through the mother's need for attention and, even in this case, the bond of love between parent and child remained strong.

Handling parents took more time than treating children. Forty years earlier, ward rounds were completed without parents, but the loss of being able to obtain a detailed history and the opportunity to ask targeted questions about symptoms would have hampered doctors in making diagnoses. Most mothers were helpful, sometimes too willing, occasionally too friendly. I needed to keep a file on one mother and seek advice about her unwanted attention via legal services.

Tallulah's mother, Mrs Jones, clearly loved her children

but as a dedicated anti-vaxxer, she fell squarely into the "pain in the arse" section, really getting my goat.

I felt for the suffering and absent Mr Jones.

Mrs Jones told me she had four children, none of them had received any vaccinations, and all of her children were alive and well. I presumed she excluded Tallulah, the ill one. She was incensed that we'd suggested it was safer to vaccinate her children rather than let nature take its course. I was used to this. I just wished that Mr and Mrs Jones lived somewhere else.

Mrs Jones was not stupid. But I couldn't understand how she could be so blind to what was such an incredible, simple, safe, cheap and potentially life-saving routine and well-established procedure. UNICEF had recently blamed the growing number of measles outbreaks on waning rates of immunisation. Measles can be a devastating and lethal condition. I'd seen dozens of children die from the disease — admittedly while working in Papua New Guinea, but young children nevertheless. Immunisation not only protects the child, but also those around the child through herd immunity. It really isn't that complicated. I couldn't help but feel frustrated.

Seat belts kill a few unlucky people, perhaps those dozing off and slipping over a cliff, but they save many more. Equally, immunisation might kill the exceptionally unfortunate child, but save millions more from avoidable death and disability. There is no conspiracy involved in trying to protect the public, and if Mrs Jones struggled to grasp that concept, then I felt she should trust those who understood the principles involved. She greeted my arrival with pursed lips, fixed my eyes and began:

"Do you know how much mercury each vaccination has?"

"No."

"Do you realise how much money the pharmaceutical companies make from vaccinations each year?"

"No."

"Are you aware of the tax benefits the Government receives from deals with Big Pharma?"

"No."

"Do you know how many members of parliament receive hospitality or direct payment from Big Pharma?"

"No."

I tapped my pager in frustration, unconsciously urging it to awake from its slumbers. It had never been my friend and, true to form, it remained stubbornly mute.

"Have you read Andrew Wakefield's research?"[33]

"Yes, I have."

Discredited nonsense, I wanted to say, but she left me no opportunity. This was the Mrs Jones show. She was more abrasive than Jeremy Paxman.

"If vaccinations are so important, why are all my children still alive?" she said.

This conversation was going nowhere, so we were going to have to disagree. I concurred that vaccinations could have side effects and, yes, rarely they could cause significant harm, but overall, I said, I was convinced they were an important advance for which we should be grateful.

Mrs Jones did a double-take when I said I'd seen many children die from measles. That medical snippet obviously didn't make *The Mail on Sunday*. But I had to give her credit, her follow up caught me on the hop. She folded her

---

33. *In 1998 Andrew Wakefield published a paper in The Lancet falsely claiming a link between the MMR vaccine and autism. In 2010, the GMC found him guilty of dishonesty and flouting ethics proposals and struck him off the medical register.*

arms, visibly bristling, and said, "I suppose you are against waterbirths as well?" Had someone tipped Mrs Jones off? As a matter of fact, I was, but accepted that many women found the experience of giving birth in water helped the pain of childbirth.

"Well, let me tell you. All of my four children are not only unvaccinated, but they were also all waterbirths, and all are absolutely fine." Mrs Jones had gathered a head of steam. I didn't dare mention her daughter Tallulah, who was looking more unwell by the minute, and appeared in need of an urgent clinical assessment.

"And you are probably against natural childbirth as well," she said.

Ah, natural childbirth; now you mention it ... Both my father's mother and his grandmother had died in *natural* childbirth. A century on and the latest fad of *waterbirths* had been promoted as a shining example of a *natural childbirth*. It sounds beautiful and moving, so intimate, giving birth as nature intended. But nature is cruel and parturition is the most hazardous event in the lives of both the mother and the baby. It is perilous. Like rock-climbing without ropes, cycling without a helmet, or driving without a seat belt, giving birth naturally might well be the preferred option, but for the associated risks. To my knowledge, none of my forebears had ever given birth under water. I suppose we might have evolved from fish, but I didn't think mentioning that would help my current predicament. Call me traditional but however hard I try, I fail to see how a human waterbirth can be described as *natural*. I chose not to mention the recent reports from both the American Academy of Pediatrics and the American College of Obstetricians and Gynecologists. These stated that women should not be offered routine underwater delivery, and that this mode of delivery ought to be limited to medical studies. I said I would look up mercury and the Pharma involvement in vaccinations (I didn't) and Mrs Jones said she would reconsider vaccinations for her children (I doubt she did). Exhausted and increasingly frustrated with having to be so fucking polite, I headed off to the sanctity and calm of the special care baby unit, where I was told there was a problem with a baby who had nearly died during my verbal assault from Mrs Jones.

I felt safer behind the baby unit's security doors. Calmness descended and frustration ebbed away. Mrs Jones couldn't get to me here. My blood pressure eased as the nurses asked me to see a mother who was distraught, having accidentally squashed her newborn baby Jack beside her in bed.

Jack had been discovered pale and lifeless an hour earlier, but after resuscitation he was looking normal. He'd had a lucky escape. Jack handled beautifully when I examined him and I reassured his mother that all was fine and we expected him to have come to no harm. Unfortunately, Mrs Jones had short-circuited my vocabulary.

"I'm sure Jack will make a full recovery. Don't worry. Pigs do it all the time," I said, the shock of what I was saying moulding my features as the words spilled out.

I really shouldn't have said that. I gasped; Jack's mother laughed. Sanity restored and no offence taken. Both Jack and Tallulah recovered. I reckoned Jack had a bright future but felt sorry for Tallulah.

One more clinic before I escaped the frontline. The last patient was an unsettled two-year-old. No problem, I'd developed a technique for this circumstance that always worked. When young children were agitated, I'd ask the mother to sit them on her lap, while I pretended to listen to her chest with my stethoscope. Great system, one slight flaw. As I leant forward to place my stethoscope a few inches away from the mother, she lifted up her blouse, exposing her bare breasts. Terrified at this close encounter in my clinic, I shouted "Down!" Ooo Missus, a Frankie Howard moment, something straight out of *Carry On Doctor*.

*

My fiftieth birthday approached; cricket therapy needed. Eight of us headed off to Cape Town, having arranged to meet up at the Test match in Newlands. We still had Strauss, Cook, KP and Jimmy Anderson but they had Smith, Kallis, Morkel and Steyn. On the fifth and final day England were in deep trouble, 170 runs astray, with South Africa needing just the one wicket to win. The England bowler, Onions, had to face the final six deliveries from the brilliant Morkel. Onions had already saved the previous Test match at Johannesburg, blocking the final six balls from the ferociously fast Ntini. Could Onions do it again? He did. A classic example of a thrilling draw. What a pity we missed it. We'd left an hour before the end, certain of England losing and wary about driving at night. So, having flown 8,000 miles to watch the cricket, we sat in a petrol station, listening to the radio, counting down the last six balls.

*

On return from holiday, the Mid Staffs inquiry kicked off and yet another White Paper was published. Ironically this one was called *Building the National Care Service*. With £20bn of savings listed, I wondered whether it might have been better labelled "Dismantling the National Care Service". Again, the patients offered respite from the developing Government/management axis of evil. The clinic was running on time when I decided to do a more thorough examination than usual on a four-year-old boy, who'd been referred in after contracting a urine infection. Amazing what you can find if you look and, I suppose, what you might miss if you don't. Bertie's liver edge should have been barely palpable, but extended down below his right rib cage by three of my finger-widths, six centimetres. Further investigations found kidney cysts, fitting a diagnosis of Caroli's syndrome. Caroli is a rare inherited condition, one that I had never heard of before encountering it. It can result in widened bile ducts in the liver and liver fibrosis. This disorder only occurs in one in a million children. In this case it was probably unconnected to Bertie's urine infection. Bertie would be at risk of gall stones and infections in his gall bladder throughout his life. If the liver fibrosis worsened Bertie could develop dilated veins in his gullet, with the potential for life-threatening bleeds.

All this from one deeper-than-usual examination. Bertie's parents had been relaxed when they arrived and now, within a short time-frame, they were coming to terms with the news that their son had a serious, complicated and lifelong health issue. Bertie's care became more troublesome as his parents were averse to traditional medicine, preferring alternative remedies. Fine with me, to some extent. But not acceptable when some unqualified "consultant" gave inaccurate, misleading, unverifiable, expensive advice about a condition they knew little or nothing about.

Bertie's family had found someone who claimed he could identify the chemical imbalance causing the condition by assessing the muscle tone in Bertie's limbs. Total bollocks. It never ceases to amaze me how intelligent and loving parents, such as Bertie's, can spend a small fortune receiving perilous advice that risks their child's health. I made a note to expose this charlatan. Traditional medicine is imperfect, but it's usually carefully performed by people who've done their research and who are not out to make a quick buck.

The following post-clinic lunch discussion with colleagues was a combination of thoughts about the new TV drama, *Game of Thrones*, and a whinge about our own mothers' increasing tactlessness with age. But I also received wise counsel not to interfere in Bertie's quack's advice, before being interrupted by a bleep.

"Please come and review an interesting twelve-year-old girl on the ward." On arrival, Abi had a stiff neck and a temperature, both signs of meningitis, but, intriguingly, she seemed well. She'd had the symptoms for over a week, so bacterial meningitis wasn't a realistic diagnosis. Abi would have been critically ill, if not dead, if her brain had been bathed in *traditional bacteria* for that length of time. By *traditional*, I mean the common bacteria that are widely reported in the press: meningococcus, e-coli, pneumococcus and streptococcus.

I adjudged Abi well enough to tolerate a lumbar puncture. Performing this procedure in an extremely sick child can kill, if there's too much pressure, as there's a risk of pushing the brain downward, through the small hole at the base of the skull. The needle was inserted into the fluid supporting her spinal cord, just below the level where Abi's spinal cord ended. Instead of gin-clear fluid, as it should have been, a single thick, slightly opaque globule, formed at the hub of the needle, before reluctantly dropping into the sterile container. Probably no increased pressure then. Powerful antibiotics that cover most bacterial infections in children were started as we awaited specific information from the laboratory that would reveal the cause of Abi's meningitis. It was Lyme disease. Just mentioning the word

Lyme filled my heart with dread. It is a fascinating disease. Sadly, however, the loons — you know, the same lot that imagine immunisation as a worldwide conspiracy to cause harm — had recently taken the condition to their hearts. Confusion on how to diagnose, misinformation on how to treat, and disagreement on who not to treat had led to a mini-economy around Lyme. Fortunately, we had access to a local, internationally respected, reference laboratory, and so were guided by a dedicated team of Lyme disease experts.

Discovered in Lyme, Connecticut, US, the disease presents classically as a red spot, mimicking the bull's-eye on a dartboard, expanding in a circular fashion, to thirty centimetres or more. A rash can follow, lasting up to three months. The bacteria that cause Lyme disease live in hard-bodied tick parasites carried on the hide of deer. Not all ticks are carriers. Thankfully this was one parasitic disease that I'd so far avoided.

34

ZOE

It's under a year since the Cape Town cricket and I'm wondering if the psychiatrist could have been mistaken. Maybe I am mad. Who else would depart for cricket Down Under, and a quadrennial humiliation? Once more we'd be taking on the Aussies in Perth. My certainty that our luck would change was absolute on this, my sixth trip. We had Strauss and Anderson, also KP and Swanny and I knew we would be OK. We'd already drawn in Brisbane and won, by over an innings, in Adelaide. We were 1–0 up and on a roll. This was going to be my moment. I could feel it in every bone in my body, apart from the round-shaped one at the top, and what did that have to do with anything?

At the cricket ground there was no shade, the sun blazed and the locals, not used to losing, snarled. Twenty-four thousand baying sandgropers and a few pink, pissed Poms. Four years and nothing much had changed. Hold on, we won the toss and decided to put Australia in to bat. Madness, or just over confidence? But maybe a correct decision, as Australia were quickly in trouble. Then their best bowler top scored – there's always one. Australia made a decent first innings total and England lost by over 250 runs. How was that possible? My sixth loss on the trot.

Back to work and more shenanigans among those in offices with nothing better to do than to play with graph paper. Some of them decided it would be entertaining to draw circles around the hospital and label them as exclusion zones. We were informed that if a staff member lived within a radius of two miles within this newly prescribed zone, permission to park a car was going to be rescinded. Staff who lived locally would not be allowed to use their own vehicles and would have to walk or catch a bus to work. The same rules applied for everyone. Midge made that clear.

"We are all equal," he said, knowing his own parking space was safe. So much for the on-call system. Midge and his managers lived further afield. They weren't needed on site in minutes, if at all, so it didn't matter to them, they were protected. But it mattered to those of us who felt obliged to be near their patients. Using a piece of string on the map, I anxiously drew a circle, sketching in Midge's exclusion zone. Bollocks! With good intent, I'd bought my house locally, so when on call I could get in to see the sick children quickly. Other consultants, because of the less urgent nature of their specialty, felt they didn't need to live close by, either that or they didn't worry about the risks of residing further away and had bought in more rural locations. Managers could live anywhere. I feared previous non-conformance with management had marked me down as a trouble causer. It would be a fight, but I was ready.

Louise, the senior epilepsy nurse, angry at the impact management's new exclusion zone was having upon me, offered to sacrifice her car parking space. Louise cared, sometimes too much. That week her dog, Bonzo, had developed a limp and, after examination by the vet, Bonzo's front paw was gently removed, from beneath his collar. Limp gone.

I couldn't tease Louise though. She'd just saved my blushes, by reviewing a parents' video of their two-year-old daughter Zoe, who appeared to be having unusual seizures. I wasn't sure what label to give Zoe's curious and atypical fits. What investigations to order, which drugs to start? In the video, Zoe moved her lower body rhythmically, before grunting, lying back and falling asleep. Louise knowingly smiled and explained. "This is classic paediatric masturbation. Politely referred to as self-gratification." Zoe's parents were horrified. Her mother took the news more stoically than her father who, like many men, believed that masturbation was limited to adults and a pastime restricted to the male of the species. He hesitantly asked whether this could be a precursor to his daughter developing into a sex-mad teenager.

I couldn't accept Louise's offer of the parking space, but was consoled that support continued to pour in and from unexpected quarters, even from within management.

Will, our paediatric department manager, was one of a rare breed and appeared genuinely angry. He straightened his already vertical pencil tie, pushed his narrow shoulders back, and reassured me that he would resolve this, even threatening to lie down outside the chief executive's office until Midge relented and handed over a parking permit.

A senior orthopaedic consultant then perjured himself. He stated that my knees were so bad that walking three miles a day would damage them beyond repair. Management caved in. However, the damage was done. I saw it as a Pyrrhic victory and, heading off to clinic, I wondered what future retribution lay ahead. Parking, like health, was a seemingly trivial matter until you lost it.

Losing it was exactly what Finn and his parents wanted. Finn was five years old and at 50 kg was the healthy weight for a boy ten years older. The GP's referral letter was more in hope than expectation. On reading it I doubted I would be able to help, or indeed that I would get too involved. As I called his name, I was surprised. Finn's parents weren't fat. Finn wasn't tucking into a bag of crisps, awaiting his next packet of biscuits. On examination, Finn was massive. Not a medical term and not one to put in the notes, but he was a giant. I was not surprised that his external genitalia were hard to find. I was unsure whether Finn had a genuine micropenis or just the appearance of one because of his rolls of fat. I was, however, surprised that Finn was of normal height and, most of all, he unexpectedly convinced me that he really wanted to lose weight. Finn and his family were endearing and desperate. I decided to believe his parents' painstakingly documented food diaries and exercise records and, although aware it was unlikely that investigations would reveal anything abnormal, I arranged a screen of chromosomal and hormonal tests.

Over lunch I discussed the case with a friend fascinated by fat. Like Louise, but for different reasons, Harry, a fellow paediatric consultant, was feeling sheepish. Training for a marathon, Harry, another blue-dot objector, had tried to run through his chest pain, before being thrown into the car by a desperate wife and taken to accident and emergency. Investigations confirmed a narrowing of Harry's main coronary artery, probably caused by fat. Harry mulled over his oversized plate of fried fish and chips, liberally sprinkled with salt.

"Check hippopotamuses and leptin," he said. I'd never heard of leptin, nor of its connection with hippopotamuses. Harry explained it was a hormone released from fat that sent messages to the brain and regulated appetite. For the former, Harry meant the hippocampus, part of the brain with leptin receptors, not hippopotamuses. Had I misheard Harry, was he confused, or was he teasing me?

Blue-dot Harry recommended a national leptin expert who gratefully took over Finn's care, exploring a possible congenital deficiency. Sadly for us all, we couldn't identify any cause for Finn's obesity. But at least I'd tried. Fat had many more layers than I'd realised. We were joined by two other paediatric consultant colleagues. The first was Owain, a diehard capitalist, married to a communist. Owain was frequently spotted sneaking back after lunch for pudding. The other was Ned, my recent saviour at the job planning battle, who'd once been subjected to my mother's frosty temperament in the canteen. Ned had sat down beside her, only to be greeted with "I do so rarely get the opportunity to see my son alone." Ned had glanced at me sympathetically, gobbled down his lunch, and fled.

The four of us headed off together, a pod of paediatricians, to hear what the medical director had to say about the new process of appraisal and revalidation. Blue-dot Harry appeared more concerned about his car than any new management interference. I suppose we all were. Harry had already suffered four flat tyres and three breakdowns on the way to work this year, and we still had most of the year in front of us.

The role of the medical director had changed much over the past twenty years. On my appointment this was a career ambition for many new consultants, myself included.

The MD was the senior doctor on site, paternalistic, fair but firm and traditionally sitting ninety per cent on the medical side of the fence. But now the incumbent risked being closer to that of a management stooge and champion brown-noser.

The MD explained, to a silent, tense, consultant body, that appraisal would involve an annual review of our individual workload, progress made and problems faced. To be followed every five years by a more searching, revalidating of our right to work. It would be backed up by proof of 250 hours of continuing professional development (CPD), patient surveys and 360-degree appraisals. In other words, a process straight out of the human resources handbook (HR would call it a toolkit), adopted by "with it" corporate organisations everywhere. Was it right for us? The question is academic.

It didn't help that this was on the back of a recent day of statutory and mandatory training; a brain-numbingly boring day, as management cancelled clinics and force- fed the consultant body the uniform, sterile and standardised diet of "right on" work bumf that goes in one ear, and out the other: fire safety awareness, health and safety, infection control, equality and diversity, information governance, safeguarding adults, safeguarding children, consent and patient experience, complaints training and conflict resolution, manual handling and finally, adverse incident reporting. Within three years, this was expanded further to include: lone worker, control of substances hazardous to health (COSHH), reporting injuries, diseases and dangerous occurrences (RIDDOR), preventing radicalisation (Prevent) and countering fraud in the NHS. Presentations were churned out on PowerPoint to a distracted group of clinicians with glazed expressions, who wanted to see patients. It all made me yearn for our trusted approach of see one, do one, teach one. Barely anything learnt in these deathly tedious sessions and mounting frustration as a result. A brave colleague cleared the air, asking why death certificates of "Travellers" had to be given priority. Dangerous territory. "It's cultural," was the curt answer. I supposed they needed certificates in a hurry in case they wanted to up and off. The rest of us can wait. It's not as if we're going anywhere, especially when we're dead. But we might start to smell. Should I mention that? No, best to keep shtum. I can't. Asking a question is almost a compulsion, something building in the throat and the vocal cords, with all the force of a giant burp.

"Excuse me, is it acceptable to leave one group within the hospital unprotected, when you are providing protection to other different sectors within the workforce?" I asked.

"Yes," came the answer, "Indirect discrimination by the accidental isolation of a group of employees is permitted."

Beep, beep, beep. Beep, beep, beep ... Oh thank you God! Escape from this drip, drip of banality, worse than water torture. But — a sting in the tail. Having missed the equality and diversity session, I sat in my office to complete the now-obligatory online training module. A few Yes/No questions to grind through, before the pain and ambiguity of the multiple-choice questions.

- Is it an adequate allowance for disability to have a ramp alongside standard steps?

- At an appointments interview, can one mention an obvious current pregnancy?

- Can one target patients of Mediterranean origin for haemoglobinopathy screening?

- Is poor communication, due to ethnic origin, a reason for non-appointment?

I didn't have a clue. Still don't.

Now for the multiple choice questions (MCQs). An easy one to start with.

- A patient arrives in a wheelchair without a manual handling assessment — who might be able to give you more information about the handling needs of the patient?
  - a. The finance department
  - b. The patient
  - c. The patient's GP
  - d. The moving and handling advisory service

What can I say?

The pass mark was eighty per cent and I scored fifty. I'd overlooked the need to watch a forty-five-minute training module before the test. No matter. I'd marked down the correct answers, to the first MCQ, on a scrap of paper. Time for the re-take. What! I'd now scored less. I hadn't noticed the questions had changed.

The principles of revalidation — making sure we are up to scratch with professional developments — may be noble, but we knew the devil would be in the detail. When the coronavirus pandemic struck, this deeply flawed process was halted. The pause caused no proven detriment to patient safety or standards of care and the Department of Health admitted that revalidation had cost £1bn over the previous ten years. How valid was that? Our immediate concerns were the expense and validity of the process, and the time involved clearing these hurdles, taking us away from seeing patients. It's fair to say we were deeply suspicious of the introduction of revalidation. Would it be used to identify incompetent doctors, or could it become a witch hunt, used to settle scores or promote status? And did we really need to spend 250 hours of CPD every five years?

It was clear this new system would result in a seismic shift in the role of a consultant. I let off steam by taking down a beech tree at the bottom of the garden. The tree was dead, couldn't be too difficult a job. Not trusting my approach to health and safety protocols, H supervised. I told her to stand back. "Stay clear or you may hurt yourself," I said. The red bow saw made good progress through most of the trunk, before I lassoed a high branch and gave a firm tug on the rope.

CRACK

From high up, five feet of tree trunk came crashing down onto my head. I woke up with a mouth full of dirt, and a towel stuck to my bloody scalp, before being helped up to the house for a medical inspection.

"It looks bad. You'll have to go to accident and emergency," H said. Maybe I should have paid more attention to the health and safety lecture. Maybe H should have boned up on "safeguarding children." Back from hospital, to the hospital. Someone, somewhere, but nobody knew who, or where, had decided that one of the three local hospitals had to close.

In theory, to improve care. In reality we all knew the reason — to save money. We wished management could be honest and explain it was all about finance. That would be a comprehensible stance, rather than dressing up a decision in thinly disguised lies. Who were they fooling? The attempt at closing a local hospital inevitably created division and conflict among the consultants. All believed passionately that their departments were the best. Dismissing a rival hospital, one senior clinician declared: "I wouldn't let my dog be treated there." Had he been to see a vet recently? Dogs can get amazing care.

Staff were asked to suggest a name for the new mega-hospital and I proposed Surrey Hospitals Independent Trust – at least that would ensure a classy acronym. SHIT.

Management was having none of this. They used the language of urgency as a tool for suppression. Divided we'd fallen, and before we'd had the opportunity to marshal our arguments, management had called a meeting at twenty-four hours' notice. Clinics would need to be cancelled. The management consultants had played this game many times and gambled correctly that clinicians would be reluctant to inconvenience patients, so couldn't and wouldn't cancel their fully booked clinics.

*

The preamble sounded dynamic, inclusive, important, urgent, expensive. A facilitator stood up. Sharp-suited, spotty, Brut aftershave, out of university for all of five years. He confidently addressed all assembled about how the NHS worked and how it could be improved. As if we didn't know. Richard, a senior colleague seated by me, had suffered enough. Clearing his throat, he rose quietly and announced that he wished to make a statement.

"If I may. I have worked in the NHS for forty years and the local region for thirty years. I have an idea whereby I believe one hospital might not have to close after all and that we could all work better together." Richard continued by explaining how care could be improved by developing more common shared streams for patients, across the three hospital sites.

Sharp Suit twitched. "Stop right there," he said, raising his hand to Richard like a traffic policeman. If I'd had a better voice, been more of a man than a mouse, I would have stood by Richard, and belted back the *Meat Loaf* lyrics: *I gotta know right now. Before we go any further.*

"I am so disappointed in you Richard," the facilitator said. "Don't go there, Richard. If you go down that line

Richard, you will have wasted all of the ground we have gained today, Richard."

Richard sat down and buried his head in his hands.

Rumour had it that five million pounds was spent on this project, including £200,000 on a visit to the US, to see how the Americans closed a hospital. A different country, a different continent, a different health model. So different that the trip had to be either brilliant, or simply plain stupid.

Over a decade later Sharp Suit and his management consultants have spent their fees, and there are no plans to shut any of these three hospitals.

35

GOATS

Patients were always — well nearly always — a welcome break from the politics. H, however, wasn't in a good mood. Watching the Queen leap out of a helicopter to open the London Olympics had helped, but not enough. The gloom worsened at a lecture on depression. Both she and the GP sitting next to her had identified with all of the traits on the slide, highlighting signs of burnout and depression. General practice was frustrating H, as much as hospital politics was affecting me. It had been bad enough for H that the previous day she'd been phoned by a woman's partner and on arrival at the house had to wend her way upstairs avoiding piles of cat shit. Upstairs lay a twenty-stone, bed-bound woman, lying on the sofa, knickers off, awaiting examination. H's next home visit was to a woman described as having a panic attack. On arrival, H found the patient sitting up in bed, puffing away on a cigarette, surrounded by six smoking relatives. H opened the windows, evicted the family, reached for the woman's sleeping tablets, gave her a pill and left.

H's frustrations at general practice aggravated the pressures at home. I started to wonder whether the Victor Meldrew GP had been right, and that we all moved relentlessly and unavoidably towards congenital grumpiness. I, too, was grumpy.

My annual appraisal was looming. Appraisals appeared a time-consuming and pointless annual exercise beloved by jobsworths in human resources. They were loathed by the majority of clinicians.

With my appraisal approaching, I noted my resuscitation training validity was expiring, and I knew I couldn't wriggle out of doing a refresher. I hated these courses. I liked to think I was competent and calm in the event of a proper resuscitation. But I wasn't great with dummies. Fifteen other candidates signed in for the three-day resuscitation course. The four older and more experienced students, all now in our fifties and sixties, gravitated towards the coffee machine and huddled together like worried goats. We were fearful of looking stupid if we were unable to remember the fancy algorithms that were now compulsory practice. Decision-making and the order in which treatment was given, the pathway, had to be done exactly as ordained. No leeway or variation was allowed, whatever the situation. If only medicine was so easy. Memorising a pathway from total ignorance is an effective way of learning a novel system, it is a lot more difficult after thirty years of real-life exposure, of treating critically ill children and babies.

One by one the old goats were summoned to contribute. None had yet been culled. Last of all, it was my turn to be questioned and challenged in front of the other candidates by a twenty-five-year-old greenhorn with one year's experience of paediatrics and a well-stuffed blouse. I found the chemise distracting. The buttons were straining but not yet popping, not like our eyes. The "patient", a life-sized white plastic dummy, was supposed to be a twelve-year-old girl with severe diabetes. I was told her tests revealed a blood sugar that was very high, at forty-two, and an acid level perilously raised. Having been in this situation in the real world many times, I was confident that, with careful management, this patient would do well. I started to explain what I would do, when, from the corner of my eye, I saw I was in trouble. The old goats in the pen were shaking their heads at me, mouthing "No."

Distracted, possibly by the bursting blouse, I had blurted out that I would ventilate the child. Which I would not have done. That would have been ridiculous. But I had sensory overload and my brain had misfired. It was like the mind blanking in the presence of Rachel Riley on *Countdown*. Who wouldn't be in a fluster in such circumstances? The junior doctor explained why I was wrong and, gave a blow-by-blow account of what the text books said should be done, to which I agreed.

The following week, six in the morning.

Beep, beep, beep. Beep, beep, beep. "Emergency special care."

Accustomed to being given no details, I didn't call to ask any questions. With sadness and resignation, I rolled out of bed, threw some clothes on, stumbled down the stairs, up the garden steps, to the pavement and my car. I was wearing a raincoat, carrying a torch, hoping to avoid any dog mess. On arrival on the baby unit, I saw two-week-old Noah was struggling on his ventilator. His chest wasn't moving well and his blood gases confirmed his plight. The junior doctor was aware something was amiss. Still chipper from being asked to be an instructor on his resuscitation course, he was adamant that he'd successfully placed the tube through Noah's vocal cords. I hadn't been invested with such responsibility on the course, either because I was no good or, perhaps, because I didn't believe in following instructions to the letter. I did, however, prefer to site the end of the ventilation tube correctly, so it sat above the level where the trachea splits into the two main airways. Clever clogs had pushed the breathing pipe too far down through Noah's cords, meaning Noah was being ventilated into a single lung. A quick snip through the ties holding the tube in place, a centimetre pulled back, and all was sorted. Just in time to go home for an odour-free shirt and a cup of tea, before running the morning ward round.

After the handover, I slipped off to the loo to insert my new hearing aid. Why the need to hide this procedure? What's the shame of being hard of hearing? Ms Yellow-Specs hadn't been bashful about her disability. The ward round was straightforward, speedy, with no sign of Mrs Jones. A blessed relief from the regimented constraints of the resuscitation course, refreshingly distant from car parks, hospital mergers and junior doctors with speckled blouses. This was my world, doing what I did best. Bugger the rest. On to special care, where a male newborn needed a careful review, having been delivered the night before, as we'd been sorting Noah's ventilator. Aiden had been born at term, with no problems identified prior to birth or during his delivery. His first twelve hours had been uneventful, until it became clear he couldn't tolerate milk feeds. Aiden looked well, but was remarkably floppy (hypotonic) and unusual in appearance. Aiden didn't look like he had Down's syndrome, where floppiness was a classical sign, but clearly something was wrong. I didn't think Aiden was a girl, but he had an exceptionally small penis, an underdeveloped scrotum and undescended testes, so it was possible. There was no doubt, when held in my palm, Aiden was uncommonly limp, so something significant was going on. But what?

Genetic testing confirmed Aiden had a condition called Prader-Willi, a fault on chromosome fifteen. The condition interferes with the hypothalamus (not the hippopotamus) and its role of controlling the appetite. Classically, Prader-Willi babies have hypotonia, small hands and feet, almond-shaped eyes and a thin upper lip. The condition is linked at birth to a weak cry, poor suck, small genitals (hypogonadism) and undescended testes (cryptorchidism). Developmental delay, obesity and a tendency to temper tantrums and stubbornness can emerge later.

In female newborns, there isn't much to see, genitally, but the condition can present with delayed periods, often after the woman's thirtieth birthday. Infertility for both sexes is the norm, but replacement of sex hormones can help. So Aiden was genetically programmed to be sterile, later developing the eating habits of a Labrador, breaking into fridges and larders, endlessly snacking and becoming morbidly obese. Aiden was lucky, however. He was born into a loving family and he always brightened my day when I saw him in clinic over the years. I couldn't help but tease him and his mother. Each time I saw Aiden, I asked him to promise me that he would take some form of daily exercise. "Yes, yes, yes," he'd say, meaning, "No, no, no."

My tactics were pointless. Aiden's weight soared relentlessly upwards, through the percentiles on his growth charts. But maybe Aiden enjoyed the visits. I certainly appreciated seeing him and his family. On one visit, his mother and I avoided talking about her son, and instead focused on chatting about the Welsh rugby front row's recent trip in a golf buggy down the M4 motorway. Aiden patiently tapped away on his iPad, glancing at us both, wondering what was going on. I confess, it wasn't me who had suspected Aiden had Prader-Willi syndrome. The diagnosis had been suggested to me by a much cleverer colleague. Team work was not only satisfying and educational, but also essential for the safe diagnosis and management of complicated patients. One has to listen to colleagues, even those on different wavelengths.

That day there was unusual tension at lunch, as Blue-dot Harry discussed an alternative approach to a slightly abnormal newborn heel prick Guthrie test. These sessions were being eyed enviously by other specialties and suspiciously by management, who failed to understand they offered respite, and an important opportunity to run thoughts and ideas past each other. Sixty years earlier Dr Robert Guthrie had devised a screening test to identify phenylketonuria, an inherited metabolic condition, resulting in raised levels of phenylalanine in the blood. Left untreated, this condition results in brain damage but, diagnosed early, it's curable by diet alone. The Guthrie test is performed after forty-eight hours of age as *in utero*, the placenta clears any abnormally high blood levels of phenylalanine. This means that any earlier test risks being misleadingly reported as normal.

This simple procedure turned a devastating inherited condition into a minor nuisance. The test has evolved over the past half century so that it is carried out now on day five of life, and includes eight other screening tests: for hypothyroidism, sickle cell disease, cystic fibrosis, and five other rare inherited metabolic conditions.

The lunchtime problem was that Harry was less worried than another consultant over a marginally abnormal thyroid blood test result. The debate could have extended to a whole day's conference, and was not my territory, but fascinating and useful. I knew where my sympathies lay, but as my pager went off once more, I made my excuses, and left to resolve whatever the beast demanded.

Jackson had been born two months premature and was struggling to feed, ingesting only half the calories he needed daily. Any increase in the rate of feeding caused abdominal distension and vomiting. My colleague Owain, the one who liked puddings, wondered whether Jackson had a narrowing of his intestines. I was more interested in Jackson's fractured cry and queried whether his vocal cords were abnormal. Neither Owain nor I were particularly interested in each other's concerns, but we both listened politely, while remaining fixated on our own areas. We were both right. We were both wrong. The cause of Jackson's problems was identified months later when a few faint scars were first seen on his skin. Jackson had suffered from congenital chickenpox. Jackson's mother hadn't been aware she'd contracted the infection in pregnancy as her disease had remained hidden (subclinical). She'd had no rash, no spots, no scabs, but inside her womb the infection had done serious damage to her unborn child. Jackson's vocal cords had been paralysed. The infection had also scarred his small bowel, leaving Jackson with a narrowed lower gut, an intestinal stricture. I'd never heard of congenital chickenpox. There seemed no end to what I didn't know, and despite working exclusively in paediatrics for over thirty years, I continued to be amazed.

Beep, beep, beep. Beep, beep, beep.

A female consultant colleague was upset. She'd been called to a disciplinary hearing for allegedly not answering her pager. There are multiple reasons that could lead to a pager not being answered. The least likely of all possible excuses is that the consultant, hearing the pager, decides to ignore it. In over three decades of being lumbered with these beasts, I'd never witnessed one being disregarded. There are a whole variety of causes behind failing to respond to a pager, including no message sent, wrong pager contacted, pager flat, pager in place of poor reception, beep not heard and pager temporarily unknowingly misplaced. Beep, beep, effing, beep! It frustrated us senior clinicians that the junior doctors were protected from bullying, but the consultants were considered fair game and enjoyed minimal protection. My colleague was understandably aggrieved. This was a slight upon her character, and she was worried that the process was going to waste many hours and cause her endless grief. After a two-month-long investigation, involving written statements and interviews, damage to her health, self-esteem and confidence, the panel — inquisition more like — heard from the member of staff who had made the original complaint: "I'm sorry, I got into a tizzy and maybe I didn't send a second bleep out," she said.

The Conservatives were back in power, under Prime Minister David Cameron.

Andrew Lansley was appointed the new Health Secretary. Sunny uplands? I shouldn't have been so naive. Lansley courted controversy by allowing representations of fast food and drink manufacturers to have influence on health-related bills. Big businesses investing in the NHS would expect a return for their money. Why not? It smacked of privatisation by the back door. *The Independent* newspaper interviewed Professor Simon Capewell, a member of Lansley's Public Health Commission, who warned that the "Government's plan to 'work together' with manufacturers to introduce voluntary cuts to fat, sugar and salt levels in food, was like 'putting Dracula in charge of the blood bank.'" Professor Capewell continued: "Andrew Lansley, in my opinion, is guilty of gross dereliction of duty in relation to public health."

Next, in publishing the "Health and Social Care Bill", Lansley prepared GPs to manage Primary Care Trusts and to start controlling hospital budgets, thus weakening the medical profession on the principle of divide and rule. Turning the screw further, Lansley and Cameron decided that GP consortia would be given eighty per cent of the health service funding available and that the GPs could then decide on what hospital services they "bought".

GPs were flattered with their new power, but hospital doctors felt the tail was now wagging the dog. The Royal College of Nursing and the British Medical Association both passed a motion of no confidence in Lansley. Then, Strategic Health Authorities and Primary Care Trusts were abolished. Did anyone understand or care what was going on? Ten years later, in 2021, the Government would try to unravel this mess —with breathtaking timing — announcing another NHS reorganisation, in the middle of the coronavirus pandemic. The witches were at large in Munchkinland, the Emerald City in decay, and the yellow brick road was going nowhere.

I looked forward to a weekend free of anything political, not least avoiding any discussion on the proposal to reduce doctors' pensions. After appraisal, revalidation, car parking exclusion zones, junior doctors' working rights, clinical awards, and the threat of hospital mergers, this assault upon our treasured pensions was one step too many. Friday lunch started well, chatting over my new role as an anti-smoking champion. The aim was to pressurise the Government into introducing new legislation to ban smoking in cars when a child was present. The past thirty years had brought about a significant cultural shift. People no longer smoked in airplanes, trains or restaurants, but they could still do so in private cars, even when children were enclosed in their smoky confines. There was little consensus on this, even among our consultant paediatricians.

The arguments against legislation focused on the loss of liberty and the inability to enforce any new law — not much different than those over seat belts and mobile phone use, then. My view was that in-car smoking, when others are present, is a dirty, selfish habit, with second-hand smoke forced upon those who can't object, child passengers for example, exposing them to harm. I believed that, with a change in the law, there was a good chance that common sense, rather than enforcement by officers of the law, could change people's behaviour. Polite consensus was reached over coffee, before we returned to discussing the relentless onslaught upon our pensions. I could feel the wearing pressure — the first inkling I was starting to think of the end game.

My weekend started in the curry house, when Dominic, a friend who was something in the City, started berating doctors and their "puffed-up pensions". Dominic didn't seem to care that, including the employer's share of contributions, doctors paid in a quarter of their salary into their retirement plans. Who in the private sector does this, I asked? I was brandishing a piece of torn chapati as I set into him. Waving the chapati like a parliamentary order paper, I told Dominic that in my view "The Government hoodwinked the press, who fooled the public into believing doctors had gold-plated *unfunded* pensions, hence cleverly taking the focus off the politicians and their much better pensions."

Dominic listened politely. I went on, gathering steam: "The term 'unfunded' is critical to any informed debate — as this word receives much publicity, but deliberately misleads the public. Unfunded implies that no money is paid in, but it doesn't mean that. Unfunded actually means that the money paid in to the doctors' pension fund is not ring-fenced. It is *not* placed in a defined pension pot." Dominic's onion bhaji had nearly gone. But I hadn't finished my chapati's worth.

"The voluntary contributions paid by the doctors, about fourteen per cent of their salaries, does not go into any safe haven but, instead, goes into the Government's general taxation pot."

Dominic shook his head. Then stretched his neck. Was he choking or disagreeing? He was probably bored stiff. Dull? Probably. Important? Definitely. No matter. I was warming up. Sod the chapati.

"More of the doctors' money goes in from these voluntary doctors' contributions, year on year, than is taken out by retired doctors. OK. I know, that's how pensions work, the doctors are no different — apart from their contributions being absorbed by the general taxation pot and not being secured in an auditable, visible, tangible mixture of shares, gilts, bonds and cash."

Dominic ordered another lager and his chicken tikka arrived. My aloo chaat was now cold and had been removed. I bleated on, unstoppable.

"The idea is that we work, at a reduced rate, and are rewarded at the end of our service with a good pension. You need to realise, Dominic, that a doctor in the private sector could earn the same amount that a full-time doctor does working in the NHS, in a quarter of the time." Dominic's third pint arrived and I had chest pain. Reflux, probably.

Assuming my new role as "The curry house bore", I told Dominic to "Compare the pension rules of five key public sector areas: Parliament, police, nurses, doctors and teachers. If you are going to criticise doctors' pensions, you should be aware of the facts around the two most important areas, those of contributions and accrual rates. The contributions paid in by these public servants range from eleven to fourteen per cent with the politicians paying in the least and the doctors paying in equal most."

I'd lost Dominic. I don't think he cared anymore. I didn't really blame him. I'm not sure I cared any more. I knew I should stop, but I couldn't. I pushed on, talking to myself now, as Dominic ordered a fourth pint. To my final point, about accrual – how quickly the pension increases. It was clear that politicians' pensions accrued a lot faster.

"So don't you talk to me about our too good fucking pensions," I said.

But where was Dominic? Dominic had gone. He had even left his pint. Bollocks, I hadn't even started on H's gripes with her position within the NHS pension scheme. Locum doctors were easy prey for the Government. Nobody stood up for them.

If H worked as a locum GP on Mondays, Tuesdays and Wednesdays, but died on a Thursday, H would not be regarded as being *in pensionable service* at death, and would only be eligible for significantly reduced benefits. Even if H's clinics were fully booked for the next three months, H had to die between 8 a.m. on a Monday and 6 p.m. on a Wednesday. Hard to plan for. I think that's called an anomaly, certainly a travesty. How bizarre can you get? And what a way to show such lack of appreciation for this essential cog within the NHS workforce. Still no Dominic. Dominic had fled. I was alone with the sitar string music, so tucked into Dominic's enlarging pool of coconut ice cream, paid our bill, and made a quiet exit.

Cricket saved my sanity once again. What else was there? Two years had passed and the English Ashes series were back in full swing. England had won the first Test by fourteen runs. We couldn't win in Australia, but surely we would win with home advantage at Lords. No cooking of eggs and bacon here, instead it was worn symbolically on the garishly striped MCC ties and blazers.

London was as hot as Perth. I couldn't find any shade on the pavilion balcony. Age, or maybe management, had started to take its toll on my scalp and there was a thinning patch on top, like the Lord's wicket on the final day of a Test match. The invasive tonsure on the top of my head was lobster pink and hurting. A moderately clean white hanky, knotted on all four corners, as if on a Brighton beach in the 1960s, offered respite.

Bzzz, bzzz, bzzz. Bzzz, bzzz, bzzz.

A text to my mobile phone interrupted my somnolescence.

"Watch out, four Sky cameras on you," messaged a friend from an adjacent stand.

The following day, the cricket journalist David Hopps reported:

'Bell prevents meltdown but Smith turns up heat. It was a sweltering summer's day with the prospect that Lord's would stage one of the hottest Tests – perhaps the hottest – in its history. And in this scorching atmosphere, so warm, by Gad, that a spectator was spied wearing a knotted handkerchief in the pavilion, Ian Bell produced his third Ashes hundred in succession to try and guard against an England calamity on the first day of the second Investec Test.'

Fame at last.

36

PING-PONG

It wasn't long before the Government started to lean harder on trust management.

Like Sir Eric Geddes ninety years earlier, while First Lord of the Admiralty, they wanted to squeeze the lemon until the pips squeak.[34] Midge felt staff had to suffer to make us realise that finances were tight. His job rested on making the books balance and, as he'd said before, "I will do whatever it takes." The pettiness manifest in this statement was breathtaking. Kettles were removed to save electricity, non-clinical areas were no longer going to be cleaned, office bins would not be emptied and car parking prices, for those staff still permitted to drive to work, would be increased by fifty per cent. Worse, outpatients had their clinic receptionists removed. There'd be nobody to meet and greet the families, to check their details were correct, to explain any unexpected issues that had arisen on the day.

---

34. *In December 1918, the British politician Sir Eric Geddes, while campaigning for re-election, referred to reparations due from Germany after the end of* WWI: *"They are going to be squeezed as a lemon is squeezed — until the pips squeak."*

"Staff have to realise that money really matters," said Midge.

What about the lawyers, so willing to cave in to the ambulance chasers? Most staff did realise; indeed, one office worker had already confessed to taking regular sick days to save on her petrol money. My secretary was refused a new earpiece on her headphones and was typing our clinic letters with a single earpiece. Goodwill had flown. Staff were annoyed.

I needed a break to clear my head and think about my future. Any break would do but this one was always weirdly special. First, outpatients, Leonin, a three-year-old boy, was driving his parents to distraction with his excessive thirst. For six weeks Leonin had been drinking from the household taps, and had shocked his parents by bending down and lapping at a puddle in the high street. When Leonin's father found him drinking the pet rabbits' water, he decided that they had to seek help. They believed this was a behavioural problem. From the GP's letter it seemed unlikely that Leonin had diabetes. There was no sugar in his urine and this raging thirst — polydipsia — had been ongoing for months. Diabetes in children usually presents in a matter of days. An examination revealed nothing unusual. It was the rabbit water and the street puddle that fascinated and alerted me.

Surely this was not behavioural. Investigations confirmed my suspicion that Leonin had diabetes insipidus — the other type of diabetes. Diabetes insipidus is an inability to concentrate urine and so, even when Leonin's body was lacking water and his body desperately needed to conserve fluid, he couldn't do so and he would keep on peeing. This meant that his body was like a fish, struggling in an emptying garden pond with a perforation in its liner. Leonin needed continuous top ups of water to survive; easily sorted with the correct medication, either a pill, nasal spray or injection, for life. Fatal without.

The last patient on the list was Barry, a nine-month-old boy. Barry's young life was blighted by severe eczema that emerged at three months of age when his mother stopped exclusive breastfeeding and started Barry on a soya-based milk. Barry had worked his way through our usual treatments. These began with a cow's milk and soya-milk-free diet, while his mother, who was continuing to give occasional breast milk top-ups, was also avoiding dairy products. We noticed a small improvement, but the eczema remained so we tried extensively hydrolysed formula milks. These products have the milk proteins broken down and are less likely to stimulate the body's allergic system. Some progress, but Barry's life still revolved around an itch-scratch cycle.

This cycle is not new. Around 1,500 BC, ancient Egyptians produced one of the earliest medical documents, the *Ebers Papyrus*, proposing fresh milk and sea salt as a remedy for itchy skin. A thousand years later, the Greek physician Hippocrates recorded treating a patient with dry, thickened, scaly skin. Nobody was exempt. Augustus, the first Roman Emperor, was plagued by a chronic itch. The first handbook on dermatological disease appeared in 1572, when the Italian physician Girolamo Mercuriale published *De morbis cutaneis*. A century later, the British dermatologist, Daniel Turner described itchiness as a sign of being "impure". Religious influences underpinned so much of society in that era. It was not a good time to itch. Then, at the beginning of the twentieth century, a breakthrough.

Histamine was discovered by Sir Henry Hallett Dale.[35] Stored throughout the body, histamine resides mainly in mast cells. Its release is stimulated by the allergy antibody, immunoglobulin E. Histamine and mast cells may be the top culprits for the itch-scratch cycle, but there are many other agents involved.

Itch has four different potential sources: skin (dermatological or pruritoceptive); systemic (diseases of the kidneys, blood or liver); neuropathic (damaged nerves) and psychogenic. Barry's parents were distraught at his frantic scratching, preventing his and their sleep. Hand mitts had helped, but Barry remained agitated and his body was covered with scratches and scabs. From first awakening, to an exhausted sleep, Barry scratched. Through the scars and patches of thickened skin, healthy, pale pink tissue shone, like a beacon of hope, a reminder of normality. We had to avoid his skin becoming dry, so soap was banned from the house. Emollients were applied throughout the day, making Barry greasy, with his clothes stained and difficult to wash. Aware of the potential hazards of steroids in these creams, we needed to apply them cautiously. The steroid strength, nevertheless, was rising to a concerning level, making his vulnerable epidermis thin, fragile, and exposed to the risks from steroid absorption through broken skin.

For the past three months the outpatient sister had applied wet wraps to rehydrate and calm Barry's damaged tissue. Wet, warm, soothing, tubular bandages were wound over a layer of grease and steroid cream, covered with a layer of dry gauze. Still Barry scratched. The expectation was that this would improve with time, but it was a millstone for

---

35. *A chemical found in many cells, which in an allergic response can produce itching, diarrhoea, vomiting and difficulty in breathing.*

both Barry and his family, and treating him had become a frustrating and time-consuming burden. Through no fault of anyone, he'd become what we call a "heartsink" patient. Barry's parents had trawled the internet for help and they requested tests.

But allergy testing lacks precision, leaving it vulnerable to medical charlatans. As an eight-year-old child, while living on our Sussex farm, I'd been through that mill with expensive and pointless skin tests for severe hay fever. Fifty years later the causes of allergy were better understood but narrowing down the causes from a bewildering array of tests remained something of a dark art.

Barry's blood tests confirmed both a raised eosinophil level and immunoglobulin E. But we all knew he was atopic (producing an exaggerated immune response); we didn't need tests to show us that. What was the point? Perhaps I did these tests out of an expectation from his family that I would take his condition seriously, or maybe I was hunting in vainglorious hope for some rare condition, such as Wiskott-Aldrich.[36]

Further blood tests included specific radioallergosorbent tests (RASTs). These check for a raised immunoglobulin E antibody to substances implicated with eczema, allergy and itch: house dust mite (HDM), cat, dog, mixed grasses and trees. In Barry all of these were raised. But there were no pets at home and no trees in the garden.

I had to do something; it was expected of me. Preventative measures to reduce the home HDM load were instituted. These included allergen-proof bed covers, removal of carpets, and freezing Barry's soft toys. Certainly, I felt better, but would Barry?

---

36. *An X-linked disorder, associated with severe eczema, low platelets and a poorly functioning immune system.*

I mused over whether in another fifty years, a single drop of blood might cheaply and reliably screen dozens of the top allergens. But the link between a positive RAST, a proven clinical significance, and a sensible option for intervention, was seldom strong. We had so much information, but how relevant was any of it? Still Barry itched. Referral to skin prick testing had been deferred to a later date, Barry's skin was too damaged to inject irritants, and we had enough to work on.

Medical treatment is seldom an exact science. Six weeks earlier Barry had been moved to a strict exclusion diet with a low-allergy, amino-acid-based formula. This milk cost three times that of the standard cow's milk formula and was only available by prescription. Another burden for his family, and the NHS's straining budget. Groaning, I stood up from my desk, poked my head down the clinic corridor and called Barry's parents. What's this? A smile breaking out on his mother's pained face? Thank God. The sight of Barry's name had already started me scratching.

Scratching my head, thinking of what my possible next steps for his management might be. Psychogenic itch no less. Examining Barry, I found his skin was less angry, no longer swollen and now a paler shade of red. More importantly, he was less agitated and, his parents appeared ten years younger, their eye-bags smaller, their eye-rings paler. Pats on the back, all round. Relief that at last we had a breakthrough.

Barry remained under dietetic supervision for the next three years and his outpatient reviews became less frequent, and enjoyable rather than stressful. Barry's name faded from my heartsink list, but other patients soon replaced him. So what was it that led to Barry's improvement? One intervention or a series of remedies? This is the most frustrating aspect of treatment. We don't always know. The bottom line though, is that both Barry and I stopped scratching. We have to settle for that.

Yes, it was that time again, the planets were aligned, and I was off to Perth for my habitual sporting humiliation. My record so far was dismal: seen six, lost six. Like most disasters, there was a positive side, as each time we lost a Test match I gained a few more Australian friends. Their curiosity pricked, the locals had begun seeking out the masochistic Pom who flew thousands of miles to suffer sunburn, drink watered-down lager, and get abused by hostile fans only to see his team ritually thrashed. I'd become a kind of fairground attraction: "Look it's our lucky Pom. G'day mate. We're bound to win."

This time, however, I was calm and brimming with confidence. I knew it had to be my seventh time lucky. Seven was the world's lucky number: seven colours in a rainbow, seven continents, seven seas, not to mention James Bond. Maybe I'd be in seventh heaven. By the time I arrived England were two Tests down and struggling at the WACA, it was clear that normal service had resumed. Unusually, I was in relative comfort, having scrounged some pavilion family tickets from a friend who knew one of the Australian Test players. After an hour of air-conditioned comfort I left the pavilion to sit with the real locals. As I sat down on the grass to watch England chase an unlikely target of 500, Alastair Cook, our captain and world cricket legend, was bowled, for a first ball golden duck. His first and last in a Test match. Even worse, he was bowled by a part-time bowler. Cook walked off, only thirty yards away, bat under arm, silently shaking his head. In front of me a massive feral local jumped up, frothing at the mouth, with watered-down beer dribbling into his curly red beard. He screamed at Cook: "You fucking cunt, you couldn't even play for Yandanooka seconds."

My switch hadn't properly gone since the schoolboy assault at Wellington, when I was fifteen. But it did now. I stood up, sighed, walked slowly up to red beard and jabbed him hard, with my right middle and index fingers, in the centre of his lower back. Where I'd normally insert the lumbar puncture needle.

A hush descended. Two thousand bloodshot eyes focused on me. I uttered what I feared might be my last words for a while.

"You need to learn how to behave and you need to learn how to win." I turned away and sat down on the grass, awaiting a pummelling. Nothing happened.

Returning to my seat in the pavilion for another small watery lager, I sadly accepted that the locals had lost the plot.

They'd forgotten that this was *cricket*, the beautiful game. My seventh trip and my seventh loss. Except, this time it didn't matter. It wasn't sport anymore. I didn't care and would never return to the WACA. England went back just once more, and lost again before the fixture was moved. I'd bailed out at a sensible time and nobody could call my decision premature.

Tom Fordyce, the Chief Sports writer for the BBC summed it up eloquently:

'Farewell to the WACA. English cricket's graveyard. The WACA remains implacable. Frozen in that period between the stark 1970s and bellicose 1980s when sitting out in 42C heat with your top off was considered a good idea, when air conditioning was for executive offices and sun cream for lightweights.'

On my return, my goody-two-shoes consultant colleague, Ned, asked me to be the lead for the newborn baby services. I didn't have any special skills around care of the newborn, but the role helped me focus once more on clinical work and the team gelled. Hard working and talented, they only required a bit of support and a voice to represent them when faced with the madness of management. There were inevitable financial storms and, as the lead, I had to conceal my blue dot and pretend to care about the finances that seldom stacked up. A funding imbalance arose. The special care baby unit was £400,000 in credit, but the children's outpatients was £200,000 below target. Both were in the same budget. I thought that should help, but the strong showing in the baby unit was ignored, and paediatric outpatients were singled out, and firmly in the cross-hairs. Maybe the tariffs — the payments for service provided — didn't balance the necessary costs incurred in delivering such care. On exploring this further, we discovered a different reason.

Management had forgotten to allow for any annual leave for the staff in paediatric outpatients. Six consultants, working an average of three clinics each a week, should have provided just over 700 clinics a year when allowance was made for leave; not the figure of 900 clinics, assumed by management. The figure was only achievable if nobody took time off. Little wonder outpatients was below target.

The target was off target. Having solved the apparent inefficiency in outpatients, I still struggled to understand why we were so financially strong on the baby unit.

It shouldn't have mattered. We were doing well. But paediatrics had taught me to pay attention to detail, maybe to nitpick, and, although it was to our benefit, it didn't make sense. I needed an answer.

Then the penny dropped. At this time the regional newborn intensive care unit was persisting in pushing hard to take over the care of our well babies, born between twenty-eight and thirty weeks. Knowing that management likes to focus on easy-to-measure parameters, I suspected that finance, rather than safety, lay behind this.

Money is made to measure. Quality is hard to measure. Babies born in this gestational range usually don't need much intensive care. But they do need months of non-intensive support, mainly around their need for temperature control and assistance in feeding. So these babies cost little to run, but are "good earners" if kept. Ridiculous, but this is what happens when you allow market economics free rein in baby care. Both sides knew there was no clinical need for the regional unit to take our babies.

A recently published and peer-reviewed national audit had scored our baby unit top in the whole country for this group of moderately premature babies. Not because we were the best in the land, but we were competent, and our mothers were in unusually robust health.

The neighbouring trust kept badgering. They insisted that we transfer these well babies to them, but I kept resisting the growing pressure to acquiesce. I didn't feel that shunting premature babies around the country was in the mothers', babies', ambulance service's or national interests. This was baby care, not pass-the-parcel. But this was also baby war and I wasn't popular. At last, suspicions were answered; a confession. The underlying explanation *was* financial. The reason the other trust needed our babies was that the funding for these well premature babies was over generous. This exaggerated national tariff was required to subsidise the inadequate national funding the other trust received for managing their other, much sicker and more premature, critically ill babies. This explained why our balance sheets were so good. I suggested a better outcome would be for the financial arrangements (tariffs) to be changed, rather than hundreds of babies moved for no good clinical reason. Moving babies to balance the books was a perversion of economics. There was a pause in their demands. Temporary exception contracts were agreed. They would bide their time till this tricky customer left, and a more malleable opponent/colleague arrived. When that happened baby ping-pong could become a whole new sport.

Then suddenly, out of nowhere, the shit really hit the fan. A paediatric consultant colleague was in grave difficulty. He had two significant problems, possibly connected. He was too bright and had irritated clinicians in a London hospital.

Previous IQ tests had put him in the 160-plus bracket.

Over one hundred years earlier, the English statistician Francis Galton had made the first crude attempt at creating a standard to assess a person's intelligence. He thought, erroneously, intelligence was all about reaction time. The intelligence quotient, or IQ, was a US invention, developed not long after WWI. People still obsess about IQ today but what does it really measure? More than anything it's problem-solving abilities. What of musical intelligence? Or footballing intelligence? Intelligence is a slippery concept. Anyway, by traditional measures, my colleague was a bright chap, possibly too clever for his own good. Accused of over-investigating and over-treating his patients, his notes were reviewed by teams of external experts. His choice of antiepileptics, duration of treatment and investigations ordered were scrutinised and challenged.

Finding the correct balance between performing too few investigations and exposing a patient to avoidable risk, against over treating a child with the ensuing burden of tests, side effects of medication and costs, is akin to walking a tightrope with a balancing pole. The pole can't be shorter on one side. Colleagues were pressurised to make legally binding statements. Few were keen to do so and the paediatric department risked being torn apart.

I wriggled out of making a statement as, having been asked by him to be an advisor, I was a sounding board and party to confidential information, so this was accepted as a potential conflict of interest. A very capable clinician, then, was cornered by going against the establishment. He wouldn't back down. We made repeated attempts at a compromise, but he wouldn't shift from his beliefs.

Lawyers ground their snouts into the trough of misery but despite the pressure imposed upon him, he stayed firm. Maybe he was disillusioned, but he stuck to his principles. There could only be one outcome. The NHS lost a talent, we lost a colleague and, most importantly, his patients lost their clinician and friend.

Why did everything have to be brought down to the average and the banal? The NHS, like any organisation, needs talented people and some of these can be mercurial. Hospital care deserved better than the homogenised mush into which it was being driven.

37

CHRISTMAS

Christmas, and the private sector began to wind down for festivities. The X *Factor* winner Ben Haenow was the Christmas chart topper with "Something I Need". Hospital staff were also in need, engaged in what we call internal trading, to ensure safe cover for the patients. I was on call again. Since one had to work either Christmas or New Year and as the latter was my birthday, I'd worked fifteen of the past twenty Christmases. So not the most wonderful time of the year for me. I sat with the night team in the scruffy handover room, drinking instant coffee from a dirty mug, looking at reindeer pullovers, waiting for the day registrar to arrive. We expected the children's ward to be quiet.

With only two women in labour and seven children on the ward, none of them very unwell, I told the night registrar to go home and enjoy Christmas with her family. After an hour the day registrar still hadn't arrived and the nurses warned me that the parents were getting tetchy. Parents, patients, nurses and midwives were all impatient for me to get moving as, quite reasonably, families wanted to be discharged home to enjoy their own Christmases. I abandoned hope of having a registrar to accompany me, sent the senior house officer (SHO) to the postnatal wards, and kicked off on the children's ward alone.

The round was straightforward with most sent home. Then, as I started on the special care baby unit, the SHO popped her head around the corner and said she was needed in theatre for an emergency Caesarian section, breech delivery. Both ward rounds completed, no major issues, I sat down, had my first cold sausage roll and called the hospital manager, explaining that the paediatric day registrar had not arrived. There was no apparent explanation. The manager said that the hospital had booked a locum doctor. I was unconvinced and wondered whether it was just another way to save money, an easy efficiency saving. As I grazed on donated salt and vinegar crisps, chocolate biscuits and a second cold sausage roll, the MD joined me. There was little love lost between us, but we were in this mess together, so we steered clear of mergers and revalidation and made small talk about the patients. He didn't understand paediatrics and although it helped me to have a medical colleague to bounce problems off, specifically issues with fifteen-year-old Portia, I would have preferred other company. Portia was one of three children whom I couldn't discharge. I knew she would be stuck here a while. Nobody wanted to take Portia home. She'd been admitted the previous Thursday afternoon with anorexia nervosa. The chance of finding a safe and appropriate place for Portia to be treated before the following Tuesday was negligible.

There was an eating disorder team, but they didn't work bank holidays, or weekends, or, it seemed, Fridays or Mondays, or any nights. The team itself was quite ordered in most respects. They certainly enjoyed their food. What they didn't enjoy was our phone calls seeking a suitable inpatient bed somewhere. Anywhere. What *we* didn't enjoy was their stalling tactic, of demanding a list of further tests that *we* might do on *their* patient. They knew their service was inadequate and that made them defensive, aggressively so.

Like most problems within the health service, it wasn't really the fault of the individuals working within the eating disorder team. It was another system failure. The real issue was a lack of central funding resulting in too few available beds and too few trained staff. Those left holding the can got the flak, and when this got too heavy, they voted with their feet, and an already poor service risked further deterioration. Portia had severe anorexia, with complex needs. A busy district general ward was not an appropriate environment for her. She was stuck in a bed, squeezed between a child coughing with pneumonia on one side and a sick diabetic on the other. As the MD overdosed on chocolate biscuits, I wondered what our country was doing to its teenage girls. It was not unusual to have three deliberate self-harmers and a child with anorexia on the ward at any one time. Invariably they were girls. Ward rounds usually ended with a list of children to run past social services, eating disorder teams and psychiatrists. Teenage boys also have their problems but tend to express them in different ways, with extreme risk-taking, excessive drinking, or an occasional violent episode. Girls, on the other hand, tend to develop eating disorders, overdose, or cut. It didn't help that most paediatricians had minimal training or understanding of psychiatric conditions. My Yuletide patience was wearing thin.

Portia weighed 33 kg, but didn't believe she was underweight. Her body mass index was fourteen, putting her in the extreme category for anorexia. When Portia was admitted most of her vital signs and blood tests were low — temperature, blood pressure, heart rate, potassium and phosphate. We had to be alert, starvation had affected the nerve conduction within her heart, and Portia was at risk of a fatal arrhythmia.

The time it takes the pumping chambers of the heart to depolarise and repolarise, to contract and relax, should be under half of one second. Portia's heart conduction time was dangerously long, and worryingly slow, at over 0.6 seconds. Like a concentration camp victim, Portia would need careful re-feeding. If we failed to find a safe place, I feared Portia would still be on the ward when I returned as consultant of the week in five weeks' time.

The MD polished off the ward's packet of McVitie's Chocolate Digestives, said "Good luck" and left. The only packet left for me was bloody Rich Tea — said it all. But before I headed to my office, I needed to think over another girl's management. Fourteen-year-old Penny had been admitted two days previously under the care of a consultant colleague. Penny had been complaining of sleepiness and a constant, throbbing, morning headache. Examination of her eyes confirmed a swelling of her optic discs (papilloedema). A brain scan found nothing unusual. A lumbar puncture confirmed normal cerebrospinal fluid (CSF), with no growth on culture, but, on measuring the CSF pressure, so-called manometry, this was found to be raised significantly at thirty-five centimetres. Normal CSF opening pressure is twenty centimetres of water or less. Penny had idiopathic intracranial hypertension (IIH), previously labelled as benign intracranial hypertension, or pseudotumour cerebri. There was nothing malignant, but little that was benign about the condition either. Penny's sight was under threat. Options to reduce the pressure around her brain included medication, repeat lumbar punctures, a surgical procedure to drain the excessive fluid, or the slicing open of her optic nerve. It was reassuring that Penny's visual fields were normal, so our plan was to sit tight over Christmas, unless her symptoms worsened.

Penny was placed on a short course of steroids to help her headaches and reduce the risk to her sight, a treatment that, bizarrely, was also a cause of IIH. How can that be? Added to her steroids were diuretics to help remove any excess fluid. Our hope was that, on this regime, repeated lumbar punctures or more drastic surgery, could be avoided and her sight protected. On the ward round Penny smiled. Her headaches were better. Was she being honest or conning me in the hope of avoiding a repeat lumbar puncture? There was no certain way of knowing without repeating the procedure. The nurses reported Penny had been comfortable overnight and I decided it was reasonable to stick with the ward handover plan, and hold off a repeat lumbar puncture until Christmas had passed.

I left the ward, and took a cup of coffee to my office to look at a different worry.

On the middle of the desk sat a brown A4 envelope, one I'd been avoiding opening. The day was already ruined, no Christmas card this. I opened the envelope and slid out the contents, a twenty-two-page Equiniti 360 Clinical analysis of my work as a paediatrician. This summarised what my colleagues and patients *really* thought about me. I felt too old for a school report and hoped my flagging morale wouldn't be dealt another blow by harsh criticism. This was deep and personal, potentially trashing self-confidence and terminally undermining my position. The report covered sixteen colleagues' assessments of my performance:

diagnostic skills, technical ability, management of complex problems, use of resources, reliability, availability when needed, time management, spoken English, commitment, keeping up-to-date, role in education, communication with colleagues, communication with patients, manners, compassion, respect of other clinicians, leadership skills, ability to delegate, probity and, finally, my health.

All twenty attributes were graded between zero and four, from "I have concerns", upwards through "Below expectations" to "Good" and finally, "Outstanding".

They mapped out on a histogram that I could compare with my previous self-assessment. The HR people just loved this stuff. And for what? Did we really change so much from year to year? And what did a "bad" score mean? Was I supposed to concentrate on my weaknesses, at the expense of my strengths? We all have different work styles. Surely the real proof of our competence is the outcome of our work? Additionally, in a similar format, were responses from twenty-six patients on whether I was: polite, listened, allowed questions, answered questions, explained simply, involved parents in decision-making, gave them confidence, was respectful of views, asked permission before examination, respected privacy and dignity and, finally, whether I made them feel better able to understand and manage their condition and care. Eleven criteria, again graded zero to four, from "Definitely not", through to "Yes, definitely".

I scrolled thought the histograms. Nothing disturbing. Then on to the free text section where my weaknesses and flaws would be there in bold print. Nothing too bad. What did I expect? These tests were designed to keep the jobsworths busy. If the bad apples hadn't been sifted out after thirty years, where would we be?

I caught myself wondering how the infamous Harold

Shipman would have performed in these tests — efficient patient handling — tick. Carry on doctor.

I didn't mind the odd dig from colleagues. Who wouldn't receive such? "Occasionally gets flustered over poor staffing levels." Damned right. I would be angry. "He needs to be more decisive." Maybe. I liked listening to others' opinions. Is that a weakness?

Maybe it is. You decide.

There was one I couldn't understand. "I do not feel I have worked with him closely enough to comment — sorry." What did that mean? I had carefully chosen the sixteen colleagues, and I knew them all well. Maybe a reluctance to be critical? To my relief, the feedback from the families was universally supportive. Without that I might have thrown in the towel there and then. Fortunately for me, Mrs Jones, the anti-vaxxer, hadn't been given a form to fill. If she had, my histogram might have painted a different picture.

Pregnant ladies and sick children started piling up and Christmas was spent rushing from the postnatal ward, to accident and emergency, to the labour ward and back to the children's ward, alone. But I was relieved. The work-style report hadn't been as traumatic for me as it had been for some. H bleeped me at lunchtime, "What's happening? It's Christmas Day!" Engrossed in the analysis of my report and sorting patients, I'd forgotten to call her. So H was also having Christmas lunch alone. But at least she had Wanda the dog for company, and some hot food to enjoy. I had Rich Tea biscuits and the soggy end of one had just broken off in my tea. Were these the world's worst dunking biscuits? Quite the opposite, said the *Daily Mirror*, where Rich Tea was reported as going strong after twenty seconds and was crowned king of dunking.[37]

---

37. *Ruki Sayid, the Daily Mirror, March 12th 2014.*

Eight hours later, the night registrar returned and I trudged home with my pager.

Weary and fed up, slumping down in front of the tv I was still niggled about the locum registrar no-show. I decided that I had to find out why this had happened. Frustratingly, consultants seemed so powerless and vulnerable. I needed to discover the reason my Christmas was once again truly stuffed.

Tucking up in bed I hoped I wouldn't be woken at three in the morning. It was gently snowing at the top of our hill and I doubted my car would get round the bend. The previous year I'd had to walk in to work on Christmas Day but I didn't fancy that in the middle of the night.

The remainder of the weekend went by in a blur and when they'd returned to work, stuffed with turkey and all the trimmings, I called the management team, who confirmed that they had booked a locum. I phoned the locum agency. "Yes, a locum had been booked by the hospital, but the doctor, Muftah, was injured crashing his car, driving his brother to the airport. Most unfortunate, sorry." This sounded too good an excuse. It was, after all, Christmas when festive fibs proliferated. I'd become a reluctant expert at analysing Christmas excuses from staff and locums and suspected it was me, not Muftah's brother, being taken for the ride. Previous Christmas excuses had included:

"Sorry, the plane was cancelled. I'm stuck in India."

"Sorry, my child is sick."

"Sorry, my sister's mother is ill, and she needs my support."

"Sorry, I have to stay at home. My husband has been called in to work by his office."

This alleged car crash was just too damned convenient.

Something wasn't right. I just couldn't put my finger on it. I asked the agency for the police incident report number. I had to check, as if Muftah had let us down, with no adequate excuse, I'd consider reporting him to the GMC for unprofessional conduct, jeopardising patient safety.

I made a diary note and phoned the locum agency every month. No incident number was forthcoming. As time passed, my determination increased. October arrived and we started to discuss the fast-approaching Christmas rota. It looked like me again.

Another call to the agency, and they finally cracked. "I am so very sorry, we haven't told you the truth. You've been lied to." The managing director of the agency continued, explaining that he'd now fully investigated the sequence of events and that Muftah *had* appropriately cancelled the locum, a fortnight before Christmas.

The agency had forgotten to tell our hospital's human resources department and, by way of an apology, they sent me a cheque for £500, which I deposited in the paediatric staff fund for the purchase of Rich Tea biscuits.

38

FRANKIE

Beep, beep, beep. Beep, beep, beep. Beep. Effing. Beep. Aaaaaaaaaaaah. Leave me alone. It was late on a Saturday evening, bath time, and the registrar wanted me to visit the ward to talk to some parents. Their baby was perfectly healthy, but they were distraught and I was needed. Their first child had just been born, at term, and nobody knew what sex the baby was and, more urgently, what to call it. Why not Frankie, from the gender neutral one-stop-shop? Then I could finish my bath. My yellow plastic duck was called Frankie. Well, it was now. I left it floating in the bubbles.

It was a relief to be able to discuss the reasons for the phone call, prior to driving in, rather than just charge in with no idea of what lay ahead. This gave me essential thinking time prior to my arrival as the so-called expert. Although its parents wouldn't have to name the child for up to a year, I was aware of the legislation that gave parents only six weeks to register the birth. There would be angst about what to tell relatives, with friends calling and congratulating them, asking whether their newborn baby was a son, or a daughter. What else is there to say about a newborn? There's the name, the weight and that's about it. Few would comprehend a truthful answer of "We don't know." Maybe Frankie wasn't such a bad idea after all.

It's unusual, but hardly rare, to be born with an indeterminate sex and there are many different causes. The baby can either be a girl with a large clitoris and a potentially life-threatening hormonal issue, or a boy with undescended testes and a deformed penis, a severe form of hypospadias, when the penile urethra opens somewhere it shouldn't. The further this opening, or what doctors prefer to call the exit, is from the correct spot at the tip of the penis, the harder this deformity is to correct. The only clinical emergency is if the baby is a girl with a high level of steroids, and a clitoris that looks like a penis. If that's the case, then there's a chance that her electrolytes might be significantly awry, and urgent life-saving hormonal treatment could be needed. However, I understood that the real emergency was what to tell the parents and, equally important, was what I suggested they told their family and friends. I scratched the Frankie idea. Truth be told, I didn't know any Frankies.

I suspected their baby was a daughter and suggested they responded to enquiries by saying that the paediatric team saw a handful of similar cases of ambiguous genitalia every year. Further tests were needed to clarify the situation. Definitive test results would become available within a few days. Hardly baby talk. I didn't say, but might have said: "Maybe just stalling folks with Frankie or some other gender-neutral name might be easier. Alex, Bobbie, Charlie, Chris, Lou, Nick, Sam, Toni — quite a bit of choice these days." Then the parents could clear up any confusion when we'd cleared it up ourselves. For some reason the lyrics of "A Boy Named Sue" by Johnny Cash were floating through my head. The baby would need to be monitored in hospital until the test results were available. Baby Frankie remained well, the electrolytes didn't go haywire and later chromosomal analysis confirmed a normal baby girl. How about Sue, then?

A paediatric endocrinologist advised on treatment and agreed to continue the management of her care. She was predicted to live a full and normal life with whatever name her parents settled on.

Back home, just as I was parking my car. *Beep, beep, beep. Beep, beep, beep.* Beep, effing, beep.

Called in again, for a straightforward severe asthma. Equally dangerous, but much easier to handle. As I was administering the intravenous magnesium, the child coughed and vomited onto my shirt. Partly digested pieces of chicken brushed off onto the linoleum floor. She appeared stable so I drove home to a dark, quiet house, where not even Wanda the dog stirred. The bathwater from hours earlier was still there, icy cold, and Frankie the duck was upended among the few remaining bubbles.

Within the NHS, protocols and guidelines were spreading like Downing Street parties in the COVID-19 crisis. But all was not straightforward. It troubled me that the National Institute for Clinical Excellence (NICE) was using out-of-date guidelines. This body had been created to provide national guidance and advice to improve health care throughout the UK. On the back of meetings of experts, NICE produced algorithms of treatment plans, rigid templates to be followed slavishly, and sent these to hospitals and GPs nationwide. The documents were a useful framework and guide, but were not always up to date, nor were they always appropriate and none addressed cases such as Frankie's. These protocols would start as contemporaneous best practice but, after taking years to agree, they would often end as historical examples of out-of-date care. The pace of change in medicine is that fast. Adding to the bureaucracy, if I practiced paediatrics outside of these recommendations, I needed to fill in exemption forms, explaining why I disagreed with the national experts. It meant that management knew who to point the finger at if things went wrong.

Exasperated, I tracked down and questioned the lead author of a piece of guidance on the management of bronchiolitis that, to my mind, seemed overly cautious and potentially detrimental to patient wellbeing.

"Don't you think we should use ninety-two per cent oxygen saturation, as opposed to ninety-five per cent, as a threshold for discharge home?" I asked.

"Yes Charles, you are right, but we won't be updating these for three years."

Arguing over three per cent for a decision on discharge? Yes. It mattered for several reasons, not least since it would prolong the duration of stay for babies admitted with bronchiolitis and who, once stabilised, should be at home with their parents. In the UK, every winter, thousands of days of inpatient care were provided for babies with saturations of ninety-three and ninety-four per cent, who would be better off discharged from the hospital (a saving for the NHS too, though economics did not come into this equation). My colleagues agreed with my stance and we followed our revised local guidelines without any clinical harm to the patients or later consequences for me.

Then Jeremy Hunt was appointed the new Health Secretary. I'd met Hunt before and thought he'd be a good choice. However, it didn't help that he'd co-authored a book suggesting the NHS should be replaced by a system where "People pay money into personal health accounts, which they could then use to shop around for care from public and private providers." This was not well received by many of the million staff working in the NHS. Hunt was also keen on spending money expanding homeopathy services. And, for some reason that was not medical but maybe personal, Hunt aimed to reduce the upper limit for abortion from twenty-four weeks from conception to twelve weeks. That sounded way beyond his brief. Who cared what his private, religious or ethical views were? Hunt was a politician, not the Dalai Lama. To hell with his personal views. Hunt needed to remember he was a public servant and that the NHS was not a plaything for him, or any other health secretary.

To cap it all, at a time of hospital managers averaging six per cent pay rises, Hunt refused to honour the one per cent pay increase recommended for hospital medical staff. His lack of respect for the medical profession was exposed further when he suggested parents go online to look up their children's rashes, in order to diagnose meningitis. Did Hunt have secret medical ambitions? If so, he could undergo the years of training and study like the rest of us. Without making any plans, Hunt then demanded a push for seven-day services, fancifully claiming that the "Monday to Friday culture" caused between 6,000 and 11,000 avoidable deaths a year, due to understaffing at weekends. The claim even sparked a response from the theoretical physicist, Stephen Hawking, who disagreed with Hunt's analysis. The data had been misrepresented, said Hawking. Hunt was using papers that hadn't been properly peer reviewed and had cherry picked figures to support his stance.

Their intellectual battle could only have one winner. Hawking then took Hunt to court over the "Backdoor privatisation of the NHS", not that the court action diminished Hunt's self-belief. When Stephen Hawking died, Hunt tweeted: "He was still a hero to me as one of our greatest ever thinkers – he inspired with his courage as well as his words." Other tweeters found Hunt's "faux-sympathy nauseating", "empty" and "hollow".

When finally costed, the estimated bill for a seven-day NHS was nearly £1bn. More importantly, despite there not being enough doctors and nurses to fill the current workforce requirements, the NHS would need another 7,000 frontline clinical staff.

The Government followed this up by claiming it had made an £8bn cash injection into the NHS, which was later confirmed as £4bn. How could their figures be at such a deviance? Little made sense and nothing added up.

The House of Commons public accounts committee reported that "no coherent attempt" had been made by Hunt's team to elaborate on the proposal and that the seven-day plans were "completely uncosted". Awash with new power, Hunt then imposed a new junior doctor contract, and became reviled across the NHS.[38] I worried for the junior doctors and for their patients. Junior doctors took strike action, putting trusts in a precarious position. Under pressure from the Government to save money, our trust asked consultants whether they'd supported the juniors' strike action. When questioned, I admitted I had.

When pushed further to describe the action I'd taken, I explained I'd worked an extra, unpaid, paediatric

---

38. *The new contract included plans to scrap overtime rates for junior doctors working between 7 a.m. and 10 p.m. (excluding Sundays). At ballot 98% of juniors voted for full strike action.*

outpatient clinic, covering a junior doctor who was on strike. Management couldn't work out what to do about that. It would be hard to dock my pay, for doing more clinical work, unpaid.

Hunt was unstoppable. "NHS Improvement" was launched and plans were made to create another new quango, "Sustainability and Transformation boards". Most of the thinking, I'm sure, went into the headings — nice words and good money for those who worked on the steering boards. Some people just love sitting on committees. Few of us cared any more. Even fewer understood the differences between the quangos and the boards, nor what these new bodies did. We sat in the canteen like defeated troops, demoralised and staring into space. Thankfully something much more interesting and important had arisen on the children's ward.

Simon, a fourteen-year-old boy, had been admitted with a priapism — an erection that fails to subside. Simon had suffered from this erection for a day and a half, and that's a surgical emergency. Untreated, this condition could result in a damaging erection, lasting for weeks.

The average adult penis is designed to stay erect for thirty minutes. Sex therapy surveys suggest even that is too long, with ideal intercourse lasting between two and ten minutes. The day before, a highly embarrassed Simon had gone with his mother to see his GP. His GP was female, and Simon refused to show her his erection. Returning home in silence, Simon thought of eating Brussels sprouts, while having repeated cold showers. Nothing would make the damned thing go floppy.

On admission, Simon's penis had been standing to attention for thirty-six hours and was showing no signs of imminent droop. It's an emergency after four hours. Nobody had ever told me that. Not that it mattered. Common causes of a prolonged erection include prior injection of the penis with the drug alprostadil (Prostaglandin E1), sickle cell disease, leukaemia, antidepressants and anxiolytics. The problem is that the penile tissue under high pressure, like a diabetic's gangrenous toe or when the bowel twists, is deprived of oxygen, causing the tissue within to die. The patient risks never being able to achieve an erection again. At the tender age of fourteen this would be a catastrophe for Simon.

Simon was on no drugs, he denied injecting anything into his penis and his blood tests were all normal. In theatre his penis was drained by a wide bore catheter inserted into his penile vessels, releasing the pressure, flushing out all the accumulated blood clots. Simon would have to wait a few months to see if he could achieve another erection. Only time would tell if Simon's penis was going to be fully functional again. The surgeon worried Simon might need an implant later, resulting in a permanently semi-stiff penis, *a lazy lob*, for the rest of his life. I never found out. Most people — people like yourself, perhaps, reading this book — are seeking neat outcomes, stories that have an ending, but medicine isn't like that. Hospital patients come and go and we can't track each and every patient's long-term outcome. Frustrating, but that's the way it is. I'd like to think that Simon's penis behaved itself for the rest of its life, or as much as any penis does.

Another patient soon came to rescue my sanity. They always did. Phillipa, a thirty-eight-year-old woman, was carrying identical twins (monozygotic) in her first pregnancy. Pretty commonplace. However, one of her twins, sharing the single placenta, was stealing the blood from the other — a severe case of a twin-twin blood transfusion. At the monthly multidisciplinary meeting the obstetricians and paediatricians debated whether fetal laser surgery was necessary for the babies, while still in the womb. As with most procedures, an argument could be made for either option. The procedure would involve inserting a camera into Phillipa's uterus and the sac the babies shared, before firing a laser beam to block the connecting blood vessels that were causing the trouble. Phillipa aided the decision by deciding it was too risky. "I'd prefer to take my, and their, chances," she said. "Let nature decide."

They soon delivered. One twin weighed 3.8 kg and the other 1.2 kg. Two boys, the big one purple and the small one white. The one I was worried about was the big purple boy, the one who had taken the blood, the "recipient" or "thief". He was the one likely to get ill from the consequences of his excessive and thick blood, with possible heart failure, jaundice and a low blood sugar. With too much blood to pump, some of this needed to be removed urgently, heart drugs given, sugar monitored and phototherapy started. He responded to treatment and then a new conundrum arose. The thief was ready for discharge but his smaller twin was below the minimum discharge-home weight. According to the rules the options included one of: keeping in hospital a perfectly well baby so that he remained with his growing twin or, sending the bigger baby home and so separating the pair or, allowing both home together — even though one baby remained below the agreed minimum discharge weight. A fudge. I was happy with that.

Twins fascinated me. Brought up on a farm, I was aware of superfecundation, when two or more eggs are fertilised during the same menstrual cycle, through different acts of sexual intercourse, not always from the same male animal. It's quite common in cats and dogs, with multiple sires fertilising the same female. It's surprisingly common in humans too. It's estimated that about ten per cent of non-identical (dizygotic) human twins are born following multiple acts of intercourse in one menstrual cycle. And one in 400 sets of non-identical human twins have different fathers.

I was more interested in twins arising from superfetation. This term applies to a female who ovulates and conceives again, despite already being pregnant, weeks or months after the first conception. Common in hares and badgers, this is incredibly rare in humans and nearly always occurs while undergoing fertility treatment.

Might this explain some apparent twin-twin transfusions and the size differences?

Of course not, a ridiculous thought. The diagnosis was clear from the antenatal scans. The only explanation was that I was losing it. My mind spinning over Hunt and the thief, and the thief and Hunt, mixed with superfecundation and superfetation.

The pressure was building.

39

CHRISTINA

Back in outpatients, the morning clinic was running late. The lunchtime X-ray meeting had started and, as I had a few patients to discuss there, I felt under time pressure. The last outpatient was Antonin, a nine-month-old French boy, with a troublesome cough. I was wary, as medicine across the Channel is different. French parents take their children to see a paediatrician in the community, just as families in the UK visit their GP. Parental expectations, therefore, are different. But this sounded routine, unlikely to be anything too worrying, time-consuming or taxing. I lifted up Antonin's Babygro to listen to his back. Oh no. No. No! Antonin had a rectangular bruise, six inches by three, green-brown in colour, sited slap-bang in the middle of his upper back. Slap marks?

Antonin's mother seemed genuinely surprised. She said she'd never seen this bruise before. Forget the X-ray meeting, more direct questioning was essential. She told me that Antonin had never bruised abnormally, he'd had no accidents and she cared for him every day, bar one afternoon a week when Antonin was looked after by a childminder. There were no blood thinning agents within the house, such as rat poison or warfarin, and no relevant past medical or family history. It didn't make sense. This was serious. Antonin's mother asked if she could call the childminder to discuss the bruise. I suspected the police would rather she didn't. But she was keen to do so and it seemed presumptive of me to refuse her request. I wondered where my boundaries were, and when the court case would be heard. Our courses didn't cover this part of safeguarding. On the mother's mobile phone Antonin's childminder insisted that she'd never seen the bruise, nor any other marks on him. There was no explanation. I was fearful we were looking at a deliberately inflicted injury, a baby-beating. There was always a chance the bruising could be due to low platelets, a clotting problem or leukaemia. But I doubted it. The most likely explanation was that Antonin had been given a hard whack, and his mother agreed. She called her husband and explained why Antonin had to be admitted. I was perplexed. The mother's manner was exemplary. If she'd done this to her son, she was a master of deception. The ward sister came down to clinic and Antonin was admitted to a place of safety. That allowed time to extend investigations, while Antonin was protected from potential further harm.

Beep, beep, beep. Beep, beep, beep.

It was the haematology consultant. "Antonin has severe haemophilia, classic haemophilia type A," he said. Antonin's life changed in four words. Antonin lacked a protein that helps blood clot. The defect is carried on the X chromosome and is usually inherited, but sometimes occurs by a spontaneous mutation. Unlike females, who have two, males have only one X chromosome, so boys lack the benefit of a correcting, back-up, second X chromosome.[39] Most female fetuses with two abnormal X chromosomes die before birth. Women with one abnormal X chromosome become carriers. These so-called carriers can have slightly abnormal clotting and a quarter have resulting symptoms. However, in one third of people with haemophilia, including Antonin's family, there is no family history of abnormal clotting. Antonin had inherited his life-threatening abnormality from his asymptomatic mother's abnormal X chromosome. He'd require a lifetime of clotting factor therapy and be prone to troublesome and painful bleeds to his joints and possibly his brain.

While the clinicians had been busy sorting patients, Lewis, a member of our senior management team, had also been busy. Busy stealing from the NHS. Schadenfreude spread amongst clinicians on hearing shouting in the management corridor. Lewis should have done his homework. It rarely pays to steal. After receiving bribes totalling £80,000 in exchange for lucrative IT software contracts, Lewis was jailed for three-and-a-half years. Sentencing Lewis, Judge Climie said, "Those charged with the financial management of the system are holding the very purse strings that can ultimately prevent pain and suffering or even death of patients." Lewis took the NHS for a ride, even paying off a £7,000 horse-stabling debt. Depressing, that as clinicians worked under close scrutiny of the smallest request for equipment, or a doctor overlooking a beeping pager, say, one of those trusted with managing the show had been feathering his own nest. Depressing, but not surprising. Then another shock, an email marked urgent, announcing

---

39. *Most females are XX and most males XY. Females with Turner's syndrome are XO, with only one X chromosome, and males with Klinefelter syndrome are XXY, with two X chromosomes.*

a £20m deficit. This is the NHS, remember? The public sector where debt is no more than a conceptual comparator. It's not, and never was, a business model. That's the whole problem in a nutshell.

A new manager had been appointed to solve the immediate shortfall. I didn't know who he was, possibly someone recruited from Marvel Comics' *Guardians of the Galaxy* I'd guess. After tapping away on his calculator, the manager's solution was to divide the trust's total deficit, pro-rata, equally, between each individual hospital department. Previous debts and past performances were now to be ignored. We were told that "the past has gone." A well-performing department was going to be treated exactly the same as an inefficient and poorly managed one. The new bean counter was to continue in post to ensure each department saved the amount demanded. Clearly, he was an X-Man, but which one? Not Wolverine. I couldn't handle Wolverine, not in outpatients. I might as well have howled at the moon, for all the good I could do in the face of this shapeshifting management.

At the same time an email landed, confirming that, despite our concerns, the merging of hospitals was going ahead. "There is no alternative," they said. My view was that if the Government wanted to close a hospital, they should do the dirty work themselves, not set hospitals against each other while standing back, cravenly watching from afar. This was a central management decision, made in Whitehall. They should take the steps themselves — not shunt the grubby deed down the line.

Much howling at the moon. I was not alone. Management bingo again became popular. In the second, refined, version we incorporated some of the newer phrases, from the endless supply of nonsense management speak: *Caldicott, commissioning, facilitator, outside the box,*

PALS, provider, revalidation, service level agreement, service user, stakeholder, transformation, valuable NHS resources.

The therapy helped. But I still had enough insight to be aware that if everything around one seems insane, then one should first check on one's own sanity. Once more mumbling "Catch-22", I looked in the mirror. Worryingly, I was beginning to look a little mad, like Chief Inspector Dreyfus in the *Pink Panther* films. I had the usual signs of ageing. But the eyes looked different. Less depth. Empty. Was that a twitch? I recalled H giggling on a GP course, when a slide was put up, showing the signs of burn out. It wasn't funny, but she recognised all of the symptoms in herself and I wondered if I was going the same way.

Departments came under tighter scrutiny and the paediatric monthly business meetings were becoming uncomfortable. The issue was not with the individuals but with the system. I had a particular issue with the way the finances were structured around paediatric surgery. We couldn't solve the trust's £20m deficit, but maybe we could do something to ease the pain. I knew I was sounding like a broken record, but I couldn't help myself. I could see management's nictitating membranes flashing as I spoke. I was being humoured, played with, like a trout on a fly; sniggered at for my persistence and my refusal to turn a blind eye or deaf ear. A junior manager explained the model all NHS trusts worked to. Each hospital received an income for providing care based upon a tariff decided by NHS England and NHS Improvement.[40] This national

---

40. *At this time NHS England was responsible for commissioning NHS services and setting strategies, whereas NHS Improvement was responsible for regulating NHS providers (hospital trusts). From 2018 they agreed to work together more closely, but legislation prevented a formal merger.*

tariff was designed to set the prices and rules for hospitals (and others) to deliver efficient and cost-effective care.

Local modifications, pricing and payment rules were permitted. Where there were no national figures, prices were determined locally between commissioners and providers. The national tariff document extended to over a hundred pages of impenetrable jargon.

For example, describing the method of pricing Best Practice Tariff (BPT), it stated:

'Using the modelled APC/OPROC or OPATT price (without BPT adjustments) at the starting point then setting a fixed differential between BPT and non-BPT price. This differential can take the form of a percentage of APC or OPATT base price or can be an absolute value, setting the level so that the BPTs are cost neutral at HRG level.'

The poor sod, having to work with such a manual. If that didn't make you ill, nothing would. The manager knew we were befuddled, so he explained further. All of the costs of the care of children with surgical needs who were admitted to our ward, were charged to the paediatric department. All of the tariff from any treatment, was given to the surgical directorate. Paediatrics supplied the beds, the fluids, the drugs, the nurses and the physiotherapists for free. Surgery supplied a quick snip and snip, and occasionally — in more complex cases — a longer snip, snip and extra snip. And the department of surgery took all the money. Management struggled to see why this seemed unreasonable. Nor why I cared. Good point. Why did I care? It was all taxpayers' money. This division in the finances should have been irrelevant. But it wasn't. I wouldn't have minded, apart from the consequences of the later analysis of this incorrect data.

The resulting balance sheets led to unreasonable blame and pressure being directed towards the paediatric department — *for poor financial performance* — while, at the same time, felicitations rained down upon surgery, for providing such a *strong performance*. We continued to miscommunicate and I became increasingly frustrated. Foolishly I decided to take this up as a challenge, raising the matter at the departmental business meeting. Every month, for two years. No progress was made.

I took the issue to the chief executive and the head of finance. Both said they "fully understood and agreed with me", and promised the anomaly would be corrected. It wasn't. I didn't expect it to be. This was a battle that couldn't be won. I continued to bleat. Mainly for entertainment and self-parody and therein joined the enlarging flock of disillusioned clinicians.

Back on the baby unit, an oversized baby. Born a week late and, at 5.9 kg, Jonnie was BIG. In pregnancy his mother had suffered from poorly controlled diabetes, with high blood sugars, which had crossed the placenta and into Jonnie in the womb. Jonnie responded by making more insulin and getting fat. During delivery Jonnie had become wedged in the birth canal. A ventouse suction cap failed to move him on, and Jonnie needed traction via forceps blades applied to his head. The procedure stretched the nerves in Jonnie's neck, causing an Erb's palsy, resulting in a flexed left wrist and a weak left arm, hanging loosely by his side. Later tests would ascertain the severity of the lesion and whether physiotherapy alone would suffice or whether primary nerve surgery repair was needed. Jonnie was unlucky. His mother had tried all she could to manage her diabetes, but sometimes sugar control goes out of control in pregnancy.

As predicted, after birth Jonnie's inappropriately high insulin level made his sugar levels worryingly low. But he also had significant jaundice and premature lung disease, even though he wasn't premature. I was confident Jonnie would do well, but my immediate worry was his low glucose. Treatment plan decided, sugar infusion started and home for supper. H had prepared spaghetti bolognese, a simple favourite and a meal that can cope with the flexibility demanded of on-call cuisine.

*

Beep, beep, beep. Beep, beep, beep. Please stop bleeping me. Christina, a sixteen-year-old diabetic girl had been admitted to accident and emergency in a ketoacidotic coma, another condition linked to an imbalance of insulin. Christina was maintaining her airway, but struggling to stay conscious. She was drowsy, with a raised sugar level of over forty. Her blood was too acidic, making her breathing abnormally fast and laboured as she expelled carbon dioxide trying to rid her body of the excess acid.

Thirty years tending diabetic children had given me confidence in its management. The paediatric registrar's plan seemed perfect to me, she was spot on. I congratulated her and thought that was the end of the matter. How wrong I was. Another consultant — not a paediatrician — butted in and wanted Christina managed differently. Loud, brash and inexperienced in this area, this consultant was more forceful than me, and insisted on filling Christina up with fluid. A reasonable approach for an adult patient, as diabetic patients do dehydrate, but neither appropriate nor safe for a child. As the old paediatric saying goes, "Children are not small adults".

I knew that giving this extra fluid to Christina would risk her developing cerebral oedema, resulting in possible permanent brain damage or death. The registrar and I agreed that we had to go slowly with the fluids, and that there was no rush. I told the registrar I fully supported her management plan. I said I would come in if she became worried.

Beep, beep, beep. Beep, beep, beep. Beep effing effing beep. AAAAAAAAAAAH!

Please let me finish the reheated spaghetti bolognese. The accident and emergency consultant was on the phone now. An experienced clinician and a smart doctor, he was calling to confirm my stance that I supported my registrar, since the other consultant remained unhappy with my management. I repeated our plan, said that I was confident that our approach was right for Christina and that I believed the other consultant was wrong. I told him that Christina would be under the care of one of us but not both, and that if she remained under my umbrella, I would follow the guidelines, which were the ones I was accustomed to, that I trusted, and that I'd every confidence in. I said I was happy to talk to the individual who was contradicting and challenging our plan. The A&E consultant paused.

"Charles, if it was my daughter, I'd rather trust you," he said. Christina went home after making a full and uneventful recovery.

A week later Blue-dot Harry crept up to me to say there'd been a complaint about my management of Christina. The issues were investigated and the complainer directed to read the published national guidelines for the treatment of diabetes *in children*. There was no apology. No thanks for saving his bacon.

This and other politicking was wearing me down. Rihanna released "Work", as I concluded I needed release from work. I didn't want it and I didn't need it. Full-time consulting was just too much hassle. I didn't want to fight any more.

The trust was still hooked on efficiency savings, so there was no objection to my reducing my contract and moving to a three-day week. So long as I did the full amount of on call, with no reduction in night, weekend or bank holiday duties.

If they'd reined in the on call, I might have looked more optimistically to the future.

But they didn't.

So part-time it would be, but for how long?

40

STEVEN

Beep, beep, beep. Beep, beep, beep. "Emergency. Accident and Emergency. Come now."

"Please" would have been appreciated. A few clinical details would have been better.

Part-time work had made no difference to the frequency of my nights of on call, or these unwelcome disruptions. It still felt a slog, and I still hated the pager. Why was there no time for niceties, or for passing on clinically useful information? Having been in post as a consultant paediatrician for over twenty years, I'd come to view this abrupt approach to hailing a consultant as poor practice. There is always an opportunity to talk and, when things are really bad or confused, to pause.

Groaning, I rolled out of bed, dressed, picked the sleep from the corners of my eyes, bared my tongue to the mirror, and charged off in the car, wondering whether to risk speeding. What was the problem? Why did they never give me any useful information? I hoped it wouldn't be a metabolic baby.

Parking outside of accident and emergency, I grabbed my ID badge and went in, dreading what I'd find. I knew it would be bad. Were my flies done up? Was there a spot on my nose? Was there a crusty yellow bogey hanging on an untrimmed, greying, nasal hair? I didn't have time to check.

I knew it would either be an unnecessary panic call, in which case I'd be irritated, or a really sick child, in which case I'd be worried. Neither alternative would result in any further sleep for me tonight. "Paediatric resus" was shouted as, panting, I walked through the emergency department. Gathering my thoughts and my breath. Why was I short of breath? I'd only walked twenty yards from the emergency parking bays to the designated paediatric resuscitation cubicle. Excitement? Fear? Something else? Approaching the pale green, washable, drawn curtains, I took another deep breath and stepped into a scene from a horror film. Back home my bed was still warm and one or both of my house companions were asleep, snoring and farting away in the warmth and privacy of their beds.

In front of me were four consultants, two junior doctors, two nurses, two parents and Steven — a screaming, blue, angry nine-month-old baby boy. One consultant was drilling a hole into Steven's tibia, the big bone in the lower leg, with what looked like a Black & Decker cordless drill. A second consultant was attempting to insert a line into Steven's radial artery, on the soft, tender underside of his exposed right wrist — an exceptionally painful procedure. A third consultant was barking instructions to the junior doctors. Demanding blood tests, X-rays and a cocktail of antibiotics to treat the crop of non-blanching spots that his mother, herself a doctor, had first noticed an hour earlier. The fourth consultant was at the head end, making sure Steven's airway was safe.

Steven's airway looked fine to me. He was, after all, screaming. Fighting for his life.

Terrified and disempowered, Steven's mother sobbed quietly, sitting alone by his bed. On Steven's shoulder, each of the purple spots that had prompted this terrible sequence of events looked about five millimetres in diameter. But I couldn't be sure. There were too many staff crowded around Steven's body for me to examine him. Doctors and nurses spoke over each other, exchanging a crossfire of possible treatments and investigations, each suggestion competing with the next, paying no heed to either Steven's mother or to me. On a bedside whiteboard, a nurse penned the times that fluids were given and drugs administered. This created a critical timeline for all to see, invaluable in guiding continuing treatment and in aiding a decision on when to admit defeat and stop the resuscitation on Steven. I could see Steven had only arrived twenty-five minutes earlier.

Steven, meanwhile, was held down, screaming, pausing to gather breath, then screaming even more fiercely. I introduced myself and watched the appalling scene for thirty seconds. Doing nothing. Believe me, that really is the hardest task. Having seen hundreds of sick children, it dawned on me that something was seriously wrong. But what?

Suddenly, I knew what it was. If Steven was so ill, why was he putting up such a good fight? That's not the usual response of an unwell, septic child. The pain of the drilling into his leg bone, with no anaesthetic, and the attempted insertion of an arterial line into his wrist must have been unbearable. Steven was in agony and, like us, he didn't understand what was going on. "Who's in charge?" I asked.

They all looked up, looked at each other, then looked

at me, as it occurred to each of them that perhaps I was. So I had to do something. If only H.G.Wells's chemicals had been available in the resuscitation trolley, I would have taken a swig, become as transparent as The Invisible Man and, like him, sought solitude in the West Sussex hamlet of Iping. I didn't have this option, so muttered, "Please all stop. Let his mother cuddle him."

As the staff turned in one, the sixteen pupils of the thirty-two-limbed resuscitation beast constricted. This could be my downfall. This would be the end of any residual credibility at work. No matter. I'd survived over twenty years as a consultant. Not a bad stint in the circumstances. I feared the possibility of Steven dying of septicaemia and of my trying to explain my decision later to the coroner, barristers and judge.

"So doctor," the prosecuting barrister would eye me over his horn-rimmed spectacles, "what line of reasoning induced you to disregard the combined eighty years of hospital experience of the four senior clinicians attending Steven, when you dragged yourself out of your warm bed, left your comfortable home, and arrived at your usual place of work?"

"Sock it to sepsis" would be changed to "Sock it to the consultant". *Sock it to Sepsis* was the latest fad. There was even a World Sepsis Day, complete with a team of enthusiastic fundraisers. The respected medical journal, *The Lancet,* reported that one-in-five deaths throughout the world was caused by sepsis. In the UK alone more than 50,000 people died every year from the condition.

Research had demonstrated that aggressive treatment in the "golden hour", the first sixty minutes, could halve the risk of death. Posters were plastered to the hospital walls, highlighting the signs of sepsis. These include a raised respiratory or heart rate, blotchy skin and poor temperature control. In paediatrics, the biggest fear is that of discovering non-blanching spots — as in Steven — which might mean meningococcal sepsis, a condition that can kill in hours. The medical director had taken the campaign to heart and was busy promoting awareness by marching up and down the hospital corridors plastering posters to the walls, parading garishly striped socks and a pair of down-at-heel brothel creepers.

Steven stopped screaming. He sobbed quietly. His heart rate came back to normal.

His respiratory rate came back to normal. He pinked up and was no longer blue. I felt sick. I had to give my consultant colleagues the time and space to gather themselves, and left the area, saying I'd be back in ten minutes and to call me if Steven deteriorated. I sat in my car, cradling the pager in my hands, staring out of the windscreen at the parked ambulances in front. Checking my watch every fifteen seconds, as the car vibrated to Queen's "I Want To Break Free".

Ten minutes later, I returned to find silence and drawn curtains. Surely Steven wasn't dead? Everyone had departed the crime scene, apart from a nurse, tidying up the mess left behind.

Steven was sitting on his mother's lap. He was kept overnight then discharged home next morning, on no treatment. Steven's spots had probably been caused by a trivial virus. Why was there this overreaction? I suspect a combination of Steven having a medical parent, combined with herd mentality, whereby one clinician, in a pack of doctors and nurses, raises the *possibility* of a patient suffering from a potentially life-threatening condition, and nobody dares to disagree.

41

EMILY

I'm pleased Steven has been sorted. But I worry at the depth of my frustration around the complaint of my management of Christina. She's made a full recovery. We've done the right thing. Why does it bother me so much? Agonising about areas that I have no control over is unhelpful. It just makes a challenging role more stressful. I realise this. But I just can't get Christina out of my head. I suppose it is that I don't expect such a flawed and underhand approach from a fellow clinician that smacks of one-upmanship, as if winning the argument is more important than settling on the most efficacious treatment. What's happening to us? Staring out of the office window, as the droplets race each other down the glass pane, my reflections are disrupted by the electronic incubus on my waist.

Beep, beep, beep. Beep, beep, beep.

A baby on the postnatal wards needs my review. Lulu's parents want to go home. She is their fourth child, born after an uneventful pregnancy and an easy delivery. Everything is perfect. Except, it isn't. The senior house officer has been thorough, checking Lulu's eyes, mouth, nose, ears, chest, heart, abdomen, genitals, anus, hips, spine and skin; all appear normal. However, the doctor is concerned that Lulu handles strangely. It's immediately evident that something is amiss. When I lay her, face down, on my right palm, Lulu's four limbs dangle, with no flexion, at the pale blue ward lino below. Lulu makes no effort to raise her head.

Floppiness is a surprisingly consistent feature of Down's syndrome. But it's also present in many other conditions. Examining Lulu, I note she has other subtle features of Down's, her eyes, hands and feet in particular. It's not an exact science. But I'm pretty certain nevertheless. Most parents are anxious when a consultant is called to examine their baby, especially in these circumstances. These parents are different. Relaxed and content. I fear this will make the shock of my explanation harder for us all. To discuss my findings and to propose a plan, I sit the parents down in a quiet room. I explain that Lulu has unusual creases on her palms, an abnormal gap between her first and second toes, is floppy, and has indications in her eyes and mouth, that point towards a likely diagnosis of Down's syndrome. Her father sees the pain etched upon my face. He smiles kindly.

"Doctor. What you do not understand is that I have three other children, who all look like Lulu. In the country I come from, all children look like this," he says.

He reassures me that my mistake is understandable. No offence has been taken. In spite of Lulu's parents' conviction that their daughter is normal, they're prepared to humour us, permitting a check of her chromosomes. Lulu stays in hospital establishing feeds, awaiting the result. Three days later we have the answer.

Lulu's chromosomal analysis confirm an extra chromosome twenty-one. She is positive for Down's syndrome. As I open the door, I see Lulu's father cradling Lulu in his arms, humming a soft melody.

"Doctor, it doesn't matter to us. We will love her all the same. We will bring Lulu up, just like all of our other children."

Lulu was blessed to be born into such an amazing family; and fortunate to be born at a time when disability was beginning to be better understood, rather than something to be avoided and shunned.

Throughout history, and in particular in the past fifty years, the attitude of society towards disability has changed profoundly. In medieval times, a disabled child was seen as a punishment for sin. In Tudor England, either devils or astronomical catastrophes were blamed. The eighteenth century saw a proliferation of private madhouses, run by unqualified "mad doctors". Those inside "suffering" from learning disabilities were labelled as idiots. The nineteenth century welcomed the asylum model. At the outbreak of the twentieth century, these UK lunatic asylums had expanded to provide accommodation to over 100,000 people, safely hidden from view, out of sight, out of mind, in some 120 institutions. They were like prisons, with an area inside their perimeters for exercise, and a private burial ground to dispose of any evidence.

At the end of WWI, the UK awoke to a reformed national conscience, when over a million disabled soldiers returned from the battlefields, and the 1918 *Education Act* was passed making schooling compulsory for all disabled children.

A quarter of a century and another war later, the Government passed the 1944 *Disabled Persons (Employment) Act*. This was the first piece of UK legislation designed to guard the rights of disabled people as a group, guaranteeing legal protection for the most vulnerable in society. The worm was turning, however slowly. It took another fifty years for the *Disability Discrimination Act* to be passed in 1995. Now was a better time to be born with a disability. Lulu was lucky indeed.

Beep, beep, beep. Beep, beep, beep.

My thoughts disrupted again. This sounds urgent. Emily, a critically unwell two-week-old baby girl, lies unresponsive in accident and emergency. She's collapsed after a routine breastfeed. Emily is pale, motionless, grunting, with a deep pulling in of her breast bone and between her ribs. I need to act fast. In my head, I run through the reasons for a collapse. Unusually, her story is unhelpful. Emily had been discharged home after a normal birth seven days earlier. The perfect baby girl with no relevant family history. Then suddenly, inexplicably, she collapses. Ah ha. I am wrong. There is a clue in the history. The word *suddenly* is critical. I shift my memory bank to search for the causes of an unexplained and sudden collapse in a newborn child.

Non-accidental injury (NAI)

I hope Emily isn't the victim of shaken baby syndrome. An unlikely diagnosis, but I know that I can't let my guard down, so I park this possibility for now and run through the others.

Gut

Emily hasn't vomited or passed blood rectally. I doubt she has a twisted or obstructed gut. Her abdomen looks normal, with no obvious distension.

Brain

Emily probably hasn't fitted. It seems unlikely that she's had a big bleed into her brain. Unless she's been shaken.

Lungs

Emily isn't on any solids. She hasn't had anything substantial to choke on. She is, however, breathing too fast and too shallow. I expect that pattern is purely a secondary phenomenon to her affliction. Not the real cause of her acute crisis.

Infection

This seems extremely improbable. Emily has gone from being perfectly well to moribund in under five minutes. *Sock it to Sepsis* may be the latest fad, but I don't buy that one for Emily.

Metabolic

Hope not. Her sugar level is normal. But she is acidotic. So that's a possible diagnosis. I'm weak at metabolic differential diagnoses. If she has that I will need to ask a "doctor smarty-pants" for help.

Her parents stand, distraught, pale, silent, by the bed. Staring at me. I in turn stare at Emily. Open-eyed, Emily stares at nobody. Naked, spread wide like a star, her short life in the balance. We are both exposed, becalmed in a sea of silence. Nobody dares speak. I am at a total loss. I know that I have to sort this and I have to sort it now.

I lay my hands on Emily and try to think harder and deeper. What on earth is going on? HELP. Come on. Sort it out. AHHHHHH. Thank God. My hands give it away. The cause is not on my initial check list. It's cardiac. Of course it is. My hands are cold. Her legs are freezing. The diagnosis is instant.

Emily has been born with a complete blockage of her aorta — the main blood vessel supplying blood from her heart to her entire body. When she had been discharged, Emily had left with another abnormality, a balancing, undetected and open duct. A bypass. A blood vessel that all babies have in the womb. This duct usually closes at birth, when normal air breathing circulation starts. Emily's duct, however, had, stayed open after birth, hiding the aortic obstruction from us all. Emily's blood had exited her heart and travelled through this duct, past the unnoticed obstruction. The problem only arose when the duct suddenly shut. Immediately cutting off the blood supply to her gut, her kidneys, her liver, her legs and her skin. Treatment was now relatively straightforward. Emily was ventilated, given drugs to make her duct re-open, and urgently transferred to London, for life-saving heart surgery. Another lucky girl.

Unknown to me, my last weekend of COW arrives. *Beep, beep, beep. Beep, beep, beep.* Four in the morning. NOOOOOOOOOOO! I struggle out of bed. Trying not to wake up H or Wanda, I gently settle the loo lid down, sit on it, head in my hands, and call the hospital switchboard. I'm put through to the labour ward and they summon me in immediately. Usual story. No story. No apology or explanation for the rude awakening. Driving in, I start muttering to myself. This insensible and indifferent approach makes my blood boil. How callous can they get? A quick summary could optimise the chances of the child. Do they not have the tiniest shred of respect for the child's life or my skills, my professional needs, not to mention my emotional and physical well-being?

Thirty years earlier, as a fresh-faced paediatric senior house officer in Sussex, I'd never anticipated this would be happening, at this age and this stage of my career.

I'd imagined a cluster of admiring colleagues, awaiting my pronouncements, showing respect, smiling, shaking my hand, patting me on the shoulder, sharing jokes, suggesting a game of golf, chatting about the good times. Well, at least some of that.

How has it come to this? It doesn't help that I have absolutely no idea what the call is about. Is it a real emergency? Can I speed? Can I go through a red light? Puffy-eyed, with a stale taste in my mouth (I really must have reflux), I charge up to the labour ward where I approach a large huddle gathered around a baby. Asking the rubberneckers to leave, I look down at an apparently perfectly healthy, slightly premature, maybe approaching 2 kg, male newborn. What the hell is this about? The baby is breathing by himself. He has a good colour, reasonable tone and, on further examination, I can find nothing amiss. Indeed, there is nothing amiss, but the story is amazing nevertheless.

Thomas's mother had enjoyed an uneventful pregnancy. When she went into labour, six weeks prematurely, the baby's heart tracing showed fetal distress. A Caesarian section was performed and, to everyone's astonishment, Thomas was not in the womb. The womb was empty. This was an abdominal pregnancy. Thomas had been conceived as an ectopic pregnancy and, by serendipity, his life, and maybe that of his mother too, had been saved when he fell out of the end of her fallopian tube.

Thomas had then attached himself to his mother's bowel apron, inside her abdomen, growing there for approaching eight months, in his own amniotic sac, unknown to all, undetected by all of his hospital scans — truly extraordinary. The mother and father of all ectopic pregnancies. A lucky boy. But why was I needed to see Thomas at four in the morning? This was a hospital, not *Ripley's Believe It or Not*! My job wasn't to gawp at the extraordinary, but to diagnose and fix things.

Needing privacy, I shuffle off to my office. I want to explain that calling me in at this time of night impacts not just on my health, but also on the service I offer. The next morning, I will be as stale as my breath. I pause, it will be pointless to do so. All the other, younger, staff are on eight- or twelve-hour rotas. This is the highlight of their shift. They are excited by such an incredible birth. Of course they are.

I've never before come across this *ex utero* phenomenon. On the internet I find an article which identifies a baby who was born in similar circumstances and of a similar gestation. Research has found no other cases. The report states that an abdominal pregnancy can implant on the bowel or its attachments, including the spleen, liver or diaphragm. This offers intriguing potential for pregnancies to proceed for women with no uterus. Indeed, it raises the possibility of men carrying a baby. Steady on.

This is dangerous territory. Back to bed for all of two hours. Struggling to sleep,

I wonder when the first man will have a baby, and if he will be called "mother", or Sue. I come to the conclusion that it doesn't matter. This only reinforces my belief that many rare conditions are not reported and are probably more common than we realise. Outpatients starts in three hours. I don't report this case. I don't have the energy. I just can't be bothered. Another wonder lost to medical science. Now in my mid-fifties, I am better at supervising, teaching, keeping a sanity check on management and making diagnoses. Better at these tasks, than in putting up drips at three in the morning or examining normal babies at four in the morning. The writing is on the wall. The end is nigh. The man on the high street with his placard — that is for me.

At this time the NHS is losing senior doctors at an alarming rate. At the local negotiating committee I put forward an idea that I hope will help retain senior doctors.

A proposal that might make a small contribution towards saving the NHS from collapse. And keep me in a job. I suggest that after a doctor's fifty-fifth birthday, or maybe after thirty years of acute on call, consultants should come off, or at least do less night-time on call. Human Resources responds with a straight bat, forward defensive, well-practiced, hand up, no run.

"Do you know that in the UK there are more age discrimination cases taken out by younger people against older people, than the other way round?" she says.

What has that to do with anything? I think the answer qualifies as a rhetorical question, but don't say so. I also doubt it is true. But I keep quiet as I worry that they already think that I'm a smart-arse.

Management's persistent creation of barriers to any suggestion is wearisome and depressing. I can't understand why my proposal is dismissed out of hand and isn't explored further. What is their problem? No problem. It is clear there are more younger workers within the hospital, and management don't give a shit for older employees who attract higher salaries on the basis of seniority, and who are less malleable due to their decades of experience. Irrelevant that this group are better diagnosticians, more efficient in running outpatients and in discharging patients. Getting fed up? Leaving soon? How sad. Management tears: those of a crocodile as it consumes its prey. Unperturbed, more in hope than expectation, and perhaps as a subconscious last resort, at the next paediatric business meeting, I propose a new consultant on-call rota. This will involve the younger consultants doing a bit more of on call early on in their career, but in the future, when older, coming off the on call. Colleagues listen politely. Eyes shift away from mine, focusing on imaginary flies on the ceiling. A newly appointed consultant looks up. He tweaks his specs.

"What's in it for me?" he says.

I consider telling him "More than you can possibly imagine." But it is pointless. If he is unable to see the future payback, there is no hope left.

Unfortunately, at this time, I collapse twice. I don't trip. I just fall over. Fascinating. But concerning. It doesn't feel like I imagine a brain tumour might. I feel well. Examinations by H and my GP are both normal. It happens a third time and, on re-examination, the GP's test for otoconia proves positive. In middle age it is quite common for the balance parts of the inner ear to get filled up with tiny bits of debris. These can tickle the delicate hairs that orientate one's perceived position, leading to many symptoms, including falls. *Otoconia.* You could have knocked me over with a feather. No, really, you could. Yet again, something I knew nothing about.

I settle down to outpatients. The clinic has been interesting and enjoyable. It is satisfying, reassuring the last-but-one set of parents that their three-year-old's breath-holding is innocent. Their video shows Alexander frowning, before crying, opening his mouth, going blue and stiff for a minute. Then jerking all over. Alexander clearly has a strong personality. It is easy to comfort the family that Alexander will grow out of this habit within a couple of years and develop normally, with no investigations or treatment needed.

Then, as I am shutting down the computer, the last mother arrives, thirty minutes late. Just as I am about to leave the clinic, she rolls in with her four-year-old son. Having battled to stay on time and looking forward to having something to eat, I am irritated. I wonder what the excuse will be this time. I expect the car park will feature prominently. That is still a shambles. Blocking staff from parking at work hasn't helped the problem at all.

The GP's referral requests I give advice to this mother, who wants to discuss her objections to the proposed immunisation of her child. Today she'd be called an anti-vaxxer. The GP is transparently exasperated and clearly embarrassed at such an apparently weak referral. I suspect the GP has little option and that, if only we didn't care so much, medicine could be so much easier.

The mother *knows* vaccinations are *dangerous*. My heart sinks. Here we go again. Not another Mrs Jones. Please. Please. This is likely to be a tricky conversation with minimal chance of success. I prepare my usual approach; I have to try. To break the ice, but also because she hasn't apologised, despite arriving at the time her appointment was scheduled to finish, I ask whether the hospital's car parking problems have caused her to be so late.

"No. I thought I might be even later. I was very lucky with the parking today. The problem was that my rabbit sitter turned up late."

42

THE DARK SIDE

It didn't take me long to rationalise. My decision to resign was right. Management confirmed it later that month.

A consultant's post can end in one of four ways — death on the job, the sack, resignation or retirement. I'd witnessed all of these. But because I'd resigned, rather than retired, and despite over twenty years of service as a consultant to the trust, I discovered that I was not going to be given the trust's usual tea party. I was delighted. I'd been to too many of these sorry affairs. They ranged from uncomfortable to excruciating. This final act of meanness was reassuring, validating my decision. Even better, my clinical colleagues had prepared a triple celebration for my departure. First, we had an outing to town, complete with embarrassing speeches, then a dragon boat race on the River Thames, and, finally, a wedding ball. I was the only man in the race, so I was told to wear a wig and get my nails painted. I liked the look. But I was surprised to discover that four of the team couldn't swim. We celebrated finishing last by having a drink near London's Waterloo station. At the bar in my frilly tutu dress, bewigged and with purple nails, standing over six feet tall and weighing over 90 kg, I was approached by a man. We started chatting. Then, a deep roar erupted from the back of the pub.

"Watch out Jim. I think it's a bloke."

*

Christmas came, and although there was no on call to barter, it appeared I was still needed. This time as Elvis at a fancy dress ball at the civic hall. I wondered what other costumes would appear. It was a set up. I was not only the sole Elvis, but also the only guest in fancy dress. A surprise mock wedding followed, with my marrying the baby unit's receptionist. Harry, my blue-dot-hippopotamus consultant colleague, was drafted in as my emergency best man, with the other paediatricians, Ned and Owain as ushers. Then the compère arrived. Dressed as Elvis. My colleagues later claimed that the Elvis doppelgänger was a bizarre coincidence and there'd been no deliberate set-up. Who cared? It was the thought that counted and, having left the bride on her special day, as I wove my way home down the high street, fellow revellers were delighted to find Elvis alive, and they couldn't care less about the other Elvis. One Elvis would do. Two would be one too many.

I missed the hospital banter, my clinical colleagues, and the teamwork. In spite of my criticisms, I'd met a few excellent managers, and accepted clinicians could be tricky. So was my opinion of the dark side reasonable? I'd find out in a management role in a different hospital.

Greg, a colourful, larger-than-life senior manager, appointed me as the hospital "chief sneak", a kind of right-hand man. Greg had an impossible task and needed someone to share his misery. Diligent, dutiful and caring, Greg knew he had no chance. Insurmountable piles of reports, incidents, complaints and demands filled his cramped office. The only colour was that of his waistcoat.

As time ran out, committees paused halfway through their agendas, and that was that. Even with most members absent, it happened for no good reason. Imagine running outpatients that way. Nothing ran on time. Greg and I worked effectively together. I had a plan and I was getting close to addressing a problem with the consultants' working practices. Then our project was abruptly called to a halt. Greg informed me apologetically that he'd been instructed from "on high" to stop our work. No explanation. The shock of being ordered to cease this project was softened by a promise of a resolution to the job-planning problems within three months. Greg left the trust and, unsurprisingly, two years later, the issue was left unresolved. Yet another example of management stasis.

Deemed to be failing everywhere, the hospital was exposed to constant attack from the Government. An experienced clinician was needed and I celebrated the offer of a place on the board, buying some new underpants and a collared shirt. The board members were talented. Most had good intentions, few had current clinical experience, but each had a different agenda. From the start I noticed an uncomfortable focus on management's personal remuneration packages, needing to be *competitive* and *attractive*. Meaning high. So this was what happened in board meetings. A newly appointed manager's pay scale was discussed. The board was informed that to draw in "talent" — what HR like to call good people — this had already been set at twenty per cent above the national average. I felt a need, a responsibility, an obligation, to challenge this. Wasn't that my role after all? Or was I supposed to be just another yes-man?

Management salaries were continuing to increase at over five per cent a year, with clinicians' earnings lagging well behind, at below one per cent per annum.

"Twenty per cent, is this right?" I asked.

The answer disappointed me. In so many ways.

"You have to realise, that's how it is, Charles," the chief executive said.

But, why did I have to do anything? Those days had gone, and why was it like that? Friends told me that committees and HR use pay data to ratchet up management wages. It's been happening for years, all part of our sick system. Boards appoint pay advisors to do this work for them and the advisors, knowing on which side their bread is buttered, ensure that their comparison studies are weighted towards higher salaries. No one wants to be on the lower percentile, so they go for the mean or the upper percentile —that's how the ratchet works. That's the management way, but not the system used for general employees. The unionised workers must stick in a pay demand and argue their case as ever. I assumed the forest of magic money trees was flourishing and, wanting some of its bounty shared around, I suggested a trust supplement be considered. One to attract clinical staff. Remember, the ones who treat patients? A colleague on the board failed to understand, or didn't care about, or comprehend, hypocrisy.

"You can't do that. That would create an internal market," she said.

At the monthly board meetings opinions were aired and "listened" to. Then pressure was applied to any outliers' opinions. Usually mine. The sole aim appeared to be for the board to reach a unanimous consensus. Like many a totalitarian state, there was a fear that any differences risked looking like weaknesses. The Soviets used to call it factionalism and suppressed it, usually with a knock on the door in the night.

My repeated drawing of attention to the poor quality and inaccuracy of the trust data, drew a consistent response.

"You must look at the bigger picture Charles, not the detail."

Responses of "have to", "can't" and "must" concerned me. It was clear that we were all being encouraged, maybe even coerced, into groupthink. Kafkaesque? Orwellian? Take your pick. I was accustomed to paying attention to fine detail, and I'd been trained to stand back and review the whole scenario, so this discouragement appeared unhelpful and patronising. I believed that paying attention to the finer points often resulted in better outcomes. It might have been OK in number 10 Downing Street, but I doubted that the Johnsonian "don't worry about the detail" approach was pinned up on the office walls of NASA, Washington DC or in the headquarters of the UK Atomic Energy Authority in Oxfordshire.

Like nearly all NHS hospitals, the trust's finances were in a mess, through little fault of the organisation. That, however, couldn't be suggested, as self-flagellation and self-recrimination were openly promoted. Woe is us. There was just too much clinical work to be done and, despite too many staff on the payroll, many clinical posts remained unfilled. The books didn't, and couldn't, balance. With an ageing population, more surgical interventions available, novel costly medical treatments being provided, combined with an increasingly demanding and knowledgeable *customer base*, our dire financial situation was inevitable. It was a microcosm of the NHS at large. The most dramatic change was anticipated to be in the over eighty-five-year-olds. This population was expected to double, to over three million, in twenty years and treble within forty years. By then, one in fourteen of the UK population, over five million people, would be in deep old age. And they'd need health care in a disproportionate share to that of the rest of the population. The old were the looming iceberg and we couldn't avoid it.

An overbearing NHS England (NHSE) and NHS Improvement (NHSI) analysed reams of inaccurate data and spat back impossible targets. Little consideration was given to being honest, admitting the problem, or discussing the option of rationing health care. No one was prepared to think the unthinkable. As a clinician, I'd been blissfully unaware that hospital management got it in the neck, day in, day out, from persistent bullying and harassment further up the food chain. I genuinely felt for them. Their jobs were thankless. The final straw was the appointment of private consultants, parasites employed to make lists of how to save the trust money. For a cost of nearly £1m, these people, who would borrow your watch to tell you the time, cut and pasted from previous lucrative contracts, making suggestions and offering training to staff. These advisers knew less about how hospitals worked than most of those working within them. Young, pretty, clueless and inexperienced, and those were just the boys. We must have appeared to them like the wise, burnt-out old turkeys that we'd all become. Ripe for plucking.

Eager to help the board's finances and reduce this squandering of our scarce funding, I uncovered an academic article on the waste these management consultants caused. Published in *Policy and Politics*, the title said it all: "NHS management consultants proven to worsen a service already under pressure".[41] The article was detailed and balanced, reporting on work from three separate sources,

---

41. *Policy and Politics Professor Ian Kirkpatrick et al March 2018.*

looking at over a hundred UK hospital trusts spanning a four-year period.

Researchers found that each UK trust spent, on average, over £1m on consultants. One trust had spent over £5m. Costs were spiralling out of control. The amount the NHS spent on this shabby lot had doubled over the previous four years, to over £600m a year. This occurred despite assurances from the Government that a brake would be applied. None was and the coronavirus pandemic of 2020–22 provided them with even greater scope. Did anyone spot the irony of a £145 million contract awarded to Deloitte, for "designing and creating a sustainable workforce solution"?[42] Though they were employed to stop waste, the consultants themselves were identified as the biggest waste. I was now even more alone on the board for raising this issue. They really didn't want to know. Slowly it dawned. Why had I been so slow? The advantage to the board of employing management consultants became clear. It gave senior management in the executive *time*, a priceless commodity. The external "expert advice" kept the individual managers in their posts for that bit longer, accruing their pensions, planning their escapes. It gave an impression of their being willing to learn, their wanting to achieve the impossible by engaging the support from the "best national talent" available. The self-deception was breathtaking, unbelievable had I not witnessed it with my own eyes and ears. Most importantly, it kept the quangos quiet and ensured the board's monthly pay cheques.

Those supposedly running the show, NHS England and NHS Improvement, employed people who persistently and openly harassed senior hospital management. The meddling from these quangos created a significant drain on

42. *Private Eye March 2021.*

management and clinician time and energy. This warped, corrosive culture came right from the top, passing through the system like an unpleasant case of dysentery.

They not only bullied trust managers, but also made their jobs more difficult and, in so doing, interfered with patient care. They rained down visits and demands, often with short notice, another deliberately unsettling tactic. The edicts from NHSE/NHSI were impossible to achieve. They might as well have been running a military boot camp, ordering those under their power to paint coal white. Senior members of our board were stuck between a rock and a hard place. With nowhere to hide, tensions rose. Weekend and late-night phone calls badgered the trust hierarchy. Nobody was exempt. At last, I understood. Much of the management lunacy I'd witnessed as a clinician came directly from the Government. The trust executive had an impossible task. I'd never realised. It wasn't their fault. As the board was harangued into coming up with a *creatively* low annual budget deficit figure, I could see that an English cricket win at the WACA was more likely. However, an agreement on an artificially small annual deficit had to be reached. Acceptance of this unrealistic target succeeded in temporarily placating NHSE/NHSI, allowing the board a short period of peace, before it again became clear that the target was unachievable. Then a new cycle of haranguing and harassment kicked off. It was worse than paying protection money to the Mafia. They would always come knocking.

July 2018, seventy years since the birth of the NHS. Party time. The chief executive passed a tray around, cautioning "Only one muffin each." Next to the tray was a single, yellow paper cup. The cup was for us to offer donations, for the muffins.

Time for me to "Muff off" too.

43

GRACE RETURNS

It's five years since I resigned, and Grace will be approaching her sixth birthday.

Grace's parents have asked to meet me, and are coming to my new home for lunch.

A winter storm has stripped the dead branches off the riverside trees. Most of the canopy is blighted by ash dieback. They will need felling soon. Snow is forecast.

I feel anxious and slightly awkward. Throughout my career I had stuck to a simple inviolable rule — do not meet the parents of your patients outside of work. But those days are over. I know Grace appeared normal when I last saw her in outpatients, but she was still only a babe in arms. What if there was something I'd missed? How would she be five years on?

A black Audi draws up, and I turn the kettle on. So British to seek solace in tea.

The doorbell rings. Grace bounces in, sporting a glittering gold headband, followed by her smiling parents. She hands me a drawing of a noseless, pink-faced, big-footed angel, wearing an orange three-pointed crown, mirroring a trio of inverted 99 Mr Whippys. The detail is well beyond that of an average six-year-old.

"She's very caring and close to her brother and sister," her mother says.

"She never gives up," says her father, before repeating "she *never* gives up".

I agree.

Grace never gave up.

Grace's Angel

Five happy mothers on the neonatal ward,
Mount Hagen hospital, Papua New Guinea, 1989.

Frank and Beachball, amongst the villagers at a Sepik Haus Tambaran,
January 1990.

The hospital fundraising team approach the summit of Kilimanjaro,
February 2001.

The Vicar and The Brick,
Aconcagua,
February 2003.

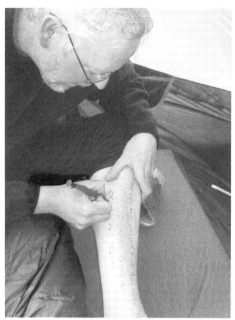

Dick inscribing his leg,
Aconcagua,
February 2003.

Dick and me suffering at altitude near the summit of Aconcagua,
February 2003.

PV, on a Brisbane beach, preparing for the Test match ahead,
November 2006.

At the WACA, proving The Ashes could still be a pleasant experience,
December 2006.

REFLECTIONS

So, smart-arse. What's *your* solution to the UK healthcare problem then? How would *you* save the NHS? I don't know. My favourite phrase. I suppose the bigger question is whether the NHS is worth saving.

In 1909, the *Minority Report of the Royal Commission on the Poor Law* suggested a new system to replace the outdated ideas of the Victorian *Poor Law*. A further twenty years, and one World War later, the *Local Government Act* was passed, providing care for all. London County Council took over the responsibility of medical schools, together with over one hundred hospitals. Soon after, the WWII years necessitated the creation of the Emergency Hospital Service, dependent for the first time on the Government. After WWII, hospitals were considerably varied in style and quality, with many establishments facing financial ruin. At Paddington General Hospital, the baby cots stood on tins of oil, to stop cockroaches reaching the newborn. Something had to change. With WWII over and a Labour Government in power, Aneurin Bevan, the UK health minister, presented his *National Health Service Bill* to Parliament, with the principles of being freely available to the whole population, providing the same service to all, according to need, and providing the best health advice and treatment possible. In short — universal, comprehensive and free at the point of delivery.

Two years on, in July 1948, the NHS accepted its first patients. The previous winter had been one of the harshest on record. The country had been battered by war, its people were unhealthy and undernourished. Lack of food, lack of fuel, three months of snow, extreme cold and the worst floods for half a century had brought the nation to its knees. Bread was rationed and the meat and bacon allowance was reduced.

On the appointed day that summer, 390,000 beds were taken over by the new NHS.[43]

The *British Medical Journal* reported "The medical man, intensely individual, was becoming more and more aware of his responsibility to the community." A good time then, for the birth of Aneurin Bevan's baby. To help ease in the new system, Bevan allowed consultants to continue providing private health care, memorably claiming he was able to accomplish his goal "by stuffing the doctors' mouths with gold". There was a hidden problem though. One the Greek philosopher Epicurus had identified 2,000 years earlier, in his creation of the Inconsistent Triad, whereby three principles cannot all be upheld simultaneously, such as the problem with God and evil. God may be omnipotent, God could be omnibenevolent, but evil exists. These three propositions are inconsistent, thus at least one must be false. In 1998, fifty years after the start of the NHS, Albert Weale, Professor of Political Theory and Public Policy at University College London, wrote in the *British Medical Journal*: "The basic principle of the NHS is simply that comprehensive, high-quality medical care should be

---

43. *Reduced to 240,000 beds in 2000 and further decreased, to 165,000 beds, by the year 2019. BMJ 2021;375:n2994.*

available to all citizens on the basis of professionally judged medical need without financial barriers to access."

Professor Weale continued, "Yet, in the face of increasing healthcare costs this basic principle threatens to become what logicians call an inconsistent triad; a collection of propositions, any two of which are compatible with each other but which, when viewed together in a threesome, form a contradiction." The professor carried on, explaining the choices we must make. "Perhaps we can have only a comprehensive service of high quality, but not one available to all. Or a high-quality service freely available to all, but not comprehensive."

Other countries, aware of this inconsistency, manage the problem in different ways. In the US, for example, healthcare is of high quality but not available to all; in New Zealand, it is available to all and high quality but doesn't cover all health demands. We, in the UK, stand alone in failing to address this inconsistent triad. Instead, we try to keep every plate spinning, accompanied by the frequent sound of smashing crockery. Do *you* believe the NHS can provide the best care possible for *every* condition and for *everyone* in our nation, *free*? Really? As a doctor working in the 1980s, I believed it could, but with the advances in medicine and surgery, and an ever-increasing and elderly population, I now believe this ideal is unachievable.

The NHS has become a life-support machine, to such an extent that it has found itself on life-support, situation critical. So, to answer the earlier question of how I'd try to save the NHS, I'd focus on the letter R.

Return

Return community midwives, nurses, physiotherapists and health visitors to their pre-efficiency-savings roles and responsibilities; it makes sense to treat patients within the community whenever possible.

Replace

Replace chief executives who have no clinical experience with those who do. Accountants can count, lawyers can interpret the law, and those who deal with patients understand hospitals best. I include — not exclusively, and in alphabetical order — doctors, nurses, pharmacists, physiotherapists, porters, receptionists, secretaries — indeed anyone with hands-on experience of handling patients.

Replace the current financial model of running the NHS as a business with the reality that it is a service, like education. That way it would no longer be run by accountants focused on savings, but as a service investing in the country's future.

Reduce

Reduce protocols and legislation; you can't cover every eventuality. They are out of date the day they are printed.

Reduce litigation. It's madness to encourage a business of sticky-fingered self-promoters, hell-bent on squeezing the life-blood out of the NHS.

No-fault compensation works in Denmark, Sweden, Finland and New Zealand. Why not in the UK?

Ration

Ration healthcare; the elephant in the room. Design a cross-party, apolitical body to debate whether it is right to fund certain procedures and practices within the NHS. No longer can everything be provided for everyone free. Make a list. Be brave. Be realistic. Be open. Be honest.

Reverse

Reverse bed closures; the UK currently has approximately 2.5 beds per 1,000 of the population. France has over double, and Germany over treble that number per capita.

Ring-fence

Ring-fence NHS employees' pensions; audit the pension fund and publish the details every year.

Remove

Remove external consultants; they aren't worth their fees, and they undermine health care.

Remove the concept of revalidation; it has been tried and proven to be a waste of valuable resources. It won't stop another Shipman.

Respect

Respect the public and the staff; neither are stupid. They shouldn't be at loggerheads.

Respect the different needs of older clinical staff; and allow them the opportunity to come off onerous acute on-call rotas. It is wasteful to force them into early retirement.

Respect the burden of on call, with increased leave, if not higher salaries.

*

Stand in your gardens, clap your hands, rattle your pots and pans in a cacophony of virtue signalling if you must. It won't put bread on the table or make a down payment on a mortgage. Applause and fine words are welcome, but they're not enough.

The service is nothing without its staff. A world-beating service, if that's what *you* desire, can only be achieved through clinical excellence, training and retaining the best.

The beating heart of the NHS is, and always has been, its people.

REMEMBER

I Remember the interventions:

July 1979
Royal Commission on the NHS: identifies concerns with an ageing population and the cost of new developments.

November 1982
My first NHS reorganisation: abolishes Area Health Authorities.

February 1983
The Griffiths report: introduces general management to the NHS.

January 1986
Project 2000: reforms nurse training.

February 1986
Green Paper: *Primary health care.*

December 1987
White Paper: *Promoting better health*, expands services supplied by nurses and pharmacists.

January 1989
White Paper: *Working for patients*, offers increased patient choice. Proposes a split between purchasers and providers of care.

November 1989
My first *Children Act*: covers adoption, fostering and care homes.

April 1990
A new GP contract is agreed.

June 1990
The National Health Service and Community Care Act creates the internal market.

June 1991
White Paper: *Health of the nation*, with a focus on cancer, mental health, HIV and heart disease.

November 1991
The Patient's Charter identifies patients as "customers with rights".

November 1994
A reduction in Regional Health Authorities to eight.

January 1996
The passing of three White Papers: *Choice and Opportunity*; *Delivering the future* and *NHS: A service with ambitions*.

January 1997
Primary Care Act: gives GPs increased choice.

December 1997
White Paper: *The new NHS: Modern, dependable*.

April 1998
Creation of the *National Institute for Health and Clinical Excellence*.

June 1998
Public enquiry into Bristol Royal Infirmary's paediatric

cardiac surgery service. Identifies outcomes as important in the contracting and provision of care.

November 1998
The Acheson inquiry: suggests targets for reducing infant mortality and increasing life expectancy. A new agreement between the Department of Health and the Treasury.

December 1998
NHS Direct established: a national health phone line that offers expert information and health advice.

April 1999
End of GP fundholding and the start of Primary Care Groups.
White Paper: *Saving Lives: Our Healthier Nation.*

July 2000
The NHS Plan: a ten-year strategy to provide more doctors and nurses. The focus shifts to performance targets, decreasing waiting times and, a commitment to building schemes with an agreement on the *Private Finance Initiative.*

January 2001
The creation of the *Commission for Healthcare Improvement* with the intention, for the first time, to assess individual NHS hospitals' performance.

May 2001
Health and Social Care Act.

September 2001
The introduction of a novel hospital star rating system, whereby the quality of care provided by individual NHS hospitals is graded and published.

January 2002
My second NHS reorganisation: District Health Authorities are replaced by Strategic Health Authorities and Primary Care Trusts.

June 2002
The National Health Service Reform and Health Care Professions Act.

June 2003
New contracts for GPs and hospital consultants. GPs cease responsibility for twenty-four-hour care.

October 2003
Agenda for Change: standardising pay and conditions for most NHS staff.

November 2003
My third NHS reorganisation: *The Health and Social Care (Community Health and Standards) Act 2003* provides for the establishment of Foundation Trusts.

April 2004
The first ten *Foundation Trusts* commence.

June 2004
NHS Improvement Plan is published.

November 2004
White Paper: *Choosing Health*. Supports personalised services and increased integration between the public and private sectors.

November 2004
My second *Children Act*: with seven core aims. Safeguarding identified as everyone's responsibility, with welfare and education brought together.

March 2005
Creating a patient-led NHS.

July 2005
Commissioning a patient-led NHS.

January 2006
My fourth NHS reorganisation: SHAs reduced from twenty-eight to ten. PCTs reduced from 303 to 152. Another White Paper: *Our Health, Our Care, Our Say.*

July 2007
Professor Darzi leads a major review into London's healthcare.

June 2008
Professor Darzi outlines another ten-year plan: *High quality care for all.*

January 2009
The *NHS Constitution* is set out: with seven principles and six core values. Pledges and responsibilities defined, for both patients and staff.

April 2009
The Care Quality Commission created: regulates and inspects health and social care services.

June 2009
NHS chief executive, Sir David Nicholson, announces a need for efficiency savings of between £15bn and £20bn.

February 2010
Robert Francis's Inquiry: identifies serious failings in Mid Staffordshire, making eighteen recommendations.

March 2010
White Paper: *Building the National Care Service* is

announced but abandoned, as Labour lose the general election.

June 2010
Announcement of a public enquiry into Mid-Staffordshire NHS Foundation Trust.

July 2010
White Paper: *Equity and excellence: Liberating the NHS.*

January 2011
My fifth NHS reorganisation: *The Health and Social Care Bill* abolishes SHAs and PCTs.

March 2012
The Health and Social Care Bill: includes a new responsibility concerning legal duties around health inequalities.

June 2012
Doctors take industrial action for the first time in forty years.

July 2012
White Paper: *Care and Support.*

November 2012
Health and Social Care Act.

April 2013
Public Health England launched, replacing the Health Protection Agency. No longer an independent, non-departmental, public agency but, one that takes instructions direct from ministers.

October 2014
NHS England publish *Five Year Forward View.*

January 2015
Government announces the *Ten-Year Plan for Health and Care*. Three months after NHSE's five year forward view.

January 2016
Junior doctors vote to strike.

April 2016
Launch of *NHS Improvement*, formed by the merger of *Monitor*, which regulated NHS foundation trusts, and the *Trust Development Authority*, which oversaw other, non-foundation, trusts.

May 2016
New junior doctor contract agreed.

October 2016
Creation of *Sustainability and Transformation Plans*, with proposals for forty-four *Footprint* areas, covering the health needs of local populations.

March 2017
NHS England publish *Next steps on the Five Year Forward View*.

January 2019
A new contract is agreed for general practice and NHS England issue *The Long Term Plan*.

Finally,

I REMEMBER WHAT MATTERS

I remember the babies
Breaking the news of Carol's liver cancer
Blindly tapping Agatha's heart effusion
Worrying about Lauren's resuscitation plans
Fearfully draining James's enlarging head
Feeling Emily's ice-cold legs, and
Missing Leah's Kawasaki disease

I remember the young children
Tyler and his brain tumour
Finn's desperation to lose weight
Aiden's promises of an exercise plan
Leonin drinking from puddles
Antonin's unexplained bruise, and
Steven's piercing screams

I remember the teenagers
Mirriam's troublesome lupus
Madison's hirsutism
Jonno's sweet wrapper

Simon's priapism
Christina's diabetic crisis, and
George, the mischievous, slapping the nurses' bottoms

I remember the difficult adults
Prune's mother and her demands for an NHS helmet
Mrs Jones and her views on immunisation
Ms Yellow-Specs's aggression and hostility
The tardy mother and her rabbit sitter
The two chief executives, who just didn't understand
The two consultants, who got it wrong, and just couldn't apologise

I remember the bad times
The battles about the parking exclusion zone
The conflict about Dr F's flipping award
The misery induced by hostile job planning
The sadness at losing two colleagues
The pathetic excuses at Christmas, and
The multiple failures, where nothing else could be done

I remember the beep, beep, beep, of that damned pager
Disturbing my bath
Invading the sanctity of my ablutions
Interrupting my meals
Destroying my sleep and my dreams
Distracting my care away from sick children, and
Draining my enthusiasm for work

I remember the good times
The satisfaction at finding a solution
The friendship from clinical colleagues
The enjoyment of teaching
The never-ending learning
The trench warfare humour, and
The satisfaction of team work

And I remember the supportive parents
Helping me manage, when I was out of my depth
Supporting me, in my breaking of bad news
Laughing with me, rather than at me
Forgiving me, when I was unable to help

And finally
Trusting me, to care for their children.

UK MEDICAL HIERARCHY

Medical student
A five-year course, including two years basic medical sciences, before three years clinical training, involving seeing patients on the wards and in out patients.

House officer/F1
Following passing the final exams, a new doctor (up until 2001) obtained two junior house officer posts (HO), both of six months duration. The foundation programmes replaced this in 2001/2, when a two-year structured scheme was created, forming a bridge between medical school and specialty training. During the first year of this the junior doctor is referred to as an F1.

Crapped on by SHOs.

Senior house officer/F2
The year following the house officer HO/F1 year. Prior to 2001 these doctors were called senior house officers (SHOs) and worked at that grade for an indeterminate period. However, the role of the F2 is limited to one year only.

Crapped on by registrars.

Registrar/Senior Registrar/Specialty Training

Specialty training programmes (ST) replaced registrar training in 2007. The ST programmes last between three and eight years, depending on which hospital career the doctor chooses. Prior to these changes doctors obtained a hospital registrar post when deemed experienced enough to manage patients alone, at nights and at weekends, and then, following a successful interview, moved posts every year or two. Before 2007 many doctors remained as registrars/ senior registrars for over a decade.

Crapped on by consultants.

Consultant

Following obtaining the necessary experience and passing the specialty exam, doctors can apply to be interviewed for a consultant post. Historically this employment was for life. More recently consultants change hospitals more frequently. The buck stops here.

Crapped on by management.

And to muddle you further:

Mr/Miss/Ms or Dr?

Physicians, whatever their seniority, stay as plain old Dr for doctor throughout their career. Surgeons who pass their exams, sat while in junior doctor specialty training, become Mr/Miss or Ms. Despite the common misperception, there is *no seniority* attached to this change to their title.

Staff grade, associate specialist and specialty doctor (SAS)

A permanent post obtained by an experienced doctor. SAS doctors tend to be very "hands on". Usually, they have not passed the specialty postgraduate examination or have opted to avoid the life-style of a hospital consultant.

More important than they think they are.

Professor

During my career this role changed from one where a senior consultant was appointed to "a chair" in a hospital with a medical school, to a post more often awarded to a consultant who raises the profile, or the income, of a hospital. For example, when I started my consultant post, there was one professor and, when I left twenty-one years later, there were six.

Less important than you think they are.

ACKNOWLEDGEMENTS

I failed *use of English* at Wellington College and I couldn't have written this book without the help of a cantankerous and obstinate Yorkshireman, Dick Donkin. Properly trained in the use of our language and with an ability to deconstruct any sentence, Dick has guided me throughout this five-year project. With a dangerous combination of incurable hypochondriasis and a near complete lack of understanding of any health issue, Dick made me explain every medical conditions in, what I hope you will find, easy to understand detail.

Dick's main gripes have been my incorrect placement of commas, Enid Blyton writing, repeated use of inverted sentences and my restricted vocabulary. All true.

A typical written note I received back on a draft copy was: "You and I don't pause in the same places. Could this be a clinical anomaly? My pause, incidentally, is the right one. You have a malfunctioning pause. Probably a birth defect. Did your mother have hiccups?"

Many other friends helped in the development of this book and I am grateful to them all. In particular I received invaluable encouragement and support from Nic and Chris Allen, Philip Bowles, Rob Donkin, Dominic Flint, Ann Godden (Mother), Sheila Handelman, Adam Hill,

Julia Lampshire, Adrian Michaels, Bin William and the reviewers who found time in their busy schedules to read and comment on the manuscript.

Most importantly I would like to thank Grace's parents for their unswerving backing, Tessa Thornley for her thorough proof-reading, and Sarah Houldcroft, from Goldcrest Books, for her patience and professionalism. Sarah is a pleasure to work with.

Finally, a special mention must be made for my long-suffering other half, Toni, known in the book, and in real life, as H for Horace (as she likes hedgehogs, and might be prickly) and W, Wanda the dog, both of whom have been perplexed by the time it has taken me to write this and the negative effect this has had on my contributions to household chores and dog walks.

H and W.

ABOUT THE AUTHOR

Resignation celebration, complete with tutu.

Charles Godden studied medicine at Charing Cross Hospital, London, qualifying as a doctor in 1983. After house posts in Yorkshire and London, he worked in Jersey prior to returning to London, then moved to Australia before securing his first paediatric consultant post, in Papua New Guinea, at the age of twenty-nine. Back in the UK he was appointed to a newly created respiratory paediatric consultant post in Surrey which he held for twenty-one years.

Frustrated by what he saw as the inefficient, and not-infrequently hostile, style of management and the waste of NHS resources, Charles resigned his consultant post in 2016 and joined a different hospital trust as a non-executive director, before freelancing as an expert witness for medical defence unions.

Today Charles spends his time in West Sussex chopping wood and supporting Norwich City Football Club.

Someone has to.